Young People's Books in Series

Young People's Books in Series
Fiction and Non-Fiction, 1975-1991

Judith K. Rosenberg
with the assistance of
C. Allen Nichols

1992
LIBRARIES UNLIMITED, INC.
Englewood, Colorado

LIBRARIES UNLIMITED, INC.
P.O. Box 6633
Englewood, CO 80155-6633

Library of Congress Cataloging-in-Publication Data

Rosenberg, Judith K.
Young people's books in series : fiction and non-fiction, 1975-1991 / Judith K. Rosenberg with the assistance of C. Allen Nichols.
x, 424 p. 17x25 cm.
Includes bibliographical references and index.
ISBN 0-87287-882-1
1. Children's literature in series--Bibliography. 2. Young adult literature--Bibliography. 3. Series (Publications)--Bibliography. I. Nichols, C. Allen. II. Title.
Z1037.R688 1992
011.62--dc20 91-36646
CIP

For Kate
You light up my life,
now and always

Contents

Introduction

This book is an update of several earlier works: *Young People's Literature in Series: Fiction*, *Young People's Literature in Series: Publishers' and Non-Fiction Series*, and *Young People's Literature in Series: Fiction, Non-Fiction, and Publishers' Series, 1973-1975*. The need for a new work is obvious: much has been published in the last fifteen years in series literature, much is no longer available, and all of it can be elusive to track down.

Fiction series here include both sequels and series. They are arranged alphabetically by the author's last name, then in chronological order as they should be read. This will assist librarians and patrons trying to find "which one comes next?" in a series. When a series consists of more than three entries, they are numbered, to make access easier for the user, particularly in the case of the unending Babysitters Club, Sweet Valleys, etc. This should help the librarian whose only clue is that the reader needs #26 in the Sweet Valley High series. If the series has already been discussed in one of our earlier editions, there is an asterisk at the beginning of the series listing, and the user will find the numbering continuing from our preceding book, i.e., coverage of Paddington the Bear books will begin with #12 here. Users may find a few series that predate 1975—these were not included before.

Criteria for inclusion have been changed somewhat. With the proliferation of paperback series for children and young adults, it seems foolish to ignore them based on mediocrity, when these are the only things that some youngsters will read, many libraries now carry them, and the demand is so high. These are also often the series that are hardest to track down. Therefore, we have included as many paperback series as we could locate. There are undoubtedly some that were missed, and even more that will be added as this is being published. We expect to include those in our next update. Materials reviewed are for readers grades 3-12. The young adult material was written specifically for that age group; no attempt has been made to include adult series that might appeal to the YA reader. The annotations are intended to assist in both materials selection and reference.

While the fiction section includes all additions since 1975, whether still in print or not, the non-fiction section contains only titles currently available. The rationale is that fiction works endure and remain on library shelves even when out of print, while non-fiction collections, to remain viable and accurate, should not contain old, outdated material. The non-fiction titles are arranged alphabetically by the series title, then by author and title. "Series" with only one or two titles have not been included. When more titles are added to them, they will appear in a later edition. Access is provided by way of four indexes: a fiction series title index, a non-fiction series title index, a non-fiction series subject index, and a combined author/title index.

In evaluating the non-fiction material, close attention was paid to the format, illustrative matter, content, and author expertise.

Indexing, glossaries, and bibliographies are always mentioned, since their desirability for student use is great. Several series that are written for kindergarten-grade 2 also appear if they are truly informational. Those that are more like picture book material are not examined.

The young adult materials were reviewed by C. Allen Nichols for his qualifying M.L.S. paper at Kent State University. His assistance has been invaluable. Any omissions have been inadvertent; suggestions are welcome. Special thanks go to the staffs of the Akron-Summit County, Barberton, and Stow Public libraries, especially the inter-library loan staff (and Jim Epling, the Lowly Peon), for their assistance in obtaining the books we needed to examine; to Julia Smith and Kate Rosenberg for their advice; and to Kenyon Rosenberg for his assistance in the great computer troubles.

TIPS FOR USING THIS INDEX

If you know either author or title of any fiction or non-fiction series, start with the Combined Author/Title Index beginning on page 360. If you know the name of a series, try either the Fiction Series Title Index (p. 347) or the Non-Fiction Series Title Index (p. 351). If you want to find a series by subject, try the Non-Fiction Series Subject Index (p. 355). There is no topical access to fiction series. Finally, remember that all fiction in the main section is arranged alphabetically by author and then chronologically by publication date. The non-fiction main section is arranged alphabetically by series title, then alphabetically by author.

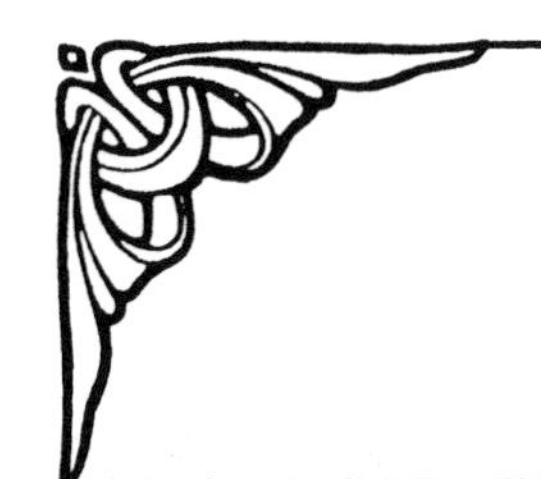

Fiction Series

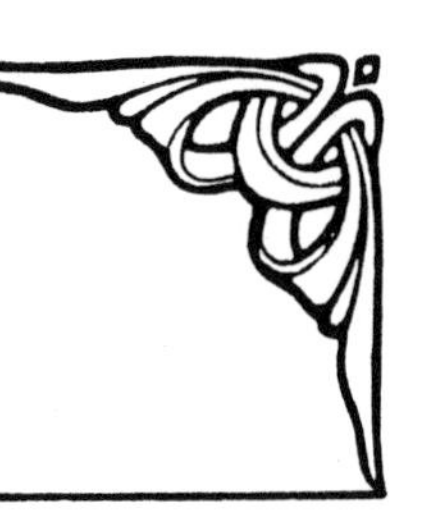

ABELS, Harriette (Galaxy 1)
Forgotten World. Crestwood, 1979
Green Invasion. Crestwood, 1979
Medical Emergency. Crestwood, 1979
Meteor from the Moon. Crestwood, 1979
Mystery on Mars. Crestwood, 1979
Planet of Ice. Crestwood, 1979
Silent Invaders. Crestwood, 1979
Strangers on NMA-6. Crestwood, 1979
Unwanted Visitors. Crestwood, 1979
There is a lot of dialogue in this sci-fi series, and the vocabulary is suitable for hi-lo readers, but the stories are simplistic with no character development. Only for reluctant readers with a sci-fi bent. Grades 3-6.

ABER, Linda Williams (Lost Girls)
Adrift. Scholastic, 1991
Alone. Scholastic, 1991
This new series differs from the usual paperback girls' offerings. Yes, there is a group of teen girls, but they are cast adrift on an island and must learn to survive on their own. In addition to personality problems, we have some adventure and survival techniques—a nice change from romance and shopping concerns.

ADAMS, Laurie, and **Allison COUDERT** (Alice Whipple Series)
1—*Alice and the Boa Constrictor*. Bantam, 1983
2—*Alice Whipple, Fifth-Grade Detective*. Bantam, 1987
3—*Alice Whipple in Wonderland*. Bantam, 1989
4—*Alice Whipple for President*. Bantam, 1990
5—*Alice Whipple Shapes Up*. Bantam, 1990
Alice is a fifth grader at a girls' school who deals with such problems as deciding what her career should be, running for school office, and the usual paperback fare for readers 8-12.

ADAMS, Nicholas (Horror High)
1—*Mr. Popularity*. Harper, 1990
2—*Resolved: You're Dead*. Harper, 1990
3—*Heartbreaker*. Harper, 1991
4—*New Kid on the Block*. Harper, 1991
5—*Hard Rock*. Harper, 1991
6—*Sudden Death*. Harper, 1991
7—*Pep Rally*. Harper, 1991
8—*Final Curtain*. Harper, 1991
Something is always happening in high school, but not normally murder. However, that is the recurring theme in this series. Each book is about a different student attending Horror High and something always happens there. This is an original paperback series that strikes a popular theme for students in grades 7-9. Fans of R. L. Stine and Christopher Pike will go for these.

ADLER, C. S.

Footsteps on the Stairs. Delacorte, 1982
Binding Ties. Delacorte, 1985

These two companion novels introduce us to stepsisters Anne and Dodie. In the first book they spend the summer together, getting to know each other, while searching for the ghosts that occupy their summer home. The second is a perky love story that has Anne falling for a rebellious teen. The tension caused between her and Dodie, and Anne's family makes this an interesting book. Written for grades 8 and above.

ADLER, C. S.

Good-bye, Pink Pig. Camelot, 1986
Help, Pink Pig! Putnam, 1990

Amanda is a shy, withdrawn child who retreats into the real-seeming world of miniatures with her tiny pink quartz pig. She does find that running away from problems does not solve them, and even fantasy places have troubles. This is a thoughtful, sensitive series for youngsters who can relate to loneliness, uncertainty, and shyness. Ages 9-12.

ADLER, C. S.

The Magic of the Glits. Camelot, 1987
Some Other Summer. Camelot, 1988

Lynette and Jeremy meet on the beach when she is seven and he is eleven. He resents having to babysit her, but they develop a special friendship. In the second book, five years have passed and they meet again, but nothing turns out as Lynette anticipated. Perceptive stories for grades 4-7.

ADLER, David (Cam Jansen Series)

1—*Cam Jansen and the Mystery of the Stolen Diamonds*. Viking, 1980
2—*Cam Jansen and the Mystery of the UFO*. Viking, 1980
3—*Cam Jansen and the Mystery of the Dinosaur Bones*. Viking, 1981
4—*Cam Jansen and the Mystery of the Television Dog*. Viking, 1981
5—*Cam Jansen and the Mystery of the Gold Coins*. Viking, 1982
6—*Cam Jansen and the Mystery of the Babe Ruth Baseball*. Viking, 1982
7—*Cam Jansen and the Mystery of the Circus Clown*. Viking, 1983
8—*Cam Jansen and the Mystery of the Monster Movie*. Viking, 1984
9—*Cam Jansen and the Mystery of the Carnival Prize*. Viking, 1984
10—*Cam Jansen and the Mystery of the Monkey House*. Viking, 1985
11—*Cam Jansen and the Mystery of the Stolen Corn Popper*. Viking, 1986
12—*Cam Jansen and the Mystery of Flight 54*. Viking, 1989

Elizabeth Jansen has been nicknamed "Cam" for "camera," because of her photographic memory. That memory comes in very handy as she solves her cases with the help of friend Eric. Mystery lovers grades 2-4 will appreciate this series, especially if they enjoy Encyclopedia Brown and Adler's Fourth Floor Twins.

ADLER, David (Fourth Floor Twins Series)

1—*The Fourth Floor Twins and the Fish Snitch Mystery*. Viking, 1985
2—*The Fourth Floor Twins and the Fortune Cookie Chase*. Viking, 1985
3—*The Fourth Floor Twins and the Disappearing Parrot Trick*. Viking, 1986
4—*The Fourth Floor Twins and the Silver Ghost Express*. Viking, 1986
5—*The Fourth Floor Twins and the Skyscraper Parade*. Viking, 1987
6—*The Fourth Floor Twins and the Sand Castle Contest*. Viking, 1988

Identical twins Donna and Diane are sisters to Eric, friend of Cam Jansen (another Adler series). To complicate life in their apartment house, they are friends with boys who are fraternal twins. The trouble that they get into thus increases exponentially! The assorted twins find mysteries wherever they go. Their mistaken ideas often lead to hilarious trouble. These are good transitional books from beginning readers to longer books. Fans of Encyclopedia Brown and Cam Jansen ages 6-9 will grab these.

ADLER, David A. (Jeffrey's Ghost Series)
Jeffrey's Ghost and the Leftover Baseball. Holt, 1984
Jeffrey's Ghost and the Fifth-Grade Dragon. Holt, 1985
Jeffrey's Ghost and the Ziffel Fair Mystery. Holt, 1987
Although Jeffrey is a fifth grader, the reading level of this series makes it more suitable for readers grades 3-5. His troubles arise from his friendship with a 200 year old ghost named Bradford. These are only so-so, with surface characterizations and predictable plot lines.

ADORJAN, Carol
The Cat Sitter Mystery. Camelot, 1986
The Copy Cat Mystery. Camelot, 1990
These aren't really mysteries—more cases of a young, overactive imagination at work. First Beth thinks her new neighbors are witches, then one of their cats disappears. Cat lovers will be attracted to these low-key books. Grades 3-6.

AIKEN, Joan (Arabel and Mortimer Series)
1—*Arabel's Raven.* Doubleday, 1974
2—*Arabel and Mortimer.* Doubleday, 1981
3—*Mortimer's Cross.* Harper, 1984
4—*Mortimer Says Nothing.* Harper, 1985
These books actually contain several related stories each about Arabel and her trouble-prone raven. Aiken is a fine writer with an offbeat sense of humor. Grades 4-7.

AIKEN, Joan (Dido Twite Series)
6—**Stolen Lake.* Delacorte, 1981
7—*Dido and Pa.* Delacorte, 1986
The wonderfully adventurous Dido Twite is back. Her travails are set in a wildly variant time period among peoples who never were (but could have been)! In one, she tries to help Queen Guinevere of New Cumbria (in Roman America) retrieve a lake that has been stolen from her. The other has Dido fighting her evil father. Excellent choices for ambitious readers grades 5 and up. Readers of these can be steered to Lloyd Alexander's Vesper Holly series.

AIKEN, Joan
Go Saddle the Sea. Doubleday, 1977
Bridle the Wind. Doubleday, 1983
Teeth of the Gale. Harper, 1988
This series more closely resembles Aiken's adult fiction than her series for children. Set in the Spain of the 1820's, all the ingredients of an historical adventure are here: political intrigue, romance, and even search for treasure. For YA historical fiction buffs.

ALDEN ALL STARS (Series)
HALLOWELL, Tommy
1—*Jester in the Backcourt.* Puffin, 1990
2—*Duel on the Diamond.* Puffin, 1990
3—*Shot from Midfield.* Puffin, 1990
4—*Last Chance Quarterback.* Puffin, 1990
HALECROFT, David
5—*Power Play.* Puffin, 1990
6—*Breaking Loose.* Puffin, 1990
7—*Wild Pitch.* Puffin, 1991
8—*Setting the Play.* Puffin, 1991
9—*Championship Summer.* Puffin, 1991
10—*Blindside Blitz.* Puffin, 1991
11—*Hotshot on Ice.* Puffin, 1991
This is a sports series featuring four friends at Alden Junior High. The boys are competitive in a variety of sports, including basketball, soccer, baseball, and football. There are so few

sports fiction books anymore, that this series should be considered for inclusion in collections catering to boys 8-12.

ALEXANDER, Lloyd (Vesper Holly Series)
1—*The Illyrian Adventure*. Dutton, 1986
2—*The El Dorado Adventure*. Dutton, 1987
3—*The Drackenberg Adventure*. Dutton, 1988
4—*The Jedera Adventure*. Dutton, 1989
5—*The Philadelphia Adventure*. Dutton, 1990
How wonderful to find such a brave, resourceful, humorous heroine as Vesper Holly. She is an orphan in search of adventure in 1872, and find it she does, following in the footsteps of her father. She begins her adventures with a search for a legendary treasure and ends up defending President Grant and other visiting dignitaries during the Philadelphia Exposition. These are excellent reads in a genre not often found in YA literature.

ALEXANDER, Lloyd (Westmark Trilogy)
Westmark. Dutton, 1981
The Kestrel. Dutton, 1982
The Beggar Queen. Dutton, 1984
Like the Prydain Chronicles, these books are set in a fantasy land, this time called Westmark. The fight between good and evil commences, and even when good seems to have overcome, and Mickle rules as wise Queen Augusta, evil once again rears its head, and past troubles must be dealt with again in the present. Excellent fare for fantasy/historical fiction buffs grades 5 and up from a master storyteller.

ALLEN, Suzanne (Scrambled Eggs)
1—*Suddenly Sisters*. Berkley, 1990
2—*Almost Starring Dad*. Berkley, 1990
3—*The Sister Plot*. Berkley, 1990
4—*The Great Treasure Hunt*. Berkley, 1990
5—*Berry and the Beanstalk*. Berkley, 1990
6—*Songbusters!* Berkley, 1990
7—*Instant Millionaires*. Berkley, 1991
The title of this series relates to the fact that two families have been merged, due to the parents' remarriage. Now there are seven kids, two parents, and thirteen pets. Sound uncomfortably like the Bradys? Right! The plot lines are about as complex, but younger paperback fans may like them. Grades 2-5.

ALMAN, Mickey (Scene of the Crime Series)
Scene of the Crime. Ivy, 1991
Murder at Midnight. Ivy, 1991
Date with Danger. Ivy, 1991
This is an exciting and involving young adult mystery series. Teens get involved with a mystery or crime and come to the rescue of their friends. Grades 7-10.

AMERICAN GIRLS (Series)
ADLER, Susan S.
1—*Meet Samantha*. Pleasant, 1986
2—*Samantha Learns a Lesson*. Pleasant, 1986
3—*Samantha's Surprise*. Pleasant, 1986
4—*Happy Birthday, Samantha!* Pleasant, 1987
5—*Samantha Saves the Day*. Pleasant, 1988
6—*Changes for Samantha*. Pleasant, 1990

SHAW, Janet
1—*Meet Kirsten*. Pleasant, 1986
2—*Kirsten Learns a Lesson*. Pleasant, 1986
3—*Kirsten's Surprise*. Pleasant, 1986
4—*Happy Birthday, Kirsten!* Pleasant, 1987
5—*Kirsten Saves the Day*. Pleasant, 1988
6—*Changes for Kirsten*. Pleasant, 1990
TRIPP, Valerie
1—*Meet Molly*. Pleasant, 1986
2—*Molly Learns a Lesson*. Pleasant, 1986
3—*Molly's Surprise*. Pleasant, 1986
4—*Happy Birthday, Molly!* Pleasant, 1987
5—*Molly Saves the Day*. Pleasant, 1988
6—*Changes for Molly*. Pleasant, 1990

1—*Meet Felicity*. Pleasant, 1991
2—*Felicity Learns a Lesson*. Pleasant, 1991
3—*Felicity's Surprise*. Pleasant, 1991
Although this series is a major marketing achievement for the publisher, which includes character dolls, clothes for dolls and girls, and crafts in addition to the books, these slim volumes have definite appeal for readers 8-12. Kirsten and her family are Swedish immigrants circa 1854; Samantha is the orphan granddaughter of a wealthy family in 1904; and Molly lives in World War II America. The Felicity books had just been announced at the time of publication, so neither author nor time period is yet available. The books use the same casts of characters; plot lines are simple but designed to give a flavor of the period. The realistic illustrations add to the effect. At the end of each volume, facts about the time period and circumstances of the story are presented. This is a very palatable way to get youngsters to read and relate to historical fiction.

ANDERSON, Mary (F*T*C* Series)
*F*T*C* Superstar*. Atheneum, 1976
*F*T*C* and Company*. Atheneum, 1979
F*T*C* stands for Freddie The Cat. He longs to go onstage, and with the help of his acting coach, Emma Pigeon, he does. The follow-up finds Freddie and friends staging *My Fair Lady* to exorcise an abandoned theater of its ghosts. Grades 4-7.

ANDERSON, Mary (Mostly Ghosts Series)
The Haunting of Hillcrest. Dell, 1987
The Leipzig Vampire. Dell, 1987
The Three Spirits of Vandermeer Manor. Dell, 1987
A brother-sister twin duo ferrets out the answers to spooky mysteries (she is psychic) in this series. Grades 4-5.

ANDERSON, Mary (Mostly Monsters Series)
1—*The Hairy Beast in the Woods*. Dell, 1989
2—*The Missing Movie Creature*. Dell, 1989
3—*The Terrible Thing in the Bottle*. Dell, 1989
4—*The Curse of the Demon*. Dell, 1989
Cassie and Barney are cousins who are thrown together and don't much like it, except they keep getting involved in spooky adventures. These are easy reading fun, and the characters' mutual distrust rings true. Grades 3-6.

APPLETON, Tom (Tom Swift Series)

1—*The Black Dragon*. Pocket, 1991
2—*The Negative Zone*. Pocket, 1991
3—*Cyborg Kickboxer*. Pocket, 1991
4—*The DNA Disaster*. Pocket, 1991

Everyone remembers Tom Swift from years ago. Well, this is Tom Jr.! He is quite a bit like his father, a brilliant inventor, but these days his playthings are incredibly hi-tech. Tom uses his many inventions, such as a flying skateboard and a personal portable stereo that does everything except cook dinner, to get him through adventure after adventure. Ages 11-15.

ARMSTRONG, Jennifer (Pets, Inc.)

1—*The Puppy Project*. Bantam, 1990
2—*Too Many Pets*. Bantam, 1990
3—*Hilary to the Rescue*. Bantam, 1990
4—*That Champion Chimp*. Bantam, 1990

Like other paperback series, this one features a group of girlfriends with a common interest—in this case, a love for animals. Some of the pets are exotic, as in the second entry, where one of the girls teaches a chimp sign language. Grades 3-6.

ASCH, Frank (Pearl the Mouse Series)

Pearl's Promise. Delacorte, 1984
Pearl's Pirates. Delacorte, 1987

Pearl is a white mouse living in a pet store. When her parents are sold, she promises to care for her brother, but when she too is sold, it seems impossible to save him from being a snake's next meal. There is a lot of humor here but also realism not usually found in anthropomorphic stories. Grades 4-6.

ASHER, Sandy (Ballet One)

1—*Best Friends Get Better*. Scholastic, 1990
2—*Pat's Promise*. Scholastic, 1990
3—*Mary in the Middle*. Scholastic, 1990
4—*Can David Do It?* Scholastic, 1991

Like the girls in the Bad News Ballet series, these eight-year-olds also take dance and share each others' ups and downs. Light reading for grades 2-4.

ASHLEY, Ellen (Center Stage)

1—*Star Struck*. Fawcett, 1990
2—*Barri, Take Two*. Fawcett, 1990
3—*Understudy*. Fawcett, 1990
4—*Lights, Camera, Action*. Fawcett, 1990
5—*Encore*. Fawcett, 1991
6—*Summer Stock*. Fawcett, 1991

Barri and her friends are interested in the stage. All are drama students at a regular high school, although their adventures often tear a page from *Fame*. For YAs.

ASIMOV, Janet, and **Isaac ASIMOV** (Norby Series)

1—*Norby, the Mixed-up Robot*. Walker, 1983
2—*Norby's Other Secret*. Walker, 1984
3—*Norby and the Lost Princess*. Walker, 1985
4—*Norby and the Invaders*. Walker, 1985
5—*Norby and the Queen's Necklace*. Walker, 1986
6—*Norby Finds a Villain*. Walker, 1987
7—*Norby and Yobo's Great Adventure*. Walker, 1989
8—*Norby Down to Earth*. Walker, 1989
9—*Norby and the Oldest Dragon*. Walker, 1990
10—*Norby and the Court Jester*. Walker, 1991

Norby is a secondhand robot that Jeff Wells originally acquired to help with teaching. Norby's many adventures have taken him to other planets and other times. The series is fast-paced with plenty of humor. They should prove entertaining for middle grade readers and reluctant readers who enjoy science fiction.

AUSTEN, Carrie (Party Line)
1—*Allie's Wild Surprise*. Berkley, 1990
2—*Julie's Boy Problem*. Berkley, 1990
3—*Becky's Super Secret*. Berkley, 1990
4—*Rosie's Popularity Plan*. Berkley, 1990
5—*Allie's Big Break*. Berkley, 1990
6—*Julie's Dream Date*. Berkley, 1990
7—*Becky Bartlett Superstar*. Berkley, 1990
8—*Rosie's Mystery on Ice*. Berkley, 1990
9—*Allie's Pizza Pool Party*. Berkley, 1991
10—*Julie's Outrageous Idea*. Berkley, 1991
11—*Becky Rides Again*. Berkley, 1991
12—*Rosie's Fashion Show*. Berkley, 1991
Like many other paperback series aimed at girls from ages 10-13, this one concentrates on four friends with a common goal: they make money by giving parties professionally—thus the series title. Their crises include having to give a sure-fire flop party for an unpopular girl and finding a party scheduled the same time as the big middle school dance.

AUSTIN, Jennifer (Cassandra Mysteries)
1—*Ticket to Danger*. Grosset, 1990
2—*Race against Time*. Grosset, 1990
3—*Mystery in Hollywood*. Grosset, 1990
4—*Treasure Beach*. Grosset, 1990
Teenage detective Cassandra Best has a pen pal from England who has involved her in travels and mysteries. What friend Alex does not know, however, is that Cassandra Best is really Cassie Jones from a small town in Ohio. The mystery/travel premise should appeal; the writing is simple and fast-moving. Reluctant readers will also enjoy these. Grades 4-7.

AVI
Night Journeys. Pantheon, 1979
Encounter in Easton. Pantheon, 1980
Peter, the stepson of a Quaker, helps two young indentured servants as they escape. After they separate, a series of events leads to tragedy for one of the runaways. These are effectively told, particularly in the telling of the plight of indentured servants, who were no better than slaves. Grades 4-6.

AVI
S.O.R. Losers. Avon, 1986
Romeo and Juliet Together (and Alive!) at Last. Avon, 1988
These books are truly funny, with believable characters. The first focuses on a team of sports losers, the second on a one-sided romance. Grades 4-7.

BABBITT, Lucy Cullyford
Oval Amulet. Harper, 1985
Children of the Maker. Farrar, 1988
This YA fantasy series follows Paragrin as she tries to find the meaning behind an amulet given her by a strange woman. She must leave her home because it restricts women's rights; eventually she set up a colony of her own, only to find she must fight her Half-Divine sister for it.

BAER, Judy (Cedar River Daydreams)
1–*Broken Promises*. Bethany, 1989
2–*Fill My Empty Heart*. Bethany, 1990
3–*The Intruder*. Bethany, 1989
4–*Jennifer's Secret*. Bethany, 1989
5–*New Girl in Town*. Bethany, 1988
6–*Silent Tears No More*. Bethany, 1989
7–*Tomorrow's Promise*. Bethany, 1990
8–*Trouble with a Capital "T"*. Bethany, 1988
9–*Yesterday's Dream*. Bethany, 1990
These are Christian alternatives to the Sweet Valley High books for young adults. They are filled with high school adventures and believable situations that are based on Christian values. Grades 6-9.

BALL, Jacqueline A. (Dino School)
1–*A Puzzle for Apatosaurus*. Harper, 1990
2–*Halloween Double Dare*. Harper, 1990
3–*Battle of the Class Clowns*. Harper, 1990
4–*Sneeze-o-saurus*. Harper, 1990
5–*A Kitten Named Cuddles*. Harper, 1991
6–*Sara's Biggest Valentine*. Harper, 1991
7–*T. Rex's Missing Tooth*. Harper, 1991
8–*Revenge of the Terror Dactyls*. Harper, 1991
In a bid to capture young readers with a yen for dinosaurs, this silly series uses dinosaurs as the stars of the plots, not as real creatures, but as if they were regular third grade kids. It works on the picture book level, but will it for the slightly more sophisticated readers grades 2-3?

BANKS, Lynne Reid (Indian in the Cupboard Series)
The Indian in the Cupboard. Doubleday, 1985
Return of the Indian. Doubleday, 1986
The Secret of the Indian. Doubleday, 1989
There are a number of books about little people (the Littles and the Borrowers, to name two), but this series has a different slant. It begins with Omri's discovery that his tiny plastic Indian can come alive. The Indian and Omri travel through time together to face real perils throughout history. These are both popular and well written, an unbeatable combination for grades 4-7.

BARGAR, Gary W.
What Happened to Mr. Forster? Clarion, 1981
Life. Is. Not. Fair. Clarion, 1984
Bargar explores two civil rights issues, during the late 1950s, in these books. In the first, Louis' favorite teacher is fired for being a homosexual. In the second, Louis is becoming popular with his classmates, but there is one problem, his good friend, DeWitt, is black and this could harm his popularity. Bargar does a good job of getting his point across, without ruining the story or making it too difficult to comprehend. Written for 13-16 year olds.

BEATTY, Patricia
Long Way to Whiskey Creek. Morrow, 1971
How Many Miles to Sundown? Morrow, 1974
Billy Be Damned Long Gone By. Morrow, 1977
Beatty's strong suit is her vivid characters and far-out adventures. In this series, several Quiney children and Nate Graber find adventure in the Southwest of the 1880s. Both girls and boys have courage, humor, and spunk. Good for historical fiction buffs, or those looking for strong female heroines. Grades 4-8.

BEATTY, Patricia

The Nickel-Plated Beauty. Morrow, 1964

Sarah and Me and the Lady from the Sea. Morrow, 1989

Beatty is a well-respected author of historical novels for children. Set just before the turn of the century in Washington state, these books follow the adventures of boisterous Sarah Kimball. Very good choices for fiction readers grades 5-7.

BEATTY, Patricia (Hannalee Series)

Turn Homeward, Hannalee. Morrow, 1984

Be Ever Hopeful, Hannalee. Morrow, 1988

The Civil War is the backdrop for *Turn Homeward, Hannalee*. Twelve-year-old Hannalee is one of 2000 textile workers shipped north by the Union Army to work in the Yankee mills. This story tells of the promise she made to make her way home again to Georgia and the family she was forced to leave behind. In the second book, Hannalee has made it back home in the war-torn South. However she has to move again, this time to Atlanta where her family hopes to make a new start. Based on true historical events, these novels are filled with the sights and sounds of the mid-1800s. Readers learn of the horrors of warfare, the changes that war can cause in people and the differing ways people fight to survive. Good for junior and senior high schoolers.

BELDEN, Wilanne Schneider

Mind-hold. Harcourt, 1987

Mind-find. Harcourt, 1988

These books center on the House of Logran, a psychic research foundation. In the first volume, Carson and his younger sister Caryl, a powerful telekinetic must survive the aftermath of an earthquake that has destroyed much of California. The second volume is the thrilling adventure of Laurel, a young girl with parapsychological powers. Both books were well received and are for students 12 and up.

BELL, Clare (Ratha Series)

Ratha's Creatures. Atheneum, 1983

Clan Ground. Dell, 1987

Ratha and Thistle Chaser. McElderry, 1990

Adults may even enjoy this series of books that are similar to the works of Jean Auel. The Ratha series is set millions of years ago, with nomadic clans living in a society based on herding forest animals. Since teens prefer reading suspenseful, action-packed stories, this series should prove to be a definite page turner for those 13 and up.

BELLAIRS, John

1 – *The Curse of the Blue Figurine*. Dial, 1983
2 – *The Mummy, the Will, and the Crypt*. Dial, 1983
3 – *The Spell of the Sorcerer's Skull*. Dial, 1984
4 – *The Revenge of the Wizard's Ghost*. Dial, 1985
5 – *The Eyes of the Killer Robot*. Dial, 1986
6 – *The Trolley to Yesterday*. Dial, 1989
7 – *The Chessmen of Doom*. Dial, 1989
8 – *The Secret of the Underground Room*. Dial, 1990

John Bellairs is truly a standout in the mystery/suspense genre. He has been nominated for the Poe Award and is uniformly well reviewed. His books combine strong characterization and plotline with adventure and truly literate writing. There is always an element of fantasy and the supernatural to spice up the broth. Readers from 5th-8th grades will enjoy these.

BELLAIRS, John

The House with a Clock in Its Walls. Dial, 1973
The Figure in the Shadows. Dial, 1975
The Letter, the Witch, and the Ring. Dial, 1976

This was the first series by suspense author Bellairs. Lewis and Uncle Jonathan are the stars as they battle ghosts and bullies with magic and real-life skills. Grades 4-7.

BELLAIRS, John

The Treasure of Alpheus Winterborn. Dial, 1985
The Dark Secret of Weatherend. Dial, 1986
The Lamp from the Warlock's Tomb. Dial, 1988

Anthony Monday is the hero of this Bellairs series. Librarians will appreciate the fact that his cohort in adventure is the town librarian. The two fight evil in 1954 Minnesota in this quality series aimed at readers grades 5-8.

BERNARD, Elizabeth (Satin Slippers)

1—*To Be a Dancer*. Fawcett, 1987
2—*Center Stage*. Fawcett, 1987
3—*Stars in Her Eyes*. Fawcett, 1987
4—*Changing Partners*. Fawcett, 1988
5—*Second Best*. Fawcett, 1988
6—*Curtain Call*. Fawcett, 1988
7—*Temptations*. Fawcett, 1988
8—*Stepping Out*. Fawcett, 1988
9—*Chance to Love*. Fawcett, 1989
10—*Rising Star*. Fawcett, 1989
11—*Starting Over*. Fawcett, 1989
12—*Summer Dance*. Fawcett, 1989

This original fiction paperback series is for young adults who have an interest in ballet. The series focuses on Leah and her attempts to become a successful professional ballerina. There is some sort of adventure and romance in each story. These are not too bad for grades 6-10.

BETANCOURT, Jeanne

1—*The Rainbow Kid*. Avon, 1983
2—*Turtle Time*. Avon, 1985
3—*Puppy Love*. Avon, 1986
4—*Crazy Christmas*. Bantam, 1988

Growing-up problems beset Aviva and her friend Josh, including her problems as a joint custody kid. Betancourt writes knowingly about youngsters coping with the real world, and this series is no exception. Ages 9-12.

BETHANCOURT, T. Ernesto (Doris Fein Series)
1—*Dr. Doom: Superstar*. Holiday, 1978
2—*Doris Fein: Superspy*. Holt, 1980
3—*Doris Fein: Quartz Boyar*. Holt, 1980
4—*Doris Fein: Phantom of the Casino*. Holt, 1981
5—*Doris Fein: The Mad Samurai*. Holt, 1981
6—*Doris Fein: Deadly Aphrodite*. Holt, 1982
7—*Doris Fein: Murder Is No Joke*. Holt, 1982
8—*Doris Fein: Dead Heat at Long Beach*. Holt, 1983
9—*Doris Fein: Legacy of Terror*. Holt, 1984
Doris is a little older than most YA heroines: she is out of high school, is a real spy, and is involved with an adult Japanese-American, both professionally and romantically. She's had some personal problems, but the main thrust here is adventure.

BLAIR, Cynthia (Pratt Twins)
1—*The Banana Split Affair*. Fawcett, 1985
2—*The Hot Fudge Sundae Affair*. Fawcett, 1985
3—*Strawberry Summer*. Fawcett, 1986
4—*The Pumpkin Principle*. Fawcett, 1986
5—*Marshmallow Masquerade*. Fawcett, 1987
6—*The Candy Cane Caper*. Fawcett, 1987
7—*Pink Lemonade Charade*. Fawcett, 1988
8—*Double Dip Disguise*. Fawcett, 1988
9—*The Popcorn Project*. Fawcett, 1989
10—*Apple Pie Affair*. Fawcett, 1989
11—*Jelly Bean Scheme*. Fawcett, 1990
12—*Lollipop Plot*. Fawcett, 1990
13—*The Coconut Connection*. Fawcett, 1991
The Pratt Twins find themselves in a number of lightweight mystery adventures. The titles will certainly grab YAs looking for a fast and easy read, as long as they are not on a diet!

BLAIR, L. E. (Girl Talk)
1—*Welcome to Junior High*. Western, 1990
2—*Face-Off!* Western, 1990
3—*The New You*. Western, 1990
4—*Rebel, Rebel*. Western, 1990
5—*It's All in the Stars*. Western, 1990
6—*The Ghost of Eagle Mountain*. Western, 1990
7—*Odd Couple*. Western, 1990
8—*Stealing the Show*. Western, 1990
9—*Peer Pressure*. Western, 1990
10—*Falling in Like*. Western, 1990
11—*Mixed Feelings*. Western, 1990
12—*Drummer Girl*. Western, 1990
Like Sweet Valley Twins, et al., this series follows a group of seventh grade girls—the snobby one, the poor one, etc., through various predictable adventures in romance, sports, etc. Grades 4-6.

BLOOM, Hanya (Vic the Vampire)
1—*School Ghoul*. Harper, 1990
2—*Science Spook*. Harper, 1990
3—*Vampire Cousins*. Harper, 1990
4—*Friendly Fangs*. Harper, 1991
What Coombs's Dorrie has done for witches, Vic may do for vampires. He is lovable and well-intentioned, and uses his powers only for good. Grades 2-4.

BLUME, Judy (Fudge Books)

3—**Superfudge*. Dutton, 1980

4—*Fudge-a-Mania*. Dutton, 1990

The mischievous Fudge Hatcher is one of the most enduring and loved characters in modern children's fiction, second only to Beverly Cleary's Ramona. Fudge's antics make his brother Peter's life a living misery, like when he decides to become a dog, or stop eating, and it's up to Peter to head him off at the pass. The arrival of a baby sister does not lighten the load, either. These are surefire hits for the 8-13 set.

BOND, Ann Sharpless

Saturdays in the City. Houghton, 1979

Adam and Noah and the Cops. Houghton, 1983

Noah and Adam are 4th grade city dwellers who experience a number of adventures. Each chapter tells about one, including a rummage sale gone wrong and a picnic that ends with them riding a horse—each facing a different direction. Fun for grades 4-6.

BOND, Michael (*Paddington the Bear Series)

12—*Paddington Takes the Test*. Houghton, 1980

13—*Paddington on Screen*. Houghton, 1982

Two new additions to this popular series featuring the cuddly star of television and the written word. Paddington is such a beloved figure that any of his books will find a ready audience. His adventures include taking a driving test and being in a magic act. Ages 8-12.

BOND, Nancy

Best of Enemies. Atheneum, 1978

A Place to Come Back To. Atheneum, 1984

Set in historic Concord, these books follow Charlotte and her friends as they face the challenges of adolescence. Their friendships begin to change more to boy-girl relationships, while Oliver finds himself rejected by his parents. Well written realistic fiction for YAs.

BOSTON, Lucy (*Green Knowe Series)

Stones of Green Knowe. Atheneum, 1976

This is the last entry in Boston's charming Green Knowe series. This time, the children she describes living at Green Knowe are from the 12th century. Green Knowe is just being built, and Roger discovers the magical stones that transport him through time to meet the other children who have inhabited the house. Grades 4-7.

BRANSCUM, Robbie (Johnny May Series)

Johnny May. Doubleday, 1975

The Adventures of Johnny May. Harper, 1984

Johnny May Grows Up. Harper, 1987

Johnny May is a gutsy heroine growing up in the Arkansas hills. She faces a slew of problems, including maybe losing her boyfriend to the more sophisticated girls of the town high school. Some readers might find the colloquial spelling difficult to read. Grades 4-8.

BRANSCUM, Robbie (Toby Series)

Toby, Granny and George. Doubleday, 1976

Toby Alone. Doubleday, 1979

Toby and Johnny Joe. Doubleday, 1979

Thirteen-year-old orphan Toby lives in the Arkansas hills with her grandmother. In her first summer there she learns a great deal about love and caring. Later, her grandmother dies and she is once again alone, except for her dog. She and Johnny Joe like each other but she puts him off. Eventually, they do get married but tragedy strikes again. Fifth grade and higher.

BRANSON, Karen

Potato Eaters. Putnam, 1979
Streets of Gold. Putnam, 1981

Maureen O'Connor and her family live in Ireland during the potato famine. The horrors of the famine and accompanying illnesses are clearly described. The second book tells of the family's emigration to the U.S. and their difficulties adapting. Good historical fiction about a neglected period for YAs.

BRENFORD, Dana (Green Street Mysteries)

1—*A Case of Poison*. Crestwood, 1988
2—*Danger in the Endless Cave*. Crestwood, 1988
3—*The Guardian of the Hopewell Treasure*. Crestwood, 1988
4—*The Kidnapped Falcon*. Crestwood, 1988
5—*Tiger on the Loose*. Crestwood, 1988
6—*Tracks in the North Woods*. Crestwood, 1988
7—*The Vanishing Stream*. Crestwood, 1988
8—*A Whale of a Rescue*. Crestwood, 1988

Three twelve year old youngsters have become an instant family with the remarriage of their parents. They call themselves the Green Street Gang, and wind up doing investigative reporting for their own newspaper. Grades 3-7 and reluctant readers.

BRITTAIN, Bill (Coven Tree Series)

1—*Devils' Donkey*. Harper, 1981
2—*Wish Giver*. Harper, 1983
3—*Dr. Dread's Wagon of Wonders*. Harper, 1987
4—*Professor Popkin's Prodigious Polish*. Harper, 1990

These stories are an unusual mix of folklore, fantasy, and the historical. Set in Coven Tree (New England), the inhabitants find themselves the "beneficiaries" of fulfilled wishes (which backfire), a boy turned into a donkey, and a rainmaker with more power than the townspeople realize. *Wish Giver* was a Newbery Honor Book. Excellent fare for the special reader. Grades 5-8.

BROOKS, Jerome

Make Me a Hero. Dutton, 1980
Naked in Winter. Orchard, 1990

Jake is twelve years old when we meet him in the first book in this twosome. He ventures out of his familiar neighborhood, meets Harry Katz, gets a job and grows a little in the process. In the second, it is four years later and Jake is out of his familiar neighborhood again. This time his parents have moved 15 miles away from his friends. He tries to maintain his friendships while developing a new romantic interest with the less than willing Roberta. Jake grows a little in this one, too. Good for grades 7-12.

BRYANT, Bonnie (Saddle Club)

1—*Horse Crazy*. Bantam, 1988
2—*Horse Shy*. Bantam, 1988
3—*Horse Sense*. Bantam, 1989
4—*Horse Power*. Bantam, 1989
5—*Trail Mate*. Bantam, 1989
6—*Dude Ranch*. Bantam, 1989
7—*Horse Play*. Bantam, 1989
8—*Horse Show*. Bantam, 1989
9—*Hoof Beat*. Bantam, 1990
10—*Riding Camp*. Bantam, 1990
11—*Horse Wise*. Bantam, 1990
12—*Rodeo Rider*. Bantam, 1990

13—*Starlight Christmas*. Bantam, 1990
14—*Sea Horse*. Bantam, 1991
15—*Team Play*. Bantam, 1991
16—*Horse Games*. Bantam, 1991
17—*Horsenapped*. Bantam, 1991

Like the popular Babysitter Club and Sweet Valley series, this has a central theme/setting: this time the girls are horse crazy twelve year olds and their adventures involve horses and people at their riding stable. For readers grades 4-7.

BUNTING, Eve (Skate Patrol Books)
Skate Patrol. Whitman, 1980
The Skate Patrol Rides Again. Whitman, 1981
The Skate Patrol and the Mystery Writer. Whitman, 1982

Milton and James are the young sleuths in this easy reading mystery series. The boys solve their mysteries with the aid of their roller skates, thus the series title. The plots are extremely simple, but Bunting is a veteran author who combines humor and well-paced adventure. The controlled vocabulary makes these good for grades 2-5, including reluctant readers.

BURCH, Robert (Ida Early Series)
Ida Early Comes Over the Mountain. Viking, 1980
Christmas with Ida Early. Viking, 1983

Ida Early simply appears at the door of the Sutton household one day looking for work. Because they have lost their mother, the Suttons do let her stay. Set in rural Georgia, Ida resembles nothing so much as an Appalachian Mary Poppins. She pops in and out of the children's lives with as many unusual and bizarre experiences as Nanny Poppins. The writing is flavorful and charming. These are must-haves for ages 8-12.

BURCH, Robert
Tyler, Wilkin and Skee. Viking, 1963
Wilkin's Ghost. Viking, 1978

Set in Georgia at the end of the Depression, these fine books focus on three brothers. Their relationships are clearly defined, but they are growing up, and family feeling gives way for the need to explore the larger world. Grades 5-8.

BYARS, Betsy (Bingo Brown Series)
The Burning Questions of Bingo Brown. Viking, 1988
Bingo Brown and the Language of Love. Viking, 1989
Bingo Brown, Gypsy Lover. Viking, 1990

Author Byars has created a delightful character in the pubescent Bingo Brown. He grapples with the continuing problems of understanding and relating to the opposite sex as he finds himself attracted to several girls at once, unable to communicate the way he would like, and finally, facing the double trauma of a long-distance romance and a new sibling. A sure bet for ages 8-12.

BYARS, Betsy (Blossom Family Series)
1—*The Not-Just-Anybody Family*. Delacorte, 1986
2—*The Blossoms Meet the Vulture Lady*. Delacorte, 1986
3—*The Blossoms and the Green Phantom*. Delacorte, 1987
4—*A Blossom Promise*. Delacorte, 1987
5—*Wanted ... Mud Blossom*. Delacorte, 1991

The Blossom family lives out west and several members (female) are involved in the rodeo circuit. The characters are eccentric, but lovable; the plots are light and fast moving, but always with a serious undercurrent. Excellent fare for grades 4-6.

BYRD, Elizabeth
I'll Get By. Viking, 1981
It Had to Be You. Viking, 1982
Heroine Kitty has a lot of verve; although set at the outset of the Depression, the period touches liven the books rather than make them difficult to read and understand. YAs should really enjoy these romances.

CALHOUN, Mary (*Katie John Series)
4—*Katie John and Heathcliff*. Harper, 1980
After an absence of almost 20 years, Katie John is back. She has just discovered boys. Having read the Brontës, she envisions herself the heroine of a real-life gothic romance, only to find that real life and fiction are very different. A likeable book about a likeable heroine for grades 4-7.

CALLEN, Larry (Four Corners Adventures)
1—*Pinch*. Little, 1975
2—*The Deadly Mandrake*. Little, 1978
3—*Sorrow's Song*. Little, 1979
4—*Muskrat War*. Little, 1980
This series has been highly rated for its humor and realistic characters and setting. Pinch is the hero, and he has to contend with hard times and swindlers, and a hunting pig competition. Grades 5-8.

CAMERON, Ann (Julian Series)
1—*The Stories Julian Tells*. Random, 1981
2—*More Stories Julian Tells*. Random, 1986
3—*Julian's Glorious Summer*. Random, 1987
4—*Julian, Secret Agent*. Random, 1988
5—*Julian, Dream Doctor*. Random, 1990
The first 2 books in this series are charming short stories about young Julian and his loving African-American family. Later entries have a controlled vocabulary and are part of Random's Stepping Stone series, aimed at ages 7-9. The first 2 books are particularly excellent for reading aloud.

CAMERON, Eleanor (Julia Redfern Books)
1—*Julia's Magic*. Dutton, 1984
2—*That Julia Redfern*. Dutton, 1982
3—*Julia and the Hand of God*. Dutton, 1977
4—*A Room Made of Windows*. Puffin, 1990
5—*The Private Worlds of Julia Redfern*. Puffin, 1990
This heartwarming series follows the young Julia through her mischievous early years, where her worst problems revolve around poison oak, on through her beloved father's death, mother's remarriage, and the successes of her sophomore year in high school. Julia is a complex, lovable heroine, and the readers grow with her. An excellent choice for ages 9-14.

CAMPBELL, Joanna (Caitlin Series)
"Love Trilogy"
1—*Loving*. Bantam, 1985
2—*Love Lost*. Bantam, 1985
3—*True Love*. Bantam, 1985
"Promise Trilogy"
1—*Tender Promises*. Bantam, 1986
2—*Promises Broken*. Bantam, 1986
3—*A New Promise*. Bantam, 1986

"Forever Trilogy"
1—*Dreams of Forever*. Bantam, 1987
2—*Forever and Always*. Bantam, 1988
3—*Together Forever*. Bantam, 1988

This series was created by Francine Pascal of Sweet Valley High fame. It chronicles the life of Caitlin from boarding school to college and after. These are normal teenage romances that also include school and the typical problems associated with that time in one's life. Grades 7 and above.

CARLSON, Natalie (*Orphelines Series)
5—*A Grandmother for the Orphelines*. Harper, 1980

The Orphelines have reappeared after a long absence. They are a large group of French orphans who consider themselves merely a large family. In this book, they decide to adopt a grandmother. There is a lot of old-fashioned charm here for ages 8-12.

CARRIS, Joan (Howard Boys Books)
1—*When the Boys Ran the House*. Lippincott, 1982
2—*Pets, Vets, and Marty Howard*. Lippincott, 1984
3—*Hedgehogs in the Closet*. Lippincott, 1988
4—*The Greatest Idea Ever*. Lippincott, 1990

There are four Howard boys, and each has his own adventure chronicled here. The first book finds the oldest, Jut, left in charge of running the household; the second finds Marty working for a vet; the third has Nick adjusting to the move to England by hiding his adopted hedgehog; and the fourth has Gus responding to the move back to Ohio with assorted schemes. Boys aged 8-12 will certainly enjoy these believable but funny adventures.

CATES, Emily (Haunting with Louisa Trilogy)
The Ghost in the Attic. Bantam, 1990
The Mystery of Misty Island Inn. Bantam, 1990
The Ghost Ferry. Bantam, 1991

These books combine fantasy with mystery. Heroine Dee finds herself orphaned and living on an island with her aunt. Her roommate turns out to be a ghostly relative who can find peace only if she can do good deeds for 4 living descendants. They are well done, with something to appeal to most readers grades 4-6.

CATLING, Patrick Skene
The Chocolate Touch. Morrow, 1979
John Midas in the Dreamtime. Morrow, 1986

In a variation of the Midas touch story, this series follows the adventures of John Midas, a young fellow who is greedy for chocolate, to the exclusion of all else. The second book follows John's adventures in Australia. Kids will definitely relate to the longing for chocolate in this humorous retelling. Grades 3-6.

CEBULASH, Mel (Carly & Co. Mysteries)
Carly & Co. Fawcett, 1989
Campground Mystery. Fawcett, 1989
Part-time Shadow. Fawcett, 1990

Teenagers Carly and Sandy (his real name is Soon Tek Ahn and he is Vietnamese) discover life in Tucson can be more exciting than they ever imagined. This paperback series is about their lives as a supersleuth duo in Arizona and the adventures and problems that arise around them. Eighth grade and up.

CEBULASH, Mel (Ruth Marini Books)
Ruth Marini of the Dodgers. Lerner, 1983
Ruth Marini: Dodger Ace. Lerner, 1983
Ruth Marini: World Series Star. Lerner, 1985

Ruth is a really outstanding baseball player—so outstanding that she becomes the first female in pro ball. These books follow her into the big leagues, through sports injury and romantic troubles to her first World Series. Girl jocks will find Ruth a good role model, with her determination and hard work overcoming sexist obstacles. For YAs.

CHAIKIN, Miriam (Yossi Books)
1—*How Yossi Beat the Evil Urge*. Harper, 1983
2—*Yossi Asks the Angels for Help*. Harper, 1985
3—*Yossi Tries to Help God*. Harper, 1987
4—*Feathers in the Wind*. Harper, 1989
Yossi is from an orthodox Jewish family where the religion and its observances are an integral part of life. These plots all turn on Yossi's views of religion: how he handles temptation, loss, gossip, and doing good deeds. Grades 4-6.

CHAIKIN, Miriam
1—*I Should Worry, I Should Care*. Harper, 1979
2—*Finders Weepers*. Harper, 1980
3—*Getting Even*. Harper, 1982
4—*Lower! Higher! You're a Liar!* Harper, 1984
5—*Friends Forever*. Harper, 1988
Molly is a Jewish girl growing up in Brooklyn in the late 1930s: her concerns revolve around home, friends, and synagogue. Jewish traditions and rituals are lovingly portrayed here as an integral part of Molly's life. Hitler's coming, and her neighborhood's concerns about the European Jews also play a part. Grades 4-6.

CHAMBERS, John
Finder. Atheneum, 1981
Showdown at Apple Hill. Atheneum, 1982
Fire Island Forfeit. Atheneum, 1984
These are YA murder mysteries that are nothing special; they do have a few YA-type problems mixed in with the mysteries, like drug abuse. OK fare for mystery readers.

CHANCE, Stephen (*Septimus Treloar Series)
3—*Stone Offering*. Nelson, 1977
This book finishes the Septimus Treloar series. This time, the former Scotland Yard detective, now a minister, is traveling in Wales, where he comes across what appears to be a series of sacrificial killings relating to an old rhyme. It is a good choice for YA mystery buffs.

CHARNAS, Suzy McKee (The Sorcery Hall Trilogy)
The Bronze King. Houghton, 1985
The Silver Glove. Bantam, 1988
The Golden Thread. Bantam, 1989
This well-known author of adult fantasy and science fiction decided to devote this series to young adults. Complete with a magical grandmother and the environs of New York City, Val Marsh comes to terms with her "family talent" to become a magical heroine. A good series for those YA sci-fi enthusiasts.

CHASE, Emily (Girls of Canby Hall)
1—*Roommates*. Scholastic, 1984
2—*Our Roommate Is Missing*. Scholastic, 1984
3—*You're No Friend of Mine*. Scholastic, 1984
4—*Keeping Secrets*. Scholastic, 1984
5—*Summer Blues*. Scholastic, 1984
6—*Best Friends Forever*. Scholastic, 1984
7—*Four Is a Crowd*. Scholastic, 1984
8—*Big Crush*. Scholastic, 1985

9—*Boy Trouble*. Scholastic, 1985
10—*Make Me a Star*. Scholastic, 1985
11—*With Friends Like That*. Scholastic, 1985
12—*Who's the New Girl?* Scholastic, 1985
13—*Here Come the Boys*. Scholastic, 1985
14—*What's a Girl to Do?* Scholastic, 1985
15—*To Tell the Truth*. Scholastic, 1985
16—*Three of a Kind*. Scholastic, 1985
17—*Graduation Day*. Scholastic, 1986
18—*Something Old, Something New*. Scholastic, 1986
19—*Making Friends*. Scholastic, 1986
20—*One Boy Too Many*. Scholastic, 1986
21—*Friends Times Three*. Scholastic, 1986
22—*Party Time*. Scholastic, 1986
23—*But She's So Cute*. Scholastic, 1987
24—*Princess Who?* Scholastic, 1987
25—*Ghost of Canby Hall*. Scholastic, 1987
26—*Help Wanted*. Scholastic, 1987
27—*Roommate and the Cowboy*. Scholastic, 1988
28—*Happy Birthday, Jane*. Scholastic, 1988
29—*A Roommate Returns*. Scholastic, 1988
30—*Surprise!* Scholastic, 1988
31—*Here Comes the Bridesmaid*. Scholastic, 1988
32—*Who's Got a Crush on Andy?* Scholastic, 1988
33—*Six Roommates and a Baby*. Scholastic, 1989

The girls in these stories are roommates at a New England boarding school. They have become fast friends and they are involved in adventures ranging from parental problems, academic difficulties and, of course, romance. This is an original paperback series that is popular in the public library. Ages 12 and above.

CHOOSE YOUR OWN ADVENTURE (Series)

PACKARD, Edward
1—*Cave of Time*. Bantam, 1979

MONTGOMERY, Raymond A.
2—*Journey under the Sea*. Bantam, 1977

TERMAN, Douglas
3—*Danger in the Desert*. Bantam, 1982

MONTGOMERY, Raymond A.
4—*Space and Beyond*. Bantam, 1979

PACKARD, Edward
5—*Mystery of Chimney Rock*. Bantam, 1979
6—*Spy Trap*. Bantam, 1989
7—*The Third Planet from Altair*. Bantam, 1981
8—*Deadwood City*. Bantam, 1980
9—*Who Killed Harlowe Thrombey?* Bantam, 1989

MONTGOMERY, Raymond A.
10—*Lost Jewels of Nabooti*. Bantam, 1981
11—*The Mystery of the Maya*. Bantam, 1981

PACKARD, Edward
12—*Inside UFO 54-40*. Bantam, 1982

MONTGOMERY, R. A.
13—*The Abominable Snowman*. Bantam, 1987

PACKARD, Edward
14—*The Forbidden Castle*. Bantam, 1982

MONTGOMERY, R. A.
15—*House of Danger*. Bantam, 1982

PACKARD, Edward
16—*Survival at Sea*. Bantam, 1982
MONTGOMERY, R. A.
17—*The Race Forever*. Bantam, 1983
PACKARD, Edward
18—*Underground Kingdom*. Bantam, 1983
BRIGHTFIELD, Richard
19—*Secret of the Pyramids*. Bantam, 1987
20—*Hyperspace*. Bantam, 1987
GOODMAN, Julius
21—*Space Patrol*. Bantam, 1983
FOLEY, Louise M.
22—*The Lost Tribe*. Bantam, 1984
MONTGOMERY, R. A.
23—*Lost on the Amazon*. Bantam, 1983
24—*Prisoner of the Ant People*. Bantam, 1983
BRIGHTFIELD, Richard
25—*The Phantom Submarine*. Bantam, 1983
GOODMAN, Julius
26—*The Horror of High Ridge*. Bantam, 1983
PACKARD, Edward
27—*Mountain Survival*. Bantam, 1984
MONTGOMERY, Raymond A.
28—*Trouble on Planet Earth*. Bantam, 1984
BRIGHTFIELD, Richard
29—*The Curse of Batterslea Hall*. Bantam, 1984
KOLTZ, Tony
30—*Vampire Express*. Bantam, 1984
GOODMAN, Julius
31—*Treasure Diver*. Bantam, 1984
BRIGHTFIELD, Richard
32—*The Dragon's Den*. Bantam, 1984
FOLEY, Louise M.
33—*The Mystery of the Highland Crest*. Bantam, 1985
GRAVER, Fred
34—*Journey to Stonehenge*. Bantam, 1984
BRIGHTFIELD, Richard
35—*The Secret Treasure of Tibet*. Bantam, 1984
MONTGOMERY, Raymond A.
36—*War with the Evil Power Master*. Bantam, 1984
LEIBOLD, Jay
37—*Sabotage*. Bantam, 1984
PACKARD, Edward
38—*Supercomputer*. Bantam, 1984
GOODMAN, Deborah L.
39—*The Throne of Zeus*. Bantam, 1985
WALLACE, Jim
40—*Search for the Mountain Gorillas*. Bantam, 1985
FOLEY, Louise
41—*The Mystery of Echo Lodge*. Bantam, 1985
LEIBOLD, Jay
42—*Grand Canyon Odyssey*. Bantam, 1985
GILLIGAN, Shannon
43—*The Mystery of Ura Senke*. Bantam, 1985
PACKARD, Edward
44—*You Are a Shark*. Bantam, 1985

BRIGHTFIELD, Richard
45–*The Deadly Shadow*. Bantam, 1985
KUSHNER, Ellen
46–*Outlaws of Sherwood Forest*. Bantam, 1985
LEIBOLD, Jay
47–*Spy for George Washington*. Bantam, 1985
FOLEY, Louise M.
48–*Danger at Anchor Mine*. Bantam, 1985
PACKARD, Edward
49–*Return to the Cave of Time*. Bantam, 1985
GOODMAN, Deborah L.
50–*The Magic of the Unicorn*. Bantam, 1985
PACKARD, Edward
51–*Ghost Hunter*. Bantam, 1987
GILLIGAN, Shannon
52–*The Case of the Silk King*. Bantam, 1986
MONRO, Louise
54–*Forest of Fear*. Bantam, 1986
GOODMAN, Deborah L.
55–*The Trumpet of Terror*. Bantam, 1986
KUSHNER, Ellen
56–*The Enchanted Kingdom*. Bantam, 1986
LEIBOLD, Jay
57–*The Antimatter Formula*. Bantam, 1986
KUSHNER, Ellen
58–*Statue of Liberty Adventure*. Bantam, 1986
KOLTZ, Tony
59–*Terror Island*. Bantam, 1986
GOODMAN, Deborah L.
60–*Vanished!* Bantam, 1986
MONTGOMERY, Raymond A.
61–*Beyond Escape*. Bantam, 1986
PACKARD, Edward
62–*Sugarcane Island*. Bantam, 1986
KUSHNER, Ellen
63–*Mystery of the Secret Room*. Bantam, 1987
SIEGMAN, Meryl
64–*Volcano!* Bantam, 1987
FOLEY, Louise M.
65–*The Mardi Gras Mystery*. Bantam, 1987
MONTGOMERY, R. A.
66–*The Secret of the Ninja*. Bantam, 1987
HODGMAN, Ann
67–*Seaside Mystery*. Bantam, 1987
PACKARD, Edward
68–*Secret of the Sun God*. Bantam, 1987
WALLACE, Jim
69–*Rock and Roll Mystery*. Bantam, 1987
BRIGHTFIELD, Richard
70–*Invaders of the Planet Earth*. Bantam, 1987
PACKARD, Edward
71–*Space Vampire*. Bantam, 1987
MONTGOMERY, Raymond A.
72–*The Brilliant Dr. Wogan*. Bantam, 1987
LEIBOLD, Jay
73–*Beyond the Great Wall*. Bantam, 1987

NEWMAN, Marc
74—*Longhorn Territory*. Bantam, 1987
BRIGHTFIELD, Richard
75—*Planet of the Dragons*. Bantam, 1988
MONTGOMERY, R. A.
76—*The* Mona Lisa *Is Missing!* Bantam, 1988
BAGLIO, Ben
77—*First Olympics*. Bantam, 1988
MONTGOMERY, R. A.
78—*Return to Atlantis*. Bantam, 1988
FOLEY, Louise M.
79—*Mystery of the Sacred Stones*. Bantam, 1988
PACKARD, Edward
80—*The Perfect Planet*. Bantam, 1988
GILLIGAN, Shannon
81—*Terror in Australia*. Bantam, 1988
BRIGHTFIELD, Richard
82—*Hurricane*. Bantam, 1988
MONTGOMERY, Raymond A.
83—*Track of the Bear*. Bantam, 1988
PACKARD, Edward
84—*You Are a Monster*. Bantam, 1988
BECKETT, Jim
85—*Inca Gold*. Bantam, 1988
KUSHNER, Ellen
86—*Knights of the Round Table*. Bantam, 1988
MONTGOMERY, R. A.
87—*Exiled to Earth*. Bantam, 1989
BRIGHTFIELD, Richard
88—*Master of Kung Fu*. Bantam, 1989
89—*South Pole Sabotage*. Bantam, 1989
PACKARD, Edward, and **R. A. MONTGOMERY**
90—*Mutiny in Space*. Bantam, 1989
PACKARD, Edward
91—*You Are a Superstar*. Bantam, 1989
LEIBOLD, Jay
92—*Return of the Ninja*. Bantam, 1989
HAMPTON, Bill, and **Luann HAMPTON**
93—*Captive!* Bantam, 1989
MONTGOMERY, R. A.
94—*Blood on the Handle*. Bantam, 1989
PACKARD, Edward
95—*You Are a Genius*. Bantam, 1989
MONTGOMERY, R. A.
96—*Stock Car Champion*. Bantam, 1990
PACKARD, Edward
97—*Through the Black Hole*. Bantam, 1990
LEIBOLD, Jay
98—*You Are a Millionaire*. Bantam, 1990
99—*Revenge of the Russian Ghost*. Bantam, 1990
PACKARD, Edward
100—*The Worst Day of Your Life*. Bantam, 1990
JOHNSON, Seddon
101—*Alien, Go Home!* Bantam, 1990
BRIGHTFIELD, Richard
102—*Master of Tae Kwon Do*. Bantam, 1990

MONTGOMERY, Ramsey
103 – *Grave Robbers*. Bantam, 1990
FOLEY, Louise
104 – *The Cobra Connection*. Bantam, 1990
GILLIGAN, Allison
105 – *The Treasure of the Onyx Dragon*. Bantam, 1990
BRIGHTFIELD, Richard
106 – *Hijacked!* Bantam, 1990
LEIBOLD, Jay
107 – *Fight for Freedom*. Bantam, 1990
PACKARD, Edward
108 – *Master of Karate*. Bantam, 1990
MONTGOMERY, R. A.
109 – *Chinese Dragons*. Bantam, 1990
PACKARD, Edward
110 – *Invaders from Within*. Bantam, 1991
MONTGOMERY, R. A.
111 – *Smoke Jumper*. Bantam, 1991
PACKARD, Edward
112 – *Skateboard Champion*. Bantam, 1991
MONTGOMERY, R. A.
113 – *The Lost Ninja*. Bantam, 1991
COMPTON, Sara
114 – *Daredevil Park*. Bantam, 1991
MONTGOMERY, R. A.
115 – *Island of Time*. Bantam, 1991
PACKARD, Edward
116 – *Kidnapped!* Bantam, 1991

Other series may imitate, but this one was the first and remains the best. The plots are often historical, and always adventurous. The reader is right in the middle; they read several pages, then choose what path they will follow. The choices continue throughout the book. Sometimes the outcome is positive, sometimes it is disastrous. Readers can go back and begin again, and the story line changes. Even the most reluctant of readers will eat these up! Grades 4-8.

CHOOSE YOUR OWN ADVENTURE (GRADES 2-5) (Series)
PACKARD, Edward
1 – *Circus*. Bantam, 1983
MONTGOMERY, R. A.
2 – *The Haunted House*. Bantam, 1981
PACKARD, Edward
3 – *Sunken Treasure*. Bantam, 1982
MONTGOMERY, R. A.
4 – *Your Very Own Robot*. Bantam, 1982
5 – *Gorga, the Space Monster*. Bantam, 1983
SAUNDERS, Susan
6 – *The Green Slime*. Bantam, 1982
PACKARD, Edward
7 – *Help! You're Shrinking!* Bantam, 1983
MONTGOMERY, R. A.
8 – *Indian Trail*. Bantam, 1983
9 – *Dream Trips*. Bantam, 1987
10 – *The Genie in the Bottle*. Bantam, 1987
SONBERG, Lynn
11 – *The Bigfoot Mystery*. Bantam, 1983

SAUNDERS, Susan
12–*Creature from Miller's Pond*. Bantam, 1983
PACKARD, Edward
13–*Jungle Safari*. Bantam, 1983
GILLIGAN, Shannon
14–*The Search for Champ*. Bantam, 1983
15–*The Three Wishes*. Bantam, 1984
RAZZI, Jim
16–*Dragons!* Bantam, 1984
SONBERG, Lynn
17–*Wild Horse Country*. Bantam, 1984
GITENSTEIN, Judy
18–*Summer Camp*. Bantam, 1984
SAUNDERS, Susan
19–*The Tower of London*. Bantam, 1984
WOODCOCK, John
20–*Trouble in Space*. Bantam, 1984
PACKARD, Edward
21–*The Evil Wizard*. Bantam, 1984
22–*Polar Bear Express*. Bantam, 1984
SPINNER, Stephanie
23–*The Mummy's Tomb*. Bantam, 1985
RAZZI, Jim
24–*The Flying Carpet*. Bantam, 1985
GOODMAN, Julius
25–*The Magic Path*. Bantam, 1985
SAUNDERS, Susan, and **Edward PACKARD**
26–*Ice Cave*. Bantam, 1987
MONTGOMERY, R. A.
27–*Fire!* Bantam, 1985
GILLIGAN, Shannon
28–*The Fairy Kidnap*. Bantam, 1985
SAUNDERS, Susan
29–*Runaway Spaceship*. Bantam, 1985
MONTGOMERY, R. A.
30–*Lost Dog*. Bantam, 1985
SAUNDERS, Susan
31–*Blizzard at Black Swan Inn*. Bantam, 1986
GILLIGAN, Shannon
32–*Haunted Harbor*. Bantam, 1986
SAUNDERS, Susan
33–*Attack of the Monster Plants*. Bantam, 1986
SAUNDERS, Susan
34–*Miss Liberty Caper*. Bantam, 1986
MONTGOMERY, R. A.
35–*The Owl Tree*. Bantam, 1986
SAUNDERS, Susan
36–*The Haunted Halloween Party*. Bantam, 1986
MONTGOMERY, Raymond A.
37–*Sand Castle*. Bantam, 1986
MONTGOMERY, R. A.
38–*Caravan*. Bantam, 1987
PACKARD, Edward
39–*The Great Easter Bunny Adventure*. Bantam, 1987

SAUNDERS, Susan
40—*The Movie Mystery*. Bantam, 1987
41—*Light on Burro Mountain*. Bantam, 1987
MONTGOMERY, R. A.
42—*Home in Time for Christmas*. Bantam, 1987
GOODMAN, Deborah L.
43—*You See the Future*. Bantam, 1988
BACH, Jennifer, and **Amy BROST**
44—*The Great Zopper Toothpaste Treasure*. Bantam, 1988
PACKARD, Edward
45—*A Day with the Dinosaurs*. Bantam, 1988
MONTGOMERY, R. A.
46—*Spooky Thanksgiving*. Bantam, 1988
SAUNDERS, Susan
47—*You Are Invisible*. Bantam, 1989
MONTGOMERY, R. A.
48—*Race of the Year*. Bantam, 1989
COMPTON, Sara
49—*Stranded!* Bantam, 1989
BAILEY, Anne
50—*You Can Make a Difference*. Bantam, 1990

Based on the highly successful Choose Your Own Adventure format written for older readers, this series is geared toward younger ones. These books are much shorter, with simpler vocabulary, but the same exciting format: adventure setting with the reader as hero/heroine, choosing the path they will follow throughout the text. Grades 2-4.

CHRISTIAN, Mary Blount (Sebastian [Super Sleuth] Series)
1—*Sebastian [Super Sleuth] and the Hair of the Dog Mystery*. Macmillan, 1982
2—*Sebastian [Super Sleuth] and the Bone to Pick Mystery*. Macmillan, 1983
3—*Sebastian [Super Sleuth] and the Crummy Yummies Caper*. Macmillan, 1983
4—*Sebastian [Super Sleuth] and the Santa Claus Caper*. Macmillan, 1984
5—*Sebastian [Super Sleuth] and the Secret of the Skewered Skier*. Macmillan, 1984
6—*Sebastian [Super Sleuth] and the Clumsy Cowboy*. Macmillan, 1985
7—*Sebastian [Super Sleuth] and the Purloined Sirloin*. Macmillan, 1986
8—*Sebastian [Super Sleuth] and the Stars-In-His-Eyes Mystery*. Macmillan, 1987
9—*Sebastian [Super Sleuth] and the Time Capsule Caper*. Macmillan, 1989
10—*Sebastian [Super Sleuth] and the Egyptian Connection*. Macmillan, 1988
11—*Sebastian [Super Sleuth] and the Mystery Patient*. Macmillan, 1989
12—*Sebastian [Super Sleuth] and the Baffling Bigfoot*. Macmillan, 1990
13—*Sebastian [Super Sleuth] and the Mystery Patient*. Macmillan, 1991

Sebastian is an anthropomorphic dog detective. His owner is a detective with the police department, and Sebastian assists on his cases without thought of reward ... and without being asked. Sebastian is cute and dog lovers grades 3-6 will love him. The short books with brief chapters and line drawings may also draw reluctant readers.

CHRISTOPHER, John (Fireball Trilogy)
Fireball. Dutton, 1981
New Found Land. Dutton, 1983
Dragon Dance. Dutton, 1986

Another fine fantasy series by master storyteller John Christopher. This one puts two boys in a parallel universe in which Rome never fell. They wind up heading for undiscovered America where they must cope with unfriendly Indians and a hostile climate. Grades 5-9.

CHRISTOPHER, John (*Tripods Trilogy)

1 – *When the Tripods Came*. Dutton, 1988

The original three books of this series, hence the trilogy, were written in the late 1960s. The titles are familiar: *The White Mountains, the City of Gold and Lead*, and *The Pool of Fire*. These science fiction adventures deal with both the good and evil in future times and are one of the most popular science fiction series ever written. This new addition is a prequel to this series and it more than holds its own. It provides a logical, ingenious, and terrifying explanation of how the Tripods were able to take over most of the world. Grades 7 and up.

CLARK, Margaret Goff (Barney Series)

Barney and the UFO. Dodd, 1979
Barney in Space. Putnam, 1981
Barney on Mars. Putnam, 1983

Orphan earth boy Barney is hoping to be adopted by the Crandalls when he happens to see a UFO. He makes friends with an alien boy, but is afraid to tell anyone for fear he will jeopardize the adoption. Subsequent adventures find him outer space bound to help his friends. Sci-fi fans ages 8-12 will enjoy these.

CLARKE, Judith (Al Capsella Series)

The Heroic Life of Al Capsella. Holt, 1988
Al Capsella and the Watchdogs. Holt, 1991

All Al wants is for his parents to be "perfectly ordinary and unobtrusive, quiet and orderly, well dressed and polite, hardworking and as wealthy as possible," but they are not. He tries hard to reform them so he then can be normal, but his mom continues to wear the same K-Mart brand sweater every day. These books provide a unique, humorous look at teen life. Ages 12 and up.

CLEARY, Beverly

Dear Mr. Henshaw. Morrow, 1983
Strider. Morrow, 1991

Arguably the most popular children's author writing, Cleary finally won the Newbery with *Dear Mr. Henshaw*. It revolves around the correspondence between a well-known author and Leigh Botts, one of his biggest fans, who also aspires to write. The new entry centers on Leigh's finding and adopting a dog, and how they both grow and mature together. Grades 4-6.

CLEARY, Beverly (Ralph the Mouse Series)

3 – **Ralph S. Mouse*. Morrow, 1982

This book continues Ralph's funny adventures in Cleary's hit series. In this one, he goes to school and winds up becoming part of a science project that backfires. This is a sure-fire winner for grades 3-6.

CLEARY, Beverly (*Ramona Series)

4 – *Ramona and Her Father*. Morrow, 1977
5 – *Ramona and Her Mother*. Morrow, 1979
6 – *Ramona Quimby, Age 8*. Morrow, 1981
7 – *Ramona Forever*. Morrow, 1984

Ramona the Incomparable stars in this series, an offshoot of Cleary's Ellen Tebbits/Henry Huggins series. Ramona is frank to a fault, and is gradually inching her way through school. Children from 3rd grade on up really relate to her, to the point where she has become a cottage industry which includes paper dolls, diaries, and even a TV show. There are so many funny gems here, these will definitely make it to classic status. Must-haves, even on the middle school level.

CLEAVER, Vera

Where the Lilies Bloom. Lippincott, 1969
Trial Valley. Lippincott, 1977

Set in the South, these books follow the trials of Mary Call as she tries to care for her siblings in the wake of their father's death. She does what she can to keep them together, as she promised, then finds her efforts in jeopardy by her own feelings for two young men. Quality material for grades 5-8.

CLIFFORD, Eth (Harvey Series)

Harvey's Horrible Snake Disaster. Houghton, 1984
Harvey's Marvelous Monkey Mystery. Houghton, 1987
Harvey's Wacky Parrot Adventure. Houghton, 1990

Harvey is normal most of the time. In fact, his life only gets out of hand when he joins forces with his cousin Nora. Part of the trouble arises because he is determined to prove his superiority to her. They encounter funny adventures and mysteries that will keep readers 8-12 entertained.

CLIFFORD, Eth (Jo-Beth and Mary Rose Mysteries)

1—*Help! I'm a Prisoner in the Library*. Houghton, 1979
2—*The Dastardly Murder of Dirty Pete*. Houghton, 1981
3—*Just Tell Me When We're Dead!* Houghton, 1983
4—*Scared Silly*. Houghton, 1988

This popular series features sisters Jo-Beth and Mary Rose and their assorted spooky adventures. There are enough shivers here, albeit tempered with humor, to delight young fans grade 3-6. Among their exploits: escaping from a locked library and investigating a famous magician.

COHEN, Barbara

The Christmas Revolution. Bantam, 1988
The Orphan Game. Bantam, 1989

Twins Emily and Sally Berg are Jewish, and the series begins when they find themselves drawn into another Jewish friend's rebellion against participating in school Christmas events. This is well written with believable characters, as is the followup volume, which focuses on the disruptive arrival of a cousin. Grades 4-6.

COLE, Jennifer (Sisters Series)

1—*Three's a Crowd*. Fawcett, 1986
2—*Too Late for Love*. Fawcett, 1986
3—*The Kiss*. Fawcett, 1986
4—*Secrets at Seventeen*. Fawcett, 1986
5—*Always a Pair*. Fawcett, 1986
6—*On Thin Ice*. Fawcett, 1986
7—*Star Quality*. Fawcett, 1987
8—*Making Waves*. Fawcett, 1987
9—*Too Many Cooks*. Fawcett, 1987
10—*Out of the Woods*. Fawcett, 1987
11—*Never a Dull Moment*. Fawcett, 1987
12—*Mollie in Love*. Fawcett, 1987
13—*College Bound*. Fawcett, 1988
14—*And Then There Were Two*. Fawcett, 1988
15—*The Boy Next Door*. Fawcett, 1988
16—*Campus Fever*. Fawcett, 1988
17—*Love Is in the Air*. Fawcett, 1989
18—*Making Up*. Fawcett, 1989

Cindy, Nicole and Mollie are sisters and best friends. They do everything together and share with each other secrets, problems, romance and more. These books are about their adventures as they grow up, go through high school and enter college. Sixth grade and up.

COLEMAN, Clay (Escape from Lost Island)
1–*Attack!* Harper, 1990
2–*Stranded!* Harper, 1990
3–*Mutiny!* Harper, 1990
4–*Discovered!* Harper, 1990
5–*Revenge!* Harper, 1991
6–*Escape!* Harper, 1991
This is an adventure series that should snare boys and reluctant readers. A group of boys are stranded because of a plane crash on an island in Micronesia. For various reasons, no attempt will be made to rescue them. The island is not deserted, and a secret project had once been tried there. Lots of room for ongoing excitement for readers grades 4-8.

COLLIER, Christopher, and **James Lincoln COLLIER** (Arabus Family Saga)
War Comes to Willy Freeman. Delacorte, 1983
Jump Ship to Freedom. Delacorte, 1981
Who Is Carrie? Delacorte, 1984
The Colliers have written a super series set during Revolutionary times and featuring a family of African-Americans who fight for freedom only to find that with the new country obtaining its liberty, they have lost theirs. Excellent choices for grades 5-8.

COLLIER FAST FICTION (Series)
GODFREY, Martyn
The Last War. Collier, 1988
IBBITSON, John
The Wimp and the Jock. Collier, 1988
KROPP, Paul
Death Ride. Collier, 1988
Jo's Search. Collier, 1988
This series of fast paced, easy reading young adult novels was designed for the reluctant reader. The words are basic, the print large and there are some pencil sketches. All of these books are less than 100 pages long. The themes run from teen alcoholism to a girl's search for her birth parents to nuclear holocaust to trying out for the high school football team.

CONE, Molly (Mishmash the Dog Series)
5–**Mishmash and the Robot*. Houghton, 1981
6–*Mishmash and the Big Fat Problem*. Houghton, 1982
Mishmash the dog returns in these adventures. Even though he now lives with teacher Miss Patch, he still gets into trouble. Among other things, he tangles with a robot, and has an attack of rivalry with a visiting pooch. Mishmash is not anthropomorphized; his reactions are normal doggy ones, and the people characters are equally believable. Fun for dog lovers grades 3-6.

CONFORD, Ellen
Dear Lovey Hart, I Am Desperate. Little, 1975
We Interrupt This Semester for an Important Bulletin. Little, 1979
Conford is a joy to read, with lots of humor and yet realistically depicted characters. Carrie handles the lovelorn column in her school newspaper. Her advice causes lots of problems for everyone, including herself. In the second book, a new girl moves in on her territory, both on the paper and in her love life. Although the kids are high schoolers, kids as young as 5th grade will enjoy them.

CONFORD, Ellen (Jenny Archer Series)
1–*A Job for Jenny Archer*. Little, 1988
2–*A Case for Jenny Archer*. Little, 1988
3–*Jenny Archer, Author*. Little, 1989
4–*What's Cooking, Jenny Archer?* Little, 1989

Part of Little's Springboard Series, these books about Jenny Archer are written for early readers grades 1-4. The stories are funny and believable within the limitations of the controlled vocabulary.

CONLY, Jane Leslie (NIMH Series)

Racso and the Rats of NIMH. Harper, 1986

R-T, Margaret, and the Rats of NIMH. Harper, 1990

Conly is the daughter of Robert O'Brien, who originated the rats of NIMH, winning a Newbery award in 1971 for *Mrs. Frisby and the Rats of NIMH*. These follow ups have been well received, praising her for maintaining both the characterizations and philosophy of the original. The movie, *The Secret of NIMH*, virtually guarantees an audience for these worthy successors. Grades 4-8.

CONSTANT, Alberta (*Miller Family Series)

3—*Does Anyone Care about Lou Emma Miller?* Crowell, 1979

In turn-of-the-century Kansas, oldest sister Lou Emma feels taken advantage of by her younger siblings. She also feels unnoticed by a boy she is particularly interested in. For those who enjoy historical novels, grades 5-8.

COOMBS, Patricia (*Dorrie the Witch Series)

13—*Dorrie and the Halloween Plot*. Lothrop, 1976

14—*Dorrie and the Screebit Ghost*. Lothrop, 1979

15—*Dorrie and the Witchville Fair*. Lothrop, 1980

16—*Dorrie and the Dreamyard Monsters*. Dell, 1982

17—*Dorrie and the Witch's Camp*. Lothrop, 1983

18—*Dorrie and the Museum Case*. Lothrop, 1986

19—*Dorrie and the Pin Witch*. Lothrop, 1989

Since 1962, author Coombs has been entertaining readers with her humorous tales of Dorrie, the apprentice witch. Children continue to enjoy her adventures, and the author's saucy illustrations add to the fun. Ages 8-10.

COONEY, Caroline B.

Camp Boy-Meets-Girl. Bantam, 1988

Camp Reunion. Bantam, 1988

Typical teen fare about counselors and campers who find romance among the mosquitoes. The second book finds them readying for a reunion. None of the new summer friends has kept in touch, so they are not sure how it will go.

COONEY, Caroline

The Fog. Scholastic, 1989

The Snow. Scholastic, 1990

The Fire. Scholastic, 1990

This trilogy is about a girl on her own and the evil she has to face in her life. The horror and suspense involved in these books are gobbled up by young adults as quickly as they hit the shelves. Popular books along the line of R. L. Stine and Christopher Pike. Seventh grade and up.

COONEY, Linda (Freshman Dorm)

1—*Freshman Dorm*. Harper, 1990

2—*Freshman Lies*. Harper, 1990

3—*Freshman Guys*. Harper, 1990

4—*Freshman Nights*. Harper, 1990

5—*Freshman Dreams*. Harper, 1991

6—*Freshman Games*. Harper, 1991

7—*Freshman Loves*. Harper, 1991

8—*Freshman Secrets*. Harper, 1991

9—*Freshman Schemes*. Harper, 1991
10—*Freshman Changes*. Harper, 1991
11—*Freshman Fling*. Harper, 1991
12—*Freshman Rivals*. Harper, 1991

Remember when you were a college freshman? Freedom, guys, best friends, guys, homework and guys. Well, we meet three close friends who are in their freshman year in this original paperback series. They grapple everything from roommates to homework to—you guessed it—guys. This is a popular draw in public libraries for grades 7-9.

COONEY, Linda (Class of...)
1—*Freshman 88*. Scholastic, 1987
2—*Freshman 89*. Scholastic, 1988
3—*Sophomore 88*. Scholastic, 1987
4—*Sophomore 89*. Scholastic, 1988
5—*Junior 88*. Scholastic, 1987
6—*Junior 89*. Scholastic, 1988
7—*Senior 88*. Scholastic, 1987
8—*Senior 89*. Scholastic, 1988

These books all seem to be related with the same characters and setting. The characters have been friends forever and are now facing the life of high school. This is a popular original paperback series for young adults 12 and older.

COONEY, Linda (Sunset High Series)
1—*Getting Experienced*. Fawcett, 1985
2—*A Chance to Make It*. Fawcett, 1985
3—*Temptations*. Fawcett, 1985
4—*Over the Edge*. Fawcett, 1986
5—*Swept Away*. Fawcett, 1986
6—*Working It Out*. Fawcett, 1986
7—*Just Friends*. Fawcett, 1986
8—*Perfect Strangers*. Fawcett, 1986
9—*No Secrets*. Fawcett, 1986
10—*The Night Before*. Fawcett, 1986

Focused on the students at mythical Sunset High, this series is filled with all that one would expect: romance, summer fun, jocks, school work and more. Grades 7 and up.

COOPER, Ilene (Kids from Kennedy Middle School)
1—*Queen of the Sixth Grade*. Morrow, 1988
2—*The Winning of Miss Lynn Ryan*. Morrow, 1987
3—*Choosing Sides*. Morrow, 1990
4—*Mean Streak*. Morrow, 1991

Various students from Kennedy Middle School go through their crises in this series. Young Carrie cannot seem to get on the good side of her teacher; Jonathan finds that his overly-demanding coach is spoiling his enjoyment of basketball. Although the "kids" are middle school age, the vocabulary and illustrations make the series more appropriate fare for grades 4-6.

COOPER, Margaret
Solution: Escape. Walker, 1980
Code Name: Clone. Walker, 1982

An unusual sci-fi series, the opener has two boys discovering each other through telepathic links. They find that they are clones in a totalitarian state. The follow up has them escaping and searching for their father, a defector with a new identity. The ideas are interesting, but the writing is rather stilted, and the characters are superficially written. Grades 4-6.

COOPER, Susan (*Dark Is Rising Sequence)

5–*Silver on the Tree*. Atheneum, 1977

The final entry in this outstanding fantasy series has the children searching for the crystal sword that will turn the tide in the last battle. Grades 5-8.

CORBETT, Scott (*Trick Books)

11–*Black Mask Trick*. Little, 1976

12–*Hangman's Ghost Trick*. Little, 1977

Kerby Maxwell began his association with Mrs. Graymalkin and magic a long time ago. These two books continue their adventures, which include helping Mrs. G. win a cooking contest by finding her missing magic ingredient. Some of the verve is missing, but 4th to 6th graders still enjoy these.

CORBETT, W. J. (Pentecost Series)

Song of Pentecost. Dutton, 1982

Pentecost, the Chosen One. Delacorte, 1987

Readers who like the O'Brien/Conly NIMH books will find these somewhat similar. The first book details how the leader must move the mice of Pentecost Farm to a new location. The second shows what happens to the group after resettlement and new problems begin, only to find the new Pentecost too deeply depressed to deal with them. The first entry won the Whitbread Award. Excellent choices for grades 5 and up.

CORCORAN, Barbara

1–*You're Allegro Dead*. Atheneum, 1981

2–*Watery Grave*. Atheneum, 1982

3–*August, Die She Must*. Atheneum, 1984

4–*Mystery on Ice*. Atheneum, 1985

Kim and Stella attend Camp Allegro. They encounter (and solve) a number of mysteries there. There are also the usual personal and boy-girl problems, but Corcoran is a veteran author with a sure touch. Grades 4-6.

COREY, Deirdre (Friends 4-Ever)

1–*P.S. We'll Miss You*. Scholastic, 1990

2–*Yours 'til the Meatball Bounces*. Scholastic, 1990

3–*2 Sweet 2 B 4-gotten*. Scholastic, 1990

4–*Remember Me When This You See*. Scholastic, 1990

5–*Sealed with a Hug*. Scholastic, 1990

6–*Friends til the Ocean Waves*. Scholastic, 1990

7–*Friends 4-Ever Minus One*. Scholastic, 1991

8–*Mysteriously Yours*. Scholastic, 1991

The Sweet Valley/Babysitters Club crowd will enjoy this similar series about a group of girl friends. Facile but popular for grades 4-6. The gimmick here revolves around collecting autographs.

CORMIER, Robert (Chocolate War Series)

The Chocolate War. Pantheon, 1974

Beyond the Chocolate War. Knopf, 1985

Cormier is one of the most thought-provoking and outstanding authors writing today in the YA field. His characters are multi-faceted, and his plots involve the reader in both the complexities of the human spirit and the disintegration of values. These two books cover one school year and examine the uses and abuses of power. Musts for all collections.

COVILLE, Bruce (Camp Haunted Hills)

How I Survived My Summer Vacation. Minstrel, 1988

Some of My Best Friends Are Monsters. Minstrel, 1988

The Dinosaur That Followed Me Home. Minstrel, 1990

Much funnier than most monster-related entries, these find kids attending a camp run by Gregory Stevens, a horror movie director. What no one realizes is that he is using the camp to try out his horrible special effects. Lots of scares and adventures follow. Grades 4-6.

COVILLE, Bruce

The Ghost in the Third Row. Bantam, 1987
The Ghost Wore Gray. Bantam, 1988

Nina and Chris seem to have a special affinity for troubled ghosts. Their first adventure involves a theater murder, the second a handsome Confederate soldier. Mildly spooky fare in an attractive paperback format should prove popular with readers 9-12.

COVILLE, Bruce (My Teacher Series)

My Teacher Is an Alien. Minstrel, 1989
My Teacher Is Still an Alien. Minstrel, 1990
My Teacher Fried My Brains. Minstrel, 1991

The titles alone will sell these books to the eight-to-twelve year old set. All kids feel that their teachers (and most adults) have just arrived from outer space. In this case, Susan is right, and she must save her classmates from a fate worse than homework.

CRESSWELL, Helen (Bagthorpe Series)

1—*Ordinary Jack*. Macmillan, 1977
2—*Absolute Zero*. Macmillan, 1978
3—*Bagthorpes Unlimited*. Macmillan, 1978
4—*Bagthorpes vs. the World*. Macmillan, 1979
5—*Bagthorpes Abroad*. Macmillan, 1984
6—*Bagthorpes Haunted*. Macmillan, 1985
7—*Bagthorpes Liberated*. Macmillan, 1989

The Bagthorpes are a very large, very eccentric English family. Most of the family are very full of themselves, often expressing what Mrs. Bagthorpe calls, "having just pride in one's own talents and accomplishments." Only Jack and his dog keep a low profile, because they are so ordinary by comparison. This family can take any minor event and turn it into a major boondoggle through their competitiveness. They search out ghosts in Wales, try to outdo one another at winning contests, and try to survive computer induced bankruptcy. This is a truly hilarious series that needs to find its audience among humor fanciers ages 8-12.

CROFFORD, Emily (Weston Family Series)

A Matter of Pride. Carolrhoda, 1981
The Blue Road. Carolrhoda, 1982

Set on a farm in Depression Arkansas, these books offer a loose collection of stories that explore the lives of the Weston family. Life is indeed tough; the children cannot afford to get attached to the baby farm animals, because they will be sold or slaughtered. But there is strong family feeling to carry them through. The plot lines are pretty strong stuff and sometimes seem more like reminiscences than actual story lines. For grades 4-6.

CROSS, Gilbert B.

Mystery at Loon Lake. Atheneum, 1986
Terror Train! Atheneum, 1987

Jeff and his adopted Vietnamese brother Nguyen find mystery and adventure. These are pretty good, with likeable heroes and a readable writing style, good for grades 4-7.

CUNNINGHAM, Julia

3—**Silent Voice*. Dutton, 1981

The mute mime, Auguste, is found nearly dead on the street by a group of other homeless urchins. He finally finds the teacher and a full scope for his talent in this final entry in the series. Grades 5-9.

CURRY, Jane

4– **Birdstone*. Atheneum, 1977

Continuing this fine fantasy series, Pooch finds a stone carved in the shape of a bird. Odd things begin to happen in his town of Apple Lock. An imaginary girl seems to come alive, and all the events may relate to an earlier time and place called Abaloc. Not easy, but worth the read for grades 5-9.

CURRY, Jane

Mindy's Mysterious Miniature. Atheneum, 1970

The Lost Farm. Atheneum, 1974

This marvelous series opens with Mindy getting a dollhouse. When her neighbor sees it, she is struck by its resemblance to her own childhood home, which suddenly disappeared one day. Professor L. L. Put turns them into miniatures as well. The second book finds Pete, whose father has stolen the house from the sinister Professor Lilliput, having to rescue his farm and family when everyone else has been reduced to miniatures. Grades 5-8.

CURRY, Jane

Parsley, Sage, Rosemary and Time. Harcourt, 1975

Magical Cupboard. Atheneum, 1976

These books are related because of the presence in each of the magic cupboard. In the first, Rosemary discovers a special sprig of thyme that literally makes time stop. In the second, the orphan Felicity moves west with the cupboard, and catches glimpses of Rosemary in 1976. Both accomplished fantasies for grades 5-8.

CURRY, Jane

Wolves of Aam. Atheneum, 1981

Shadow Dancers. Atheneum, 1983

This fantasy series follows the trials of the people of Astarlind, where strange portents hail the arrival of a new battle between good and evil. Grades 5-8.

DALY, Maureen

Acts of Love. Scholastic, 1986

First a Dream. Scholastic, 1990

The author of *Seventeenth Summer* has written these two romance novels for young adults. Retta meets and falls in love with Dallas, a "difficult boy." He is secretive and has lived a hard, nomadic life. She finds out about Dallas on her own and decides to make something out of their lives. In the second volume, Retta has moved with her family to California, and Dallas takes a summer job nearby so they can be together. But problems arise, between the two of them and with others. Both are quality romances that should be enjoyed by young adults.

DANK, Milton

The Dangerous Game. Lippincott, 1977

Game's End. Lippincott, 1979

Charles is 15 and alone in occupied Paris during World War II. He joins up with the Resistance and is thrown into the world of adult terror and betrayal. He matures quickly as he meets German soldiers and French traitors. He survives and at 19 he becomes an officer in the Free French Army and a spy for the British, as they prepare for the Allied invasion. Grades 7 and up.

DANK, Milton

Khaki Wings. Delacorte, 1980

Red Flight Two. Delacorte, 1981

Edward, 16, signs up to be a pilot for Britain during World War I. He loves the adventure but soon he is the only one left alive from his original squadron and he learns that the adventure is not quite as exhilarating as he first thought. Two years later, after being recognized for his performance and suffering a nervous breakdown, he must return to action because of heavy

British losses. He leads his old squadron and must now decide who is sent out under impossible odds. Lots of action and adventure in these two coming of age novels. Thirteen and up.

DANZIGER, Paula

The Cat Ate My Gymsuit. Delacorte, 1974
There's a Bat in Bunk Five. Delacorte, 1980

Readers will thoroughly enjoy meeting Marcy as she learns to think for herself under the tutelage of a new teacher. She eventually becomes a camp counselor, coping with romance and campers at the same time, with hilarious results. Grades 4-7.

DANZIGER, Paula

The Divorce Express. Delacorte, 1982
It's an Aardvark-Eat-Turtle World. Delacorte, 1985

This is another popular series, featuring friends Rosie and Phoebe who meet aboard the "divorce express," the train that shuttles them between parental visits. After a period of matchmaking, their parents do marry each other. Then the girls have to adjust to being "sisters." Good choice for grades 4-7.

DANZIGER, Paula

Everyone Else's Parents Said Yes. Delacorte, 1989
Make Like a Tree and Leave. Delacorte, 1990
Earth to Matthew. Delacorte, 1991

In this series, Paula Danziger utilizes an eleven year old boy named Matthew Martin. He's a highly organized computer nut with an obnoxious older sister and a health food freak mother. His latest finds him becoming interested in ecology—and a girl! These are amusing and should earn the author even more new fans. Grades 4-7.

DAVIDSON, Linda (Endless Summer)

1—*Treading Water*. Ivy, 1988
2—*Too Hot to Handle*. Ivy, 1988
3—*On the Edge*. Ivy, 1988
4—*Cool Breezes*. Ivy, 1989
5—*Changing Gears*. Ivy, 1989
6—*Fast Forward*. Ivy, 1989

Russell Stevens sees his parents off on a European vacation. He is looking forward to a summer filled with days at the beach, girl watching, and driving the new sports car he and his sister got for graduation. All goes well until he has an accident. In order to raise the money he needs to pay for the repairs, he convinces his sister to rent out the rooms in their house. They make new friends and experience all sorts of adventure and romance. Seventh grade and up.

DAVIS, Gibbs (Never Sink Nine)

1—*Walter's Lucky Socks*. Bantam, 1991
2—*Major League Melissa*. Bantam, 1991
3—*Slugger Mike*. Bantam, 1991
4—*Pete the Magnificent*. Bantam, 1991

Like the High Fives, this series features a group of sports-oriented boys, this time a baseball team. The plots are predictable but easy to digest for sports lovers grades 4-6.

DE CLEMENTS, Barthe

Five-Finger Discount. Dell, 1989
Monkey See, Monkey Do. Dell, 1990
Breaking Out. Dell, 1991

Jerry Johnson has an unusual problem in a series intended for grades 4-6—his father is a convict. A classmate discovers it, and threatens to tell. The second book finds Dad out of prison, but taking up with his old rotten friends again. By the third, Jerry has learned he must accept his parents' flaws, and tries to help friend Grace to fit into the new school climate. De Clements writes believable stories with believable characters, and is a deservedly popular author for this age group.

DE CLEMENTS, Barthe
1–*Fourth Grade Wizards*. Viking, 1988
2–*Nothing's Fair in Fifth Grade*. Viking, 1981
3–*Sixth Grade Can Really Kill You*. Viking, 1985
4–*How Do You Lose Those Ninth Grade Blues?* Viking, 1983
5–*Seventeen and In-Between*. Viking, 1984
This is one of the most popular fiction series around for 9-12 year olds. De Clements's background as teacher, counselor, and psychologist have really given her the inside track on how youngsters think and what they enjoy. There is a child in Elsie Edwards's group of friends that any reader can identify with. As she and her friends get older, the stakes get higher and their problems more adult. These are "must haves" in any collection.

DELTON, Judy (Angel Series)
1–*Back Yard Angel*. Houghton, 1983
2–*Angel in Charge*. Houghton, 1985
3–*Angel's Mother's Boyfriend*. Houghton, 1986
4–*Angel's Mother's Wedding*. Houghton, 1987
5–*Angel's Mother's Baby*. Houghton, 1989
Angel certainly has a lot on her plate. When the series begins, she finds herself increasingly responsible for the care of her five year old brother. Her worries change when her mother falls in love with a clown! The subsequent marriage and impending siblinghood add further plot developments. Delton is an accomplished writer whose characters are believable and charming. These will be sure fire hits with grades 3-6.

DELTON, Judy (Condo Kids)
1–*Hello Huckleberry Heights*. Dell, 1990
2–*Summer Showdown*. Dell, 1990
3–*The Artificial Grandma*. Dell, 1990
4–*Huckleberry Hash*. Dell, 1990
5–*Scary, Scary Huckleberry*. Dell, 1990
6–*Merry, Merry Huckleberry*. Dell, 1990
The Condo Kids are neighbors in a condominium complex who share adventures. Delton is a skilled author who infuses a formula series with fun and vigor. Grades 3-5.

DELTON, Judy (Kitty Series)
1–*Kitty from the Start*. Houghton, 1987
2–*Kitty in the Middle*. Houghton, 1979
3–*Kitty in the Summer*. Houghton, 1980
4–*Kitty in High School*. Houghton, 1984
This series follows Kitty through her days in Catholic elementary school clear into high school. The books are set during World War II, but Kitty is still a very contemporary child. Her reactions to moving, trying to raise money to win a puppy, and falling in love for the first time make for enjoyable fare for grades 3-6.

DELTON, Judy (Peewee Scouts)
1–*Cookies and Crutches*. Dell, 1988
2–*Camp Ghost-Away*. Dell, 1988
3–*Lucky Dog Days*. Dell, 1988
4–*Blue Skies, French Fries*. Dell, 1988
5–*Grumpy Pumpkins*. Dell, 1988
6–*Peanut-Butter Pilgrims*. Dell, 1988
7–*Pee Wee Christmas*. Dell, 1988

8–*That Mushy Stuff*. Dell, 1989
9–*Spring Sprouts*. Dell, 1989
10–*The Pooped Troop*. Dell, 1989
11–*The Pee Wee Jubilee*. Dell, 1989
12–*Bad, Bad Bunnies*. Dell, 1990
13–*Rosy Noses, Freezing Toes*. Dell, 1990

Delton has a light touch and a nice sense of humor that is bound to appeal to the young audience she has in mind for these simply written books. The PeeWees are boys and girls in second grade who meet at each others' homes (under parental leadership) and resemble a brownie/cub scout group. Good for readers making the transition from picture books. Grades 2-3.

DEVER, Joe (Freeway Warrior Series)
1–*Highway Holocaust*. Berkley, 1989
2–*Mountain Run*. Berkley, 1990
3–*Omega Zone*. Berkley, 1990
4–*California Countdown*. Berkley, 1990

Like Dever's Lone Wolf series, this is also interactive fiction. This is set in the future after a nuclear war. Here the reader is the Freeway Warrior, a sort of Mad Max. The format is more appropriate to older teens and adults.

DEVER, Joe, and **Gary CHALK**
"Lone Wolf Series"
1–*Flight from the Dark*. Berkley, 1986
2–*Fire on the Water*. Berkley, 1986
3–*Caverns of Kalte*. Berkley, 1986
4–*Chasm of Doom*. Berkley, 1986
5–*Shadow on the Sand*. Berkley, 1986
6–*Kingdom of Terror*. Berkley, 1987
7–*Castle of Death*. Berkley, 1987
8–*Jungle of Horrors*. Berkley, 1987
9–*Cauldron of Fear*. Berkley, 1988
10–*Dungeons of Torgar*. Berkley, 1987
11–*Prisoners of Time*. Berkley, 1989
12–*Masters of Darkness*. Berkley, 1989
"World of Lone Wolf"
1–*Grey Star the Wizard*. Berkley, 1985
2–*Forbidden City*. Berkley, 1986
3–*Beyond the Nightmare Gate*. Berkley, 1986
4–*War of the Wizards*. Berkley, 1987
"Legends of Lone Wolf"
1–*Eclipse of the Kai*. Berkley, 1990
2–*The Dark Door Opens*. Berkley, 1991
3–*Tides of Treachery*. Berkley, 1991

This role-playing series is sort of a cross between Choose Your Own Adventures and the Dungeons and Dragons-related books aimed at older teens and adults. The reader is Lone Wolf, an adventure hero set in a Medieval-style future. As in CYOA, the reader may determine which course of action the hero follows. The first series is for older teens; the last two for grades 5 and up.

DE WEESE, Gene
Black Suits from Outer Space. Putnam, 1985
The Dandelion Caper. Putnam, 1986
The Calvin Nullifier. Putnam, 1987

This sci-fi series opens with bespectacled Calvin and friend Kathy encountering aliens who vary in form from cats to men in black suits to a ten-foot hairy monster. The combination of adventure and humor will appeal to readers 8-12.

D'IGNAZIO, Fred (Chip Mitchell Series)

Chip Mitchell: The Case of the Stolen Computer Brains. Dutton, 1982
Chip Mitchell: The Case of the Robot Warriors. Dutton, 1984
Chip Mitchell: The Case of the Chocolate-Covered Bugs. Dutton, 1985

Like Encyclopedia Brown, Chip Mitchell solves 10 mysteries. Unlike Brown, Chip is a computer whiz, so his stories are full of computer activities and explanations, which should find an audience with computer-literate readers grades 4-7.

DIXON, Franklin (Hardy Boys Mystery)

1—*The Tower Treasure*. Grosset, 1927
2—*The House on the Cliff*. Grosset, 1927
3—*The Secret of the Old Mill*. Grosset, 1927
4—*The Missing Chums*. Grosset, 1930
5—*Hunting for Hidden Gold*. Grosset, 1928
6—*The Shore Road Mystery*. Grosset, 1964
7—*The Secret of the Caves*. Grosset, 1929
8—*The Mystery of Cabin Island*. Grosset, 1929
9—*The Great Airport Mystery*. Grosset, 1930
10—*What Happened at Midnight*. Grosset, 1931
11—*While the Clock Ticked*. Grosset, 1932
12—*Footprints Under the Window*. Grosset, 1933
13—*The Mark on the Door*. Grosset, 1934
14—*The Hidden Harbor Mystery*. Grosset, 1935
15—*The Sinister Signpost*. Grosset, 1936
16—*A Figure in Hiding*. Grosset, 1937
17—*The Secret Warning*. Grosset, 1938
18—*The Twisted Claw*. Grosset, 1939
19—*The Disappearing Floor*. Grosset, 1940
20—*The Mystery of the Flying Express*. Grosset, 1941
21—*The Clue of the Broken Blade*. Grosset, 1942
22—*The Flickering Torch Mystery*. Grosset, 1943
23—*The Melted Coins*. Grosset, 1944
24—*The Short-Wave Mystery*. Grosset, 1928
25—*The Secret Panel*. Grosset, 1946
26—*The Phantom Freighter*. Grosset, 1947
27—*The Secret of Skull Mountain*. Grosset, 1948
28—*The Sign of the Crooked Arrow*. Grosset, 1949
29—*The Secret of the Lost Tunnel*. Grosset, 1950
30—*The Wailing Siren Mystery*. Grosset, 1951
31—*The Secret of Wildcat Swamp*. Grosset, 1952
32—*The Crisscross Shadow*. Grosset, 1953
33—*The Yellow Feather Mystery*. Grosset, 1954
34—*The Hooded Hawk Mystery*. Grosset, 1955
35—*The Clue in the Embers*. Grosset, 1956
36—*The Secret of Pirates' Hill*. Grosset, 1957
37—*The Ghost at Skeleton Rock*. Grosset, 1958
38—*The Mystery at Devil's Paw*. Grosset, 1959
39—*The Mystery of the Chinese Junk*. Grosset, 1959
40—*The Mystery of the Desert Giant*. Grosset, 1960
41—*The Clue of the Screeching Owl*. Grosset, 1962
42—*The Viking Symbol Mystery*. Grosset, 1963
43—*The Mystery of the Aztec Warrior*. Grosset, 1964
44—*The Haunted Fort*. Grosset, 1964
45—*The Mystery of the Spiral Bridge*. Grosset, 1966
46—*The Secret Agent on Flight 101*. Grosset, 1967
47—*The Mystery of the Whale Tattoo*. Grosset, 1967

48—*The Arctic Patrol Mystery*. Grosset, 1969
49—*The Bombay Boomerang*. Grosset, 1970
50—*Danger on Vampire Trail*. Grosset, 1971
51—*The Masked Monkey*. Grosset, 1972
52—*The Shattered Helmet*. Grosset, 1973
53—*The Clue of the Hissing Serpent*. Grosset, 1974
54—*The Mysterious Caravan*. Grosset, 1975
55—*The Witchmaster's Key*. Grosset, 1976
56—*The Jungle Pyramid*. Grosset, 1977
57—*The Firebird Rocket*. Grosset, 1978
58—*The Sting of the Scorpion*. Grosset, 1979
59—*Night of the Werewolf*. Wanderer, 1979
60—*The Mystery of the Samurai Sword*. Wanderer, 1979
61—*Hardy Boys: The Pentagon Spy*. Wanderer, 1980
62—*Hardy Boys: The Apeman's Secret*. Wanderer, 1980
63—*Hardy Boys: The Mummy Case*. Wanderer, 1980
64—*Hardy Boys: Mystery of Smuggler's Cove*. Wanderer, 1980
65—*Hardy Boys: The Stone Idol*. Wanderer, 1981
66—*Hardy Boys: The Vanishing Thieves*. Wanderer, 1981
67—*Hardy Boys: The Outlaw's Silver*. Wanderer, 1981
68—*Hardy Boys: The Submarine Caper*. Wanderer, 1981
69—*The Four-Headed Dragon Mystery*. Pocket, 1981
70—*Hardy Boys: The Infinity Clue*. Wanderer, 1981
71—*Hardy Boys: Track of the Zombie*. Wanderer, 1982
72—*Hardy Boys: Voodoo Plot*. Wanderer, 1982
73—*Hardy Boys: Billion Dollar Ransom*. Wanderer, 1982
74—*Hardy Boys: Tic-Tac Terror*. Wanderer, 1982
75—*Hardy Boys: Trapped at Sea*. Wanderer, 1982
76—*Hardy Boys: Game Plan for Disaster*. Wanderer, 1982
77—*The Crimson Flame*. Wanderer, 1983
78—*Cave-In*. Wanderer, 1983
79—*Sky Sabotage*. Wanderer, 1983
80—*The Roaring River Mystery*. Wanderer, 1984
81—*Hardy Boys: Demon's Den*. Wanderer, 1984
82—*Hardy Boys: The Blackwing Puzzle*. S&S, 1984
83—*Hardy Boys: The Swamp Monster*. Wanderer, 1985
84—*Revenge of the Desert Phantom*. S&S, 1989
85—*Hardy Boys: The Skyfire Puzzle*. Wanderer, 1985
86—*The Mystery of the Silver Star*. S&S, 1987
87—*Program for Destruction*. S&S, 1987
88—*Tricky Business*. S&S, 1988
89—*The Sky Blue Frame*. S&S, 1988
90—*Danger on the Diamond*. S&S, 1988
91—*Shield of Fear*. S&S, 1988
92—*The Shadow Killers*. S&S, 1988
93—*The Serpent's Tooth Mystery*. S&S, 1988
94—*Breakdown in Axeblade*. S&S, 1989
95—*Danger on the Air*. S&S, 1989
96—*Wipeout*. S&S, 1989
97—*Cast of Criminals*. S&S, 1989
98—*Spark of Suspicion*. S&S, 1989
99—*Dungeon of Doom*. Pocket, 1989
100—*The Secret of the Island Treasure*. S&S, 1990
101—*The Money Hunt*. S&S, 1990
102—*Terminal Shock*. Pocket, 1990

103—*Million Dollar Nightmare*. S&S, 1990
104—*Tricks of the Trade*. Pocket, 1990
105—*Smoke Screen Mystery*. Minstrel, 1990
106—*Attack of the Video Villains*. Minstrel, 1991
107—*Panic on Gull Island*. Minstrel, 1991
108—*Fear on Wheels*. Minstrel, 1991
109—*The Prime Time Crime*. Minstrel, 1991

Over 60 years old, and they still look like teens! The Hardy Boys still keep rolling along. One of several entries (including Nancy Drew and the Bobbsey Twins) of the Stratemeyer Syndicate, these may be written by committee, but their popularity endures. They are certainly a good bet for reluctant readers, as well as others ages 12-14. To capture the teen market, the publishers have come up with a trendy spinoff, the Hardy Boys Casefiles.

DIXON, Franklin W. (The Hardy Boys Casefiles)
1—*Dead on Target*. Archway, 1987
2—*Evil, Inc.* Archway, 1987
3—*Cult of Crime*. Archway, 1987
4—*The Lazarus Plot*. Archway, 1987
5—*Edge of Destruction*. Archway, 1987
6—*The Crowning Terror*. Archway, 1987
7—*Deathgame*. Archway, 1987
8—*See No Evil*. Archway, 1987
9—*The Genius Thieves*. Archway, 1987
10—*Hostages of Hate*. Archway, 1987
11—*Brother against Brother*. Archway, 1988
12—*Perfect Getaway*. Archway, 1988
13—*The Borgia Disaster*. Archway, 1988
14—*Too Many Traitors*. Archway, 1988
15—*Blood Relations*. Archway, 1988
16—*Line of Fire*. Archway, 1988
17—*The Number File*. Archway, 1988
18—*A Killing in the Market*. Archway, 1988
19—*Nightmare in Angel City*. Archway, 1988
20—*Witness to Murder*. Archway, 1988
21—*Street Spies*. Archway, 1988
22—*Double Exposure*. Archway, 1988
23—*Disaster for Hire*. Archway, 1989
24—*Scene of the Crime*. Archway, 1989
25—*The Borderline Case*. Archway, 1989
26—*Trouble in the Pipeline*. Archway, 1989
27—*Nowhere to Run*. Archway, 1989
28—*Countdown to Terror*. Archway, 1989
29—*Thick as Thieves*. Archway, 1989
30—*The Deadliest Dare*. Archway, 1989
31—*Without a Trace*. Archway, 1989
32—*Blood Money*. Archway, 1989
33—*Collision Course*. Archway, 1989
34—*The Final Cut*. Archway, 1989
35—*The Dead Season*. Archway, 1990
36—*Running on Empty*. Archway, 1990
37—*Danger Zone*. Archway, 1990
38—*Diplomatic Deceit*. Archway, 1990
39—*Flesh and Blood*. Archway, 1990
40—*Fright Wave*. Archway, 1990
41—*Highway Robbery*. Archway, 1990

42—*The Last Laugh*. Archway, 1990
43—*Strategic Moves*. Archway, 1990
44—*Castle Fear*. Archway, 1990
45—*In Self Defense*. Archway, 1990
46—*Foul Play*. Archway, 1990
47—*Flight into Danger*. Archway, 1990
48—*Rock 'n' Revenge*. Archway, 1990
49—*Dirty Deeds*. Archway, 1990
50—*Power Play*. Archway, 1990
51—*Choke Hold*. Archway, 1990
52—*Uncivil War*. Archway, 1990
53—*Web of Horror*. Archway, 1990
54—*Deep Trouble*. Archway, 1991
55—*Beyond the Law*. Archway, 1991

The Hardy Boys are back! This paperback series brings the two detective brothers into the hands of an all new generation of readers. These books have a more mature Frank and Joe solving mysteries again, except now, they are living in the 1990s and are a little more up to date. These are a must for a YA collection. Good for ages 12 and up.

DIXON, Paige
May I Cross Your Golden River? Atheneum, 1975
Skipper. Atheneum, 1979

The first entry in this series is about teenage Jordan, who notices the first signs of his terminal illness at his birthday party. His brother Skipper does not understand why this has happened. In order to cope, he decides he must find the father he has never known. These two books are well done, not melodramatic. Good books for young adults 12 and older.

DONAHUE, Marilyn Cram
Straight along a Crooked Road. Walker, 1985
The Valley in Between. Walker, 1987

Emmie and her family suffer many hardships as they make the long trek from Vermont to their new home in California. The first book depicts those struggles. The second describes the homesteading, and what happens to the town when the Mormons leave and lawlessness reigns. Grades 5-7.

DRAGONFLIGHT (Series)
DE LINT, Charles
The Dreaming Place. Atheneum, 1990
SILVERBERG, Robert
Letters from Atlantis. Atheneum, 1990

Fantasy books are filled with excitement, suspense and thrilling adventure. These books are no exception. Two young time travelers return to the world of Atlantis to study the civilization in De Lint's book. Once their presence becomes known, they learn of some astonishing revelations about extraterrestrial visitation in pre-Stone Age Europe. The Silverberg book takes us into the world of evil spirits as two cousins, Ashley and Nina, come face-to-face with a fateful choice that involves life and death. These books are written by renowned fantasy authors and should be appreciated by young adults 12 and up.

DUANE, Diane
So You Want to Be a Wizard. Delacorte, 1983
Deep Wizardry. Delacorte, 1985
High Wizardry. Delacorte, 1990

On a visit to her local library, thirteen year old Nita comes across an instruction manual for the ancient art of wizardry. Readers who enjoy Diana Wynne Jones or Madeleine L'Engle will feel at home reading these three adventures. The tales are original and both funny and scary. YA.

DUFFY, James (May Gray Mysteries)
The Revolt of the Teddy Bears. Scribner, 1985
The Christmas Gang. Scribner, 1989
Although they seem like people, May Gray and her husband are French poodles—living in France. They hold people-type jobs, with May working for the police department. Her first case involved the teddy bears, several of whom now make their home with the Grays. Although the books are slim, their whimsy will be best appreciated by readers 10-13.

DUFFY, James
Missing. Scribner, 1988
The Man in the River. Scribner, 1990
Duffy has written two suspense-filled books for the 10-14 year old age group. Twelve year old Kate is picked up after school by a 'friend' of her mother's, who is actually a deranged kidnapper. Agatha Bates, a retired police officer, helps in the search for Kate and returns in the second book, to find out how Kate's father died.

DUNNAHOO, Terry (Espie Sanchez Series)
Who Cares about Espie Sanchez? Dutton, 1975
This Is Espie Sanchez. Dutton, 1976
Who Needs Espie Sanchez? Dutton, 1975
Esperanza Sanchez is a teen in the barrio and on her way to big trouble until she becomes involved with a law enforcement explorer group. Realistic problems are shown, with attention to detail and a believable background. YA.

EAST, Ben (Survival)
1—*Danger in the Air*. Crestwood, 1979
2—*Desperate Search*. Crestwood, 1979
3—*Frozen Terror*. Crestwood, 1979
4—*Mistaken Journey*. Crestwood, 1979
5—*Trapped in Devil's Hole*. Crestwood, 1979
Ben East was an editor of *Outdoor Life* magazine. These stories are real life adventures told to him and recounted by those involved. The writing is spare and factual but hardly as exciting as it could be. Marginal choices for grades 3-6.

EISENBERG, Lisa (Kate Clancy Series)
Mystery at Snowshoe Mountain Lodge. Dial, 1987
Mystery at Bluff Point Dunes. Dial, 1988
Mystery at Camp Windingo. Dial, 1991
Kate and her cousin Monty share assorted adventures-cum-mysteries at ski resorts and summer camps. Acceptable mystery fare for readers 9-12.

EISENBERG, Lisa (Lexie Series)
Leave It to Lexie. Viking, 1989
Happy Birthday, Lexie. Viking, 1991
Fourth grader Lexie often feels herself on the receiving end of things. She shares a room with her moody sister, her other sister is working entirely too hard on perfection, and her brother is a sports star. She can't even decide what to do for the talent show! Her lighthearted approach to life will capture readers grades 4-6.

ELFMAN, Blossom (Mike and Ally Mysteries)
Love Me Deadly. Fawcett, 1989
Tell Me No Lies. Fawcett, 1989
The Ghost-Sitter. Fawcett, 1990
These YA paperback mysteries are nothing special, but easy to read with the stereotypical brainy boy paired with the pretty egghead girl.

ELLIS, Lucy (Pink Parrots)

1 – *The Girls Strike Back*. Sports Illustrated, 1990
2 – *All That Jazz*. Sports Illustrated, 1990
3 – *Mixed Signals*. Sports Illustrated, 1991
4 – *Fielder's Choice*. Sports Illustrated, 1991

The Pink Parrots are an all-girl baseball team that the girls formed for themselves when they realized they were not getting equal time in the game with boy players with the same talents. Lots of sports lingo spices these up so that girl jocks will gravitate to them. Even with the sports bent, there are still the usual inter-personal problems. Grades 4-7.

ELLISON, Lucile Watkins

Butter on Both Sides. Scribner, 1979
Tie That Binds. Scribner, 1981

The author draws on her own childhood memories to fashion these stories of a large loving family living in Alabama at the turn of the century. Good and bad things happen, but the strong family ties keep them pulling together. Grades 4-6.

ELMORE, Patricia (Susannah Mysteries)

Susannah and the Blue House Mystery. Scholastic, 1990
Susannah and the Poison Green Halloween. Scholastic, 1990

Susannah and Lucy have decided to be detectives, and finally get a case when a younger classmate's grandfather disappears. Their second case involves finding a cruel prankster. These are a cut above most juvenile mysteries, with solid characterizations and well-constructed plots. Grades 4-6.

ENGDAHL, Sylvia

3 – **Doors of the Universe*. Atheneum, 1981

Noren has appeared in two previous books. In this one, he realizes that his people's efforts to synthesize metal to save themselves is misguided. The answer lies in genetics. His people are not inclined to try something so new. The mature fantasy reader will appreciate this. For YA to adult.

EWING, Kathryn

Private Matter. Harcourt, 1975
Things Won't Be the Same. Harcourt, 1980

Marcy lives with her mother, and becomes very attached to a retired neighbor couple. She loves the old man as though he is her father and is distraught when he moves away. She also must learn to adjust to her own move and new stepfather. These are movingly written for ages 8-11.

FACT AND FICTION BOOKS (Series)

RADLAUER, Ed, and **RUTH RADLAUER**

BMX Winners. Childrens, 1984
Guide Dog Winners. Childrens, 1983
Karting Winners. Childrens, 1982
Motorcycle Winners. Childrens, 1982
Soap Box Winners. Childrens, 1983

The Radlauers are primarily nonfiction writers, and this series is an attempt to teach readers about a subject by placing it within a story setting. This plus an index, glossary, and color photos make these far more informational than entertaining. A straight nonfiction approach would reach more readers.

FARLEY, Carol (Flee Jay Mysteries)
The Case of the Vanishing Villain. Avon, 1986
The Case of the Lost Lookalike. Avon, 1988
The Case of the Haunted Health Club. Avon, 1990
Flee Jay Saylor is burdened with a brilliant younger sister. They get involved in several mysteries, including one where they are held by an escaped convict. Readers are challenged to figure out the mystery before Clarice does, and all clues are tidied up in the last chapter. Grades 3-6.

FARLEY, Carol
1—*Mystery in the Ravine*. Avon, n.d.
2—*Mystery of the Fog Man*. Avon, n.d.
3—*The Case of the Fiery Message*. Avon, 1983
4—*The Mystery of the Melted Diamonds*. Avon, 1986
Cousins Kipper and Larry find themselves constantly enmeshed in mysteries and adventures. These really are exciting, plunging the reader immediately into the thick of the action—the third book opens immediately with a raging fire! Grades 4-6.

FARLEY, Walter, and **Steven FARLEY** (*Black Stallion Series)
15—*The Black Stallion Legend*. Random, 1983
16—*The Young Black Stallion*. Random, 1989
Walter Farley's son has taken his father's idea and turned it into a prequel of this ever-popular horse saga. It traces Black's life before his capture as he roams the mountains of Arabia. There are so few horse series anymore, this will be a sure hit. Ages 10-14.

FIFTH GRADE MONSTERS (Series)
GILDEN, Mel
1—*Born to Howl*. Camelot, 1987
2—*M Is for Monster*. Camelot, 1987
3—*The Pet of Frankenstein*. Camelot, 1988
HODGMAN, Ann
4—*There's a Batwing in My Lunchbox*. Camelot, 1988
GILDEN, Mel
5—*Z Is for Zombie*. Camelot, 1988
6—*Monster Mashers*. Camelot, 1989
7—*Things That Go Bark in the Park*. Camelot, 1989
8—*Yuckers!* Camelot, 1989
9—*The Monster in Creeps Head Bay*. Camelot, 1990
10—*How to Be a Vampire in One Easy Lesson*. Camelot, 1990
11—*Island of the Weird*. Camelot, 1990
12—*Werewolf Come Home*. Camelot, 1990
13—*Monster Boy*. Camelot, 1991
14—*Troll Patrol*. Camelot, 1991
15—*The Curse of the Dinosaur Bog*. Camelot, 1991
P. S. 13 has an unusual fifth-grade class comprising normal Danny Keegan, vampire C. D. Bitesky, werewolf Howie Wolfner, and Elisa and Frankie Stein. The comic-spooky combination is bound to interest a lot of readers, including reluctant ones. Fun for grades 3-6.

FIFTH GRADE STARS (Series)
NORBY, Lisa
1—*The Holly Hudnut Admiration Society*. Knopf, 1989
SAUNDERS, Susan
2—*Rent-a-Star*. Knopf, 1989
NORBY, Lisa
3—*Crazy Campout*. Knopf, 1989

SAUNDERS, Susan
4—*Twin Trouble*. Knopf, 1989
NORBY, Lisa
5—*Star Reporter*. Knopf, 1990
DOUGLAS, Anna Jo
6—*The Goofy Gamble*. Knopf, 1990
Much akin to other paperback series aimed at this age group (grades 4-7), this one features a group of girls of various personality and body types who have become friends/club members. These are all new girls in town who share the same homeroom. For fans of Sweet Valley, Babysitters, et al.

FLIPSIDE FICTION (Series)
ALLMAN, Paul
The Knot. Rosen, 1988
No Pain, No Gain. Rosen, 1987
COLE, Barbara
Alex the Great. Rosen, 1989
Don't Tell a Soul. Rosen, 1987
DUMOND, Michael
Dad Is Leaving Home. Rosen, 1987
KURLAND, Morton L.
Our Sacred Honor. Rosen, 1987
MCCLASKEY, Marilyn H.
What Kind of Name Is Juan? Rosen, 1989
RUE, Nancy
Stop in the Name of Love. Rosen, 1988
These YA novels are designed to awaken moral/ethical considerations in readers. Each story revolves around a "problem," such as teen pregnancy. Half the book presents the story from one point of view, then the other half tells it from the opposing viewpoint.

FORRESTER, John (Bestiary Trilogy)
Bestiary Mountain. Macmillan, 1985
Secret of the Round Beast. Macmillan, 1986
The Forbidden Beast. Macmillan, 1988
These three science fiction books are about twins Tamara and Drewyn. In book one, they escape the highly controlled society in which they live to find their scientist mother, on abandoned Earth. In its sequel the twins are pitted against an evil geneticist and the hordes of half-animal, half-human creatures he has made. The final entry in the trilogy completes the suspenseful buildup as the world faces a decisive battle. A nice aspect of the third book is that it includes an annotated list of main characters, enabling someone who has not read the first two, to pick it up and read on. Good for any YA science fiction collection.

FRIEDMAN, Melanie (Jennifer Series)
1—*What's Next, Jennifer?* Berkley, 1991
2—*No Way, Jennifer*. Berkley, 1991
3—*You're Crazy!* Berkley, 1991
4—*Get Real, Jennifer!* Berkley, 1991
These are typical YA romance books; Jennifer writes an advice column for her school paper, which gets her in hot water a number of times.

GARDEN, Nancy
Four Crossings. Farrar, 1981
Watersmeet. Farrar, 1983
The Door Between. Farrar, 1987

There is an element of the pagan supernatural in these YA books. They are set in Four Crossings and the action centers on an evil hermit who affects the area by controlling the weather. He is finally captured and put on trial, but the emergence of his relative complicates events.

GARDEN, Nancy (Monster Hunters)

Mystery of the Night Raiders. Farrar, 1987
Mystery of the Midnight Menace. Farrar, 1988
Mystery of the Secret Marks. Farrar, 1989

The three monster hunters have taken a pledge to explore all unsolved crimes in the belief that there are supernatural beings who could be involved. They do run up against all kinds of creatures including a werewolf. Garden is a good writer and these are far better than most monster-oriented mysteries. Grades 4-7.

GARFIELD, Leon

The Strange Affair of Adelaide Harris. Pantheon, 1971
Night of the Comet. Delacorte, 1979

Garfield writes solid historical English novels, with a gift for dialogue and a humorous touch with characters. These are no exception. Grades 5 and up.

GARNER, Alan

1—*Stone Book*. Collins, 1976
2—*Granny Reardon*. Collins, 1977
3—*Aimer Gate*. Collins, 1979
4—*Tom Fobble's Day*. Collins, 1979

This series of slim books follows four generations of an English family. The first is set during the Victorian era and introduces Mary and her father; the second tells the tale of her son Joseph; the third tells about his son Robert's desire to be a soldier; the last tells about Joseph's grandson William and what happens to his sledge during World War II. Excellent for those special YAs.

GATES, Doris (Melinda Books)

A Morgan for Melinda. Puffin, 1982
A Filly for Melinda. Puffin, 1984

Gates is a well respected author who uses, in these books, the horse story format as a background for heroine Melinda's growing up. While being responsible for her horse and filly, she must also cope with romantic entanglements and family problems. Horse lovers ages 8-12 will enjoy these.

GELMAN, Jan (Marci Books)

Marci's Secret Book of Flirting (Don't Go Out Without It). Knopf, 1990
Marci's Secret Book of Dating. Knopf, 1991

Marci is just entering middle school. Is her primary concern grades? Of course not! It is boys, and these books describe her attempts to perfect her techniques with the opposite sex. There is a nice tongue-in-cheek touch to these. Grades 4-6.

GEORGE, Jean Craighead

My Side of the Mountain. Dutton, 1967
On the Far Side of the Mountain. Dutton, 1990

Thirty-one years after the first classic book, author George has decided to revisit her hero, Sam Gribley, his falcon, and his younger sister Alice as they attempt to live on their own in the wild. The nature lore is fascinating and Sam's many fans will be glad to discover what has happened to him. Grades 5-9.

GERSON, Corinne

Oh, Brother! Macmillan, 1982
Son for a Day. Scholastic, 1983
My Grandfather the Spy. Walker, 1990

Danny is quite a people person. In the second volume of this series, he notices the "zoodaddy" syndrome: a father and child who don't seem to be having much fun together; since they don't live together anymore, they have trouble bridging the gap. He decides to act as intermediary to get these families interacting again. The newest book has Danny meeting an elderly man on a long bus trip. When the man shows up at Danny's house, Danny decides to find out more about him to help him. These will appeal to sensitive readers grades 5-8.

GIFF, Patricia Reilly (Abby Jones, Junior Detective, Mysteries)

Have You Seen Hyacinth Macaw? Dell, 1982
Loretta P. Sweeny, Where Are You? Dell, 1984
Tootsie Tanner, Why Don't You Talk? Delacorte, 1987

Anyone who has ever thought they could solve crimes will find a lot in common with Abby Jones. Unlike other kid sleuths, mysteries don't just drop into her lap. She actively goes out to find them, especially murders. She expects detecting to be her career; she keeps a detective journal; she picks up tips from her policeman friend Garcia. Her suppositions are often wrong, however, which leads to some funny scenes. Better-than-average mystery fare for grades 4-7.

GIFF, Patricia Reilly (Casey, Tracy, and Company)

1—*Fourth Grade Celebrity*. Delacorte, 1984
2—*The Girl Who Knew It All*. Delacorte, 1979
3—*Left-Handed Shortstop*. Dell, 1981
4—*The Winter Worm Business*. Dell, 1983
5—*Rat Teeth*. Dell, 1985
6—*Love from the Fifth Grade Celebrity*. Delacorte, 1986
7—*Poopsie Pomerantz, Pick up Your Feet*. Dell, 1990

Casey Valentine and Tracy Matson are sometime friends. This series uses humor intermingled with realism to portray that friendship and their lives in and out of school as they grow up. The plots flow and the characters and their feelings are most believable. Good choices for grades 3-6.

GIFF, Patricia Reilly (Kids of Polk Street School Series)

1—*The Beast in Ms. Rooney's Room*. Dell, 1984
2—*Fish Face*. Dell, 1984
3—*The Candy Corn Contest*. Dell, 1984
4—*December Secrets*. Dell, 1986
5—*In the Dinosaur's Paw*. Dell, 1985
6—*The Valentine Star*. Dell, 1985
7—*Lazy Lions, Lucky Lambs*. Dell, 1985
8—*Snaggle Doodles*. Dell, 1985
9—*Purple Climbing Days*. Dell, 1985
10—*Say "Cheese"*. Dell, 1985
11—*Sunny-side Up*. Dell, 1986
12—*Pickle Puss*. Dell, 1986
13—*Beast and the Halloween Horror*. Dell, 1990
14—*Emily Arrow Promises to Do Better This Year*. Dell, 1990
15—*Monster Rabbit Runs Amuck!* Dell, 1990
16—*Wake Up, It's Mother's Day!* Dell, 1990

Intended for beginning readers grades 1-3 this series features the ongoing adventures of a group of school kids in New York City. The slim paperback format, controlled vocabulary, and short chapters should make these good transitional material for this age group.

GIFF, Patricia Reilly

Matthew Jackson Meets the Wall. Delacorte, 1990

Matthew is one of the Kids from Polk Street School, another Giff series. This offshoot begins when Matthew is forced to move from New York to Ohio. Fans of her other series will enjoy this one as well. Grades 3-6.

GIFF, Patricia Reilly (New Kids at Polk Street School Series)

1–*Watch Out! Man-eating Snake.* Dell, 1988
2–*Fancy Feet.* Dell, 1988
3–*B-e-s-t Friends.* Dell, 1988
4–*All about Stacy.* Dell, 1988
5–*Spectacular Stone Soup.* Dell, 1989
6–*Stacy Says Good-bye.* Dell, 1989

A companion piece to her Kids of Polk Street School series, this one also features the early reading paperback format that highlights the other series. This series centers around the activities of kindergarten youngsters, and the vocabulary is easier. Grades 1-4.

GIFF, Patricia Reilly (Polka Dot Private Eye Series)

1–*The Mystery of the Blue Ring.* Dell, 1987
2–*The Riddle of the Red Purse.* Dell, 1987
3–*The Secret at Polk Street School.* Dell, 1987
4–*The Powder Puff Puzzle.* Dell, 1987
5–*The Case of the Cool-Itch Kid.* Dell, 1989
6–*Garbage Juice for Breakfast.* Dell, 1989
7–*The Trail of the Screaming Teenager.* Dell, 1990
8–*The Clue at the Zoo.* Dell, 1990

Young readers grades 2-4 will enjoy these simply written, humorous mysteries. Fans of Cam Jansen and Giff's other series for this age group will gravitate to these.

GILLIGAN, Shannon (Our Secret Gang)

1–*The Clue in the Clock Tower.* Bantam, 1991
2–*The Haunted Swamp.* Bantam, 1991
3–*The Case of the Missing Formula.* Bantam, 1991
4–*The Locker Thief.* Bantam, 1991

Here is another paperback mystery series, this one with girls running their own detective agency. Their cases are low-key, like the time they try to find the thief of a soda pop invention. Acceptable fare for grades 4-6.

GILSON, Jamie

Harvey, the Beer Can King. Lothrop, 1983
Hello, My Name Is Scrambled Eggs. Lothrop, 1985

Harvey is an ambitious kid, always in search of glory. First he decides that he will win the prize for being a Superkid, using his beer can collection to win. Then he decides that he will turn their new Vietnamese houseguest into a Harvey clone. These books are really funny, with Harvey an entertaining character that will appeal to readers 8-12.

GILSON, Jamie (Hobie Hanson Series)

1–*Thirteen Ways to Sink a Sub.* Lothrop, 1982
2–*4B Goes Wild.* Lothrop, 1983
3–*Hobie Hanson, You're Weird.* Lothrop, 1987
4–*Double Dog Dare.* Lothrop, 1988
5–*Hobie Hanson, Greatest Hero of the Mall.* Lothrop, 1989
6–*Sticks and Stones and Skeleton Bones.* Lothrop, 1991

Hobie and his friends gained attention with their efforts to get rid of a substitute teacher and have since gone on to other typically funny adventures, including the horrors of overnight camp and whiling their way through a boring summer. These are surefire hits with fans of Robert Peck and Betsy Byars. Grades 8-12.

GIPSON, Fred
3—**Little Arliss*. Harper, 1978
Arliss is Travis Coates's (*Old Yeller*) younger brother. He decides to prove how grown-up he is by catching an outlaw horse. Lots of frontier adventure here for readers grades 5 and up.

GLASER, Dianne (Amber Wellington Series)
Amber Wellington, Daredevil. Walker, 1975
Amber Wellington, Witch Watcher. Walker, 1976
Set down South, these tales follow spunky Amber into adventures in both city and country. They are okay, but the country dialect might throw some readers. Grades 4-6.

GONDOSCH, Linda
Who Needs a Bratty Brother? Dutton, 1985
The Witches of Hopper Street. Dutton, 1986
Who's Afraid of Haggerty House? Dutton, 1987
Kelly and her friends are typical girls. They feel put upon by an obnoxious brother, left out at someone else's big Halloween party—but the characters are likeable and their reactions have a realistic ring. Grades 4-6.

GORMAN, Susan (High Fives)
1—*Soccer Is a Kick*. Pocket, 1990
2—*Slam Dunk*. Pocket, 1990
3—*Home Run Stretch*. Pocket, 1991
4—*Quarterback Sneak*. Pocket, 1991
Like similar paperback series aimed at girls, this one is for boys and features a group of 6th grade boys who form a soccer team of five, thus the series title. Their woes are sports-oriented, but still revolve around parents and friends, i.e., a father whose overzealous attitude is ruining the game. Grades 4-6.

GORMLEY, Beatrice (Fifth Grade Magic Series)
Fifth Grade Magic. Dutton, 1982
More Fifth Grade Magic. Dutton, 1989
These fantasies are fun—in the first, Gretchen meets her fairy godmother, who seems more like a clerk than a magical creature. In the second, shy Amy wants to use calendar magic to make her summer a great one. Grades 4-6.

GORMLEY, Beatrice
The Magic Mean Machine. Avon, 1989
Sky Guys to White Cat. Dutton, 1991
Spencer is a bully, but an unusual one in that he is so cheerful and obnoxious at the same time. Alison longs to beat him at chess, at any price. These are entertaining, with enough of a twist from the usual paperback plot/character devices to keep them interesting. Grades 4-7.

GORMLEY, Beatrice
Mail-Order Wings. Avon, 1984
The Ghastly Glasses. Avon, 1985
These are most entertaining fantasies. In the first, Emily sends away for wings, and discovers that the price she pays for being able to fly may be too high. In the second, she has a pair of glasses that can improve anyone she looks at. Not all improvements are as good as they seem at first. Grades 4-6.

GOULD, Marilyn
Golden Daffodils. Lippincott, 1982
The Twelfth of June. Lippincott, 1986

Janis, the heroine of these novels, has cerebral palsy which she is overcoming. Readers see her relationships with others blossom, especially with her best friend Barney. There is the possibility of a romance for these two, but Barney has troubles of his own, facing lots of pressures to achieve at home, school, and in synagogue. These kids talk like real kids, and their believability makes these stories special. Grades 4-7.

GRABER, Richard

A Little Breathing Room. Harper, 1978
Pay Your Respects. Harper, 1979
Black Cow Summer. Harper, 1980

Ray Decker grows up in Minnesota during the Depression. There are financial problems, problems with the town, problems with the farms. There are also problems with a girl, as first love turns into a first sexual experience. For YAs.

GREAT EPISODES HISTORICAL FICTION SERIES (Series)

GREGORY, Kristiana
Jenny of the Tetons. Harcourt, 1989
The Legend of Jimmy Spoon. Harcourt, 1990

HILTS, Len
Timmy O'Dowd and the Big Ditch. Harcourt, 1988

JENSEN, Dorothea
The Riddle of Penncroft Farm. Harcourt, 1989

KOLLER, Jackie
Nothing to Fear. Harcourt, 1991

MELTZER, Milton
Underground Man. Harcourt, 1990

RINALDI, Ann
A Ride into Morning. Harcourt, 1991

This series takes real people and weaves a novel around the occurrences in their lives. Readers of historical fiction should enjoy the realism of the backgrounds and characters. That very realism does lead to portrayals of love and sex, although not graphically described. Grades 6 and up.

GREENE, Bette

Philip Hall Likes Me, I Reckon Maybe. Dial, 1974
Get On Out of Here, Philip Hall. Dial, 1981

Beth Lambert, a young Black girl from Arkansas tackles her world and growing up with a lot of style. She has an ongoing love-hate relationship with Philip Hall. She has a crush on him, but he is also her rival in school: she expects to earn a leadership award because she is so great, but he does instead. The first book was a Newbery Honor Book. Grades 5-8.

GREENE, Bette

The Summer of My German Soldier. Dial, 1973
Morning Is a Long Time Coming. Bantam, 1978

The first book was an ALA Notable. It is about a young girl in Arkansas during World War II who makes an unlikely and unpopular friend in a German prisoner of war. She is older in the second book, but still has not come to terms with what happened to her and Anton. She travels to Europe to meet his mother, and has her first love affair. Outstanding reading for grades 5-8.

GREENE, Constance C. (Isabelle Series)

Isabelle the Itch. Viking, 1973
Isabelle Shows Her Stuff. Viking, 1984
Isabelle and Little Orphan Frannie. Puffin, 1990

Isabelle is a spirited ten year old whose enthusiasm for life often gets her and her friends into trouble. She has an honest and forthright view of life that readers will thoroughly enjoy. Her most recent book deals with juvenile illiteracy, which Isabelle tackles with her usual energy.

GREENE, Constance (*Al Series)
3—*Your Old Pal, Al*. Dell, 1981
4—*Al(exandra) the Great*. Dell, 1982
5—*Just Plain Al*. Dell, 1988
6—*Al's Blind Date*. Dell, 1989
Al(exandra) continues to grow up. She copes with family problems created by divorce and stepfamilies and just plain growing up as unglamorous as her name. She has a deservedly sizeable following among those in grades 4-7.

GREENWALD, Sheila (Rosy Cole Series)
1—*Give Us a Great Big Smile, Rosy Cole*. Little, 1981
2—*Valentine Rosy*. Little, 1984
3—*Rosy Cole's Great American Guilt Club*. Little, 1985
4—*Write On, Rosy!* Little, 1988
Rosy is a down-to-earth heroine with a practical approach to life and a gift for telling the truth that occasionally gets her into trouble. Author Greenwald has gift for writing just the way a child would, which makes Rosy very believable, and her line drawings add a lot of zest to the proceedings. Good choices for grades 2-4.

GREENWALD, Sheila (Mariah Delany Series)
The Mariah Delany Lending Library Disaster. Houghton, 1977
Mariah Delany's Author-of-the-Month-Club. Little, 1990
To compensate for her bookish, dreamy parents, Mariah has become a paragon, however mistakenly, of practical business acumen. At least, that is what she thinks as she ignores her schoolwork and moves from one get-rich quick scheme to another. Readers grades 4-6 will find lots of laughs with the very human Mariah.

GREER, Gery, and **Bob RUDDICK** (Max Books)
Max and Me and the Time Machine. Harcourt, 1983
Max and Me and the Wild West. Harcourt, 1988
Time travel is a time-honored theme in children's books. These follow Max and Steve to the Middle Ages and the Wild West. Their adventures are funny and exciting for readers 9-12.

GUY, Rosa (Imamu Jones Books)
Disappearance. Delacorte, 1979
New Guy around the Block. Delacorte, 1983
And I Heard a Bird Sing. Delacorte, 1987
Harlem is the setting for these mysteries. Imamu Jones is a past juvenile offender and therefore the prime suspect, wrongly so, in the disappearance of a child in Brooklyn. He must help find the real criminal. In *New Guy...*, he joins up with two newcomers in the neighborhood to solve some robberies, but instead, they end up in jail on suspicion of being the burglars. These two books would be an excellent addition to a black culture collection. Young adults 12 and older.

GUY, Rosa
The Friends. Viking, 1973
Ruby. Viking, 1976
Edith Jackson. Viking, 1978
In the first book, Phyllisia and her older sister Ruby are new kids in Harlem. Phyllisia finds it difficult to adjust and make friends; her new classmates make fun of her West Indies accent. At first she does not accept Edith's friendship, but after her mother dies, she realizes Edith is her best friend. Ruby has a difficult time adjusting to her mother's death, but a friend helps

her also. Edith tries to keep her family together when she becomes old enough to leave their foster home, but soon realizes that she needs help herself. These books would be an asset to a black culture collection in a library. Good books for YAs.

HAAS, Dorothy (Peanut Butter and Jelly)
1–*New Friends*. Scholastic, 1988
2–*Peanut and Jilly Forever*. Scholastic, 1988
3–*The Haunted House*. Scholastic, 1988
4–*Trouble at Alcott School*. Scholastic, 1989
5–*Not Starring Jilly*. Scholastic, 1989
6–*Peanut in Charge*. Scholastic, 1989
7–*The Friendship Test*. Scholastic, 1990
8–*Two Friends Too Many*. Scholastic, 1990
9–*Alcott Library Is Falling Down*. Scholastic, 1991
Fans of Babysitter's Little Sister, Sweet Valley Kids, and Condo Kids will enjoy this series as well. The usual adventures abound: run-ins in a haunted house, a school play, and making new friends. The title of this series comes from the friendship of two girls named Peanut and Jilly. Grades 2-4.

HAAS, Dorothy
Poppy and the Outdoors Cat. Whitman, 1980
Tink in a Tangle. Whitman, 1983
Poppy is one of seven children–a fact that often causes her to indulge in self-pity. If there weren't so many of them crowded into a small apartment, she could have a dog of her own. Although her friend Tink has lots more money, *she* feels put upon because of her red hair. Not great literature, but acceptable fare for grades 2-5.

HALAM, Ann
The Daymaker. Orchard, 1987
Transformations. Orchard, 1988
Two fine stories by the author of adult science fiction/fantasy books. The first has a decidedly pro-female theme but both have magical doings and will be enjoyed by readers of spooky children's books, as well as fantasy fans. Written for YAs.

HALL, Lynn (Dagmar Schultz Series)
1–*The Secret Life of Dagmar Schultz*. Macmillan, 1988
2–*Dagmar Schultz and the Powers of Darkness*. Scribner, 1989
3–*Dagmar Schultz and the Angel Edna*. Scribner, 1989
4–*Dagmar Schultz and the Green-Eyed Monster*. Scribner, 1991
Dagmar is a down-to-earth thirteen year old who values the fact that her parents love her and each other even if her father is really old and plays games with his false teeth, and her mother is awfully fat. This combination of common-sense values and humor makes this series far better than the usual growing pains books. Excellent choices for grades 4-7.

HALL, Lynn (Zelda Hammersmith Series)
In Trouble Again, Zelda Hammersmith? Harcourt, 1987
Zelda Strikes Again. Harcourt, 1988
Here Comes Zelda Claus! And Other Holiday Disasters. Harcourt, 1989
Zelda is an irresistible girl; she has hair the color of cookie dough at sunset, a face loaded with freckles, and a brand of honesty that caused her to leap in front of a boy's bike and announce to him that she was his new girlfriend. These will be a surefire hit with grades 3-6.

HALLIN, Emily (Meg and Stanley Stories)
Partners. Archway, 1989
Changes. Archway, 1989
Risks. Archway, 1989

Megan and Stanley are both taking ballroom dancing lessons. Megan is preparing for her grandparents' golden anniversary party, while Stanley is trying to impress a wealthy debutante. They begin to date but have many problems in their way: parents, friends and the fact that neither know exactly what they want. Grades 6-8.

HAMILTON, Virginia (Dies Drear Series)
The House of Dies Drear. Macmillan, 1968
The Mystery of Drear House. Greenwillow, 1987
Set in Ohio, this well received series by much-honored writer Virginia Hamilton revolves around the home of abolitionist Dies Drear. The Small family eventually discovers that the home was a stop on the Underground Railroad. The second volume deals with ownership of a newly discovered archaeological treasure. Strong characterizations and plot make these musts for any collection. Grades 4-7.

HAMILTON, Virginia (The Justice Cycle)
Justice and Her Brothers. Greenwillow, 1978
Dustland. Greenwillow, 1980
The Gathering. Greenwillow, 1981
Supersensory powers link the four protagonists of these three books: Justice, her two twin brothers and a neighbor. Book one explores how these powers threaten to tear Justice's family apart. Book two sees the foursome travel through time to a place in the distant future, Dustland. Jealousy threatens to strand the group in this strange land. In the final volume, the group returns to Dustland to battle an evil power that threatens civilization. Recommended for grades 5-8.

HANSEN, Joyce
The Gift-Giver. Clarion, 1980
Yellow Bird and Me. Clarion, 1986
Doris is an inner-city child in a tough neighborhood. Her relationship with two boys, one a loner new to the neighborhood, the other the class clown, help her to adjust to the problems she and her family face. Strong picture of ghetto life. Grades 4-8.

HANSEN, Joyce
Which Way Freedom? Walker, 1986
Out from This Place. Walker, 1988
Obi was born into slavery, but escaped to the North. When the Civil War broke out, he joined the Union Army. These are very realistic novels showing the horrors of war, the accomplishments of an African American regiment, and one man's growth from slavery to freedom. Grades 5-9.

HARRELL, Janice (Andie Books)
Andie and the Boys. Archway, 1990
Dooley MacKenzie Is Totally Weird. Archway, 1990
Brace Yourself, P.J. Archway, 1990
Andie meets the boys when her mother remarries: her new stepbrother, P.J. and his friends, Chris and Dooley. In the first book, the boys scare off any potential beau for Andie. Later, Dooley's parents divorce and Andie tries to help him through that rough stage, while still looking for her "true love." Andie finds that love in Chris and that begins an uproarious period of denial to everyone that they are a "hot" item. These are funny books that should be popular in the young adult paperback collection. Grades 7-10.

HARRELL, Janice
Wild Times at Westmount High. Archway, 1990
Easy Answers. Archway, 1990
Senior Year at Last. Archway, 1990

Walk into any high school in the nation and you are walking into Westmount High. The characters are believably real and the dialogue is true to life. Harrell has written three books that accurately represent the trials and tribulations of today's teens. Young adults who are dating the "wrong" person or falling in love with their best friend's girlfriend or having problems with their parents will enjoy reading these books. Ages 12 and up.

HARRIS, Geraldine (Seven Citadels)
1—*Prince of Godborn*. Greenwillow, 1983
2—*Children of the Wind*. Greenwillow, 1983
3—*Dead Kingdom*. Greenwillow, 1983
4—*Seventh Gate*. Greenwillow, 1984
Kerish-lo-Taan and his friends pass many tests in their search/quest for the Saviour of Galkis. They must acquire seven keys, each guarded by an immortal sorcerer in order to free him. If the sorcerers give up their keys, they lose their immortality, so Kerish has to use reason, trickery, and force to obtain them. He loses much, but also gains much in experience. This is truly a remarkable series, most comparable to Lloyd Alexander's Prydain books and C. S. Lewis's Narnia tales. For ages 12 and up.

HARRIS, Robie H. (Rosie Books)
1—*Rosie's Double Dare*. Knopf, 1980
2—*Rosie's Razzle Dazzle Deal*. Knopf, 1982
3—*Rosie's Rock 'n Roll Riot*. Minstrel, 1990
4—*Rosie's Secret Spell*. Minstrel, 1991
Rosie is full of mischief and has trouble getting along with her older brother—a perfectly normal nine year old. These are acceptable family novels, but nothing special. Greenwald's Rosie Cole is a lot more entertaining than this Rosie. Grades 4-6.

HART, Bruce, and **Carol HART**
Sooner or Later. Avon, 1978
Waiting Games. Avon, 1981
Now or Never. Avon, 1991
Jessie doesn't think Michael, who is seventeen, will be interested in her if he knew her real age—fourteen. So Jessie lies, finds out he is still more than interested. These two learn what love really means in the first two books. In the newest addition to the series, Jessie prepares to enter college as Michael tries to rebuild his life without drugs. Decently written, these books are easy-to-sell romances to the young adult audience, aged 13 and up.

HAAS, E. A. (Incognito Mosquito Series)
1—*Incognito Mosquito, Private Insective*. Random, 1985
2—*Incognito Mosquito Flies Again!* Random, 1985
3—*Incognito Mosquito Takes to the Air*. Random, 1986
4—*Incognito Mosquito Makes History*. Random, 1987
Each book contains five cases the reader can try to solve before Incognito, the private insective, does. All the clues are provided, and the reader has an opportunity to solve the case before the explanation is revealed. What makes this different from the Encyclopedia Brown series are the many jokes and cartoons that grace the text. Readers grades 3-6, and reluctant readers, will find this a truly hilarious series.

HATCHIGAN, Jessica
Count Dracula, Me and Norma D. Avon, 1987
Dinosaurs Aren't Forever. Avon, 1991
Not too smart, the girls had to admit, when they were caught while trying to hold a seance in a funeral parlor after hours. That is not the least of Molly's problems, as she has to cope with her mother dating the funeral director and her father dating a friend's mother. Grades 4-6.

HAUGAARD, Erik

Messenger for Parliament. Houghton, 1976

Cromwell's Boy. Houghton, 1978

Set in England during the struggles between King Charles and Cromwell, the hero of this series is also named Oliver. He does side with his namesake and acts as a secret messenger for the Roundheads. There is a lot of philosophizing here that, accompanied by the unfamiliar time period, will limit the appeal to grades 5-8.

HAVILL, Juanita (Leona Books)

It Always Happens to Leona. Crown, 1989

Leona and Ike. Crown, 1991

Leona is a middle child with a flair for the dramatic, rather like Ramona Quimby. She feels very left out, and searches for ways to be noticed in her family. The second book follows her friendship with Ike. Above average fare for grades 4-6.

HAWES, Louise (Nelson Malone Series)

Nelson Malone Meets the Man from Mush-Nut. Avon, 1988

Nelson Malone Saves Flight 942. Avon, 1990

At first Nelson seems like any other kid. Loves candy, tired of taking the same old pet to Pet Day at school. But strange things happen to Nelson, like the time the characters leave the video game to play with him, or the time he finds his summer camp is not really located on earth. The combination of reality and slapstick fantasy should bring laughs to readers in grades 4-7.

HAYES, Sheila

The Carousel Horse. Scholastic, 1988

You've Been Away All Summer. Scholastic, 1988

Fran Davies reacts badly when she learns her mother is to be the summer cook for a rich family, especially when she meets the family's snooty daughter. Fran has lots of verve and a dramatic flair for life. Good choices for readers in grades 4-7.

HAYNES, Betsy (Fabulous Five Series)

1—*Seventh-Grade Rumors*. Bantam, 1988
2—*The Trouble with Flirting*. Bantam, 1988
3—*The Popularity Trap*. Bantam, 1988
4—*Her Honor, Katie Shannon*. Bantam, 1988
5—*The Bragging War*. Bantam, 1989
6—*The Parent Game*. Bantam, 1989
7—*Kissing Disaster*. Bantam, 1988
8—*Runaway Crisis*. Bantam, 1989
9—*The Boyfriend Dilemma*. Bantam, 1989
10—*Playing the Part*. Bantam, 1989
11—*Hit and Run*. Bantam, 1989
12—*Katie's Dating Tips*. Bantam, 1989
13—*The Christmas Countdown*. Bantam, 1989
14—*Seventh-Grade Menace*. Bantam, 1990
15—*Melanie's Identity Crisis*. Bantam, 1990
16—*The Hot-Line Emergency*. Bantam, 1990
17—*Celebrity Auction*. Bantam, 1990
18—*Teen Taxi*. Bantam, 1990
19—*The Boys-Only Club*. Bantam, 1990
20—*The Witches of Wakeman*. Bantam, 1990
21—*Jana to the Rescue*. Bantam, 1990
22—*Melanie's Valentine*. Bantam, 1991
23—*Mall Mania*. Bantam, 1991
24—*The Great TV Turn-Off*. Bantam, 1991

25—*Fabulous Five Minus One*. Bantam, 1991
26—*Laura's Secret*. Bantam, 1991

This is an offshoot of Haynes's Taffy Sinclair series, following the same set of girls as they enter junior high. The usual boy-girl problems are the primary focus here. Grades 4-7.

HAYNES, Betsy (Taffy Sinclair Series)
1—*The Against Taffy Sinclair Club*. Bantam, 1984
2—*Taffy Sinclair Strikes Again*. Bantam, 1984
3—*Taffy Sinclair, Queen of the Soaps*. Bantam, 1985
4—*Taffy Sinclair and the Romance Machine Disaster*. Bantam, 1987
5—*Blackmailed by Taffy Sinclair*. Bantam, 1987
6—*Taffy Sinclair, Baby Ashley and Me*. Bantam, 1988
7—*The Truth about Taffy Sinclair*. Bantam, 1988
8—*Taffy Sinclair and the Melanie Make-Over*. Bantam, 1988
9—*Taffy Sinclair and the Secret Admirer Epidemic*. Bantam, 1988
10—*Taffy Goes to Hollywood*. Bantam, 1990

There's one like her in every class—Miss Perfect. She's the snooty blonde with naturally curly hair. The one regular girls love to hate. That's Taffy Sinclair. This series is bound to strike a responsive chord with "regular girl" readers grades 4-7.

HAYWOOD, Carolyn (*Betsy and Eddie Series)
25—*Eddie's Menagerie*. Morrow, 1978
26—*Merry Christmas from Eddie*. Morrow, 1986
27—*Hello, Star*. Morrow, 1987
28—*Eddie's Friend Boodles*. Morrow, 1991

Here are more adventures for fans of this longtime series. Typically heartwarming school and family plotlines still abound, and this series has gotten a boost with recent paperback repackaging. The last entry may be the end of the series because Ms. Haywood died in 1990. That story is dedicated to Eddie's best friend Boodles, who has an idea for turning Poochie into a circus dog. Grades 3-6.

HEARN, Betsy
South Star. Atheneum, 1977
Home. Atheneum, 1979

Megan is the last daughter of the first giants. In the first book she must flee the Screamer, an enemy of giants, who has imprisoned her parents. In the second, she searches for the lost king, Brendan. Fantasy for grades 4-7.

HEARTSONG (Series)
CHISHOLM, Gloria
Andrea. Bethany, 1983
Jocelyn. Bethany, 1988
ELLIS, Joyce
Tiffany. Bethany, 1986
GIBSON, Eva
Colleen. Bethany, 1985
Laina. Bethany, 1986
Marty. Bethany, 1987
Melissa. Bethany, 1982
Michelle. Bethany, 1983
Sara. Bethany, 1984
GOLDING, Leila
Cynthia. Bethany, 1987
Rachel. Bethany, 1988
Shelly. Bethany, 1986
Sherri. Bethany, 1985

MITCHELL, Marcia
Jenny. Bethany, 1983
PAGE, Carol
Carrie. Bethany, 1984
Kara. Bethany, 1981
POLLINGER, Eileen
Erica. Bethany, 1985
Stacey. Bethany, 1987
WELLS, Marion
Karen. Bethany, 1983

These books are filled with action, romance, adventure and the theme of Christian commitment. The female characters show growth in their belief in God as they work towards overcoming the obstacles in their path. This is a good paperback series for students in grades 8-12.

HEIDE, Florence Parry
Banana Twist. Holiday, 1978
Banana Blitz. Holiday, 1983

Jonah finds himself lumbered with a "friend" named Goober who not only aims to be perfect, but plans to force Jonah into perfection as well. The first was an ALA Notable Book. Grades 4-6.

HEIDE, Florence Parry, and **Roxanne HEIDE** (Brillstone Series)
1—*Brillstone Break-in*. Whitman, 1977
2—*Burning Stone at Brillstone*. Whitman, 1978
3—*Fear at Brillstone*. Whitman, 1978
4—*Face at the Brillstone Window*. Whitman, 1979
5—*Black Magic at Brillstone*. Whitman, 1981
6—*Time Bomb at Brillstone*. Whitman, 1982
7—*Body in the Brillstone Garage*. Whitman, 1988

This mystery series by veteran authors Heide features the residents of the Brillstone Apartments. Characterizations are minimal, but there is plenty of action to keep the interest of those in grades 4-9 and reluctant readers. These are part of Whitman's Pilot Books, a hi-lo collection aimed at this interest group.

HEIDE, Florence Parry (*Spotlight Club Series)
3—*Mystery of the Lonely Lantern*. Whitman, 1976
4—*Mystery at Keyhold Carnival*. Whitman, 1977
5—*Mystery at Southport Cinema*. Whitman, 1978
6—*Mystery of the Forgotten Island*. Whitman, 1979
7—*Mystery of the Mummy's Mask*. Whitman, 1979
8—*Mystery of the Midnight Message*. Whitman, 1982
9—*Mystery of the Vanishing Visitor*. Whitman, 1982
10—*Mystery of the Danger Road*. Whitman, 1983

These are Pilot Books, with a controlled vocabulary that should be appealing to reluctant readers as well as other mystery buffs grades 4-8. Written by a mother/daughter team, the detectives are a group of friends both male and female whose adventures are reminiscent of the Three Investigators.

HEIDE, Florence Parry
Time's Up! Holiday, 1982
Time Flies! Holiday, 1984

Young Noah has many of the usual problems to handle—a potentially boring summer, and the imminent arrival of a new baby. His reactions are realistic but funny, and Marilyn Hafner's drawings add to the good humor. Entertaining fare for ages 8-11.

HEIDE, Florence Parry (Treehorn Books)

The Shrinking of Treehorn. Holiday, 1971
Treehorn's Treasure. Holiday, 1981
Treehorn's Wish. Holiday, 1984

Treehorn is a highly imaginative boy whose dreams and wishes often come graphically true. Although they are illustrated throughout with black and white drawings by Edward Gorey, the slim texts are really written at the third to sixth grade level. The first two of these books were ALA Notables.

HENTOFF, Nat

This School Is Driving Me Crazy. Delacorte, 1976
Does This School Have Capital Punishment? Delacorte, 1981

Sam does not want to go to the same school where his father is the headmaster, but he does and finds himself getting into trouble with faculty and friends. Then he is falsely accused of possessing marijuana. In actuality he has been framed by a bully classmate, but he could end up expelled. His class project about a renowned black jazz trumpeter may help set him free. Sam is a likeable character and these are good books. Ages 10 and older.

HERMAN, Charlotte (Max Malone Books)

Max Malone and the Great Cereal Rip-Off. Holt, 1990
Max Malone Makes a Million. Holt, 1991

Max is a feisty kid who, in the first book, decides that he's tired of being ripped-off by send-away cereal products. He decides to try some ripping off of his own. In the second book, his attempts to make money backfire: he doesn't succeed, but his best friend does. Grades 3-6.

HERMAN, Charlotte (Millie Cooper Books)

Millie Cooper, 3B. Dutton, 1985
Millie Cooper, Take a Chance. Puffin, 1990

Millie is a third grader during the mid-1940s. She is faced with the ordeal of trying to write a perfect spelling paper with a pen and ink that smear and blot at the least provocation. She lacks confidence; it seems that school is a place of special terrors and failures. Readers will certainly relate to her fears and may learn that success often comes in areas we don't value or expect. A very good bet for readers 8-12.

HERMES, Patricia

Kevin Corbett Eats Flies. Minstrel, 1987
Heads, I Win. Minstrel, 1989

Bailey's new in school, a foster child who has been passed around too much. She finds herself in league with another newcomer, Kevin Corbett, who is gaining acceptance by swallowing disgusting creatures. She eventually runs for class president and learns that her latest foster mother wants her—permanently. Funny, touching, realistic, excellent choices for grades 4-7.

HERMES, Patricia

What If They Knew? Dell, 1989
A Place for Jeremy. Harcourt, 1987

Jeremy (a girl) spends lengthy periods with her grandparents in Brooklyn because of her father's business and a subsequent adoption of a South American baby. Her first stay is complicated when she tries to hide her epilepsy from her new friends. Her resentment toward the impending baby clouds the second. In spite of this, she still has pre-teen type fun and an especially strong relationship with her grandparents. Grades 4-7.

HICKMAN, Janet

Stones. Macmillan, 1976
Thunder-Pup. Macmillan, 1981

The first book follows Garrett McKay during World War II as he wrestles with the problem of patriotism vs. human kindness as he falls in with a group of unruly friends. The second finds his sister Linnie nearing age 10. As much as she looks forward to it, she finds many disappointments, plus must contend with a guest who is stealing her thunder. These are understated, with believable situations and characters. Grades 4-7.

HICKS, Clifford (*Alvin Fernald Series)
6—*Alvin's Swap Shop*. Holt, 1976
7—*Alvin Fernald, T.V. Anchorman*. Holt, 1980
8—*The Wacky World of Alvin Fernald*. Holt, 1981
9—*Alvin Fernald, Master of a Thousand Disguises*. Holt, 1986
Alvin and his friends all think he has a Magnificent Brain. Of course, it does get him into lots of trouble, but it also gets him out. Fans of Soup will gravitate to these. Grades 4-6.

HICKS, Clifford (Peter Potts Books)
Peter Potts. Dutton, 1971
Pop and Peter Potts. Holt, 1984
The Peter Potts Book of World Records. Holt, 1987
Peter lives with his grandfather, whom everyone calls Pop, as well as his sister and her husband. Even though Pop is a grown-up, his many hobbies cause as many problems for the family as those dreamed up by any kid. Hicks's usual light touch prevails in these treats for grades 4-6.

HIGHWATER, Jamake (Ghost Horse Cycle)
Legend Days. Harper, 1984
The Ceremony of Innocence. Harper, 1985
I Wear the Morning Star. Harper, 1986
These books have won a whole slew of awards for young adult literature. Amana is a Northern Plains Indian, who as a child, is orphaned, but is rescued by a grandfather fox, who teaches her the skills of being a warrior. In *Ceremony*, she is forced to beg from whites in order to survive. In the final volume, Amana's grandson is regarded as a freak because of his heritage. He clings fiercely to his past and the myths his grandmother taught him. In particular, this book demonstrates the modern difficulties that are present for native Americans. Indian culture is strong in these three books. Highly recommended for grades 8 and above.

HILDICK, E. W. (Ghost Squad Series)
1—*Ghost Squad Breaks Through*. Dutton, 1984
2—*Ghost Squad Flies Concorde*. Dutton, 1985
3—*Ghost Squad and the Halloween Conspiracy*. Dutton, 1985
4—*Ghost Squad and the Ghoul of Grunberg*. Dutton, 1986
5—*Ghost Squad and the Prowling Hermits*. Dutton, 1987
6—*Ghost Squad and the Menace of the Malevs*. Dutton, 1988
In an unusual turn for a mystery suspense series, this one features four young ghosts who fight crime, using two live earthly intermediaries. Grades 4-6.

HILDICK, E. W. (*McGurk Series)
4—*The Case of the Nervous Newsboy*. Macmillan, 1976
5—*The Great Rabbit Rip-off*. Macmillan, 1977
6—*The Case of the Invisible Dog*. Macmillan, 1977
7—*The Case of the Secret Scribbler*. Macmillan, 1978
8—*The Case of the Phantom Frog*. Macmillan, 1979
9—*The Case of the Treetop Treasure*. Macmillan, 1980
10—*The Case of the Snowbound Spy*. Macmillan, 1980
11—*The Case of the Bashful Bank Robber*. Macmillan, 1981
12—*The Case of the Four Flying Fingers*. Macmillan, 1981
13—*The Case of the Felon's Fiddle*. Macmillan, 1982

14—*McGurk Gets Good and Mad*. Macmillan, 1982
15—*The Case of the Slingshot Sniper*. Macmillan, 1983
16—*The Case of the Vanishing Ventriloquist*. Macmillan, 1985
17—*The Case of the Muttering Mummy*. Macmillan, 1986
18—*The Case of the Wandering Weathervanes*. Macmillan, 1988
19—*The Case of the Dragon in Distress*. Macmillan, 1989
20—*The Case of the Purloined Parrot*. Macmillan, 1990
The McGurk mysteries have been around a long time. Veteran author Hildick always gives quality for budget dollar: well-plotted mysteries with humor and action for ages 9-12.

HILL, Douglas
The Blade of the Poisoner. McElderry, 1987
Master of Fiends. McElderry, 1988
A small band of magically inclined friends help Jarral in this fantasy adventure. He has been marked with the demon-tainted sword of Mephtik. Unless the prince and sword are destroyed by the next full moon, Jarral will die horribly. Successful in their first adventure, this group of friends is determined to rescue the imprisoned grand wizard. These are a lot of fun and are sure to attract readers grades 7 and up.

HILL, Douglas (Colsec Series)
Exiles of Colsec. McElderry, 1984
The Caves of Klydor. McElderry, 1985
Colsec Rebellion. McElderry, 1985
Colsec, part of the repressive Earth-wide government, gets rid of teenaged trouble makers by shipping them off to explore distant planets. On this trip, a mechanical failure crashes the spaceship on Klydor, leaving six survivors. Five are teen rebels, one is a psychotic killer. While exploring this new planet they come across the Crushers and must survive in their new environment and vanquish their new enemies. Finally, they join forces with a rebel space pilot and journey back to earth. Grades 7 and up.

HILL, Douglas
The Huntsman. McElderry, 1982
Alien Citadel. McElderry, 1984
Finn is the star of these adventure-packed science fiction novels. He is discovered wandering through the woods as a small child and adopted by a loving family. When the evil aliens come to his village and kidnap members of his family, Finn must take up the challenge and find them. On his journey he encounters many terrors and dangers he didn't know existed, and he makes an unusual friend too. In the sequel Finn and a group of friends risk their lives to rid their land of the alien creatures. Grades 7-10.

HILL, Douglas
1—*Galactic Warlord*. McElderry, 1980
2—*Deathwing Over Veynaa*. McElderry, 1981
3—*Day of the Starwind*. McElderry, 1981
4—*Planet of the Warlord*. McElderry, 1982
5—*Young Legionary*. McElderry, 1983
Keill must overcome the grief associated with the destruction of his planet in order to seek revenge on the evil being who caused the destruction. He then must take on Deathwing, part of the evil. The third adventure has Keill and the winged alien Glr trying to overtake the warlord that destroyed Keill's planet. In the final installment Keill survives a test and is selected to train as a Young Legionary. The books are fast paced and leave the reader waiting to read the next book. For YAs.

HISER, Constance

No Bean Sprouts, Please! Holiday, 1989
Ghosts in Fourth Grade. Holiday, 1991

James has problems with bully Mean Mitchell. The first book where James has acquired a magic lunchbox that changes health food into "good" junk food, should find a sympathetic audience. Grades 2-4.

HODGMAN, Ann (Lunchroom Series)

1—*Night of the 1000 Pizzas*. Berkley, 1990
2—*Frog Punch*. Berkley, 1990
3—*Cookie Caper*. Berkley, 1990
4—*French Fried Aliens*. Berkley, 1990
5—*Rubberband Stew*. Berkley, 1990
6—*The Flying Popcorn Experiment*. Berkley, 1990
7—*Invasion of the Fast Food*. Berkley, 1990
8—*Space Food*. Berkley, 1990
9—*Day of the Monster Plant*. Berkley, 1991
10—*Mutant Garbage*. Berkley, 1991

Like so many other paperback series, this one follows the school adventures of assorted youngsters who eat in the school cafeteria together. Their woes range from a runaway hamster to participating in a school play to a science fair project that gets out of hand. Easy reading for grades 3-6.

HOLL, Kristi D.

Just Like a Real Family. Atheneum, 1983
No Strings Attached. Atheneum, 1989

June is lonely, with a working mother and no friends living nearby, so she jumps at the chance to be in a foster grandparent program. She does not expect the crusty, tyrannical old man she is paired with. Their friendship does finally crystallize to the point that June and her mother move in with Franklin, but the child still has problems accepting the real man over her idealized version of family life. These present a realistic, telling picture of intergenerational family life. Grades 4-7.

HOLLANDS, Judith (The Ketchup Sisters)

1—*The Rescue of the Red-Blooded Librarian*. Minstrel, 1989
2—*The Deeds of the Desperate Campers*. Minstrel, 1990
3—*The Secret of the Haunted Doghouse*. Minstrel, 1990
4—*The Cry of the Captured Doll*. Minstrel, 1990
5—*Locked in the Screaming School*. Minstrel, 1991

The Ketchup Sisters are not really blood sisters—they pledged their true friendship in ketchup instead. They solve low-key mysteries, such as who is trying to get rid of an obnoxious camper. Grades 2-4.

HOLMES, Barbara (Charlotte Cheetham Series)

Charlotte Cheetham: Master of Disaster. Harper, 1985
Charlotte the Starlet. Harper, 1988
Charlotte Shakespeare and Annie the Great. Harper, 1989

Charlotte is quite a little liar. Some of her stories are so fantastic, she garners lots of attention. She finally decides to put her fertile imagination to work as a writer, and her adventures go on from there. Grades 3-6.

HONEYCUTT, Natalie (Jonah Twist Series)

The All-New Jonah Twist. Bradbury, 1986
The Best-Laid Plans of Jonah Twist. Bradbury, 1988

Jonah is a normal, slam-bang third grader who gets into all kinds of situations due to his failure to think things through. Somehow, his good heart always rescues him, turning one-time enemy Granville Jones into a best friend. This may or may not be good, since Granville is great at planning, but Jonah has trouble remembering all the details of these fabulous arrangements. Grades 4-6.

HOOVER, H. M. (Morrow Books)

Children of Morrow. Four Winds, 1973

Treasures of Morrow. Four Winds, 1976

This sci-fi series begins with Tia and Rabbit who have "heard" themselves called to "The Sea." In the sequel they have finally arrived at the land Tia has seen through her telepathy. They enjoy being in this new and wonderful place but have yearnings for home. These are for readers in grades 7 and up.

HOPE, Laura Lee (Bobbsey Twins Series)

1—*The Bobbsey Twins of Lakeport*. Grosset, 1989
2—*Adventure in the Country*. Grosset, 1989
3—*Secret at the Seashore*. Grosset, 1989
4—*Mystery at School*. Grosset, 1989
5—*The Mystery at Snow Lodge*. Grosset, 1990
6—*The Bobbsey Twins on a Houseboat*. Grosset, 1990
7—*Mystery at Meadowbrook*. Grosset, 1990
8—*Big Adventure at Home*. Grosset, 1990
9—*Search in the Great City*. Grosset, 1930
10—*Bobbsey Twins on Blueberry Island*. Grosset, 1930
11—*Mystery on the Deep Blue Sea*. Grosset, 1930
12—*Adventure in Washington*. Grosset, 1963
13—*Visit to the Great West*. Grosset, 1966
14—*Bobbsey Twins and the Cedar Camp Mystery*. Grosset, 1967
15—*Bobbsey Twins and the County Fair Mystery*. Grosset, 1922
16—*Camping Out*. Grosset, 1923
17—*Adventures with Baby May*. Grosset, 1968
18—*Bobbsey Twins and the Play House Secret*. Grosset, 1968
19—*Bobbsey Twins at Cloverbank*. Grosset, 1926
20—*The Mystery at Cherry Corners*. Grosset, 1971
21—*The Bobbsey Twins and Their Schoolmates*. Grosset, 1928
22—*Bobbsey Twins Treasure Hunting*. Grosset, 1929
23—*Bobbsey Twins at Spruce Lake*. Grosset, 1930
24—*Wonderful Winter Secret*. Grosset, 1931
25—*Bobbsey Twins and the Circus Surprise*. Grosset, 1932
26—*Bobbsey Twins on an Airplane Trip*. Grosset, 1933
27—*Bobbsey Twins Solve a Mystery*. Grosset, 1934
28—*Bobbsey Twins on a Ranch*. Grosset, 1935
29—*Bobbsey Twins in Eskimo Land*. Grosset, 1936
30—*Bobbsey Twins in a Radio Play*. Grosset, 1937
31—*Bobbsey Twins at Windmill Cottage*. Grosset, 1938
32—*Bobbsey Twins at Lighthouse Point*. Grosset, 1939
33—*Bobbsey Twins at Indian Hollow*. Grosset, 1940
34—*Bobbsey Twins at the Ice Carnival*. Grosset, 1941
35—*Bobbsey Twins in the Land of Cotton*. Grosset, 1942
36—*Bobbsey Twins in Echo Valley*. Grosset, 1943
37—*Bobbsey Twins on the Pony Trail*. Grosset, 1944
38—*Bobbsey Twins at Mystery Mansion*. Grosset, 1945
39—*Bobbsey Twins at Sugar Maple Hill*. Grosset, 1946
40—*Bobbsey Twins in Mexico*. Grosset, 1947
41—*Bobbsey Twins' Toy Shop*. Grosset, 1948

42—*Bobbsey Twins in Tulip Land*. Grosset, 1949
43—*Bobbsey Twins in Rainbow Valley*. Grosset, 1950
44—*Bobbsey Twins at Whitesail Harbor*. Grosset, 1951
45—*Bobbsey Twins and the Horseshoe Riddle*. Grosset, 1952
46—*Bobbsey Twins at Big Bear Pond*. Grosset, 1953
47—*Meet the Bobbsey Twins*. Grosset, 1954
48—*Bobbsey Twins on a Bicycle Trip*. Grosset, 1955
49—*Bobbsey Twins' Own Little Ferryboat*. Grosset, 1956
50—*Bobbsey Twins at Pilgrim Rock*. Grosset, 1957
51—*Forest Adventure*. Grosset, 1958
52—*Bobbsey Twins at London Tower*. Grosset, 1959
53—*Bobbsey Twins in the Mystery Cave*. Grosset, 1960
54—*Bobbsey Twins in Volcano Land*. Grosset, 1961
55—*Bobbsey Twins and the Goldfish Mystery*. Grosset, 1962
56—*Bobbsey Twins and the Big River Mystery*. Grosset, 1963
57—*Bobbsey Twins and the Greek Hat Mystery*. Grosset, 1964
58—*Search for the Green Rooster*. Grosset, 1965
59—*Bobbsey Twins and Their Camel Adventure*. Grosset, 1966
60—*Mystery of the King's Puppet*. Grosset, 1967
61—*Bobbsey Twins and the Secret of Candy Castle*. Grosset, 1968
62—*Bobbsey Twins and the Doodlebug Mystery*. Grosset, 1969
63—*Bobbsey Twins and the Talking Fox Mystery*. Grosset, 1970
64—*The Red, White and Blue Mystery*. Grosset, 1971
65—*Bobbsey Twins and Dr. Funnybone's Secret*. Grosset, 1972
66—*Bobbsey Twins and the Tagalong Giraffe*. Grosset, 1973
67—*Bobbsey Twins and the Flying Clown*. Grosset, 1974
68—*Bobbsey Twins on the Sun-Moon Cruise*. Grosset, 1975
69—*Bobbsey Twins and the Freedom Bell Mystery*. Grosset, 1976
70—*Bobbsey Twins and the Smoky Mountain Mystery*. Grosset, 1977
71—*Bobbsey Twins in a TV Mystery Show*. Grosset, 1978

The publisher is reissuing this series with new cover art and updated, more realistic illustrations. The first eight volumes are currently available in the new format. The others still have the old format. Although not as popular with youngsters as Nancy Drew and the Hardy Boys continue to be, there are still many parents who request these classic tales of two sets of twins. Ages 8-12.

HOPE, Laura Lee (Bobbsey Twins)
1—*The Blue Poodle Mystery*. Wanderer, 1980
2—*Secret in the Pirate's Cave*. Wanderer, 1980
3—*Dune Buggy Mystery*. Wanderer, 1981
4—*The Missing Pony Mystery*. Wanderer, 1981
5—*The Rose Parade Mystery*. Wanderer, 1981
6—*Camp Fire Mystery*. Wanderer, 1982
7—*Double Trouble*. Wanderer, 1983
8—*Mystery of the Laughing Dinosaur*. Wanderer, 1983
9—*The Music Box Mystery*. Wanderer, 1983
10—*The Ghost in the Computer*. Wanderer, 1984
11—*The Scarecrow Mystery*. Wanderer, 1984
12—*The Haunted House Mystery*. Wanderer, 1985
13—*The Mystery of the Hindu Temple*. Wanderer, 1985

More of the Bobbsey Twins; Wanderer updated the look and the approach. The job was continued by Simon & Schuster as well. Grades 3-6.

HOPE, Laura Lee (New Bobbsey Twins Series)

1–*The Secret of Jungle Park*. Minstrel, 1987
2–*The Case of the Runaway Money*. Minstrel, 1987
3–*The Clue That Flew Away*. Minstrel, 1987
4–*Mystery on the Mississippi*. Minstrel, 1988
5–*The Case of the Close Encounter*. Minstrel, 1988
7–*Trouble in Toyland*. Minstrel, 1988
8–*The Secret of the Stolen Puppies*. Minstrel, 1988
9–*The Clue in the Classroom*. Minstrel, 1988
10–*The Chocolate Covered Clue*. Minstrel, 1989
11–*The Case of the Crooked Contest*. Minstrel, 1989
12–*The Secret of the Sunken Treasure*. Minstrel, 1989
13–*The Case of the Crying Clown*. Minstrel, 1989
14–*The Mystery of the Missing Mummy*. Minstrel, 1989
15–*The Secret of the Stolen Clue*. Minstrel, 1989
16–*The Case of the Missing Dinosaur*. Minstrel, 1990
17–*The Case at Creepy Castle*. Minstrel, 1990
18–*Secret at Sleepaway Camp*. Minstrel, 1990
19–*Show and Tell Mystery*. Minstrel, 1990
20–*The Weird Science Mystery*. Minstrel, 1990
21–*The Great Skate Mystery*. Minstrel, 1990
22–*The Super-Duper Cookie Caper*. Minstrel, 1991
23–*The Monster Mouse Mystery*. Minstrel, 1990
24–*The Case of the Goofy Game Show*. Minstrel, 1991
25–*The Case of the Crazy Collections*. Minstrel, 1991

Publisher Simon & Schuster picked up the baton on updating the Bobbsey Twins in these paperback entries. Grades 3-6.

HOPKINS, Lee (Mama Books)

Mama. Knopf, 1977
Mama and Her Boys. Harper, 1981

Mama is quite a character. A single parent with a highly practical approach to life, she refuses to let things get her down. She is the first to tell anyone that she is always right, most of the time. Entertaining, realistic view of life in Mama's house for grades 4-7.

HOUSTON, James

Frozen Fire. McElderry, 1977
Black Diamonds. McElderry, 1982
Ice Swords. McElderry, 1985

Matthew Morgan and his Eskimo friend, Kayak, set off after Matt's father who is lost in the Arctic. The book depicts the influence of modern life on the Eskimos as the suspenseful adventure comes to a head. In the sequel the boys and Matt's father go after natural gas and oil on Prince Charles Island. Lastly, in *Ice Swords*, the two boys jump at the chance to study the migration of whales with an American scientist in the Arctic. Ages 13 and up.

HOUSTON, James

White Archer. Harcourt, 1967
Falcon Bow. McElderry, 1986

Inuit Eskimo Kungo's family has been killed by marauding Indians, so he goes to the famed expert White Archer to learn how to kill so he can exact vengeance. In the follow up he tries to avert bloodshed between the two sides when each blame the other for the scarcity of food. Houston has spent much time in Alaska and the background makes these novels outstanding. Grades 5-8.

HOWARD, Elizabeth (Paris MacKenzie Series)

1—*Mystery of the Metro*. Random, 1987
2—*Mystery of the Magician*. Random, 1987
3—*A Scent of Murder*. Random, 1987
4—*Mystery of the Deadly Diamond*. Random, 1987

Teenage Paris MacKenzie arrives in the city of the same name only to find her uncle murdered. She meets attractive Marcel Fleury, who assists her in solving that mystery, as well as several others. The third of these features famous artist Claude Monet as a character. These period mysteries are well written and plotted with the suggestion of romance to keep readers grades 4-8 interested.

HOWARD, Ellen

Sister. Atheneum, 1990
Edith Herself. Atheneum, 1987
The Chickenhouse House. Atheneum, 1991

Author Howard has drawn upon the experiences of her grandmother's farm family for these novels set in the 1880s. Two sisters born many years apart are the heroines here—the first must become an adult before her time when her mother sinks into a serious depression. The younger must move in with the elder and her family upon the death of the mother. Edith's epilepsy and others' responses to it add depth to these historical novels for ages 9-13.

HOWE, James (Bunnicula Books)

1—*Bunnicula*. Atheneum, 1979
2—*Howliday Inn*. Atheneum, 1982
3—*The Celery Stalks at Midnight*. Atheneum, 1983
4—*Nighty-Nightmare*. Atheneum, 1987
5—*The Fright before Christmas*. Atheneum, 1988
6—*Scared Silly*. Atheneum, 1989
7—*Hot Fudge*. Atheneum, 1990
8—*Creepy-Crawly Birthday*. Atheneum, 1991

This is a thoroughly charming series that has become beloved of readers, especially the first entry about the vampire bunny. Hilarious from page one, these are also great read alouds. The last four additions using these characters are written on the picture book level. Grades 3-6.

HOWE, James (Sebastian Barth Mysteries)

1—*What Eric Knew*. Atheneum, 1986
2—*Stage Fright*. Atheneum, 1986
3—*Eat Your Poison, Dear*. Atheneum, 1986
4—*Dew Drop Dead*. Atheneum, 1990

Sebastian and his friends David and Corrie find themselves involved in assorted mysteries. In addition to solving them the youngsters become involved in some important social issues like the mentally ill homeless. The youngsters come from real families with real problems: Sebastian's father may be fired and have to relocate; David's father is wrestling with an overdue manuscript and writer's block; and Corrie's minister father cannot find enough selfless volunteers to help with the nutrition program. Well above average fare for readers grades 4-8.

HUDDY, Delia

Time Piper. Greenwillow, 1979
The Humboldt Effect. Greenwillow, 1982

This unusual series deals in time travel and love as a mysterious girl follows Luke to London when he goes to study with Tom Humboldt, who may have invented a time machine. But time travelers may pay a heavy price, as the newly married Arthur and Mary discover in the sequel. Older YAs may find these fantasies interesting.

HUGHES, Dean (Angel Park All-Stars)

1—*Making the Team*. Knopf, 1990
2—*Big Base Hit*. Knopf, 1990
3—*Winning Streak*. Knopf, 1990
4—*What a Catch!* Knopf, 1990
5—*Rookie Star*. Knopf, 1990
6—*Pressure Play*. Knopf, 1990
7—*Line Drive*. Knopf, 1990
8—*Championship Game*. Knopf, 1990
9—*Superstar Team*. Knopf, 1991
10—*Stroke of Luck*. Knopf, 1991
11—*Safe at First*. Knopf, 1991
12—*Up to Bat*. Knopf, 1991
13—*Play-Off*. Knopf, 1991
14—*All Together Now*. Knopf, 1991

Sports fiction series are hard to come by; this and the Alden Park series are pretty good ones. While the other one uses a variety of sports as a backdrop, this one concentrates strictly on baseball. The third grade stars match the 7-10 year old reading level.

HUGHES, Dean (Nutty Nutshell Series)

1—*Nutty for President*. Atheneum, 1981
2—*Nutty and the Case of the Mastermind Thief*. Atheneum, 1985
3—*Nutty and the Case of the Ski Slope Spy*. Atheneum, 1985
4—*Nutty Can't Miss*. Atheneum, 1987
5—*Nutty Knows All*. Atheneum, 1988
6—*Nutty, the Movie Star*. Atheneum, 1989

Nutty is a fifth grade boy whose leadership qualities often lead himself and others into trouble. Like Soup, he wants to be class president. When he achieves this goal, he worries about losing the job and his popularity to a new boy. Not nearly as funny or "real" as Soup, yet these stories will still find an audience with grades 4-7.

HUGHES, Monica

Devil on My Back. Atheneum, 1984
The Dream Catcher. Atheneum, 1987

Tomi has looked forward to the day he would have access to the knowledge of the whole world. Now that he has achieved that level of intelligence, he doesn't understand why so few people are permitted access to it. He gets stranded outside of his domed city with the people who do not have his knowledge. The companion novel tells us about Ruth. She possesses ESP and has been getting messages calling for her to help the people of a different civilization. Grades 6-10.

HUGHES, Monica (Isis Series)

Keeper of the Isis Light. Atheneum, 1981
Guardian of Isis. Atheneum, 1982
Isis Pedlar. Atheneum, 1983

These books take place on Isis, a remote planet on which a lighthouse was built to assist space travelers. Olwen was born there and raised by Guardian, a robot, after her parents were killed. When humans arrive, Olwen has mixed feelings and when she falls in love with Mark, problems arise. Eventually Mark becomes president of the earth people but the settlers lose all of their technical knowledge. In the final volume, Moira's spaceship breaks down on Isis and her father creates havoc for the people living there. Guardian must come to Moira's aid. Junior high and up.

HUNT, Joyce (Victoria Chubb Series)

Eat Your Heart Out, Victoria Chubb. Scholastic, 1990
The Four of Us and Victoria Chubb. Scholastic, 1990

Like Taffy Sinclair, Victoria Chubb is pretty full of herself. She is a take-over kind, who does come up with good ideas, but then buffaloes everyone else into doing what she wants. Controlling her and teaching her a lesson form the basis for these enjoyable books. Grades 4-7.

HUNTER, Kristin (Lou Books)

Soul Brothers and Sister Lou. Scribner, 1975
Lou in the Limelight. Scribner, 1981

In the first book, Lou overcomes problems with and is accepted by the local gang when she becomes part of a singing group that includes some gang members. In the second book the group makes a record and is engaged to perform in Las Vegas. Lou has some difficulty coping with the stress and disloyalty from people close to the group. Both are good books for a black culture collection. Written for junior and senior high schoolers.

HUNTER, Mollie

A Sound of Chariots. Harper, 1972
Hold Onto Love. Harper, 1982

A young Scottish girl overcomes poverty and tragedy in order to become a writer. Fifteen year old Bridie lives with her grandparents. She is stifled by their attitudes and religion. She meets Peter and they begin a courtship that must overcome her grandparents' strictness and the threat of World War II. For YAs.

HURWITZ, Johanna (Aldo Series)

1—*Much Ado about Aldo*. Morrow, 1978
2—*Aldo Applesauce*. Morrow, 1979
3—*Aldo Ice Cream*. Morrow, 1981
4—*Tough-Luck Karen*. Morrow, 1982
5—*Dede Takes Charge!* Morrow, 1984
6—*Hurricane Elaine*. Morrow, 1988
7—*Aldo Peanut Butter*. Morrow, 1990

Aldo Sossi is a very earnest eight year old, anxious to make the world a better place. For example, when he learns where hamburgers come from and what a food chain involves, he becomes a vegetarian. Some of the books chronicle the adventures of other family members, like his thirteen year old sister Elaine, whose main concerns involve clothes and nail polish, and his friend DeDe, who has to adjust to her parents' new divorce. Because the characters run such a gamut in age, sex, and problems, these books will find a large and appreciative audience in readers from 8-12.

HURWITZ, Johanna (Ali Baba Bernstein Books)

The Adventures of Ali Baba Bernstein. Morrow, 1985
Hurray for Ali Baba Bernstein. Morrow, 1989

David Bernstein has decided that his life is dull. But when he changes his name to Ali Baba the adventures begin. Ali Baba notices things like jewel thieves in the neighborhood, he tries to meet the real Santa, and even invites every David Bernstein in the phone book to his new party. Eight year old David will provide a lot of laughs for readers 8-12.

HURWITZ, Johanna

1—*Busybody Nora*. Morrow, 1976
2—*Nora and Mrs. Mind-Your-Own-Business*. Morrow, 1977
3—*New Neighbors for Nora*. Morrow, 1979
4—*Rip-Roaring Russell*. Morrow, 1983
5—*Russell Rides Again*. Morrow, 1985
6—*Russell Sprouts*. Morrow, 1987

7—*Superduper Teddy*. Morrow, 1980
8—*Russell and Elisa*. Morrow, 1989
9—*"E" Is for Elisa*. Morrow, 1991

Nora is six, and her world revolves around typical six year old events: school, friends, new neighbors, babysitters. These stories about Nora and friends Russell and Teddy are simple and fun. The vocabulary is for readers 8-11, but the older kids may not enjoy reading about protagonists this much younger than themselves. Elisa is Russell's younger sister, always trying to keep up with him, as only a pesky younger sibling can.

HURWITZ, Johanna

1—*Class Clown*. Morrow, 1987
2—*Teacher's Pet*. Morrow, 1988
3—*Class President*. Morrow, 1990
4—*School's Out*. Morrow, 1991

This charming series focuses on classmates (class clown) Lucas Cott and (brain) Cricket Kaufman. One of Lucas's problems arises when Cricket bets him that he can go a whole day in school without talking. Cricket finds a new teacher does not appreciate her tattletale ways and she has to adjust to not being the smartest kid in class anymore with the arrival of a new girl. Once again, Hurwitz presents readers 8-12 with a funny, realistic group of heroes and heroines to read about.

HURWITZ, Johanna

The Hot & Cold Summer. Morrow, 1984
The Cold & Hot Winter. Morrow, 1988

Rory and Derek are the best of friends. They do everything together—except argue. Their summer is in jeopardy with the arrival of a guest, a girl named Bolivia! The boys have to admit, finally, that she is not bad for a girl, and even makes a pretty good friend. The boy/girl friendships here are presented realistically and humorously, so that both boys and girls 8-12 will definitely enjoy.

HUTCHINS, Pat

The House That Sailed Away. Morrow, 1975
Follow That Bus! Greenwillow, 1977
The Mona Lisa Mystery. Greenwillow, 1981

These English mysteries are aimed at readers grades 3-6 who not only enjoy solving a puzzle, but like a few laughs as well. Morgan and his friends from Hampstead School encounter adventure on a school picnic and a field trip. Laurence Hutchins's drawings add to the sense of fun.

INDIANA JONES SERIES (Series)

MCKAY, William

1—*Young Indiana Jones and the Plantation Treasure*. Random, 1990

MARTIN, Les

2—*Young Indiana Jones and the Tomb of Terror*. Random, 1990

MCKAY, William

3—*Young Indiana Jones and the Circle of Death*. Random, 1990

MARTIN, Les

4—*Young Indiana Jones and the Secret City*. Random, 1990
5—*Young Indiana Jones and the Princess of Peril*. Random, 1991
6—*Young Indiana Jones and the Gypsy Revenge*. Random, 1991

MCKAY, William

7—*Young Indiana Jones and the Ghostly Riders*. Random, 1991
8—*Young Indiana Jones and the Curse of the Ruby Cross*. Random, 1991

These mystery/adventures capitalize on the well-known Indiana Jones name. The tales are set in foreign locales and feature the spies, villains, and antiquities so popular in the movies. The vocabulary is easy enough to attract reluctant readers and those in grades 4-6.

JACKSON, Alison

My Brother the Star. Dutton, 1990
Crane's Rebound. Dutton, 1991

With a little brother who's a star of TV commercials, Les has problems being recognized for any achievement of his own. In the first book he does succeed in his goal of making the cut for basketball camp. In the second he runs into trouble with a bully at camp. Grades 4-6.

JACQUES, Brian

Mossflower. Philomel, 1988
Redwall. Philomel, 1987

This is a charming series set in Medieval times, but the protagonists are mice. The mice have vivid personalities ranging from the clownish novitiate Matthias to the evil Cluny the Rat. There is lots of humor and drama here as the battle lines between good and evil are drawn. This is an excellent choice for fantasy lovers grades 7 and up.

JOHNSTON, Norma

3—**The Sanctuary Tree*. Atheneum, 1977
4—*The Mustard Seed of Magic*. Atheneum, 1977
5—*A Nice Girl Like You*. Atheneum, 1980
6—*Myself and I*. Atheneum, 1981

Based on stories the author heard about relatives, the characters in this series are vivid and strong with real life problems. For example, instead of making a simple romantic choice between two boys, Saranne tries to help the one boy who feels alienated because he has learned that he is illegitimate, and the people he thought were his parents are really his grandparents. She must decide how much you can help someone else and how far your responsibility extends. For YAs.

JOHNSTON, Norma (Carlisle Chronicles)

Carlisles Hope. Bantam, 1986
To Jess, With Love and Memories. Bantam, 1986
Carlisles All. Bantam, 1986

The Carlisles are a close-knit family with their own traditions and pride. Fifteen year old Jess tells the story of her family in these three books. Her father is away a great deal because he has a foreign service job with the government. This presents some special problems to go with the usual ones associated with school and boys. Grades seven and older.

JOHNSTON, Norma

Of Time and of Seasons. Atheneum, 1975
A Striving after Wind. Atheneum, 1976

Even though Bridget didn't have a special talent, unlike the other members of her family, she was the one they looked to for assistance. Nevertheless, Bridget wants to have her own talent and tries to find one. In the sequel she tries to make her life as successful as her family's lives are. These books are set around the U.S. Civil War. They do not need to be read together and are good books for ages 12-16.

JOHNSTON, Norma

Swallow's Song. Atheneum, 1978
If You Love Me, Let Me Go. Atheneum, 1978

Allison, living in the 1920s, meets Lisa, whose family is rich and glamorous. Allison thinks that her life is awful and unexciting in comparison, but she does not realize Lisa's family has their problems too. Allison is ready to become a new person at school in the fall but that doesn't happen until Lisa shows up and together they become popular. For YAs.

JONES, Adrienne

Whistle Down a Dark Lane. Harper, 1982
A Matter of Spunk. Harper, 1983

The summer of 1921 was fated to be different. Margery and her family always went to their home in the Blue Ridge Mountains to spend the summer months, but this year her father does not go. In the first book Margery, her mother, and sister face the fact that Daddy isn't around anymore. Finally the three of them move to California to start a new life. The story shows that a lot of hard work and perseverance pays off. Junior high and up.

JONES, Diana Wynne (Chrestomancy Series)

The Lives of Christopher Chant. Knopf, 1990
Charmed Life. Knopf, 1977
Witch Week. Knopf, 1982

Jones is a consummate author of fantasy, particularly since she blends fantasy and reality so convincingly. Chrestomancy is the most important sorcerer around, but it is really not so much an individual as it is a position that any gifted child can achieve. In addition to the magic these books deal with sibling rivalry and school problems. Grades 9-12.

JONES, Diana Wynne (Dalemark Series)

The Spellcoats. Atheneum, 1979
Cart & Cwidder. Collier, 1977
Drowned Ammet. Atheneum, 1978

Although *Cart and Cwidder* was written first, *The Spellcoats* takes us into the prehistory of Dalemark, a divided land between the North and the South that is made up of earldoms, where we learn of the gods and other powers in Dalemark. The other books tell us about the stories and happenings in this fantasy land. These books have well developed characters and a believable setting. Good for YAs.

JONES, Diana Wynne

Howl's Moving Castle. Greenwillow, 1986
Castles in the Air. Morrow, 1991

Howl is supposed to be an evil wizard. He is a wizard, but a young one, a cranky one, who has had to develop a castle that moves to run away from his evil nemesis. The characters are vivid, the plots enjoyably complex, and the imagination unparalleled. Excellent for YAs or any other fantasy lovers.

JONES, Rebecca C. (Germy Books)

Germy Blew It! Dutton, 1987
Germy Blew It—Again! Holt, 1990
Germy Blew the Bugle. Little, 1990

Jeremy Bluitt has been nicknamed Germy Blew It for a very good reason. Whatever his situation, his grandiose attempts to solve problems result in continuing disaster and laughs for readers in grades 4-6.

KAYE, Marilyn (Camp Sunnyside Friends)

1—*No Boys Allowed!* Camelot, 1989
2—*Cabin Six Plays Cupid*. Camelot, 1989
3—*Color War!* Camelot, 1989
4—*New Girl in Cabin Six*. Camelot, 1989
5—*Looking for Trouble*. Camelot, 1990
6—*Katie Steals the Show*. Camelot, 1990
7—*A Witch in Cabin 6*. Camelot, 1990
8—*Too Many Counselors*. Camelot, 1990
9—*The New-and-Improved Sarah*. Camelot, 1990

10–*Erin and the Movie Star*. Camelot, 1991
11–*The Problem with Parents*. Camelot, 1991
12–*The Tennis Trap*. Camelot, 1991
13–*Big Sister Blues*. Camelot, 1991
14–*Cabin Six Halloween Party*. Camelot, 1991

Camp Sunnyside Friends have (obviously) met at camp and have numerous entanglements including meeting a movie star, and at first fostering then changing their minds about the budding romance of one girl's divorced mother and another's widowed dad. Grades 4-6.

KAYE, Marilyn (Sisters Series)
1–*Phoebe*. Harcourt, 1987
2–*Daphne*. Harcourt, 1987
3–*Cassie*. Harcourt, 1987
4–*Lydia*. Harcourt, 1987
5–*A Friend Like Phoebe*. Harcourt, 1989

These four girls are sisters about a year apart in age; each book reveals a separate personality with varieties of growing up pains. The values are obvious and the characterizations superficial, but they are easy to read and will appeal to readers of the Sebastian Sisters books. Grades 5-8.

KAYE, Marilyn (Three of a Kind Series)
1–*With Friends Like These, Who Needs Enemies*. Harper, 1990
2–*Home's a Nice Place to Visit, But I Wouldn't Want to Live There*. Harper, 1990
3–*Will the Real Becka Morgan Please Stand Up?* Harper, 1991
4–*Two's Company, Four's a Crowd*. Harper, 1991
5–*Cat Morgan, Working Girl*. Harper, 1991

In the quintessential "girlfriend with something in common" plot basis, three twelve year old orphan girls find themselves adopted by the same family. They must adjust to new parents, siblings, school, boys, you name it. Sweet Valley fans will eat these up. Grades 4-7.

KEENE, Carolyn (Nancy Drew Mysteries)
1–*The Secret of the Old Clock*. Grosset, 1930
2–*The Hidden Staircase*. Grosset, 1930
3–*The Bungalow Mystery*. Grosset, 1930
4–*The Mystery at Lilac Inn*. Grosset, 1930
5–*The Secret of Shadow Ranch*. Grosset, 1931
6–*The Secret of Red Gate Farm*. Grosset, 1931
7–*The Clue in the Diary*. Grosset, 1932
8–*Nancy's Mysterious Letter*. Grosset, 1963
9–*The Sign of the Twisted Candles*. Grosset, 1959
10–*Password to Larkspur Lane*. Grosset, 1960
11–*The Clue of the Broken Locket*. Grosset, 1943
12–*The Message in the Hollow Oak*. Grosset, 1935
13–*The Mystery of the Ivory Charm*. Grosset, 1974
14–*The Whispering Statue*. Grosset, 1937
15–*The Haunted Bridge*. Grosset, 1938
16–*The Clue of the Tapping Heels*. Grosset, 1939
17–*The Mystery of the Brass-Bound Trunk*. Grosset, 1976
18–*The Mystery of the Moss-Covered Mansion*. Grosset, 1971
19–*The Quest of the Missing Map*. Grosset, 1942
20–*The Clue in the Jewel Box*. Grosset, 1943
21–*The Secret in the Old Attic*. Grosset, 1955
22–*The Clue in the Crumbling Wall*. Grosset, 1945
23–*The Mystery of the Tolling Bell*. Grosset, 1973
24–*The Clue in the Old Album*. Grosset, 1947
25–*The Ghost of Blackwood Hall*. Grosset, 1948

26—*The Clue of the Leaning Chimney*. Grosset, 1949
27—*The Secret of the Wooden Lady*. Grosset, 1950
28—*The Clue of the Black Keys*. Grosset, 1951
29—*The Mystery at the Ski Jump*. Grosset, 1968
30—*The Clue of the Velvet Mask*. Grosset, 1953
31—*The Ringmaster's Secret*. Grosset, 1974
32—*The Scarlet Slipper Mystery*. Grosset, 1955
33—*The Witch Tree Symbol*. Grosset, 1975
34—*The Hidden Window Mystery*. Grosset, 1975
35—*The Haunted Showboat*. Grosset, 1958
36—*The Secret of the Golden Pavilion*. Grosset, 1959
37—*The Clue in the Old Stagecoach*. Grosset, 1960
38—*The Mystery of the Fire Dragon*. Grosset, 1961
39—*The Clue of the Dancing Puppet*. Grosset, 1962
40—*The Moonstone Castle Mystery*. Grosset, 1963
41—*The Clue of the Whistling Bagpipes*. Grosset, 1964
42—*The Phantom of Pine Hill*. Grosset, 1965
43—*The Mystery of the 99 Steps*. Grosset, 1965
44—*The Clue in the Crossword Cipher*. Grosset, 1967
45—*The Spider Sapphire Mystery*. Grosset, 1968
46—*The Invisible Intruder*. Grosset, 1969
47—*The Mysterious Mannequin*. Grosset, 1970
48—*The Crooked Banister*. Grosset, 1971
49—*The Secret of Mirror Bay*. Grosset, 1972
50—*The Double Jinx Mystery*. Grosset, 1973
51—*Mystery of the Glowing Eye*. Grosset, 1974
52—*The Secret of the Forgotten City*. Grosset, 1975
53—*The Sky Phantom*. Grosset, 1976
54—*The Strange Message in the Parchment*. Grosset, 1977
55—*The Mystery of Crocodile Island*. Grosset, 1978
56—*The Thirteenth Pearl*. Grosset, 1979
57—*Triple Hoax*. Wanderer, 1987
58—*Flying Saucer Mystery*. Wanderer, 1980
59—*The Secret in the Old Lace*. Wanderer, 1980
60—*The Greek Symbol Mystery*. Wanderer, 1981
61—*The Swami's Ring*. Wanderer, 1981
62—*The Kachina Doll Mystery*. Wanderer, 1981
63—*The Twin Dilemma*. Wanderer, 1981
64—*The Captive Witness*. Wanderer, 1981
65—*Mystery of the Winged Lion*. Wanderer, 1982
66—*Race against Time*. Wanderer, 1982
67—*The Sinister Omen*. Wanderer, 1982
68—*The Elusive Heiress*. Wanderer, 1982
69—*Clue in the Ancient Disguise*. Wanderer, 1982
70—*The Broken Anchor*. Wanderer, 1983
71—*The Silver Cobweb*. S&S, 1983
72—*The Haunted Carousel*. Wanderer, 1983
73—*Enemy Match*. Wanderer, 1984
74—*The Mysterious Image*. Wanderer, 1984
75—*The Emerald-Eyed Cat*. S&S, 1984
76—*The Eskimo's Secret*. Minstrel, 1985
77—*The Bluebeard Room*. Wanderer, 1985
78—*The Ghost in the Gondola*. Wanderer, 1985
79—*The Double Horror of Fenley Place*. S&S, 1987
80—*The Case of the Disappearing Diamonds*. S&S, 1987

81 – *The Mardi Gras Mystery*. S&S, 1990
82 – *The Clue in the Camera*. S&S, 1988
83 – *The Case of the Vanishing Veil*. S&S, 1988
84 – *The Joker's Revenge*. S&S, 1989
85 – *The Secret of Shady Glen*. S&S, 1989
86 – *The Mystery of Misty Canyon*. S&S, 1989
87 – *The Case of the Rising Stars*. S&S, 1990
88 – *The Search for Cindy Austin*. S&S, 1989
89 – *The Case of the Disappearing Deejay*. S&S, 1989
90 – *The Puzzle at Pineview School*. S&S, 1989
91 – *The Girl Who Couldn't Remember*. S&S, 1989
92 – *The Ghost of Craven Cove*. Minstrel, 1989
93 – *The Case of the Safecracker's Secret*. S&S, 1990
94 – *The Picture Perfect Mystery*. S&S, 1990
95 – *The Silent Suspect*. Minstrel, 1990
96 – *The Case of the Photo Finish*. S&S, 1990
97 – *The Mystery at Magnolia Mansion*. Pocket, 1990
98 – *The Haunting of Horse Island*. Minstrel, 1990
99 – *The Secret at Seven Rocks*. Minstrel, 1991
100 – *A Secret in Time*. Minstrel, 1991
101 – *The Mystery of the Missing Millionaires*. Minstrel, 1991
102 – *The Secret in the Dark*. Minstrel, 1991

Perennial queen of mysteries, Nancy Drew, continues to go strong. Long before women's lib, Nancy and her chums were solving mysteries. Not great literature, but the kind of books parents tell their kids about, and kids continue to read generation to generation, which does make them classics of a sort. Surefire hits with grades 3-7.

KEENE, Carolyn (Nancy Drew Casefiles)
1 – *Secrets Can Kill*. Archway, 1986
2 – *Deadly Intent*. Archway, 1986
3 – *Murder on Ice*. Archway, 1986
4 – *Smile and Say Murder*. Archway, 1986
5 – *Hit and Run Holiday*. Archway, 1986
6 – *White Water Terror*. Archway, 1986
7 – *Deadly Doubles*. Archway, 1987
8 – *Two Points for Murder*. Archway, 1987
9 – *False Moves*. Archway, 1987
10 – *Buried Secrets*. Archway, 1987
11 – *Heart of Danger*. Archway, 1987
12 – *Fatal Ransom*. Archway, 1987
13 – *Wings of Fear*. Archway, 1987
14 – *This Side of Evil*. Archway, 1987
15 – *Trial by Fire*. Archway, 1987
16 – *Never Say Die*. Archway, 1987
17 – *Stay Tuned for Danger*. Archway, 1987
18 – *Circle of Evil*. Archway, 1987
19 – *Sisters in Crime*. Archway, 1988
20 – *Very Deadly Sins*. Archway, 1988
21 – *Recipe for Murder*. Archway, 1988
22 – *Fatal Attraction*. Archway, 1988
23 – *Sinister Paradise*. Archway, 1988
24 – *Till Death Do Us Part*. Archway, 1988
25 – *Rich and Dangerous*. Archway, 1988
26 – *Playing with Fire*. Archway, 1988
27 – *Most Likely to Die*. Archway, 1988

28—*The Black Widow*. Archway, 1988
29—*Pure Poison*. Archway, 1988
30—*Death by Design*. Archway, 1988
31—*Trouble in Tahiti*. Archway, 1989
32—*High Marks for Malice*. Archway, 1989
33—*Danger in Disguise*. Archway, 1989
34—*Vanishing Act*. Archway, 1989
35—*Bad Medicine*. Archway, 1989
36—*Over the Edge*. Archway, 1989
37—*Last Dance*. Archway, 1989
38—*The Final Scene*. Archway, 1989
39—*The Suspect Next Door*. Archway, 1989
40—*Shadow of a Doubt*. Archway, 1989
41—*Something to Hide*. Archway, 1989
42—*The Wrong Chemistry*. Archway, 1989
43—*False Impressions*. Archway, 1990
44—*Scent of Danger*. Archway, 1990
45—*Out of Bounds*. Archway, 1990
46—*Win, Place or Die*. Archway, 1990
47—*Flirting with Danger*. Archway, 1990
48—*A Date with Deception*. A Summer of Love Trilogy #1, 1990
49—*Portrait in Crime*. A Summer of Love Trilogy #2, 1990
50—*Deep Secrets*. A Summer of Love Trilogy #3, 1990
51—*A Model Crime*. Archway, 1990
52—*Danger for Hire*. Archway, 1990
53—*Trail of Lies*. Archway, 1990
54—*Cold As Ice*. Archway, 1990
55—*Don't Look Twice*. Archway, 1991
56—*Make No Mistake*. Archway, 1991
57—*Into Thin Air*. Archway, 1991
58—*Hot Pursuit*. Archway, 1991
59—*High Risk*. Archway, 1991
60—*Poison Pen*. Archway, 1991
61—*Sweet Revenge*. Archway, 1991
62—*Easy Marks*. Archway, 1991
63—*Mixed Signals*. Archway, 1991

Just like the Hardy Boys, Nancy Drew has returned in a stylish, up-to-date series. These are situated in River Heights and are totally new stories involving America's best known teen detective. These books are only available in paperback, which makes them popular with young adults 13 and up. Adults will also read them, some for nostalgia and some because they are "clean."

KEENE, Carolyn (Dana Girls Mystery Series)
1—*Mystery of the Stone Tiger*. Grosset, 1972
2—*The Riddle of the Frozen Fountain*. Grosset, 1972
3—*The Secret of the Silver Dolphin*. Grosset, 1972
4—*Mystery of the Wax Queen*. Grosset, 1972
5—*The Secret of the Minstrel's Guitar*. Grosset, 1972
6—*The Phantom Surfer*. Grosset, 1972
7—*The Secret of the Swiss Chalet*. Grosset, 1973
8—*The Haunted Lagoon*. Grosset, 1973
9—*Mystery of the Bamboo Bird*. Grosset, 1973
10—*The Sierra Gold Mystery*. Grosset, 1973
11—*The Secret of the Lost Lake*. Grosset, 1974

12—*The Winking Ruby Mystery*. Grosset, 1974
13—*Ghosts in the Gallery*. Grosset, 1975
14—*The Curious Coronation*. Grosset, 1976
15—*The One Hundred Year Mystery*. Grosset, 1977
16—*The Mountain-Peak Mystery*. Grosset, 1978
17—*The Witch's Omen*. Grosset, 1979

Louise and Jean Dana are orphan sisters being brought up by their aunt and uncle. Like their fictional relative, Nancy Drew, they solve mysteries. These are straightforward fare but not nearly as popular as Nancy or the Hardy Boys. Grades 4-8.

KEENE, Carolyn (River Heights Series)
1—*Love Times Three*. Pocket, 1989
2—*Guilty Secrets*. Pocket, 1989
3—*Going Too Far*. Pocket, 1990
4—*Stolen Kisses*. Pocket, 1990
5—*Between the Lines*. Pocket, 1990
6—*Lessons in Love*. Pocket, 1990
7—*Cheating Hearts*. Pocket, 1990
8—*The Trouble with Love*. Pocket, 1990
9—*Lies and Whispers*. Pocket, 1991
10—*Mixed Emotions*. Pocket, 1991
11—*Broken Hearts*. Pocket, 1991
12—*Hard to Handle*. Pocket, 1991

By the syndicate that produces the Nancy Drew/Hardy Boys moneymakers, this series has so far not proven as popular. These are straight romances centering around the teens in small town River Heights. They will appeal to the paperback romance lovers nonetheless. For YA collections.

KELLER, Beverly (Desdemona Series)
No Beasts! No Children! Lothrop, 1983
Desdemona—Twelve Going on Desperate. Lothrop, 1986
Fowl Play, Desdemona. Lothrop, 1989

Aside from a perfectly awful name, Desdemona has other problems. Her father, a widower, has begun to date. Her kindergarten age twin siblings are into all kinds of mischief, the family's landlord is anxious to get rid of them. Add to this being new in town, and the usual teen hangups, and you have a series that lots of readers will be able to relate to. Grades 4-7.

KERR, Judith
When Hitler Stole Pink Rabbit. Coward, 1971
The Other Way Around. Coward, 1975
Small Person Far Away. Coward, 1978

Anna is a German-Jewish child living in Berlin when Hitler comes to power. These semi-autobiographical novels follow Anna and her family as they flee an increasingly dangerous Germany to settle eventually in England. The series ends with Anna, now grown, finding herself once more returning to Berlin and confronting her past, present, and that of both Germany and Holocaust survivors. Excellent for grades 5-9.

KERR, M. E. (Fell Series)
Fell. Harper, 1987
Fell Back. Harper, 1989

Both books have well constructed plots and good characterization. John Fell is a favorite of young adult readers for his realistic life. The books have a good mix of suspense, humor and dreams come true. The original *Fell* is an ALA Best Book for Young Adults. Both are excellent for YA collections.

KEY, Alexander (Witch Mountain Series)

Escape to Witch Mountain. Westminster, 1968
Return from Witch Mountain. Westminster, 1984

These books were the basis for two popular Disney pictures. The children, who appear to be orphans, are actually telepaths from another planet. There is lots of adventure here as an evil man tries to kidnap them to use their powers. Grades 4-6.

KIESEL, Stanley

War between the Pitiful Teachers and the Splendid Kids. Avon, 1980
Skinny Malinky Leads the War for Kidness. Avon, 1984

"The Status Quo Solidifier" is the brainchild of Mr. Foreclosure at Scratchland School and it is supposed to turn kids into Perfect Young People. But the students want no part of that. Skinny Malinky leads the battle through these two books to preserve kidness forever. These very original books are very funny and enjoyable. Young people in seventh grade and up will read these and maybe even get a few ideas of their own.

KILLIEN, Christi

Putting on An Act. Houghton, 1986
Fickle Fever. Houghton, 1988

Skeeter has a problem. She has been confiding about herself and her life to pen pal Terry. Especially about her love life with gorgeous Campbell Lancaster. Her glorious love life is all a lie, and she knows she'll be found out because Terry is moving to town. These are amusing—no deep characters or complex plotlines, but are fine pleasure reading for grades 5-8.

KLEIN, Norma

Confessions of An Only Child. Knopf, 1988
Tomboy. Knopf, 1989

Author Klein is a specialist in the "problem" novel; this series finds young Antonia rebelling at the thought of a new sibling, then facing growing up pains with boys and her period. Grades 4-6.

KLINE, Suzy (Herbie Jones Series)

1—*Herbie Jones*. Putnam, 1985
2—*What's the Matter with Herbie Jones?* Putnam, 1986
3—*Herbie Jones and the Class Gift*. Putnam, 1987
4—*Herbie Jones and the Monster Ball*. Putnam, 1988
5—*Herbie Jones and Hamburger Head*. Putnam, 1989

Herbie is an average third grader, an average reader (in the lower reading group), and an average baseball player even with the help of his Uncle Dwight. These are low key books for readers ages 8-12. They are not outstanding, but certainly passable fare for this age group, particularly boys.

KLINE, Suzy (Horrible Harry Series)

1—*Horrible Harry in Room 2B*. Viking, 1988
2—*Horrible Harry and the Ant Invasion*. Viking, 1989
3—*Horrible Harry and the Green Slime*. Viking, 1989
4—*Horrible Harry and the Christmas Surprise*. Viking, 1991

Harry is one of those kids who always seems destined for trouble despite his own best intentions. This series, written for ages 7-10, features simple vocabulary and self-contained chapters that make this more like a collection of interrelated short stories than a novel. It should prove a good transition from the "chapter" beginning reading book.

KNUDSON, R. R. (Zan Series)

1—*Zanballer*. Delacorte, 1972
2—*Zanbanger*. Harper, 1977
3—*Zanboomer*. Harper, 1978

4—*Rinehart Lifts*. Farrar, 1980
5—*Zan Hagen's Marathon*. Farrar, 1984
6—*Rinehart Shouts*. Farrar, 1987

Suzanne "Zan" Hagen is a gifted athlete. Arthur Rinehart is her opposite, a straight "A" student with no athletic ability. The two of them develop a strong friendship, each respecting the other. In the three "Zan"-titled books Arthur helps Zan fight her school against discrimination, teaches her that you don't always have to play on a team to compete and helps her reach the Olympics as a marathon runner. The two "Rinehart" books have Zan helping Arthur lift weights to prove to the school jocks that he is worthy and they together race to victory in the President's Cup Regatta. Grades 5-10.

KORMAN, Gordon (Bruno and Boots Series)
1—*This Can't Be Happening at Macdonald Hall!* Scholastic, 1979
2—*Beware the Fish!* Scholastic, 1980
3—*Go Jump in the Pool!* Scholastic, 1982
4—*The War with Mr. Wizzle*. Scholastic, 1982
5—*The Zucchini Warriors*. Scholastic, 1988
6—*Macdonald Hall Goes Hollywood*. Scholastic, 1991

Korman has been writing about Bruno and Boots for more than ten years now. He knows and enjoys the characters as much as his readers do. The boys attend prep school at Macdonald Hall, where their latest adventure finds them trying to pass off a girl as their star quarterback. The stories are laugh aloud funny and will prove popular with grades 5-8.

KRENSKY, Stephen (Wynd Family Series)
The Dragon Circle. Aladdin, 1990
The Witching Hour. Aladdin, 1990
A Ghostly Business. Aladdin, 1990

The Wynd children are all magical, but to the good. They use their talents to foil nasty ghosts, spells that misfire, and evil witches. This is an amusing series that will entertain fantasy readers 8-12.

LANDON, Lucinda (Meg Mackintosh Series)
1—*Meg Mackintosh and the Case of the Missing Babe Ruth Baseball*. Little, 1986
2—*Meg Mackintosh and the Case of the Curious Whale Watch*. Little, 1987
3—*Meg Mackintosh and the Mystery at the Medieval Castle*. Little, 1989
4—*Meg Mackintosh and the Mystery at Camp Creepy*. Little, 1990

Sleuth Meg is the heroine of these easy to read mysteries. Each book is a full-length story written at the grade 2-4 level. There are points in the story where some clues are presented and the reader is asked for input.

LANGTON, Jane (*Hall Children Series)
4—*The Fledgling*. Harper, 1980
5—*The Fragile Flag*. Harper, 1984

The fantasy adventures of the Hall children continue here. *The Fledgling* was a Newbery Honor book. Although the plots are not based on real events, the message they carry, like the meaning of patriotism and the horror of war, are both real and important. This outstanding series is for grades 4-8.

LAWLOR, Laurie (Addie Books)
Addie across the Prairie. Whitman, 1986
Addie's Dakota Winter. Whitman, 1989

Young Addie is upset to learn her father has decided to move the family from Iowa, especially since she was going to learn cursive this year. She is even more dismayed at the severe brutality of the Dakota prairie. Gradually she comes to adjust and see the beauty around her. Author Lawlor makes the rigors faced by the early pioneers come very much to life. Addie is an appealing heroine for readers grades 4-7.

LE GUIN, Ursula K. (Catwings Books)
Catwings. Orchard, 1988
Catwings Return. Orchard, 1989
Catwings are exactly what they sound like—four tabby kittens with wings. Raised by their mother in a slum, they finally escape to the country. In the sequel they return to find their mother. These tiny books with their fantastical heroes will be a nice bridge from picture books to longer novels for readers grades 3-6.

LE GUIN, Ursula K. (*Earthsea Books)
4—*Tehanu*. Atheneum, 1990
Tehanu represents the final book of the highly recommended Earthsea series. Tenar is an aging widow when she is called to the deathbed of her friend, the mage Ogion. His final words send Tenar on a journey through her former life to find an orphaned child's true identity and worth. Seventh grade and up.

L'ENGLE, Madeleine (*Austin Family)
5—*Ring of Endless Light*. Farrar, 1980
This is Madeleine L'Engle's fifth book dealing with the Austin family and is as appealing as the others. In this addition, 16 year old Vicki narrates the time spent with her grandfather as he lives his last days. This Newbery Honor Book is strongly recommended for junior high and up.

L'ENGLE, Madeleine
1—*The Arm and the Starfish*. Farrar, 1965
2—*Dragons in the Water*. Farrar, 1976
3—*House Like a Lotus*. Farrar, 1984
4—*An Acceptable Time*. Farrar, 1989
In *Arm* Adam, a prospective Berkeley freshman and brilliant student of marine biology, gets a job with Dr. O'Keefe. Adam becomes involved in a number of mysteries. In the second book O'Keefe and his family are traveling aboard a freighter when one of the passengers is murdered. The family becomes involved in solving the crime. Many of the characters in this book and its prequel are seen in L'Engle's Time Trilogy series. Grades 6-10.

L'ENGLE, Madeleine (*Time Series)
3—*Swiftly Tilting Planet*. Dell, 1978
4—*Many Waters*. Farrar, 1986
This series continues the Time Trilogy begun with *A Wrinkle in Time*. The Murry family continues their time traveling in an effort to repair a broken time link; then the twins find themselves in a pre-Flood world. The characters in this series interweave with the O'Keefe family in another L'Engle series during their travels. Outstanding choices for grades 5-9.

LEONARD, Constance
1—*The Marina Mystery*. Putnam, 1981
2—*Stowaway*. Putnam, 1983
3—*Aground*. Putnam, 1984
4—*Strange Waters*. Putnam, 1984
Tracy James and boyfriend Peter always seem to get in over their heads in "watery" adventures. First they get involved in a smuggling caper. Then there is a stowaway aboard her boat. Having gone home to Maine, Tracy gets involved with a Utopian cult in *Aground*. Lastly, the two characters end up in Greece where they get themselves tangled up in a museum robbery and murder. Readers will find it easy to cruise along with Tracy and her adventures. Junior high and up.

LEPPARD, Lois Gladys (Mandie Series)

1—*Mandie and the Secret Tunnel*. Bethany, 1983
2—*Mandie and the Cherokee Legend*. Bethany, 1983
3—*Mandie and the Ghost Bandits*. Bethany, 1984
4—*Mandie and the Forbidden Attic*. Bethany, 1985
5—*Mandie and the Trunk's Secret*. Bethany, 1985
6—*Mandie and the Medicine Man*. Bethany, 1986
7—*Mandie and the Charleston Phantom*. Bethany, 1986
8—*Mandie and the Abandoned Mine*. Bethany, 1987
9—*Mandie and the Hidden Treasure*. Bethany, 1987
10—*Mandie and the Mysterious Bells*. Bethany, 1988
11—*Mandie and the Holiday Surprise*. Bethany, 1988
12—*Mandie and the Washington Nightmare*. Bethany, 1989
13—*Mandie and the Midnight Journey*. Bethany, 1989
14—*Mandie and the Shipboard Mystery*. Bethany, 1989
15—*Mandie and the Foreign Spies*. Bethany, 1990
16—*Mandie and the Silent Catacombs*. Bethany, 1990

Set in 1900, this series follows Mandie as she copes with assorted mysteries and teen angst. These are Christian fiction, and there is not too much available in series format for this group of readers. Grades 5-8.

LEROE, Ellen (Cupid Delaney Series)

Have a Heart, Cupid Delaney. Lodestar, 1986
Meet Your Match, Cupid Delaney. Lodestar, 1990

Cupid Delaney is just what the name implies ... a real cupid. She is trying to earn her wings from the Love Bureau and sets out to make matches. Naturally things do not go as planned when the chosen partners do not seem to be as good a match as Cupid thinks is possible. There is humor here for those YAs who enjoy a light romantic read.

LEROE, Ellen

Robot Romance. Harper, 1985
Robot Raiders. Harper, 1987

Silicon Computer High School would be an interesting place to be a student. You see, there are both human and robot students there. Bixby is a new student and is an upsetting influence to the students and to MAX, the computerized school administrator. Havoc reaches high proportions as Bixby's beautiful humanoid short circuits the whole school. The next book finds Bixby involved with NASA, MIT, an anti-computer faction, and MAX. These farces are fun reads! ...*Raiders* was chosen as a Best Book for the Teen Age. Junior high schoolers will like these two.

LEVY, Elizabeth

Frankenstein Moved in on the Fourth Floor. Harper, 1979
Dracula Is a Pain in the Neck. Harper, 1983

Levy's humorous touch is at work here with brothers Robert and Sam. In the first book the boys become increasingly convinced that one of their neighbors is a monster, in the second Robert's Dracula doll begins to evince peculiar powers. Very popular with ages 7-10.

LEVY, Elizabeth (Gymnasts Series)

1—*The Beginners*. Scholastic, 1988
2—*First Meet*. Scholastic, 1988
3—*Nobody's Perfect*. Scholastic, 1988
4—*The Winner*. Scholastic, 1988
5—*Trouble with Elizabeth*. Scholastic, 1989
6—*Bad Break*. Scholastic, 1989
7—*Tumbling Ghosts*. Scholastic, 1989

8—*Captain of the Team*. Scholastic, 1989
9—*Crush on the Coach*. Scholastic, 1990
10—*Boys in the Gym*. Scholastic, 1990
11—*Mystery at the Meet*. Scholastic, 1990
12—*Out of Control*. Scholastic, 1990
13—*First Date*. Scholastic, 1990
14—*World-Class Gymnast*. Scholastic, 1990
15—*Nasty Competition*. Scholastic, 1991
16—*Fear of Falling*. Scholastic, 1991
17—*Gymnast Commandos*. Scholastic, 1991
18—*The New Coach?* Scholastic, 1991
19—*Tough at the Top*. Scholastic, 1991

Fans of the Babysitters and Sweet Valley Twins will find this series appealing. The girls here are gymnasts on an intermediate team of intermediate ability. There are the usual interpersonal problems. Grades 3-6.

LEVY, Elizabeth (Magic Mystery Series)
The Case of the Gobbling Squash. S&S, 1988
The Case of the Mind-Reading Mommies. S&S, 1989
The Case of the Tattletale Heart. S&S, 1990
The Case of the Dummy with Cold Eyes. S&S, 1991

These easy reading mysteries aimed at readers 7-9 feature two realistic, likeable youngsters, Kate and Max. In the first book Kate advertises as a detective during a school fund raiser. Max is a magician whose bunny has disappeared. Each book ends with a chapter on how to do Max's tricks.

LEVY, Elizabeth (Something Queer Books)
1—*Something Queer Is Going On*. Dell, 1982
2—*Something Queer on Vacation*. Dell, 1982
3—*Something Queer at the Haunted School*. Dell, 1983
4—*Something Queer at the Lemonade Stand*. Dell, 1983
5—*Something Queer at the Ball Park*. Dell, 1984
6—*Something Queer at the Library*. Dell, 1984
7—*Something Queer in Rock 'N Roll*. Delacorte, 1987
8—*Something Queer at the Birthday Party*. Dell, 1991

Although these books have large illustrations and seem like picture books, the text is longer than picture book norm, and the text is geared to 7-9 year old reading skills. Like the books by Adler and Markham, these are humorous mysteries featuring a set of sleuths. Mordecai Gerstein's cartoon-like illustrations add a lot of pizzaz.

LEWIS, Linda (Linda Stories)
1—*2 Young 2 Go 4 Boys*. Minstrel, 1988
2—*We Hate Everything but Boys*. Minstrel, 1989
3—*Tomboy Terror in Bunk 109*. Minstrel, 1989
4—*Want to Trade Two Brothers for a Cat?* Minstrel, 1989
5—*We Love Only Older Boys*. Minstrel, 1989
6—*My Heart Belongs to That Boy*. Minstrel, 1989
7—*Is There Life after Boys?* Minstrel, 1989
8—*All for the Love of That Boy*. Minstrel, 1989
9—*Dedicated to the Boy I Love*. Minstrel, 1990
10—*Loving Two Is Hard to Do*. Minstrel, 1990

Beginning when Linda is still in elementary school this series follows her into high school and through her ongoing romance with a troubled boy. Their up-and-down relationship causes her parents to dislike the boy even more than his questionable past alone would cause. Teens will relate to Linda and her adolescent woes.

LINDBERGH, Anne (Pineapple Place Series)
The People of Pineapple Place. Camelot, 1990
The Prisoner of Pineapple Place. Camelot, 1990
Here is a fantasy series with a charming twist. Pineapple Place is a fantasy street that can move through time and place, and often does. The residents never change or age. They are invisible to those in the "real" world, except to a select few. One of the select is August, miserable after his parents' divorce and subsequent move. His involvement with the residents of Pineapple Place helps him to adjust. In the second book a permanent resident of Pineapple Place, Jeremiah, is tired of life the way it is. Things look up when a "real" girl becomes aware of his existence. She can see him in mirrors. This is a well written series that should find a ready audience in fantasy lovers in grades 4-7.

LINDGREN, Astrid (*Pippi Longstocking Series)
4–*Pippi on the Run*. Viking, 1976
This is the last in the Pippi Longstocking series to date, and is just as enjoyable as the earlier works. Pippi is an endearing tomboy, enormously strong and independent, whose popularity has extended to movie stardom. This is a must addition to collections for readers 8-12.

LINDQUIST, Marie (Texas Promises Series)
Dreams at Dawn. Bantam, 1987
Untamed Heart. Bantam, 1987
Hidden Longings. Bantam, 1987
A full-blown western series with female lead characters are the basis for the books. Maggie, Charlotte, and Teyah are friends and rivals in post-Civil War Texas. They must learn to deal with the harsh realities of frontier life and still find time for the promise of love. Each book focuses on the adventures of one of the three friends. For grades seven and up.

LINGARD, Joan
5– **Hostages to Fortune*. Nelson, 1977
Set in strife ridden Ireland, Protestant Sadie and Catholic Kevin first met in a skirmish when they were children. When they meet again as teens, they fall in love. They eventually marry but face many problems. To escape, they move to England, but their problems remain. In this new book, they lose their rented farm when it is sold by the owner. They must move again but they are still confronting the same problems. This is a good book, realistically portrayed, that discusses bigotry and the lack of understanding by others. For YAs.

LINGARD, Joan
Clearance. Nelson, 1974
Resettling. Nelson, 1975
Pilgrimage. Nelson, 1976
Set in Scotland at the time of the Clearances of the 1840s, this series follows young Maggie as she and her family are forced to leave their home. Eventually she, along with her boyfriend James, travels to the Scottish glen her relatives were expelled from in the Clearances of the 1840s. They are pulled into a number of adventures and learn more than they expected. For YAs.

LIPSYTE, Robert
One Fat Summer. Harper, 1977
Summer Rules. Harper, 1979
The Summerboy. Harper, 1982

Bobby Marks is fourteen years old. He is overweight and hates summer. He is always getting picked on by a group of hecklers because of his weight, but he finds out that a hero doesn't have to be thin. Two years later Bobby gets a summer job as a camp counselor. He meets his first love and learns how to make difficult decisions. We last see Bobby when he is eighteen. He has another summer job in a laundry where the working conditions are substandard. He must also cope with the fact that his best friend is pregnant with his boss's child. These books are very funny and are a joy to read. Seventh grade and above.

LITTLE, Jean

From Anna. Harper, 1972
Listen for the Singing. Dutton, 1977

Anna is awkward and makes many mistakes. When her vision problem is finally diagnosed, life changes for the better even though it means glasses and a special school. When she goes to high school she fears the change, and finds it worse than expected, because her teacher is prejudiced against anyone with a German surname like hers. Little is a sensitive writer with a sure touch. Grades 4-7.

LITTLE, Jean

3—**Hey World, Here I Am!* Harper, 1989

Author Little states in a preface to this book that she thought Kate was a minor character in one of her other books, only to find that Kate was so compelling she forced the author to write another book all about her. And after an absence of eighteen years she is back! This one collects a lot of Kate's poems and jottings that readers should find fun, revealing, and thought-provoking. An unusual, very well done entry for grades 4-6.

LORD, Athena V. (Z.A.P. and Zoe Series)

Today's Special: Z.A.P. and Zoe. Macmillan, 1984
The Luck of Z.A.P. and Zoe. Macmillan, 1987

Z.A.P. stands for Zachary Athanasius Poulous, an eleven year old boy of Greek extraction. He and four year old sister, Zoe, live in a small town in New York in 1939. Zach is pretty sharp—he knows enough not to tell an outright lie unless completely unavoidable. But he's not sharp enough to protect himself from his little sister. Entertaining period piece for grades 4-6.

LOWRY, Lois (Anastasia Series)

1—*Anastasia Krupnik*. Houghton, 1979
2—*Anastasia Again!* Houghton, 1981
3—*Anastasia at Your Service*. Houghton, 1982
4—*Anastasia, Ask Your Analyst*. Houghton, 1983
5—*Anastasia on Her Own*. Houghton, 1985
6—*Anastasia Has the Answers*. Houghton, 1986
7—*Anastasia's Chosen Career*. Houghton, 1987
8—*All about Sam*. Houghton, 1988
9—*Anastasia at This Address*. Houghton, 1991

Lowry is a popular author with kids because of her lifelike characters, believable dialogue, and light touch with a plot. Heroine Anastasia Krupnik goes through so many "typical" phases, there is not a child alive who will not identify with her. The series begins with Anastasia's reaction to the news that she is finally (and unwillingly) going to become a big sister. She faces a wrenching move, being left in charge of the house, and even psychoanalysis! An outstanding entree for grades 4-7.

LOWRY, Lois

The One Hundredth Thing about Caroline. Houghton, 1983
Switcharound. Houghton, 1985
Your Move, J.P.! Houghton, 1990

This entertaining series follows the adventures of Caroline, her older brother J.P., and their friend Stacy. Lowry is a pastmistress at portraying realistic kids in believable situations. Her dialogue is funny and the plots will keep readers coming back for more. Ages 8-12.

MACGREGOR, Ellen (*Miss Pickerell Series)
10—*Miss Pickerell Takes the Bull by the Horns*. McGraw, 1976
11—*Miss Pickerell and the Supertanker*. McGraw, 1978
12—*Miss Pickerell Tackles the Energy Crisis*. McGraw, 1980
13—*Miss Pickerell and the Blue Whales*. McGraw, 1983
In recent years, Miss Pickerell's scientific bent has turned toward ecology, as she handles oil spills, fuel shortages, and endangered species. Recently her authorship has been taken over by Dora Pantell. Grades 4-6.

MAGUIRE, Jack (Many Lives of Underfoot the Cat)
Trouble and More Trouble. Minstrel, 1991
Hit the Road and Strike It Rich. Minstrel, 1991
Surprise and Double Surprise. Minstrel, 1991
Each book features two adventures of Underfoot, so named because of his tendency to be continually in the way. These are short, easy reads that will help younger readers bridge the gap from chapter books to full length stories. Grades 2-4.

MAGUIRE, Jesse (Nowhere High)
1—*Just Friends*. Ivy, 1990
2—*Nowhere High*. Ivy, 1990
3—*On the Edge*. Ivy, 1990
If you do not fit in with a group at Ernest Norwell (Nowhere) High, you are on your own. In these books we take a look at the lives of two "Nowhere" outsiders and the friendship that develops between them. As their relationship progresses other outsiders begin to drop by the abandoned railroad station where they hang out. This ragtag group forms a special bond of friendship. In the back of each book there is a list of national help line phone numbers for kids to call if they are in the need of help. Grades 7-12.

MALCOLM, Jahnna N. (Bad News Ballet)
1—*The Terrible Tryouts*. Scholastic, 1989
2—*Battle of the Bunheads*. Scholastic, 1989
3—*Stupid Cupids*. Scholastic, 1989
4—*Who Framed Mary Bubnik?* Scholastic, 1989
5—*Blubberina*. Scholastic, 1989
6—*Save D.A.D.* Scholastic, 1990
7—*The King and Us*. Scholastic, 1990
8—*Camp Clodhopper*. Scholastic, 1990
9—*Boo Who?* Scholastic, 1990
10—*A Dog Named Toe Shoe*. Scholastic, 1991
Girls 8-12 will follow the adventures of the five misfit friends who take hated ballet classes at the Deerfield (OH) Academy of Dance. Fans of the Babysitters Club and Sweet Valley will find these a painless way to while away their reading time.

MALCOLM, Johanna (Hart & Soul)
1—*Kill the Story*. Bantam, 1990
2—*Play Dead*. Bantam, 1990
3—*Speak No Evil*. Bantam, 1990
4—*Get the Pictures*. Bantam, 1990
5—*Too Hot to Handle*. Bantam, 1991
6—*Signed, Sealed and Delivered*. Bantam, 1991
7—*House of Fear*. Bantam, 1991
8—*Run for Your Life*. Bantam, 1991

Amanda Hart is the sophisticated editor-in-chief of the Sutter Academy *Spectator*. Mickey Soul is the street tough, good looking guy from the other side of town. He has his own messenger service and is called upon to deliver a newspaper story to the printer for Amanda in the first book. Well, he is mugged and the story stolen, so they join forces to solve the mystery. There are similar adventures in the other books. Grades 7-10.

MALCOLM, Jahnna (Rock 'n Rebels)

Makin' the Grade. Bantam, 1991
Sticking Together. Bantam, 1991

This new series will ring a responsive chord: the protagonists (male!) form a band called the Rebels. They come out with a hit song but must deal with a promoter who wants to package them slickly, ala New Kids. They go on the road only to find the stresses of performing and constant proximity create more problems. These are packaged to appeal to girls, but should also appeal to boys grades 4-6.

MANES, Stephen

Be a Perfect Person in Just Three Days! Houghton, 1982
Make Four Million Dollars by Next Thursday! Bantam, 1991

Dr. K. Pinkerton Silverfish is a remarkable mentor. In the first book, he teaches Jason how to be perfect by having him do a number of ridiculous stunts. The upshot is that at the end of three days he has looked so idiotic, he never worries about not being perfect again. The follow-up takes much the same route: among other things, Jason is advised to pin dollar bills to himself to attract more money. These silly books are sure to strike a chord with any reader who needs to have things put in perspective. Hilarious choices for grades 3-7.

MANES, Stephen (Hooples Series)

The Hooples' Haunted House. Delacorte, 1981
The Hooples on the Highway. Avon, 1985
The Hooples' Horrible Holiday. Avon, 1986

The Hooples are a funny family whose trips always seem to go awry. They encounter a Thanksgiving power failure, a vacation in what seems to be a haunted house, and trouble getting to a ball game. These will amuse readers grades 4-6.

MANES, Stephen (Oscar Noodleman Series)

That Game from Outer Space. Dutton, 1983
The Oscar Noodleman Television Network. Dutton, 1984
Chicken Trek. Dutton, 1987

Oscar is a most unusual boy whose adventures are quite fantastical. For example, in the second book he takes over a TV network with a little help from an alien. Even his problem solving skills are remarkable: he owes a cousin megabucks, so he decides to raise it by entering a coast-to-coast chicken eating contest. Funny, funny, funny for grades 3-6.

MARKHAM, Marion M.

1—*The Halloween Candy Mystery*. Houghton, 1982
2—*The Christmas Present Mystery*. Houghton, 1984
3—*The Thanksgiving Day Parade Mystery*. Houghton, 1986
4—*The Birthday Party Mystery*. Houghton, 1989
5—*The April Fool's Day Mystery*. Houghton, 1991

These are simple holiday related mysteries for those just past the beginning reader stage. There is a bit of humor and adventure for twins Mickey and Kate. These will attract the same crowd that enjoys Adler's Fourth Floor Twins. Grades 2-4.

MARSHALL, Kirk (Hoops)

1–*Fast Breaks*. Ballantine, 1989
2–*Longshot Center*. Ballantine, 1989
3–*Backboard Battle*. Ballantine, 1989
4–*Half-Court Hero*. Ballantine, 1989
5–*Tourney Fever*. Ballantine, 1989
6–*Pressure Play*. Ballantine, 1989

Brian Davis is the leader on the Jefferson Patriots' basketball team. We meet him and his teammates as this series takes a look at one season in the life of the team. Marshall has the team battle through injuries, grade problems and other real life scenarios as the Patriots, with Brian at the lead, battle their way to their State Championship game. This is a good series for reluctant readers. Grade 6 and up.

MARTIN, Ann (Babysitters Club)

1–*Kristy's Great Idea*. Scholastic, 1986
2–*Claudia and the Phantom Phone Calls*. Scholastic, 1986
3–*The Truth about Stacey*. Scholastic, 1986
4–*Mary Anne Saves the Day*. Scholastic, 1987
5–*Dawn and the Impossible Three*. Scholastic, 1987
6–*Kristy's Big Day*. Scholastic, 1987
7–*Claudia and Mean Janine*. Scholastic, 1987
8–*Boy Crazy Stacey*. Scholastic, 1987
9–*The Ghost at Dawn's House*. Scholastic, 1988
10–*Logan Likes Mary Anne*. Scholastic, 1988
11–*Kristy and the Snobs*. Scholastic, 1988
12–*Claudia and the New Girl*. Scholastic, 1988
13–*Good-bye, Stacey, Good-bye*. Scholastic, 1988
14–*Hello Mallory*. Scholastic, 1988
15–*Little Miss Stoneybrook and Dawn*. Scholastic, 1988
16–*Jessi's Secret Language*. Scholastic, 1988
17–*Mary Anne's Bad Luck Mystery*. Scholastic, 1988
18–*Stacey's Mistake*. Scholastic, 1988
19–*Claudia and the Bad Joke*. Scholastic, 1988
20–*Kristy and the Walking Disaster*. Scholastic, 1989
21–*Mallory and the Trouble with Twins*. Scholastic, 1989
22–*Jessi Ramsey, Pet-Sitter*. Scholastic, 1989
23–*Dawn on the Coast*. Scholastic, 1989
24–*Kristy and the Mother's Day Surprise*. Scholastic, 1989
25–*Mary Anne and the Search for Tigger*. Scholastic, 1989
26–*Claudia and the Sad Good-bye*. Scholastic, 1989
27–*Jessi and the Superbrat*. Scholastic, 1989
28–*Welcome Back, Stacey*. Scholastic, 1989
29–*Mallory and the Mystery Diary*. Scholastic, 1989
30–*Mary Anne and the Great Romance*. Scholastic, 1990
31–*Dawn's Wicked Stepsister*. Scholastic, 1990
32–*Kristy and the Secret of Susan*. Scholastic, 1990
33–*Claudia and the Great Search*. Scholastic, 1990
34–*Mary Anne and Too Many Boys*. Scholastic, 1990
35–*Stacey and the Mystery of Stoneybrook*. Scholastic, 1990
36–*Jessi's Baby-sitter*. Scholastic, 1990
37–*Dawn and the Older Boy*. Scholastic, 1990
38–*Kristy's Mystery Admirer*. Scholastic, 1990
39–*Poor Mallory*. Scholastic, 1990
40–*Claudia and the Middle School Mystery*. Scholastic, 1991
41–*Mary Anne vs. Logan*. Scholastic, 1991

42—*Jessi and the Dance School Phantom*. Scholastic, 1991
43—*Stacey's Emergency*. Scholastic, 1991
44—*Dawn and the Big Sleepover*. Scholastic, 1991
45—*Kristy and the Baby Parade*. Scholastic, 1991
46—*Mary Anne Misses Logan*. Scholastic, 1991
47—*Mallory on Strike*. Scholastic, 1991

Second in popularity only to the Sweet Valley saga, this one is a major player for preteens. The babysitters are now on video and TV so this popularity will undoubtedly increase. The storylines focus on the activities of teens Dawn, Claudia, Stacey, and the other members of the club. Some of the stories revolve around babysitting adventures, but most involve the girls in the usual teen concerns.

MARTIN, Ann (Babysitters Little Sister)
1—*Karen's Witch*. Scholastic, 1988
2—*Karen's Roller Skates*. Scholastic, 1988
3—*Karen's Worst Day*. Scholastic, 1989
4—*Karen's Kittycat Club*. Scholastic, 1989
5—*Karen's School Picture*. Scholastic, 1989
6—*Karen's Little Sister*. Scholastic, 1989
7—*Karen's Birthday*. Scholastic, 1990
8—*Karen's Haircut*. Scholastic, 1990
9—*Karen's Sleepover*. Scholastic, 1990
10—*Karen's Grandmothers*. Scholastic, 1990
11—*Karen's Prize*. Scholastic, 1990
12—*Karen's Ghost*. Scholastic, 1990
13—*Karen's Surprise*. Scholastic, 1990
14—*Karen's Wish*. Scholastic, 1990
15—*Karen's in Love*. Scholastic, 1991
16—*Karen's Goldfish*. Scholastic, 1991
17—*Karen's Brothers*. Scholastic, 1991
18—*Karen's Home Run*. Scholastic, 1991
19—*Karen's Good-bye*. Scholastic, 1991
20—*Karen's Carnival*. Scholastic, 1991
21—*Karen's New Teacher*. Scholastic, 1991

Like the Sweet Valley Kids' publisher, Scholastic has brought out a younger version of the Babysitters to catch the seven to nine year old set. Instead of being the sitter, though, little Karen is the sittee. These are palatable enough fare in a very popular format.

MARZOLLO, Jean (39 Kids on the Block)
1—*The Green Ghost of Appleville*. Scholastic, 1989
2—*The Best Present Ever*. Scholastic, 1989
3—*Roses Are Pink and You Stink!* Scholastic, 1990
4—*The Best Friends Club*. Scholastic, 1990
5—*Chicken Pox Strikes Again*. Scholastic, 1990
6—*My Sister the Blabbermouth*. Scholastic, 1990

As the series title implies there is a wide range of kids (total *39*!) who live on Baldwin Street, ranging in age from babies to teenagers. Different groups of kids and their adventures appear in each book. The vocabulary and sentence structure are suitable for grades 2-4.

MATAS, Carol
Lisa's War. Scribner, 1987
Code Name Kris. Scribner, 1990

Matas chronicles the lives of three young adults growing up in occupied Denmark during World War II. Lisa's brother, Stefan, joins the Danish resistance. She becomes a secret messenger. Her adventures end as she and Stefan escape to Sweden. Jesper, Stefan's resistance friend, is left behind under the code name Kris. Stefan returns on an assignment and both are captured by the Germans. Matas based these novels on the experiences shared by her relatives. These two books are for young adults.

MAZER, Norma Fox

1–*A, My Name Is Ami*. Scholastic, 1987
2–*B, My Name Is Bunny*. Scholastic, 1987
3–*C, My Name Is Cal*. Scholastic, 1990
4–*D, My Name Is Danita*. Scholastic, 1991

Mazer is a well respected author of YA novels. These are aimed at a slightly younger crowd of 9-12, and will definitely find a niche with them. Each novel centers on a youngster and his or her friendships and family relationships. There are parental and romantic problems that kids will relate to. Good choices.

MAZER, Harry

Dollar Man. Delacorte, 1974
I Love You, Stupid. Crowell, 1981

Fourteen year old Marcus Rosenbloom must find and confront his real father to establish his own identity. Three years later he feels that the only thing missing from his life and keeping him from being a man is sex. What he doesn't understand is that things are not that simple. In particular, the last book is very perceptive and funny. Good books for seventh graders and older.

MCARTHUR, Nancy (Plant That Ate Dirty Socks Books)

The Plant That Ate Dirty Socks. Camelot, 1988
The Return of the Plant That Ate Dirty Socks. Camelot, 1990

Michael and Norman have a problem. They share a room. Michael is a slob, while Norman is super-neat, which leads to lots of friction. In fact, both boys probably overdo just to get each other's goat. It seems that their problem may be solved when they acquire a plant that eats dirty socks. Seems like every mother's dream, but things get out of hand. These books are truly hilarious and will find a natural audience among both neatniks and slobs. Grades 4-7.

MCBRIER, Page, and **Michael MCBRIER** (Oliver and Co. Series)

1–*Oliver and the Lucky Duck*. Troll, 1986
2–*Adventure in the Haunted House*. Troll, 1986
3–*Oliver's Lucky Day*. Troll, 1986
4–*Secret of the Old Garage*. Troll, 1986
5–*Secret of the Missing Camel*. Troll, 1987
6–*Oliver and the Runaway Alligator*. Troll, 1987
7–*Oliver's High-Flying Adventure*. Troll, 1987
8–*Oliver's Backyard Circus*. Troll, 1987
9–*Oliver and the Amazing Spy*. Troll, 1988
10–*Oliver's Barnyard Blues*. Troll, 1988
11–*Getting Oliver's Goat*. Troll, 1988
12–*Oliver Smells Trouble*. Troll, 1988

These are nothing special–just the usual paperback adventures with Oliver and friends. Grades 4-6.

MCBRIER, Page (Treehouse Times Series)

1–*Under Twelve Not Allowed*. Camelot, 1989
2–*Kickball Crisis*. Camelot, 1989
3–*Spaghetti Breath*. Camelot, 1989
4–*First Course Trouble*. Camelot, 1990
5–*Daphne Takes Charge*. Camelot, 1990
6–*The Press Mess*. Camelot, 1990
7–*Rats!* Camelot, 1990
8–*The Great Rip-Off*. Camelot, 1990
9–*Stinky Business*. Camelot, 1991

Like the Babysitters Club, Bad News Ballet, and a number of other paperback series, this one features a group of girls of predictable sizes and personality types with a common interest: these girls run their own newspaper and their adventures involve the investigative reporting that they do. For genre fans grades 4-6.

MCCAFFREY, Anne (Harper Hall Trilogy)
Dragonsong. Atheneum, 1976
Dragonsinger. Atheneum, 1977
Dragondrums. Atheneum, 1979
We first meet Menolly in *Dragonsong* (an ALA Best) as she tries to become Pern's first female Harper. She also discovers the legendary fire lizards who had helped to save her world. Eventually she becomes an apprentice in Harper Hall, then a journeyman. In the final book of the series McCaffrey focuses on Menolly's young protege, Piemur, a singer whose life changes when his voice changes. These are popular and deservedly so. Well written and intriguing, these are strongly recommended for libraries. The Pern books continue, but are written more for adults. Grades 6 and up.

MCDANIEL, Lurlene
Somewhere between Life and Death. Bantam, 1991
Time to Let Go. Bantam, 1991
From the author of the popular children's book *Six Months to Live*, comes these two books that deal with euthanasia and the grief associated with it. Erin is distraught when an automobile accident places her sister in the hospital on life support with no hope of recovery. In the second book Amy is haunted by violent headaches and must complete the grieving process for her sister before continuing on with her own life. For YAs.

MCEVOY, Seth, and **Laure SMITH** (The New Kids on the Block)
1—*Backstage Surprise*. Archway, 1990
2—*Block Party*. Archway, 1991
3—*Workin' Out*. Archway, 1991
4—*On Tour*. Archway, 1991
5—*Between Brothers*. Archway, 1991
6—*On Stage*. Archway, 1991
7—*Where's Joe?* Archway, 1991
8—*Peace Out*. Archway, 1991
The most popular and successfully marketed singing group of this generation now has their own series of books. As of this writing their phenomenon has quieted a little, but the books about them are still highly popular in the public library. Each book focuses on a different New Kid with a storyline written especially for them. Not too high on the quality scale but popularity will probably necessitate a purchase. Ages 10 and up.

MCFANN, Jane
Maybe by Then I'll Understand. Avon, 1987
One More Chance. Avon, 1988
One Step Short. Avon, 1990
For Cath life really becomes confusing when she starts dating the "wrong" boy and her mother begins to date Mr. Right. Later Cath defends the strange new boy in her class from her best friends and she suspects her old flame is responsible for the accident that kills her best friend's boyfriend. Original paperbacks for seventh graders and above.

MCGUIRE, Leslie (Fred Books)
Fred to the Rescue. Fawcett, 1991
Fred in Charge. Fawcett, 1991
Fred and the Pet Show Panic. Fawcett, 1991
Fred Saves the Day. Fawcett, 1991

Fred is a St. Bernard who feels very human. He is very helpful, which his breed is known for, but his help often comes at inopportune moments and results in more problems than it solves. These are funny and Fred is an appealing hero. Grades 2-4.

MCHUGH, Elisabet

Beethoven's Cat. Atheneum, 1988
Wiggie Wins the West. Atheneum, 1989

Fans of Howe's Bunnicula series should enjoy this one. Athough the puns are missing, there is still plenty of fun in these tales told by Wiggie, a family cat who first fancies himself the reincarnation of Beethoven, then thinks he may be reincarnated from pioneer stock. Grades 4-6.

MCHUGH, Elizabeth

Raising a Mother Isn't Easy. Greenwillow, 1983
Karen's Sister. Greenwillow, 1983
Karen and Vicki. Greenwillow, 1984

Karen is a Korean orphan who has been adopted by a very self-sufficient veterinarian. Karen decides to play matchmaker. She winds up first with another adopted sister, then finally a new dad with a family of his own. Author McHugh is an adoptive parent, so she knows whereof she writes. The characters are both realistic and charming. Grades 4-6.

MCINERNY, Judith (Judge Benjamin Series)

Judge Benjamin, Superdog. Holiday, 1982
Judge Benjamin, Superdog Secret. Holiday, 1983
Judge Benjamin, Superdog Rescue. Holiday, 1984
Judge Benjamin, Superdog Surprise. Holiday, 1985
Judge Benjamin, Superdog Gift. Holiday, 1986

The author based this series on her own dog and family. The dog tells the stories. He seems to have a pretty adult-people type attitude and his "family" contains a pregnant mother and bourbon-drinking grandma. Mishmash and Bunnicula's Harold have a lot more charm. Grades 4-6.

MCKEAN, Thomas

The Anti-Peggy Plot. Camelot, 1986
Vampire Vacation. Camelot, 1986
The Search for Sara Sanderson. Camelot, 1987

The second book finds the Smith kids investigating a supposed vampire haunting at their vacation hotel. The other two books concentrate more on real life, like when they try to drive off Dad's new girlfriend and her obnoxious dog, then find the perfect new wife for Dad. These really are fun and the author has a wry writing style that will keep the interest of grades 4-7.

MCKENNA, Colleen O'Shaughnessy (Murphy Family Series)

1—*Too Many Murphys*. Scholastic, 1988
2—*Fourth Grade Is a Jinx*. Scholastic, 1989
3—*Fifth Grade: Here Comes Trouble*. Scholastic, 1989
4—*Eenie, Meanie, Murphy, No!* Scholastic, 1990
5—*Murphy's Island*. Scholastic, 1990
6—*The Truth about Sixth Grade*. Scholastic, 1991

Collette is the oldest of the four Murphy children. At age eight she feels put upon by her younger siblings. She often wishes she were an only child. She faces other problems, including having her own mother as a substitute teacher, and attending her first boy-girl party. Children in the 8-12 age bracket will easily relate to her difficulties in these entertaining stories.

MCKILLIP, Patricia

Moon-flash. Atheneum, 1984

The Moon and the Face. Atheneum, 1985

The Moon-flash is an annual symbol of life and joy to Kyreol's people. During this year's ceremony she is going to become betrothed to Korre. Things don't work out as she expects and she is full of questions. She and her best friend take a long journey and discover there is more about the world than they ever imagined. Four years later having been trained in the space center, they go on their own separate journeys: Kyreol crash lands on a distant moon and must work hard to survive while Terje journeys back to the Riverworld from where they came, and must adjust to his new role. Grades 7 and up.

MCKILLIP, Patricia A.

The Riddle-Master of Hed. Atheneum, 1976

Heir of Sea and Fire. Ballantine, 1987

Harpist in the Wind. Atheneum, 1979

Morgan is the prince of the simple farmers of Hed and a proven riddle master, solving riddles from the long ago when the wizards vanished from the earth and all knowledge was left behind in the form of riddles. Evil forces are brewing and Morgan must seek the High One in these high fantasy works. Along with him is Deth, the High One's Harper, as together they trek towards their goal. Grades seven and up.

MCKINLEY, Robin

The Hero and the Crown. Atheneum, 1984

The Blue Sword. Atheneum, 1983

McKinley has established herself as a master of fantasy. *The Hero and the Crown*, a Newbery Award winner, is a prequel and serves as an introduction for readers to the mythical Kingdom of Damar. Aerin is the only child of the Damar king but she needs to prove herself. She receives help from Luthe, the wizard, and the Blue Sword. In *The Blue Sword*, Harry leaves her home to see where the Free Hillfolk (the last remaining Damarians) live. She sees the magic of the people and the Sword as she rides into battle to meet her destiny. This is a Newbery Honor Book. This series is highly recommended for students from 5th grade up.

MCMULLAN, Kate (Lila Fenwick Series)

The Great Ideas of Lila Fenwick. Dial, 1986

The Great Advice from Lila Fenwick. Dial, 1988

Fifth grader Lila Fenwick is famous among her friends for her Great Ideas—her solutions to their problems. To find a lost guinea pig, try acting like one. Her ideas extend to making money fast, and even into the pre-teen realm of talking to boys. Lila is a spunky, likeable heroine that will be a good choice for fans of Constance Greene and Lois Lowry. Ages 8-12.

MEYER, Caroline (Hotline Series)

1—*Because of Lissa*. Bantam, 1990

2—*The Problem with Sidney*. Bantam, 1990

3—*Gillian's Choice*. Bantam, 1991

4—*The Two Faces of Adam*. Bantam, 1991

A topical series about a group of young adults that form a hotline to help kids in crisis. Each book focuses on a character introduced in the first book and depicts a conflict or issue, the hotline involvement, and the resolution of the problem. Teen pregnancy and teen runaways are two of the topics covered. At the end of each book is a list of national hotlines the reader can call if they are in need of help. Also, there is some information for the reader concerning what to do if they are in a crisis. For YAs.

MEYERS, Susan (P.J. Clover Series)
1–*P.J. Clover, Private Eye: The Case of the Stolen Laundry*. Wanderer, 1981
2–*P.J. Clover, Private Eye: The Case of the Missing Mouse*. Lodestar, 1985
3–*P.J. Clover, Private Eye: The Case of the Borrowed Baby*. Lodestar, 1988
4–*P.J. Clover, Private Eye: The Case of the Halloween Hoot*. Lodestar, 1990
Fifth grader P.J. (Pamela Jean) Clover runs a detective agency ala Encyclopedia Brown. Rather than detailing a series of cases, her books present just one mystery at a time. The puzzles involve such things as missing laundry and a missing Mickey Mouse bank. For mystery fans grades 4-6.

MILLENNIUM SCIENCE FICTION (Series)
ANDERSON, Poul
The Year of the Ransom. Walker, 1988
DEHAVEN, Tom
Joe Gosh. Walker, 1988
GERROLD, David
Chess with a Dragon. Walker, 1987
KURTZ, Katherine
The Legacy of Lehr. Walker, 1986
LONGYEAR, Barry B.
The Homecoming. Walker, 1989
LUPOFF, Richard A.
The Forever City. Walker, 1988
MAYHAR, Ardath
A Place of Silver Science. Walker, 1988
SILVERBERG, Robert
Project Pendulum. Walker, 1987
WU, William F.
Hong on the Range. Walker, 1989
ZELAZNY, Roger
A Dark Traveling. Walker, 1987
Intended for young adults, this series mixes both sci-fi and fantasy entries by veteran writers like Anderson and Silverberg with proven YA writers like Mayhar. The basic themes including time travel, parallel worlds, and alien life are covered. The illustrators are well-known fantasy or graphic artists. Sci-fi fans will enjoy these (both YA and adults), and they will also serve as quality introductions to new readers of the genre.

MILLER, Judi
Ghost in My Soup. Bantam, 1985
Ghost a la Mode. Bantam, 1989
Scott has moved and is having trouble fitting in. He wangles his way into a club, but he still is not accepted because the other boys did not really want him as a member. Helping him with his problems is a friendly ghost. Grades 3-6.

MILLER, Marvin (You Be the Jury Series)
You Be the Jury. Scholastic, 1987
You Be the Jury: Courtroom II. Scholastic, 1989
You Be the Jury: Courtroom III. Scholastic, 1990
Fans of Encyclopedia Brown will find these an interesting variation. Instead of solving a mystery as a detective, the readers find themselves a juror, with evidence being presented. Clues are in both written and visual evidence and the readers must render a verdict. At the end of each case the real verdict (and the reasons why) are given. There are ten cases per book. Grades 4-8.

MINES, Jeanette

Reckless. Avon, 1983

Risking It. Avon, 1988

J.T. and Sam were meant for each other, but right from the beginning there was trouble. Everyone has it out for Sam, J.T.'s brother warns her against him, he gets suspended and he becomes a drinker, he drives too fast, he becomes reckless. J.T. thought she could save him but it is too late and Sam is killed. Three years later J.T. is falling in love again, but he may be bigger trouble than Sam. These two are paperback originals for ages 12 and up.

MOHR, Nicholasa

Felita. Dial, 1979

Going Home. Dial, 1986

Felita is a popular little girl in her neighborhood but she doesn't know what will happen when she moves. Nor does she know how she will manage to keep her friends in the old neighborhood. She is an appealing Spanish-American heroine for grades 4-7.

MONSELL, Mary Elise (Mr. Pin Series)

The Mysterious Cases of Mr. Pin. Atheneum, 1989

Mr. Pin: The Chocolate Files. Atheneum, 1990

The mysterious Mr. Pin is a detective who moves from the South Pole to Chicago to solve crime. He has one weakness—chocolate, especially chocolate ice cream. The catch is that Mr. Pin is a penguin, a fact which no one really notices. The story line is simple, but aside from the initial premise, nothing special. Acceptable fare for grades 3-6.

MONTGOMERY, R. A. (Trio: Rebels in the New World)

1—*Traitors from Within*. Bantam, 1990

2—*Crossing Enemy Lines*. Bantam, 1990

3—*Almost Lost*. Bantam, 1990

4—*Hidden Evil*. Bantam, 1990

5—*Escape from China*. Bantam, 1990

It is the year 2015. A war between China and Russia devastated the world and has left the U.S. divided into two territories. One is evil, the other is dedicated to upholding all that America once stood for. They fight to protect their freedoms and the members of TRIO are their elite fighting force. Grades 7 and up.

MONTGOMERY, Robert (Gary Carter's Iron Mask)

1—*Home Run*. Troll, 1990

2—*Grand Slam*. Troll, 1990

3—*Triple Play*. Troll, 1990

4—*MVP*. Troll, 1990

5—*Hitting Streak*. Troll, 1990

6—*The Show*. Troll, 1990

This is a series for baseball players and fans that is filled with drama and action. Readers follow Robbie Belmont's rise from high school star to possible major league player. This series was written with consultation from major league star Gary Carter. Grades 5-9.

MOORE, Robin

The Bread Sister of Sinking Creek. Lippincott, 1990

Maggie among the Seneca. Lippincott, 1990

All the realism of the hardships of frontier life is captured in this series. Maggie is a sixteen year old Irish immigrant. In search of her Aunt, she sets out west, only to be captured by Indians. She winds up marrying and bearing a child, only to lose both husband and baby with the advent of marauding soldiers. Those who saw *Dances with Wolves* will find these equally fascinating. Grades 5-9.

MOOSER, Stephen (Creepy Creatures Club)
1—*Monsters in the Outfield*. Dell, 1989
2—*My Halloween Boyfriend*. Dell, 1989
3—*Monster Holiday*. Dell, 1989
4—*The Fright-Face Contest*. Dell, 1989
5—*That's So Funny, I Forgot to Laugh*. Dell, 1990
6—*Crazy Mixed-up Valentines*. Dell, 1990
7—*Monster of the Year*. Dell, 1990
8—*Secrets of Scary Fun*. Dell, 1990
9—*The Night of the Vampire Kitty*. Dell, 1991
10—*The Man Who Ate a Car and Tons of Other Weird Stories*. Dell, 1991
Young independent readers (grades 2-4) will find a lot to like in this funny series that follows a group of school friends with a love of monsters in common. Each book ends with a series of jokes.

MOOSER, Stephen
The Hitchhiking Vampire. Delacorte, 1989
It's a Weird, Weird School. Delacorte, 1989
When Jamie puts her mind to something the effects can be monumental. For example, the weird looking hitchhiker she and her brother pick up becomes their honorary grandfather. Then, due to problems with the local school, she becomes the new principal! Under the light tone, some serious topics are dealt with here. For grades 4-7.

MORGAN, Alison
All Kinds of Prickles. Nelson, 1980
Paul's Kite. Atheneum, 1981
Paul was abandoned as an infant by his mother, but when his grandfather dies, Paul is sent from rural Wales to London to be with her. She continues to ignore him and pretends he is not her child. How Paul manages on his own to make friends and a place for himself is movingly told. Grades 4-7.

MORGAN SWIFT MYSTERIES (Series)
HUGHES, Sara
1—*Morgan Swift and the Kidnapped Goddess*. Ballantine, 1985
2—*Morgan Swift and the Treasure of Crocodile Key*. Ballantine, 1985
LESLEY, Martine
3—*Morgan Swift and the Mindmaster*. Random, 1985
4—*Morgan Swift and the Trail of the Jaguar*. Random, 1985
5—*Morgan Swift and the Riddle of the Sphinx*. Random, 1986
SAUNDERS, Susan
6—*Morgan Swift and the Lake of Diamonds*. Random, 1986
Morgan is a high school science teacher with a touch of clairvoyance and a talent for sleuthing. Grades 5-9.

MORRIS, Dave (Teenage Mutant Ninja Turtles)
1—*Buried Treasure*. Dell, 1990
2—*Dinosaur Farm*. Dell, 1990
3—*Red Herrings*. Dell, 1990
4—*Six-Guns and Shurikens*. Dell, 1990
5—*Sky High*. Dell, 1990
6—*Splinter to the Fore*. Dell, 1991
This spinoff series will be a surefire hit with the legion of fans the Turtles have. Grades 3-6.

MURPHY, Jill (Worst Witch Series)

The Worst Witch. Viking, 1989
The Worst Witch Strikes Again. Viking, 1989
A Bad Spell for the Worst Witch. Viking, 1989

Clumsy Mildred is doing poorly at the witch academy. Despised as she is, she still manages to save the day when she vanquishes plotters against the academy. A new recruit gets Mildred into even more scrapes later on. These are funny books for readers 8-12 who can relate to Mildred's hilarious unintentional mistakes.

MURPHY, Shirley (Dragonbards Trilogy)

Nightpool. Harper, 1985
The Ivory Lyre. Harper, 1987
The Dragonbards. Harper, 1988

A pawn in the hands of his father's killer, Tebriel is used as bait to capture a singing dragon (the symbol of freedom). He is injured in a battle by those who are trying to rescue him, but survives and discovers hidden talents within himself. In the second volume he must fight the Dark forces. He is able to weave a magical spell that can free people's minds from evil. Finally Teb comes face to face with the leader of the Dark forces. Only the strongest will survive. Murphy's dragons are among the most appealing in fantasy. Twelve and older.

MURPHY, Shirley

1—*Ring of Fire*. Atheneum, 1977
2—*Wolf Bell*. Atheneum, 1979
3—*Castle of Hape*. Atheneum, 1980
4—*Caves of Fire and Ice*. Atheneum, 1980

These books introduce fantasy fans to the children of Ynell and their destinies. Thorn learns that he has the power of seeing. This could mean death but he bands together with Zephyr to free themselves and to save the children of Ynell. In the later books Ramad and friends search for the Rune Stone to save Ere and they must work to rid the planet of the evil monster, Hape. In the series finale Ramad aids the heroes from the many ages of Ere. These are recommended for ages 10-16.

MYERS, Walter Dean (Arrow Adventure Series)

The Hidden Shrine. Puffin, 1985
Ambush in the Amazon. Puffin, 1986
Duel in the Desert. Puffin, 1986

Chris and Ken Arrow travel worldwide with their anthropologist mother. Each book begins with the boys smack in the middle of investigating a crime in some exciting foreign locale. The locations and adventure are pluses, but other than that, these are par for the course mysteries for grades 4-7.

NABB, Magdalen (Josie Smith Books)

Josie Smith. Macmillan, 1989
Josie Smith at the Seashore. McElderry, 1990

The first novel was a runner-up for the *Guardian*'s Children's Fiction Award. Josie is a young English girl with simple experiences written in a simple style. Some of the English expressions have been changed to make reading easier for Americans grades 2-4.

NAMIOKA, Lensey

1—*The Samurai and the Long-Nosed Devils*. McKay, 1976
2—*White Serpent Castle*. McKay, 1976
3—*Valley of the Broken Cherry Trees*. Delacorte, 1980
4—*Village of the Vampire Cat*. Delacorte, 1981

This is a complex series that takes a look at 16th Century feudal Japan. Zenta and Matsuzo are samurai without a master. Their first adventure begins when they find themselves in the middle of a political struggle that could mean death. Next they arrive at a castle during a fight for a warlord's territory. They help the rightful owner secure his power. Their other adventures include becoming involved with the mystery of why sacred cherry trees are being mutilated and helping their former teacher's village fight a band of killers. For YAs.

NAYLOR, Phyllis Reynolds (Alice Series)
The Agony of Alice. Atheneum, 1985
Alice in Rapture, Sort of—. Atheneum, 1989
Reluctantly Alice. Atheneum, 1991
Unlike Naylor's other books, these are not spooky, but instead follow Alice as she heads into adolescence. She is an appealing heroine, who can see the humor in most situations. She worries about finding the right role model, boys, and being popular. Grades 4-7.

NAYLOR, Phyllis Reynolds (Bessledorf Series)
The Mad Gasser of Bessledorf Street. Atheneum, 1983
The Bodies in the Bessledorf Hotel. Atheneum, 1986
Bernie and the Bessledorf Ghost. Atheneum, 1990
Bernie Magruder and his family run the Bessledorf Hotel. In these adventures they have had to contend with a mad gasser, dead bodies that appear and disappear from guest rooms, and a young ghost. The plots are entertaining enough although the characters are not particularly well drawn. Grades 3-6.

NAYLOR, Phyllis Reynolds (Witch Series)
1—*Witch's Sister*. Macmillan, 1980
2—*Witch Water*. Dell, 1977
3—*The Witch Herself*. Dell, 1978
4—*The Witch's Eye*. Delacorte, 1990
5—*Witch Weed*. Delacorte, 1991
This series chronicles Lynn and Mouse's efforts to thwart Mrs. Tuggle, an evil witch who lives in their neighborhood. Unfortunately no one else believes them. Unlike other series, this one portrays the witch as truly evil, not just cute or eccentric or misunderstood. Many children do want to read scary books, and these will fit the bill. Grades 4-8.

NAYLOR, Phyllis (York Trilogy)
Shadows on the Wall. Atheneum, 1980
Faces in the Water. Atheneum, 1981
Footprints at the Window. Atheneum, 1981
Dan Roberts is searching for answers: what is the disease that attacks some members of his family in middle age, and will he get it, and what was his relationship to a gypsy from York, England during the 4th century? This last question is particularly interesting, because he is seeing one of those gypsies in 20th century Pennsylvania. There is fantasy here but the underlying messages of commitment, courage, and loyalty are universal. These should be read in sequence. Grades 5-9.

NEWMAN, Robert
1—*The Case of the Baker Street Irregulars*. Atheneum, 1978
2—*The Case of the Vanishing Corpse*. Atheneum, 1980
3—*The Case of the Somerville Secret*. Atheneum, 1981
4—*The Case of the Threatened King*. Atheneum, 1982
5—*The Case of the Murdered Players*. Atheneum, 1985
6—*The Case of the Indian Curse*. Atheneum, 1986
7—*The Case of the Watching Boy*. Atheneum, 1987

Andrew, friend Sara, and his stepfather Peter Wyatt of Scotland Yard, are engaged in many mysteries, including kidnappings, the cult of Kali, and even Sherlock Holmes. Well plotted and fast paced, the turn-of-the-century English setting will add charm for readers grades 4-8.

NEY, John (Ox Books)

Ox under Pressure. Lippincott, 1976
Ox and the Prime-Time Kid. Pineapple, 1985

Ox leads a very unconventional life as the son of two very rich parents. At 17 he is already used to life in the fast lane, but in *Ox under Pressure*, he pauses to think about the wild life he has led in the past and what that may mean for his future. In his newest escapade, he helps a confused kid look for his mother and come to terms with drug problems. These are funny books with a serious message. Good for ages 12-16.

NICHOLS, Paul (Blitz Series)

1—*Rookie Quarterback*. Ballantine, 1989
2—*Tough Tackle*. Ballantine, 1989
3—*Guts and Glory*. Ballantine, 1989
4—*Team Spirit*. Ballantine, 1989
5—*End-Zone Express*. Ballantine, 1989
6—*Touchdown*. Ballantine, 1989
7—*Champions*. Ballantine, 1989
8—*On the Road*. Ballantine, 1989
9—*Making the Team*. Ballantine, 1989
10—*Blitz*. Ballantine, 1989

Nichols takes us through a high school football season with the Tucker High Tigers. The team is labeled as losers after previous poor seasons. However, they come back and win it all, but not without overcoming a few problems. These books take a look at the highs and lows of high school football. Good for reluctant readers, grade 6 and up.

NIELSEN, Shelly (Victoria Series)

1—*Just Victoria*. Cook, 1986
2—*More Victoria*. Cook, 1986
3—*Take a Bow, Victoria*. Cook, 1986
4—*Only Kidding, Victoria*. Cook, 1986

The usual young-girl-growing-up fare, including a forced vacation away from friends and an impending (and embarrassing) baby. Grades 4-6.

NIMMO, Jenny

The Snow Spider. Dutton, 1987
Orchard of the Crescent Moon. Dutton, 1989
The Chestnut Soldier. Dutton, 1990

Set in Wales, this series combines the realities of today with Welsh folklore and myth. Gwyn, Emlyn, and Nia all possess gifts and magical talismans they are unaware of and do not know how to use. Through the course of the series they come to value themselves and others, even when the magic might lead to their own destruction. The unusual names and Welsh phrases may daunt some readers, but die-hard fantasy readers may enjoy these. Ages 11-14.

NIXON, Joan Lowery (Hollywood Daughters: A Family Trilogy)

Star Baby. Bantam, 1989
Overnight Sensation. Bantam, 1990
Encore. Bantam, 1990

Fifty years of Hollywood history are retold in this series from a popular young adult author. Through the lives of "Cookie" Baynes, her daughter and granddaughter, we see the ups and downs of living and working in the most glamorous city in America. An engaging series with good characterizations, it should be well read by young adults ages 14-18.

NIXON, Joan Lowery (Maggie Series)
Maggie, Too. Harcourt, 1985
And Maggie Makes Three. Harcourt, 1986
Maggie Forevermore. Harcourt, 1987
Maggie has been shunted from school to school and relative to relative. She longs to really belong somewhere and make friends. Her problems in adjusting to family and school relationships are realistically and humorously dealt with by veteran author Nixon. Very good choices for grades 4-7.

NIXON, Joan Lowery (Nic Nacs and the Nic Nac News)
1—*The Mystery Box*. Dell, 1991
2—*Watch Out for Dinosaurs!* Dell, 1991
3—*Honeycutt Street Celebrities*. Dell, 1991
4—*Haunted House on Honeycutt Street*. Dell, 1991
A younger version of the Treetop Times kids, this group of youngsters are also writing their own newspaper. These are easy reading paperbacks for grades 2-4.

NORTH, Rick (Young Astronauts)
1—*Young Astronauts*. Zebra, 1990
2—*Ready for Blastoff!* Zebra, 1990
3—*Space Blazers*. Zebra, 1990
4—*Destination Mars*. Zebra, 1991
5—*Space Pioneers*. Zebra, 1991
6—*Citizens of Mars*. Zebra, 1991
A lot of kids wonder what space travel would be like, and even wish they could experience it for themselves. That is exactly what this series tries to do. A group of youngsters are working astronauts, and readers travel with them on their missions. This is not so much science fiction as science possibility, which should have an appreciative audience among those grades 4-8.

NORTON, Alice Mary (Star Ka'at Series)
1—*Star Ka'at*. Walker, 1976
2—*Star Ka'at's World*. Walker, 1978
3—*Star Ka'at and the Plant People*. Walker, 1979
4—*Star Ka'ats and the Winged Warriors*. Walker, 1981
Norton is a quality science fiction writer. This series for younger readers (ages 8-12) will prove a nice introduction to the genre. Jim and Elly Mae are unwanted children who find two equally unwanted cats. What they don't realize is that the cats are really Ka'ats, aliens who have inhabited earth for some time, and who, along with the children, face fearsome tasks.

NORTON, Andre (*Witch World Series)
7—*Crystal Gryphon*. Atheneum, 1972
8—*Gryphon in Glory*. Atheneum, 1984
9—*Gryphon's Eyrie*. Atheneum, 1984
Norton began this saga in the early 70s with *Crystal Gryphon* and *Jargoon Pard*. Those books introduced readers to Kerovan and his bride Joisan and told the story of their fight to save their people. In these final two volumes, they battle the Dark Evil. Kerovan is on a secret journey and Joisan sets out to find him. The crystal globe he has given her contains a gryphon which possesses some wonderful powers. In the last book, Kerovan finally fulfills his destiny and defeats the Dark Evil. Highly recommended for young adults 12 and older.

NORTON, Andre
3—**Year of the Unicorn*. Viking, 1965
This is the last entry in this science fiction series about Murdoc and his search for the Zero stone. Norton is a veteran writer with lots of young fans. Grades 4-7.

NORTON, Mary (*Borrowers Series)
6—*The Borrowers Avenged*. Harcourt, 1982
The Borrowers' latest adventure finds them looking for a new, safe home after escaping from the villainous Platters. They settle in the abandoned rectory (with some relatives), but the Platters track them down. This is a wonderful addition to the quintessential series about "tiny people." Grades 4-7.

O'DELL, Scott
Captive. Houghton, 1979
Feathered Serpent. Houghton, 1981
The Amethyst Ring. Houghton, 1983
Julian Escobar is a young Spanish seminarian who comes to the Americas with the conquistadores in the 16th century. He experiences battles, the ravaging of the natives by the conquerors, and the Indians' savagery. He even becomes the living incarnation of a Mayan god. He becomes a merchant and eventually winds up with Pizarro in Peru. O'Dell is a superb writer who impeccably researches his period and builds strong characters and plots. Grades 5 and up.

O'DELL, Scott
Island of the Blue Dolphins. Houghton, 1960
Zia. Houghton, 1976
Island of the Blue Dolphins is a Newbery winner that follows Karana and her brother as they struggle to survive alone on an island. The second book takes place after her rescue and focuses on her niece, Zia, as she struggles with prejudice. Grades 5-8.

OLSEN, Violet
The Growing Season. Atheneum, 1982
The View from the Pighouse Roof. Atheneum, 1987
Set in Iowa during the Depression, these books find Marie Carlson wanting desperately to grow up as she worries about her absent married sister on the road with her husband searching for work. Worthy offerings for grades 4-7.

ORGEL, Doris (Becky Suslow Books)
1—*My War with Mrs. Galloway*. Viking, 1985
2—*Whiskers Once and Always*. Viking, 1986
3—*Midnight Soup and a Witch's Hat*. Viking, 1987
4—*Starring Becky Suslow*. Viking, 1989
Becky Suslow is a feisty youngster. Her concerns range from learning to get along with a difficult neighbor, to the death of her cat. Author Orgel has a true-to-life sensitive touch with all the growing up issues that Becky faces. Good choices for ages 8-12.

PANTELL, Dora (Miss Pickerell Series)
14—**Miss Pickerell and the War of the Computers*. Watts, 1984
15—*Miss Pickerell and the Lost World*. Watts, 1986
Although veteran author MacGregor is gone, Miss Pickerell goes on with a new author. She is still contending with her nieces and nephews while adventuring in scientific realms. The first book tackles artificial intelligence; the second, the possibility that there is a "lost world" that an unusual creature must be returned to or she will die. Grades 4-6.

PARISH, Peggy (*Roberts Family Series)
5—*Hermit Dan*. Dell, 1981
6—*The Ghosts of Cougar Island*. Dell, 1986
These are easy reading mysteries that continue the adventures of the Roberts kids. This time they explore the secret of a "ghost" and investigate the behavior of a local hermit who keeps a box buried in the dunes. Acceptable for grades 3-6.

PARK, Barbara

Don't Make Me Smile. Avon, 1983

My Mother Got Married (and Other Disasters). Knopf, 1989

This series is not thigh-slapping funny like Skinnybones, but there is still Park's trademark humorous touch. Charles's problems are a little tougher: his parents' divorce and all the changes it brings. Very good choices for readers (especially boys) grades 3-6.

PARK, Barbara (Skinnybones Books)

Skinnybones. Knopf, 1982

Almost Starring Skinnybones. Knopf, 1988

The misadventures of Alex "Skinnybones" Frankovich have proven very popular with readers. The first book finds him a sports washout, while the second finds him on his way to TV commercial fame. These books are laugh aloud choices. Excellent for grades 3-7.

PARKER, Cam

Camp Off-the-Wall. Camelot, 1987

A Horse in New York. Camelot, 1989

Tiffin faces the usual adventures at camp. When she returns home, she learns her summer horse will be destroyed if she can't find it a home. So she agrees to have it shipped to her in New York, without telling her parents. Predictable fare for grades 4-6.

PARKINSON, Ethelyn (*Rupert Piper Series)

6—*Rupert Piper and the Dear, Dear Birds.* Abingdon, 1976

7—*Rupert Piper and the Boy Who Could Knit.* Abingdon, 1979

Rupert seems pretty dated and one dimensional now. He and his clean-cut, earnest friends are not very believable, and their concerns, like learning to accept a boy named Shirley who knits, and a girl named Jamie who is a tomboy, will probably not hold the interest of today's kids. Grades 4-6.

PASCAL, Francine

Hangin' Out with Cici. Penguin, 1977

My First Love and Other Disasters. Viking, 1979

Love and Betrayal and Hold the Mayo! Dell, 1986

The first book will have a lot of appeal—Victoria goes back in time and sees how wild her strict mom was as a kid! The second book is an ALA Best Book for YAs. In it we read about Victoria who, not yet 15, has her eye on the man of her dreams, while serving as a mother's helper on Fire Island. Of course, he doesn't even know who she is. The sequel is fast paced as Victoria finds love even more complicated than she had thought, in the midst of teenage defeats and ecstasies at summer camp. Ages 12-18.

PASCAL, Francine (Sweet Valley Saga)

1—*The Wakefields of Sweet Valley.* Bantam, 1991

The incredibly popular Sweet Valley books have spawned another series. This one is in the nature of a popular adult genre, the family generational saga. Here the reader is introduced to the forebears of the twins, beginning in 1860 when the matriarch sales from Sweden, following through the Roaring Twenties and through the courtship of the girls' parents. Surefire material for YAs.

PASCAL, Francine (Sweet Valley Kids)

1—*Surprise! Surprise!* Bantam, 1989

2—*Runaway Hamster.* Bantam, 1989

3—*The Twins Mystery Teacher.* Bantam, 1990

4—*Elizabeth's Valentine.* Bantam, 1990

5—*Jessica's Cat Trick.* Bantam, 1990

6—*Lila's Secret.* Bantam, 1990

7–*Jessica's Big Mistake*. Bantam, 1990
8–*Jessica's Zoo Adventure*. Bantam, 1990
9–*Elizabeth's Super-Selling Lemonade*. Bantam, 1990
10–*The Twins and the Wild West*. Bantam, 1990
11–*Crybaby Lois*. Bantam, 1990
12–*Sweet Valley Trick or Treat*. Bantam, 1990
13–*Starring Winston Egbert*. Bantam, 1990
14–*Jessica the Babysitter*. Bantam, 1991
15–*Fearless Elizabeth*. Bantam, 1991
16–*Jessica the TV Star*. Bantam, 1991
17–*Caroline's Mystery Dolls*. Bantam, 1991
18–*Bossy Steven*. Bantam, 1991
19–*Karen's Good-Bye*. Bantam, 1991
20–*The Twins Go to the Hospital*. Bantam, 1991
21–*Jessica and the Spelling Bee*. Bantam, 1991
22–*Sweet Valley Slumber Party*. Bantam, 1991

Elizabeth and Jessica Wakefield are second grade twins whose lives are chronicled here for the youngest Sweet Valley fans. A popular series duo, this will appeal to younger sisters grades 2-4.

PASCAL, Francine (Sweet Valley Twins)
1–*Best Friends*. Bantam, 1986
2–*Teacher's Pet*. Bantam, 1986
3–*Haunted House*. Bantam, 1986
4–*Choosing Sides*. Bantam, 1986
5–*Sneaking Out*. Bantam, 1986
6–*The New Girl*. Bantam, 1987
7–*Three's a Crowd*. Bantam, 1987
8–*First Place*. Bantam, 1987
9–*Against the Rules*. Bantam, 1987
10–*One of the Gang*. Bantam, 1987
11–*Buried Treasure*. Bantam, 1987
12–*Keeping Secrets*. Bantam, 1987
13–*Stretching the Truth*. Bantam, 1987
14–*Tug of War*. Bantam, 1988
15–*The Older Boy*. Bantam, 1988
16–*Second Best*. Bantam, 1988
17–*Boys against the Girls*. Bantam, 1988
18–*Center of Attention*. Bantam, 1988
19–*The Bully*. Bantam, 1988
20–*Playing Hooky*. Bantam, 1988
21–*Left Behind*. Bantam, 1988
22–*Out of Place*. Bantam, 1988
23–*Claim to Fame*. Bantam, 1988
24–*Jumping to Conclusions*. Bantam, 1988
25–*Standing Out*. Bantam, 1989
26–*Taking Charge*. Bantam, 1989
27–*Teamwork*. Bantam, 1989
28–*April Fool!* Bantam, 1989
29–*Jessica and the Brat Attack*. Bantam, 1989
30–*Princess Elizabeth*. Bantam, 1989
31–*Jessica's Bad Idea*. Bantam, 1989
32–*Jessica on Stage*. Bantam, 1990
33–*Elizabeth's New Hero*. Bantam, 1990
34–*Jessica, the Rock Star*. Bantam, 1990

35–*Amy's Pen Pal*. Bantam, 1990
36–*Mary Is Missing*. Bantam, 1990
37–*War between the Twins*. Bantam, 1990
38–*Lois Strikes Back*. Bantam, 1990
39–*Jessica and the Money Mix-up*. Bantam, 1990
40–*Danny Means Trouble*. Bantam, 1990
41–*The Twins Get Caught*. Bantam, 1990
42–*Jessica's Secret*. Bantam, 1990
43–*Elizabeth's First Kiss*. Bantam, 1990
44–*Amy Moves In*. Bantam, 1991
45–*Lucy Takes the Reins*. Bantam, 1991
46–*Mademoiselle Jessica*. Bantam, 1991
47–*Jessica's New Look*. Bantam, 1991
48–*Mandy Miller Fights Back*. Bantam, 1991
49–*The Twins' Little Sister*. Bantam, 1991
50–*Jessica and the Secret Star*. Bantam, 1991
51–*Elizabeth the Impossible*. Bantam, 1991
52–*Booster Boycott*. Bantam, 1991

The Sweet Valley girls, Jessica and Elizabeth are slightly older here. They are in middle school, but their target reading audience is grades 4-6. Super popular can't-miss series–even reluctant readers will try these.

PASCAL, Francine (Sweet Valley High)
1–*Double Love*. Bantam, 1985
2–*Secrets*. Bantam, 1985
3–*Playing with Fire*. Bantam, 1985
4–*Power Play*. Bantam, 1985
5–*All Night Long*. Bantam, 1985
6–*Dangerous Love*. Bantam, 1985
7–*Dear Sister*. Bantam, 1985
8–*Heartbreaker*. Bantam, 1985
9–*Racing Hearts*. Bantam, 1985
10–*Wrong Kind of Girl*. Bantam, 1985
11–*Too Good to Be True*. Bantam, 1985
12–*When Love Dies*. Bantam, 1986
13–*Kidnapped*. Bantam, 1986
14–*Deceptions*. Bantam, 1986
15–*Promises*. Bantam, 1986
16–*Rags to Riches*. Bantam, 1986
17–*Love Letters*. Bantam, 1986
18–*Head Over Heels*. Bantam, 1986
19–*Showdown*. Bantam, 1986
20–*Crash Landing!* Bantam, 1986
21–*Runaway*. Bantam, 1986
22–*Too Much in Love*. Bantam, 1986
23–*Say Goodbye*. Bantam, 1986
24–*Memories*. Bantam, 1987
25–*Nowhere to Run*. Bantam, 1987
26–*Hostage!* Bantam, 1987
27–*Lovestruck*. Bantam, 1987
28–*Alone in the Crowd*. Bantam, 1987
29–*Bitter Rivals*. Bantam, 1987
30–*Jealous Lies*. Bantam, 1987
31–*Taking Sides*. Bantam, 1987
32–*The New Jessica*. Bantam, 1987

33—*Starting Over*. Bantam, 1987
34—*Forbidden Love*. Bantam, 1987
35—*Out of Control*. Bantam, 1987
36—*Last Chance*. Bantam, 1988
37—*Rumors*. Bantam, 1988
38—*Leaving Home*. Bantam, 1988
39—*Secret Admirer*. Bantam, 1988
40—*On the Edge*. Bantam, 1988
41—*Outcast*. Bantam, 1988
42—*Caught in the Middle*. Bantam, 1988
43—*Hard Choices*. Bantam, 1988
44—*Pretenses*. Bantam, 1988
45—*Family Secrets*. Bantam, 1988
46—*Decisions*. Bantam, 1988
47—*Troublemaker*. Bantam, 1988
48—*Slam Book Fever*. Bantam, 1989
49—*Playing for Keeps*. Bantam, 1989
50—*Out of Reach*. Bantam, 1989
51—*Against the Odds*. Bantam, 1989
52—*White Lies*. Bantam, 1989
53—*Second Chance*. Bantam, 1989
54—*Two-Boy Weekend*. Bantam, 1989
55—*Perfect Shot*. Bantam, 1989
56—*Lost at Sea*. Bantam, 1989
57—*Teacher Crush*. Bantam, 1989
58—*Brokenhearted*. Bantam, 1989
59—*In Love Again*. Bantam, 1989
60—*That Fatal Night*. Bantam, 1990
61—*Boy Trouble*. Bantam, 1990
62—*Who's Who?* Bantam, 1990
63—*The New Elizabeth*. Bantam, 1990
64—*The Ghost of Tricia Martin*. Bantam, 1990
65—*Trouble at Home*. Bantam, 1990
66—*Who's to Blame?* Bantam, 1990
67—*The Parent Plot*. Bantam, 1990
68—*The Love Bet*. Bantam, 1990
69—*Friend against Friend*. Bantam, 1990
70—*Ms. Quarterback*. Bantam, 1990
71—*Starring Jessica*. Bantam, 1991
72—*Rock Star's Girl*. Bantam, 1991
73—*Regina's Legacy*. Bantam, 1991
74—*The Perfect Girl*. Bantam, 1991
75—*Amy's True Love*. Bantam, 1991
76—*Miss Sweet Teen Valley*. Bantam, 1991
77—*Cheating to Win*. Bantam, 1991
78—*The Dating Game*. Bantam, 1991

Super Editions

1—*Perfect Summer*. Bantam, 1985
2—*Special Christmas*. Bantam, 1985
3—*Spring Break*. Bantam, 1986
4—*Malibu Summer*. Bantam, 1986
5—*Winter Carnival*. Bantam, 1986
6—*Spring Fever*. Bantam, 1987

Super Thrillers

1—*Double Jeopardy*. Bantam, 1987
2—*On the Run*. Bantam, 1988
3—*No Place to Run*. Bantam, 1988
4—*Deadly Summer*. Bantam, 1989

Super Star

1—*Lila's Story*. Bantam, 1989
2—*Bruce's Story*. Bantam, 1990
3—*Enid's Story*. Bantam, 1990

Follow the lives, loves, adventures and misadventures of the students at Sweet Valley High. This series is probably the most popular among young adults that is available. Not the greatest young adult books ever written (although probably the best marketed), but teenagers cannot get enough. A new title is published monthly. These books should be in public libraries.

PAULSEN, Gary

Hatchet. Bradbury, 1987
The River. Delacorte, 1991

Teenager Brian Robeson finds himself alone in the wilderness after his plane crashes. He learns to survive the hard way. The sequel finds him teaching survival technique classes, where he once again finds himself trapped in the wilderness, this time with a wounded student. Very well written, excellent adventure fare for YAs.

PECK, Richard (Blossom Culp Series)

1—*The Ghost Belonged to Me*. Viking, 1975
2—*Ghosts I Have Been*. Viking, 1977
3—*The Dreadful Future of Blossom Culp*. Delacorte, 1983
4—*Blossom Culp and the Sleep of Death*. Delacorte, 1986

Blossom Culp is burdened with a spiritualist mother and finds herself a kind of outcast among her peers. Because she truly has second sight, she becomes involved in quieting ghosts and forestalling the machinations of her archenemy, Letty Shambaugh. Blossom's friend and helper, Alexander Armsworth, helps her to adjust to her abilities and to high school. This series can be both funny and moving, a nice change of pace from the usual YA fare.

PECK, Robert Newton (Arly Books)

Arly. Walker, 1989
Arly's Run. Walker, 1991

Set in Florida in 1927, the first book finds Arly the son of an illiterate migrant worker, illiterate himself. Hope finally raises its head when he meets a teacher, although tragedy still dogs him. The sequel finds Arly captured as a slave, branded, and sent to work in the fields until he escapes. These are powerful books, all for upper elementary readers, all the more so because of author Peck's plea to remember that migrant workers still endure this today.

PECK, Robert Newton (*Soup Series)

3—*Soup for President*. Knopf, 1978
4—*Soup's Drum*. Knopf, 1980
5—*Soup on Wheels*. Knopf, 1981
6—*Soup in the Saddle*. Knopf, 1983
7—*Soup's Goat*. Knopf, 1984
8—*Soup on Ice*. Knopf, 1985
9—*Soup on Fire*. Delacorte, 1987
10—*Soup's Uncle*. Delacorte, 1988
11—*Soup's Hoop*. Delacorte, 1990
12—*Little Soup's Hayride*. Dell, 1991

Rob and Soup continue their adventures in these additions to the popular series. Set in the 1930s, their exploits still ring a bell with kids of today, with the author's affection and sense of humor proving infectious. For those who enjoy small town friendship stories, these are a sure bet. Grades 4-7.

PECK, Robert Newton (Trig Series)

1—*Trig*. Little, 1977
2—*Trig Sees Red*. Little, 1978
3—*Trig Goes Ape*. Little, 1980
4—*Trig or Treat*. Little, 1982

For younger readers than Soup, Trig is a gutsy heroine. She lives in the small town of Clodsburg, where her exploits are too well-known, including her efforts to rid the town of its first stop light so that her policeman friend will not lose his job. Readers will laugh aloud at her adventures. Grades 3-6.

PELLOWSKI, Anne

1—*First Farm in the Valley: Anna's Story*. Philomel, 1982
2—*Winding Valley Farm: Annie's Story*. Philomel, 1982
3—*Stairstep Farm: Anna Rose's Story*. Philomel, 1981
4—*Willow Wind Farm: Betsy's Story*. Philomel, 1981
5—*Betsy's Up and Down Year*. Philomel, 1983

Set in Wisconsin, this series follows girls in the Korb family through several generations of living on the farm: Anna begins the saga in the 1870s, and Betsy ends it (so far) in modern times. These books have real old-fashioned charm and family values, just like the Betsy-Tacy books that little Betsy enjoys so much. Grades 4-6.

PERL, Lila (Fat Glenda Series)

1—*Me and Fat Glenda*. Houghton, 1972
2—*Hey, Remember Fat Glenda?* Houghton, 1981
3—*Fat Glenda's Summer Romance*. Clarion, 1986
4—*Fat Glenda Turns 14*. Clarion, 1991

Fat Glenda is going to find a lot of readers. For one reason or another, many kids feel inferior to their peers, whether due to weight, or shyness, or whatever. Glenda really tries to overcome her weight problems, but because they are tied in with her emotional responses, it is always tough. Excellent for ages 11-14.

PETERSEN, P. J.

Would You Settle for Improbable? Delacorte, 1982
Here's to the Sophomores. Delacorte, 1984

Michael and his buddies are asked to befriend a new student, Arnold, who is fresh from juvenile hall. At first it is not easy, but the whole class begins to accept Arnold, until he is accused of a crime. In the follow up novel Michael thinks tenth grade is going to be great, but soon things go out of control. These are humorous, well told stories. The first is an ALA Best Book for Young Adults. Good additions for junior high schoolers.

PETERSON, John (Littles Series)

1—*The Littles*. Scholastic, 1986
2—*The Littles and the Big Storm*. Scholastic, 1988
3—*The Littles and the Trash Tinies*. Scholastic, 1988
4—*The Littles to the Rescue*. Scholastic, 1981
5—*Tom Little's Great Halloween Scare*. Scholastic, 1986
6—*The Littles and Their Friends*. Scholastic, 1981
7—*The Littles Give a Party*. Scholastic, 1974
8—*The Littles Go Exploring*. Scholastic, 1978
9—*The Littles Go to School*. Scholastic, 1985
10—*The Littles Have a Wedding*. Scholastic, 1972
11—*The Littles' Scrapbook*. Scholastic, 1987
12—*The Littles Take a Trip*. Scholastic, 1972
13—*The Littles and the Lost Children*. Scholastic, 1991

Not as classy as the Borrowers, the Littles are poor relations, but very popular ones, in the "little people" genre. They even had a brief stint on TV. Grades 3-6.

PEYTON, K. M. (*Flambards Series)

4—*Flambards Divided*. Philomel, 1981

World War I is almost over. Christina, now a widow with a baby, as well as the new owner of Flambards, decides to marry Dick, her former stablehand. The difference in their stations persists, as well as her troublesome feelings for her cousin. Fans of the PBS series and YAs will be eager for this sequel.

PEYTON, K. M. (*Pennington Series)

5—*The Team*. Crowell, 1976

6—*Marion's Angels*. Oxford, 1979

Ruth has outgrown her horse, Fly-by-Night, and buys another. She is told her new horse is too much animal for her, so she must now prove people wrong. This part of the Pennington series retells Ruth's story before she meets Patrick and they marry. The sixth entry takes place after their forced marriage due to her pregnancy. They must work together to raise money to restore the church. They are successful but their marriage may not fare as well. These are highly recommended for young adults 12-16.

PEYTON, K. M.

Prove Yourself a Hero. Collins, 1977

A Midsummer Night's Death. Collins, 1978

Free Rein. Philomel, 1983

Peyton explores the little-probed area of psychological suspense in these two insightful books. Jonathan deals with the mental pressures associated with being a released kidnap victim in the first and he attempts to find the truth behind the death of his teacher in the second. The third finds him helping to train a horse for England's Grand National race. Both are filled with exciting scenes and clear characterization. They should be enjoyed by 12-16 year olds.

PFEFFER, Susan Beth

April Upstairs. Holt, 1990

Darcy Downstairs. Holt, 1990

Darcy and April are cousins who wind up living in the same apartment building. Their friendship with each other blooms, but at the expense of their other friendships. Although the writing is intended for ages 9-12, the cover art and ages of the heroines may really appeal to YA readers.

PFEFFER, Susan Beth (Kid Power Books)

Kid Power. Scholastic, 1982

Kid Power Strikes Back. Scholastic, 1987

Janie is a great role model for girls: an entrepreneur interested in starting and running her own business, and not afraid of hard work, she organizes her friends for an odd-jobs business. She faces problems and setbacks with humor under the deft hand of author Pfeffer. Grades 4-6.

PFEFFER, Susan Beth

Rewind to Yesterday. Delacorte, 1988

Future Forward. Delacorte, 1989

Twins Scott and Kelly discover that their new VCR can take them through time. In the first book they go back to help a friend's grandfather during a robbery; in the second Scott's plan to travel back and win the lottery backfires. Lightweight fare for ages 9-12.

PFEFFER, Susan Beth (Sebastian Sisters Quintet)

1—*Evvie at Sixteen*. Bantam, 1988

2—*Thea at Sixteen*. Bantam, 1988

3—*Claire at Sixteen*. Bantam, 1989

4—*Sybil at Sixteen*. Bantam, 1989

5—*Meg at Sixteen*. Bantam, 1990

Ranging from teen love to growing up to a loved one's death, these five titles review a year in the life of each of the Sebastian Sisters. Pfeffer uses the occasion of each sister's birthday to relate a different story that any teen could be familiar with. It should be well read by 7th graders and up.

PIERCE, Meredith

Darkangel. Little, 1982

Gathering of Gargoyles. Little, 1984

The Pearl of the Soul of the World. Joy Street Books, 1990

Aeriel must choose between destroying her vampire master for his evil deeds or saving him for the goodness she sees in him. She must battle the evil White Witch for control of Irrylath and the other mortals that have been enslaved by her. To do this she must find an ancient artifact to discover the meaning of life. In the last volume of the trilogy, Aeriel must use the magic that has been given to her in order to achieve her destiny. She must also confront the White Witch, face to face. *Darkangel* was selected as an ALA Best Book for Young Adults. These are masterfully written and are recommended for grades 8-12.

PIERCE, Tamora (Song of the Lioness)

1—*Alanna: The First Adventure*. Atheneum, 1983

2—*In the Hand of the Goddess*. Atheneum, 1984

3—*The Woman Who Rides Like a Man*. Atheneum, 1986

4—*Lioness Rampant*. Atheneum, 1988

Alanna switches places with her brother in order to be trained to become a warrior. She succeeds through a tremendous amount of effort and eventually saves the life of Jonathan, the king's son. This series follows her adventures as a knight, her relationship with Jonathan and her battle for her own destiny in her male-oriented world. Grades 7 and up.

PIKE, Christopher (Final Friends)

1—*The Party*. Pocket, 1988

2—*The Dance*. Pocket, 1988

3—*The Graduation*. Pocket, 1989

"It was their last year of school.... Maybe the last year of their lives," so reads the cover of the first book in this series by the most well-known of a new breed of young adult authors. These books are extremely popular with the 13-18 year olds who enjoy suspense, mystery, twistabout plots, murder and any other bit of intrigue imaginable. The books keep the attention of the reader and are musts for public libraries.

PINKWATER, Daniel Manus (Blue Moose Books)

Blue Moose. Putnam, 1975

The Return of the Moose. Putnam, 1979

The moose is not only big and blue, it also talks. It also appreciates Mr. Breton's chowder so much that it moves in with him and becomes maitre d' at the restaurant. This tall tale/fantasy will have readers laughing aloud. By the way, Mr. Breton resembles author/illustrator Pinkwater. For ages 7-10.

PINKWATER, Daniel (Snarkout Boys)

Snarkout Boys and the Avocado of Death. Lothrop, 1982

Snarkout Boys and the Baconburg Horror. Lothrop, 1984

The Snarkout Boys are so-called because of their proclivity for sneaking out of the house while everyone is sleeping to have an adventure. They wind up tangling with various monsters, but the plots defy description, laced as they are with Pinkwater's one-liners and zany sense of humor. These are real belly-laughers for grades 4-7.

PLATT, Kin (*Chloris Series)

Chloris and the Weirdos. Bradbury, 1988

Readers met Chloris in 1973 with the publication of *Chloris and the Creeps*. She was eleven and had problems accepting her stepfather because of the feelings she still had for her father. We meet her again at 14 in *Chloris and the Freaks* (1975). She believes that her dead father wants her mother to divorce her stepfather and she decides to help this come about. Meanwhile, she considers her sister Jenny a freak. In the new addition to the series, 13 year old Jenny falls in love with Harold, whom Chloris calls a weirdo. These are for the middle school student.

PLATT, Kin

3—**Ghost of Hellsfire Street*. Delacorte, 1980

Steve and his dog Sinbad are back in the middle of trouble again as they try to expose a shady contender for sheriff, solve the riddle of the peculiar goings-on at Hellsfire House, and lay a ghost to rest. Grades 4-7.

PORTRAITS COLLECTION (Series)

QUIN-HARKIN, Janet

1—*Summer Heat*. Fawcett, 1990

KAYE, Marilyn

2—*Attitude*. Fawcett, 1990

BLAKE, Susan

3—*Stealing Josh*. Fawcett, 1991

SCHWEMM, Diane

4—*Always*. Fawcett, 1991

SOMMERS, Beverly

5—*The Uncertainty Principle*. Fawcett, 1991

FEIL, Hila

6—*Between Friends*. Fawcett, 1991

The Portraits Collection takes a look at the many problems faced by young adults in today's world. Whether it is the loss of a loved one, falling in love, or making decisions on your own, the subject is discussed in this series. Each centers on a different main female character. Grades 7 and up.

POTTER, Marian

Blatherskite. Morrow, 1980

A Chance Wild Apple. Morrow, 1982

Maureen is an irrepressible ten year old, despite growing up during the Depression. She has to continually fight her over-active mouth as she tries to brighten the lives of those around her. She hopes to help her family by developing a new strain of apple from a wild one that she has found. For history buffs ages 10-12.

PRATCHETT, Terry

Truckers. Delacorte, 1990

Diggers. Delacorte, 1991

Wings. Delacorte, 1991

Rather like a cross between the Borrowers and the rats of NIMH, the nomes are tiny people living beneath the floorboards of a department store, unaware that there is any other way of life. Natural phenomena have the aura of legend to them, but they must face all that and more with the news that their world will be demolished. The writing is almost poetical, begging to be read aloud. These will be a real treat for older fantasy lovers, grades 5-9.

PRINCE, Alison

Sinister Airfield. Morrow, 1983

Night Landings. Morrow, 1984

Set in England, this series finds three kids up to their eyeballs in mysteries. One involves the appearance, then disappearance of a dead body, along with the odd behavior of a peculiar gamekeeper, and cattle rustling. Acceptable fare for ages 10-13.

PROVOST, Gary, and **Gail LEVINE-PROVOST**

Good If It Goes. Berkley, 1985

David and Max. Jewish Publication Society, 1988

This husband and wife team won the National Jewish Books Award for the first book in this series. Both books are centered around David Newman's thirteenth birthday. The first reviews his preparation for his Bar Mitzvah and his organization of a basketball league for short kids. The second discusses his grandfather's death and what David learned from him. Good books for young people ages 10-15.

PULLMAN, Philip

The Ruby in the Smoke. Knopf, 1985

Shadow in the North. Knopf, 1988

The Tiger in the Well. Knopf, 1990

Sally becomes involved with a deadly series of events in the London of 1872 in the *Ruby*. The second book has her older and working in business fighting the corrupt financial practices of Europe. *Tiger* concludes the trilogy and pits Sally against a familiar evil, in the fight for her life. These mystery novels are well done, with especially well developed characters that are easy to identify with. All are ALA Best Books for Young Adults. Ages 14 and up.

QUIN-HARKIN, Janet (Friends Series)

Starring Tess and Ali. Harper, 1991

Tess & Ali and the Teeny Bikini. Harper, 1991

An original paperback series from Quin-Harkin. These books review the ups and downs of friendship between two adolescent girls. Grades 7-10.

QUIN-HARKIN, Janet (Sugar and Spice Series)

1—*Two Girls, One Boy*. Ballantine, 1987
2—*Trading Places*. Ballantine, 1987
3—*Dear Cousin*. Ballantine, 1987
4—*Nothing in Common*. Ballantine, 1987
5—*Flip Side*. Ballantine, 1987
6—*Tug of War*. Ballantine, 1987
7—*Surf's Up*. Ballantine, 1987
8—*Double Take*. Ballantine, 1987
9—*Make Me a Star*. Ballantine, 1988
10—*Big Sisters*. Ballantine, 1988
11—*Out in the Cold*. Ballantine, 1988
12—*It's My Turn*. Ballantine, 1988
13—*Home Sweet Home*. Ballantine, 1988
14—*Dream Come True*. Ballantine, 1988
15—*Campus Cousins*. Ballantine, 1989
16—*Road Trip*. Ballantine, 1989
17—*One Step Too Far*. Ballantine, 1989
18—*Having a Ball*. Ballantine, 1989

Iowan Crissy goes to San Francisco to spend a year with her cousin, Caroline. It starts out as a disaster but then things begin to fall into place, when they both look for jobs, audition for the school play, and fall in and out of love. These are dreamy stories and will probably circulate well in a library. Grades 8-12.

RADIN, Ruth Yaffe (Tac Series)
Tac's Island. Macmillan, 1986
Tac's Turn. Macmillan, 1987
These two books are a human version of the town mouse/country mouse tale. Steve meets Tac while vacationing on an island off the coast of Virginia in the first book. Their friendship develops as Tac shows Steve the ways of his home. The second books finds Tac returning home with Steve, while Steve silently worries that his visitor won't fit in. Grades 3-6.

RAGZ, M. M.
Eyeballs for Breakfast. Minstrel, 1990
Stiff Competition. Minstrel, 1991
Murphy is getting grief from his friends, who think he has a crush on the snooty new girl, Ashley. He knows he doesn't, although the second book finds him trying out for the basketball team to impress her. The title of the first refers to the no-yolk breakfast his health-food nut Dad keeps fixing. These are funny and more realistic than most paperback entries for grades 4-6.

RANDALL, Carrie (Dear Diary)
1—*The Party*. Scholastic, 1989
2—*The Secret*. Scholastic, 1990
3—*The Dance*. Scholastic, 1990
4—*The Mystery*. Scholastic, 1991
5—*The Roommate*. Scholastic, 1991
6—*The Lie*. Scholastic, 1991
Lizzie confides in her diary about the events of her life, especially about her best friend Nancy and worst enemy Samantha. Typical lightweight fare for grades 4-6.

RANSOM, Candice F. (Kobie Series)
1—*Almost Ten and a Half*. Scholastic, 1990
2—*Going on Twelve*. Scholastic, 1988
3—*Thirteen*. Scholastic, 1986
4—*Fourteen and Holding*. Scholastic, 1987
5—*Fifteen at Last*. Scholastic, 1987
Readers get to live Kobie's life, preteen through teen years, with her. The series begins with her and a friend trying to build a roller coaster and takes her to high school and first love. Popular choices for grades 4-7.

RANSOM, Candice F. (My Sister Series)
My Sister, the Meanie. Scholastic, 1988
My Sister, the Traitor. Scholastic, 1989
My Sister, the Creep. Scholastic, 1990
Seventh grader Jackie sees her older sister Sharon as beautiful and popular. If only her sister would share her expertise, Jackie could be too. Readers grades 4-8 will relate to the sibling strife that veteran author Ransom writes about. This will prove as popular as Ransom's other books.

RAZZI, Jim (Spine Chillers)
The Ghost in the Mirror. Grosset, 1990
Creature Feature. Grosset, 1990
These are actually collections of 4 spooky short stories per volume aimed at grades 3-6. Youthful horror fans (and reluctant readers) not expecting *Friday the 13th* gore will eat them up.

REUTER, Bjarne (Buster Series)

Buster's World. Dutton, 1980

Buster, the Sheikh of Hope Street. Dutton, 1991

Written by a popular Danish author, this series revolves about Buster, who is not much good at math, but is great at magic! He is picked on until his talent for entertaining comes to the fore. (A word of caution, the opening scene takes place in a boys' locker room with somewhat graphic dialogue.) The sequel finds Buster hoping to be in the school play but instead winding up working backstage. Acceptable for grades 4-6.

RICHLER, Mordecai (Jacob Two-Two Books)

Jacob Two-Two Meets the Hooded Fang. Bantam, 1987

Jacob Two-Two and the Dinosaur. Bantam, 1988

Jacob Two-Two has two of most things including sisters and brothers. He is also 2+2+2 years old, and he has to repeat things twice to be noticed. Most kids feel ignored and scared, and they will find inspiration in the humor here as Jacob overcomes his fears and shows them for the childish things they really are. Ages 8-12.

RINALDI, Ann

But in the Fall I'm Leaving. Holiday, 1985

Good Side of My Heart. Holiday, 1987

Brie lives with her father, but it is very difficult. She decides to move to California and live with her mother, until she learns a secret about her family's past. Later she begins dating Josh against her father's wishes. She is very much in love with him but then he tells her he is homosexual. She needs to come to grips with that revelation and with some additional family difficulties. These are two excellent books for YAs.

RINALDI, Ann

Term Paper. Walker, 1980

Promises Are for Keeping. Walker, 1981

Nicki is a freshman who comes to terms with her father's death only after her brother Tony, the new English teacher, assigns her a paper on the subject. In the sequel, Nicki takes some birth control pills from her older brother's, a doctor, desk. The pills are not for her but she cannot tell him that when he confronts her. As punishment, she must volunteer at the local hospital. She begins to realize that you must accept responsibility for your own actions. The characters in these two books are well developed and believable. Grades 6-9.

ROBERTS, Willo Davis (Minden Series)

The Minden Curse. Atheneum, 1978

More Minden Curses. Aladdin, 1990

The Minden Curse is some mystical ability that puts Danny Minden, his dog Leroy, or his grandfather at the scene of any exciting event that occurs. Consequently, they get mixed up in all kinds of trouble, including finding a vicious lost cat and spending time in a haunted house. Roberts is a mistress of writing spooky books with a touch of humor and plenty of realism. These are for readers grades 4-7.

ROBERTSON, Keith (*Henry Reed Series)

5—*Henry Reed's Think Tank*. Viking, 1986

In the first Henry Reed book in 16 years, Henry and his friend Midge have decided that what Grover's Corner needs is a think tank to solve everyone's problems. He and Midge, of course, will be the thinkers. Their projects include weaning Mrs. Shultz away from her health food craze and back to the kind of food her kids like and convincing bothersome guests that it is time to go home. Henry's offhand narration of their exploits adds to the humor of the situations and solutions. For ages 8-12.

ROBINSON, Nancy K. (Angela Series)
1—*Mom, You're Fired!* Scholastic, 1983
2—*Oh, Honestly, Angela!* Scholastic, 1985
3—*Angela, Private Citizen*. Scholastic, 1989
4—*Angela and the Broken Heart*. Scholastic, 1991
Angela is an unusually socially responsible six year old. Her older sister Tina begins by telling her about the less fortunate. Angela decides to help by furnishing stuffed animals to the poor. In a later outing, she sends in taxes, hoping the government will buy soap for a poor child. The family interrelationships are portrayed realistically and with good values, but the characters are often one-dimensional. Aimed at ages 8-11.

ROBINSON, Nancy K. (Veronica Series)
Veronica the Show-Off. Scholastic, 1982
Veronica Knows Best. Scholastic, 1987
Veronica Meets Her Match. Scholastic, 1990
In the first book Veronica has moved to a new school and is having trouble making friends. To get attention she makes things up. In the second entry Veronica ruins her father's wedding plans. Youngsters ages 8-11 will identify with her problems in overenthusiasm and being accepted. This is a pleasant series for this age group.

ROCKWELL, Thomas
How to Eat Fried Worms. Dell, 1988
How to Fight a Girl. Dell, 1988
Billy finds himself in a tough position: to win a bet (for enough money for a trail bike), he has to eat 15 worms. In the second book he has to foil a group of kids out to cut him down to size. The first is particularly popular, and makes a great book talk—use gummy worms to illustrate! Grades 4-6.

RODGERS, Mary
3— **Summer Switch*. Harper, 1982
Following up on her highly successful *Freaky Friday*, which had a mother/daughter body switch, author Rodgers this time has a father/son switch. Although this book did precede all those movies about body switching, this one was made into a TV movie. Popular subject for grades 4-6.

RODGERS, Raboo
Magnum Fault. Houghton, 1984
The Rainbow Factor. Houghton, 1985
Cody Burke loves his dog Riley, flying, and the outdoors. In *Magnum Fault* Cody and Jill solve a mystery that begins with the disappearance of her father and ends with the drying up of Cody's favorite canoeing river. *The Rainbow Factor* sends Cody off on another action-filled mystery, this time with Audrey, that includes a hint of romance and lots of adventure. Above-average books for YAs in eighth grade and up.

ROGERS, Jean
Dinosaurs Are 568. Greenwillow, 1988
Raymond's Best Summer. Greenwillow, 1990
Raymond is a first grader who definitely does not want to go to school in the first volume. The second finds him learning to swim in a very different way during summer vacation. These are fun in a low-key way for grades 2-4.

ROOS, Stephen (Life and Times of the Kids from New Eden)
1—*My Horrible Secret*. Dell, 1983
2—*The Terrible Truth*. Delacorte, 1983
3—*My Secret Admirer*. Delacorte, 1984
4—*Twelve-Year-Old Vows Revenge!* Delacorte, 1990

Kids will find a lot of laughs in this series about a group of youngsters in the town of New Eden, particularly friendly rivals Shirley and Claire. They compete for grades, boys, even in the business world. Grades 4-7.

ROOS, Stephen (Plymouth Island Series)
1—*The Fair-Weather Friends*. Atheneum, 1986
2—*Thirteenth Summer*. Atheneum, 1987
3—*My Favorite Ghost*. Atheneum, 1988
4—*And the Winner Is....* Atheneum, 1989
These books center around a group of kids living on Plymouth Island: vain Phoebe, whose family loses their money; Pink, who yearns to see what life is like off the island; Derek, whose money-making scheme to exploit the island ghost causes many problems; and Kit, who must adjust to changing friendships. Grades 4-7.

RUBINSTEIN, Gillian
Space Demons. Dial, 1986
Skymaze. Orchard, 1991
Andrew has never played a computer game that required such skill and that was so exciting to play. Space Demons did not come with instructions and he is shocked when he is hurled through the screen and finds out that he is now part of the game. The game reflects many conflicts that he and his friends encounter in real life. In the next book, Andrew's friends disappear. Could it be that Skymaze, the newest computer game, has spirited them away? They must use their deepest strengths to come out ahead in this real life computer game. Grades 6-9.

RUCKMAN, Ivy (Melba Series)
Melba the Brain. Dell, 1991
Melba the Mummy. Dell, 1991
Melba is a highly intelligent youngster who borders on nerd-dom. She daydreams about the hypotenuses of triangles! Somehow she is taken to another planet where animals are the primary inhabitants and humans are on the endangered list. She and the animals try to save endangered species here on earth. With the revitalized interest in planet earth, these should prove quality choices for grades 4-6.

SACHAR, Louis (Wayside School Series)
1—*Sideways Stories from Wayside School*. Camelot, 1990
2—*Wayside School Is Falling Down*. Camelot, 1990
3—*Sideways Arithmetic from Wayside School*. Scholastic, 1989
This is a highly unusual series set in an unusual school, where nothing is done the way it is in most schools. Arithmetic is done with letters rather than numbers and there are thirty stories, including the 19th, which doesn't really exist. Readers will find themselves laughing and stimulated at the same time. The short chapters make these an ideal transition for middle readers, ages 8-12.

SACHS, Elizabeth-Ann
Just Like Always. Atheneum, 1981
I Love You, Janie Tannenbaum. Aladdin, 1990
Two very different girls find themselves roommates with little in common except their scoliosis. One is a practical tomboy, the other a dreamer living in a fantasy world. The sequel, originally published as *Where Are You, Cow Patty?*, has the girls meeting again a year and a half after the hospital stay. There is a lot of humor here and the girls are portrayed realistically. The plots are believably handled and will find a ready audience with readers 8-12, especially those with scoliosis themselves.

SACHS, Marilyn

The Bear's House. Doubleday, 1971
Fran Ellen's House. Dutton, 1987

Unlike so many authors, Sachs' characters and their problems are heartbreakingly real. Fran Ellen has suffered a lot: her father deserted the family, her mother became ill, and the family split up. The second book finds them reunited after a year, but they have all changed and grown apart. They must rebuild their relationships with each other. Excellent choices for grades 4-9.

SAUNDERS, Susan (Bad News Bunny Series)

1—*Third-Prize Surprise*. Simon & Schuster, 1987
2—*Back to Nature*. Simon & Schuster, 1987
3—*Stop the Presses*. Simon & Schuster, 1987
4—*Who's Got a Secret?* Simon & Schuster, 1987
5—*Caught in the Act*. Simon & Schuster, 1987
6—*Narrow Escape*. Simon & Schuster, 1987

Robot the rabbit is an inhabitant of the fourth grade science corner in Jason's class. This rabbit talks and loves junk food—any kid's dream! Jason tries to keep others from learning this secret, but his efforts often lead to more trouble. Easy reading fun for those who enjoy humorous school/animal tales. Grades 3-5.

SAUNDERS, Susan (Sleepover Friends)

1—*Patti's Luck*. Scholastic, 1987
2—*Starring Stephanie*. Scholastic, 1987
3—*Kate's Surprise*. Scholastic, 1987
4—*Patti's New Look*. Scholastic, 1988
5—*Lauren's Big Mix-Up*. Scholastic, 1988
6—*Kate's Camp-Out*. Scholastic, 1988
7—*Stephanie Strikes Back*. Scholastic, 1988
8—*Lauren's Treasure*. Scholastic, 1988
9—*No More Sleepovers, Patti?* Scholastic, 1988
10—*Lauren's Sleepover Exchange*. Scholastic, 1989
11—*Stephanie's Family Secret*. Scholastic, 1989
12—*Kate's Sleepover Disaster*. Scholastic, 1989
13—*Patti's Secret Wish*. Scholastic, 1989
14—*Lauren Takes Charge*. Scholastic, 1989
15—*Stephanie's Big Story*. Scholastic, 1989
16—*Kate's Crush*. Scholastic, 1989
17—*Patti Gets Even*. Scholastic, 1989
18—*Stephanie and the Magician*. Scholastic, 1989
19—*The Great Kate*. Scholastic, 1989
20—*Lauren in the Middle*. Scholastic, 1990
21—*Starstruck Stephanie*. Scholastic, 1990
22—*The Trouble with Patti*. Scholastic, 1990
23—*Kate's Surprise Visitor*. Scholastic, 1990
24—*Lauren's New Friend*. Scholastic, 1990
25—*Stephanie and the Wedding*. Scholastic, 1990
26—*The New Kate*. Scholastic, 1990
27—*Where's Patti?* Scholastic, 1990
28—*Lauren's New Address*. Scholastic, 1990
29—*Kate the Boss*. Scholastic, 1990
30—*Big Sister Stephanie*. Scholastic, 1990
31—*Lauren's After School Job*. Scholastic, 1990
32—*A Valentine for Patti*. Scholastic, 1990
33—*Lauren's Double Disaster*. Scholastic, 1991

34—*Kate the Winner!* Scholastic, 1991
35—*The New Stephanie*. Scholastic, 1991
36—*Presenting Patti*. Scholastic, 1991
37—*Lauren Saves the Day*. Scholastic, 1991
38—*Patti's City Adventure*. Scholastic, 1991

Another popular paperback series for girls ages 8-12. Four friends spend a lot of time on overnights at each others' homes and even travel out of state for adventures. Easy reading, cotton candy type fare that will be popular with fans of the Babysitters Club and Sweet Valley Twins.

SCHOCH, Tim

Flash Fry, Private Eye. Avon, 1986
Cat Attack! Avon, 1988

Flash's adventures are retold by his associate, Private Nose Scratch, his dog. These are funnier than most mysteries, and Scratch is most likeable. Good fun for grades 4-6.

SCHWARTZ, Joel L. (Upchuck Series)

Upchuck Summer. Dell, 1983
Best Friends Don't Come in Threes. Dell, 1985
Upchuck Summer's Revenge. Delacorte, 1990

Set during successive summers at camp, this hilarious series has been a surefire hit with readers 8-12. There is a little romance, a lot of slapstick humor, and believable characters and plots. There is an ongoing rivalry between hero Richie and another counselor. Nerdy Chuck, trying to help out, always causes trouble. A good choice for any collection.

SEBESTYEN, Ouida

Words by Heart. Little, 1979
On Fire. Little, 1988

Lena tries to fulfill her papa's dream of a better life for his family. She works hard to succeed in school, not knowing that she is unleashing a string of prejudices that ultimately kills her father. Eventually she must learn to forgive her father's killer. This first book is powerfully written and was selected as an ALA Best Book for Young Adults. The companion novel centers on a dangerous strike in a frontier mining town, where Sammy's feelings toward his older brother change. His brother is Tater, who is having a difficult time coping with having killed Lena's father. For YAs.

SELDEN, George (Chester Cricket Series)

1—**Harry Kitten and Tucker Mouse*. Farrar, 1986
5—*Chester Cricket's Pigeon Ride*. Farrar, 1981
6—*Chester Cricket's New Home*. Farrar, 1983
7—*The Old Meadow*. Farrar, 1987

Harry Kitten and Tucker Mouse is actually a prequel to this fine series. These beloved characters who first met to the lovely sounds of Chester Cricket's music, continue their adventures, including an aerial tour of New York City, and a search for a new home for the musical cricket. Grades 4-6.

SENN, Steve

Spacebread. Atheneum, 1981
Born of Flame. Atheneum, 1982

Spacebread is a white, Persian-style cat from another planet. She roams the galaxy waiting for trouble to come to her. She becomes involved with many species and adventures. There is a bit of Star Wars to the descriptions of the aliens, but charm ends there and the many odd terms could prove confusing except for die-hard science fiction buffs. Grades 4-6.

SHACHTMAN, Tom (Daniel Au Fond Trilogy)
Beachmaster. H. Holt & Co., 1988
Wavebender. H. Holt & Co., 1989
These books have been compared to *Watership Down*, because the stories revolve around a sea lion named Daniel, who seeks to make the sea safe for his own kind not only from predators, but also from the increasing danger of pollution. Grades 4-7.

SHARMAT, Marjorie
He Noticed I'm Alive. Delacorte, 1985
Two Guys Noticed Me. Delacorte, 1985
Jody really likes Matt, but her father is dating Matt's mom. When Matt asks her out she is not sure if she wants to go—it might make her father more serious about his mother, which Jody doesn't want. Eventually her father makes plans to marry and that is when her mother, who has previously disappeared, returns. This causes problems for everyone! These are very lighthearted but entertaining books. Sixth grade and up.

SHARMAT, Marjorie (Gorgeous Series)
How to Meet a Gorgeous Guy. Delacorte, 1983
How to Meet a Gorgeous Girl. Delacorte, 1984
How to Have a Gorgeous Wedding. Dell, 1989
Shari is the "star" of an article entitled "How to Meet a Gorgeous Guy" to be published in a new teen magazine. She gets a date with handsome senior Mark, but problems arise as she tries to hold onto him. In the "male" version of the series, Mark is dying to know who the girl is behind the make-up counter. When he finds a book, *How to Meet a Gorgeous Girl*, he thinks his problems are over, but boy, is he wrong! These are better written than most YA romances. The characters are entertaining and believable. Grades 7-10.

SHARMAT, Marjorie, and **Andrew SHARMAT** (The Kids on the Bus)
1—*School Bus Cat*. Harper, 1990
2—*The Cooking Class*. Harper, 1991
3—*Bully on the Bus*. Harper, 1991
4—*The Secret Notebook*. Harper, 1991
Veteran author Sharmat here writes with her son, presenting the school joys and woes of a group of elementary school kids who take the same bus to school. These are good for younger readers grades 2-4.

SHARMAT, Marjorie (*Maggie Marmelstein Series)
3—*Mysteriously Yours, Maggie Marmelstein*. Harper, 1982
The determined Maggie Marmelstein is at it again. This time she is determined to win the spot as the mystery columnist on the school paper. She does win the column and decides to use the column to help improve others' lives. Really good fun with a spunky heroine. Grades 4-6.

SHARMAT, Marjorie (Sorority Sisters)
1—*For Members Only*. Dell, 1986
2—*Snobs Beware*. Dell, 1986
3—*I Think I'm Falling in Love*. Dell, 1986
4—*Fighting Over Me*. Dell, 1986
5—*Nobody Knows How Scared I Am*. Dell, 1987
6—*Here Comes Mr. Right*. Dell, 1987
7—*Getting Closer*. Dell, 1987
8—*I'm Going to Get Your Boyfriend*. Dell, 1987
The exclusive sorority at Palm Canyon High School is Chi Kappa. This is another original paperback series about life in high school, with a twist. This time a sorority is the focus of events and friendships. Grades 7 and up.

SHARP, Margery (*Miss Bianca Series)
8—*Bernard the Brave*. Little, 1977
9—*Bernard into Battle*. Little, 1978
The beloved Miss Bianca, now a Disney movie star, gives way a bit here to her stalwart companion in danger, Bernard. He, too, takes on any foe, regardless of size or the chance of success. These are charming adventure series, told with a graceful wit. They also make good read-aloud material. Grades 4-6.

SHEFFER, H. R. (Teammates)
The Last Meet. Crestwood, 1981
Moto-Cross Monkey. Crestwood, 1981
Partners on Wheels. Crestwood, 1981
Sara Sells Soccer. Crestwood, 1981
Second-String Nobody. Crestwood, 1981
Street-Hockey Lady. Crestwood, 1981
Swim for Pride. Crestwood, 1981
Two at the Net. Crestwood, 1981
Weekend in the Dunes. Crestwood, 1981
Winner on the Court. Crestwood, 1981
These books involve different characters involved in a variety of sports. They are aimed at reluctant readers with a sports bent. The controlled vocabulary with teen heroes both male and female participating as winners in a variety of sports make these decent choices, although the plots and writing are less than riveting. Grades 4-8.

SHELDON, Ann (Linda Craig Adventures)
1—*The Golden Secret*. Minstrel, 1988
2—*A Star for Linda*. Minstrel, 1988
3—*The Silver Stallion*. Minstrel, 1988
4—*The Crystal Trail*. Minstrel, 1988
5—*The Glimmering Ghost*. Minstrel, 1989
6—*The Ride to Gold Canyon*. Minstrel, 1989
7—*A Horse for Jackie*. Minstrel, 1989
8—*A Star in the Saddle*. Minstrel, 1989
9—*The Riding Club*. Minstrel, 1989
10—*Anything for Kelly*. Minstrel, 1989
11—*Everybody's Favorite*. Minstrel, 1990
12—*Kathy in Charge*. Minstrel, 1990
Linda lives on a ranch with her grandparents and her horse, Amber. Some of the plots involve mysteries, some involve trouble with friends, but all are very "horsey," so that girls who enjoy the Saddle Club Series will also like these. Grades 4-6.

SHELDON, Ann (Linda Craig Series)
1—*The Palomino Mystery*. Wanderer, 1981
2—*The Secret of Rancho del Sol*. Wanderer, 1981
3—*The Clue on the Desert Trail*. Wanderer, 1981
4—*The Mystery of Horseshoe Canyon*. Wanderer, 1981
5—*The Mystery in Mexico*. Wanderer, 1981
6—*The Ghost Town Treasure*. Wanderer, 1982
7—*The Haunted Valley*. Wanderer, 1982
8—*Secret of the Old Sleigh*. Wanderer, 1983
9—*The Emperor's Pony*. Wanderer, 1983
These are an earlier incarnation for Linda, still set on the ranch with grandparents and horse. These accent the mystery more than the horse lore, and vaguely resemble a younger Nancy Drew on horseback. Grades 4-6.

SHURA, Mary F.

Chester. Dodd, 1980
Eleanor. Dodd, 1983
Jefferson. Dodd, 1984

These three children are siblings whose arrival disrupts the entire neighborhood—even the school. It begins with Chester, who has freckles on his freckles. It only takes him a week to change things. These stories are entertainingly written, with lots of humor and believable characterizations. Ages 8-12.

SHURA, Mary F.

Kate's Book. Scholastic, 1989
Kate's House. Scholastic, 1990

In 1843, Kate and her family, along with others, have decided to make the long trek from sunny Ohio, the land of milk and honey. These books detail the trip and settling in. Both the joys and hardships of pioneer life are seen through the eyes of a realistically portrayed heroine. Grades 4-7.

SIEGAL, Aranka

Upon the Head of the Goat. Farrar, 1981
Grace in the Wilderness. Farrar, 1985

The first of these two books chronicles the true life experiences of Piri, from 1939-1944, in Hungary. A very sensitive book, it details her family's destruction during the Holocaust. The second is a fictionalized account of Piri's life after release from Bergen-Belsen. Well told, the books were written for 14 year olds and up.

SIEGEL, Barbara, and **Scott SIEGEL** (Firebrats)

1—*The Burning Land*. Archway, 1988
2—*Survivors*. Archway, 1988
3—*Thunder Mountain*. Archway, 1988
4—*Shockwave*. Archway, 1988

Matt and Dani were deep underground when the nuclear missiles of World War III hit. They survived but are now faced with the constant threat of their new world. They need to learn how to forage for food and outwit gangs of bloodthirsty people. This science fiction series contains action-filled plots and an interesting story that can provoke discussion. Good for a public or school library. Grades 7 and up.

SIMON, Seymour (Einstein Anderson Series)

1—*Einstein Anderson, Science Sleuth*. Puffin, 1986
2—*Einstein Anderson Shocks His Friends*. Puffin, 1986
3—*Einstein Anderson Makes Up for Lost Time*. Puffin, 1986
4—*Einstein Anderson Tells a Comet's Tale*. Puffin, 1987
5—*Einstein Anderson Goes to Bat*. Puffin, 1987
6—*Einstein Anderson Lights Up the Sky*. Puffin, 1987
7—*Einstein Anderson Sees through the Invisible Man*. Puffin, 1987

Einstein Anderson is to science what Encyclopedia Brown is to mysteries. Each book has 10 puzzles that Einstein solves using his knowledge of various fields of science. The reader has an opportunity to solve the problem before Einstein reveals how he figured it out. This is an entertaining way to reinforce what kids are learning in school. Ages 8-12.

SINGER, Marilyn

Fido Frame-up. Warne, 1983
A Nose for Trouble. Holt, 1985

Like the Flash Fry series, this one also features a detective and his faithful dog, Samantha Spayed. She is firmly convinced that the detective talent rests with her. She may be right, because her detective is thirty-six years old! Grades 4-6.

SINGER, Marilyn (Sam and Dave Mysteries)

1–*The Case of the Sabotaged School Play*. Harper, 1984
2–*Leroy Is Missing*. Harper, 1984
3–*The Case of the Cackling Car*. Harper, 1985
4–*Clue in Code*. Harper, 1985
5–*The Case of the Fixed Election*. Harper, 1989
6–*The Hoax Is on You*. Harper, 1989

Twins Sam and Dave solve various mysteries, including finding missing jewelry and discovering who fixed a school election. The plots move quickly and all the clues are there for the reader to try to outwit the boys. Grades 4-6.

SINGER, Marilyn

Tarantulas on the Brain. Harper, 1982
Lizzie Silver of Sherwood Forest. Harper, 1986

Lizzie gets these obsessions: first she yearns to buy her very own tarantula, then she becomes a Robin Hood fan, and when she sees a live counterpart at a Medieval fair, she decides she must be one of the Merry Men. Youngsters who really, really want things will easily identify with the multi-faceted Lizzie as she attempts to make her various dreams come true. Terrific choices for grades 4-7.

SKOLSKY, Mindy

1–*Whistling Teakettle*. Harper, 1977
2–*Carnival and Kopeck*. Harper, 1979
3–*Hannah Is a Palindrome*. Harper, 1980
4–*Hannah and the Best Father on Route 9W*. Harper, 1982

Hannah is a young Jewish girl growing up on the Hudson River in 1932. These stories follow Hannah and her family through simple everyday events: grandma moving nearby, trouble with a bully, and spiffing up the restaurant to win an award. She is an appealing heroine and the period and family life are lovingly portrayed. Grades 4-6.

SLEPIAN, Janice

Alfred Summer. Macmillan, 1980
Lester's Turn. Macmillan, 1981

In an unusual series, Alfred, who has cerebral palsy, becomes friends with severely retarded Lester. Both of them become involved with another boy and girl in building a boat on which all four misfits hope to escape their currently untenable lives. These sensitively written works are for the discriminating reader in grades 5-8.

SLOTE, Alfred

1–*My Robot Buddy*. Lippincott, 1975
2–*My Trip to Alpha I*. Lippincott, 1978
3–*C.O.L.A.R.* Lippincott, 1981
4–*Omega Station*. Lippincott, 1983
5–*Trouble on Janus*. Lippincott, 1985

Fans of Norby will also go for this series, which features a boy and his robot. Although set in the future, the family still worries about missing PTA meetings. There is lots of adventure mixed with a generous helping of humor. Grades 4-6.

SLOTE, Alfred

Moving In. Lippincott, 1988
A Friend Like That. Lippincott, 1988

Life changes for the Miller family when their new housekeeper moves in. Robby winds up acting as matchmaker between her and friend Beth's father. New problems crop up, though, when they move and Robby worries about his father remarrying. The characters are realistically portrayed, and these should find a ready audience with grades 4-7.

SMARIDGE, Norah

1–*Secret of the Brownstone House*. Dodd, 1977
2–*Mystery at Greystone Hall*. Dodd, 1979
3–*The Mystery in the Old Mansions*. Putnam, 1981
4–*The Mysteries in the Commune*. Putnam, 1982

Robin finds herself in different locations each summer as her parents travel. She manages to discover mystery and adventure each time. These are easy to read and will attract preteen readers.

SMITH, Doris Buchanan

Last Was Lloyd. Viking, 1981
The First Hard Times. Viking, 1983

Smith has been foster mother to over 20 children and her knowledge of what makes troubled children tick is very evident in her writing. In the first book Lloyd is a pampered mama's boy whose clutziness at school is a response to the bullying he faces there. He finally decides to seek friendship and become independent from mother. The second book follows the troubled adjustment of his friend Ancil, whose mother has remarried and moved them all following a whirlwind courtship. Ancil rebels, feeling that someone has to be there in case her MIA father ever reappears from Vietnam. A very perceptive duo for ages 8-12.

SMITH, L. J.

The Night of the Solstice. Macmillan, 1987
Heart of Valor. Macmillan, 1990

Fantasy lovers will revel in this series that follows a family of children as their lives intertwine with Morgana, the guardian of a portal to a parallel universe. The series combines reality with Arthurian legend in a unique blend. The first book would reach a wider audience were it not for the very unappealing cover art. Grades 5-9.

SMITH, Susan (Best Friends)

1–*Sonya Begonia and the Eleventh Birthday Blues*. Pocket, 1988
2–*Angela and the King-size Crusade*. Pocket, 1988
3–*Dawn Selby, Super Sleuth*. Pocket, 1988
4–*Terri the Great*. Pocket, 1989
5–*Sonya and the Chain Letter Gang*. Pocket, 1989
6–*Angela and the Greatest Guy in the World*. Pocket, 1989
7–*$100,000 Dawn*. Pocket, 1990
8–*The Terrible Terri Rumors*. Pocket, 1990
9–*Linda and the Little White Lies*. Pocket, 1990
10–*Sonya and the Haunting of Room 16A*. Pocket, 1990
11–*Angela and the Great Book Battle*. Pocket, 1990
12–*Dynamite Dawn vs. Terrific Terri*. Pocket, 1991
13–*Who's Out to Get Linda?* Pocket, 1991
14–*Terri and the Shopping Mall Disaster*. Pocket, 1991
15–*The Sonya and Howard Wars*. Pocket, 1991
16–*Angela and the Accidental On-Purpose Romance*. Pocket, 1991

Another in a long line of Babysitter Club clones. The usual set of girl friends faces the usual problems, like a visiting friend who does not fit in with the crowd. Grades 4-6.

SMITH, Susan (Samantha Slade Series)

1–*Monster-Sitter*. Archway, 1987
2–*Confessions of a Teenage Frog*. Archway, 1987
3–*Our Friend, Public Nuisance, No. 1*. Archway, 1987
4–*The Terrors of Rock and Roll*. Archway, 1988

This paperback series is a cross between the Babysitters Club, because Samantha is a sitter, and the various monster series, because her sittees are monsters. Their weird house and unusual talents lead to both trouble and fun. Grades 4-6.

SNYDER, Zilpha Keatley

Below the Root. Atheneum, 1975
And All Between. Atheneum, 1976
Until the Celebration. Atheneum, 1977

This is an excellent fantasy series, very different from Snyder's other work. There are two different people, those who live in lofty trees, and those who face starvation underground. This can be read purely for the adventure, but deeper thinkers will see the parallels of haves and have-nots, privilege and power used to keep others subservient. Excellent choices for grades 5-9.

SNYDER, Zilpha Keatley (Stanley Family)

1—*The Headless Cupid*. Dell, 1985
2—*The Famous Stanley Kidnapping Case*. Dell, 1985
3—*Blair's Nightmare*. Dell, 1985
4—*Janie's Private Eyes*. Dell, 1988

Snyder is a very good author, so these family mysteries are well above average. The settings are unusual, with one taking place in Italy, another one at a seance. These also read aloud well. Grades 4-6.

SOBOL, Donald J. (Encyclopedia Brown Series)

13—*Encyclopedia Brown and the Case of the Midnight Visitor*. Lodestar, 1977
14—*Encyclopedia Brown Carries On*. Four Winds, 1980
15—*Encyclopedia Brown Sets the Pace*. Macmillan, 1982
16—*Encyclopedia Brown and the Case of the Exploding Plumbing*. Scholastic, 1984
17—*Encyclopedia Brown and the Case of the Mysterious Handprints*. Scholastic, 1985.
18—*Encyclopedia Brown and the Case of the Treasure Hunt*. Scholastic, 1988
19—*Encyclopedia Brown and the Case of the Disgusting Sneakers*. Scholastic, 1990
20—*Encyclopedia Brown's Book of Strange But True Crimes*. Scholastic, 1991

Veteran boy detective Encyclopedia Brown still rides high. These easy to read, short mysteries remain popular with the 8-12 year old set. The format remains the same: ten cases with all clues intact for the reader to solve if they can; answers and reasons why at the end. Also good to use with reluctant readers.

SOMMER-BODENBURG, Angela (Vampire Series)

1—*My Friend the Vampire*. Dial, 1984
2—*The Vampire Moves In*. Dial, 1984
3—*The Vampire Takes a Trip*. Dial, 1985
4—*The Vampire on the Farm*. Dial, 1985
5—*The Vampire in Love*. Dial, 1991

Tony makes friends with a vampire named Rudolph. This should be really neat, but instead causes nothing but problems when Rudolph moves in. These are translated from the German. While these are acceptable, Mooser and Anderson both have monster series with more pizzaz than this one for the same age group. Grades 4-6.

SORENSON, Jane (Jennifer Books)

1—*It's Me, Jennifer*. Standard, 1984
2—*It's Your Move, Jennifer*. Standard, 1984
3—*Jennifer's New Life*. Standard, 1984
4—*Jennifer Says Good-Bye*. Standard, 1984
5—*Boy Friend*. Standard, 1985
6—*Once Upon a Friendship*. Standard, 1985
7—*Fifteen Hands*. Standard, 1985
8—*In Another Land*. Standard, 1985
9—*The New Pete*. Standard, 1986
10—*Out with the In Crowd*. Standard, 1986
11—*Another Jennifer*. Standard, 1986
12—*Family Crisis*. Standard, 1986

Jennifer is a teen from fairly affluent surroundings who faces a number of problems with friends and family, including a move and family illness. Jennifer is also a member of her church youth group, and since these are Christian novels, God plays a large part in her life. There is a large audience out there for these kinds of books. Although the heroine is older, the age group these are aimed at is 8-12.

SOUTHALL, Ivan

King of the Sticks. Greenwillow, 1979
Golden Goose. Greenwillow, 1981

Written almost poetically, these books follow Custard, an Australian boy with the gift of divination. He becomes the target for several unscrupulous people who want to use his gift for their own purposes. For the special reader, grades 5-8.

SPEEDSTERS

APABLASA, Bill, and **Lisa THIESING**
Rhymin' Simon and the Mystery of the Fat Cat. Dutton, 1991
BENDALL-BRUNELLO, John
The Seven-and-a-Half Labors of Hercules. Dutton, 1991
CHRISTIE, Sally, and **Peter KAVANAUGH**
Mean and Mighty Me. Dutton, 1991
FEDER, Paula Kurzband
Did You Lose the Car Again? Dutton, 1991
IMPEY, Rose, and **Jolyne KNOX**
Desperate for a Dog. Dutton, 1989
No-Name Dog. Dutton, 1990
PETERSEN, P. J., and **Betsy JAMES**
The Fireplug Is First Base. Dutton, 1990
WEST, Colin
Shape Up, Monty! Dutton, 1991

The Speedster Series is written for grades 2-5, with a beginning reading vocabulary and lots of black and white illustrations to appeal to readers breaking away from picture books as well as older ones in need of simple vocabulary. The books are under 60 pages, the stories are breezy and humorous.

SPINELLI, Jerry

Space Station Seventh Grade. Little, 1982
Jason and Marceline. Little, 1986

Jason learns a great deal about growing up during seventh grade. He experiences zits, sports, girls, and locker room shows. When he becomes a freshman his friendship with Marceline develops into a romance. He finds out there is more to the relationship than just making out. *Space Station...* is considered the boys' version of Judy Blume's *Are You There God, It's Me, Margaret*. Both are refreshing and would be good in a collection for grades 7-10.

SPRINGSTUBB, Tricia (Eunice Gottlieb Series)

Which Way to the Nearest Wilderness. Little, 1984
Eunice Gottlieb and the Unwhitewashed Truth about Life. Delacorte, 1987
Eunice (the Egg Salad) Gottlieb. Little, 1988

Eunice is the middle child, so she is often overlooked in her mother's concern for her over-emotional older sister and withdrawn younger brother. Meeting a best friend certainly helps because they do so much together, until first a boy, then a new-found talent in gymnastics intrude. These are fun entries with appealing, entertaining heroines. Grades 4-7.

SPRINGSTUBB, Tricia (Lulu Books)

With a Name Like Lulu, Who Needs More Trouble? Delacorte, 1989
Lulu vs. Love. Delacorte, 1990

There is an unusual premise to this series. Eleven year old Lulu is best friends with nineteen year old unwed mother Tilda. Tilda coaches Lulu for baseball, while Lulu babysits for her. While the author uses a light tone, the subject matter and the way the plots are handled make these more series and more suitable for YAs than younger readers.

SPRINGBOARD BOOKS (Series)

AUCH, Mary Jane

Angel and Me and the Bayside Bombers. Little, 1989

CHRISTOPHER, Matt

The Hit-Away Kid. Little, 1988

The Spy on Third Base. Little, 1988

CONFORD, Ellen

A Job for Jenny Archer. Little, 1988

A Case for Jenny Archer. Little, 1988

Jenny Archer, Author. Little, 1989

Jenny Archer to the Rescue. Little, 1990

What's Cooking, Jenny Archer? Little, 1989

DUNCAN, Lois

Wonder Kid Meets the Evil Lunch Snatcher. Little, 1988

GONDOSCH, Linda

The Monsters of Marble Avenue. Little, 1988

KOLLER, Jackie French

The Dragonling. Little, 1990

Impy for Always. Little, 1989

Like the Step-Up series, this one is intended as the next controlled vocabulary step after beginning readers. Not short stories, but full-length novels, these are sprinkled with occasional illustrations and a fair amount of humor to keep the interest of readers grades 1-4.

STANDIFORD, Natalie (Space Dog Books)

1—*Space Dog and Roy*. Camelot, 1990

2—*Space Dog and the Pet Show*. Camelot, 1990

3—*Space Dog the Hero*. Camelot, 1991

4—*Space Dog in Trouble*. Camelot, 1991

Space Dog is an extraterrestrial who has taken canine form, but can think and speak just like earth folks. Younger sci-fi lovers grades 2-4 may enjoy these.

STANLEY, George

The Ukrainian Egg Mystery. Avon, 1986

The Italian Spaghetti Mystery. Avon, 1987

The Mexican Tamale Mystery. Avon, 1991

This funny series follows the escapades of Miss Westminster and her students, one of whom is from Atlanta and is appropriately named Augusta Savannah. The girls wind up tackling a lot of silly things, including a spaghetti making plant that goes crazy. These are great fun for those who like to laugh as well as mystery buffs. Grades 4-6.

STAUNTON, Ted (Greenapple Street Geniuses Series)

Maggie and Me. Viking, 1990

Greenapple Street Blues. Viking, 1990

This is a popular Canadian series that loses nothing in the transition to U.S. shores. The genius of the duo is Maggie. Nobody messes with her because she thinks up such great revenge plots. Her stooge is Cyril, and he usually winds up carrying out her outrageous schemes. There are plenty of laughs in this friendship for ages 8-12.

STEINER, Barbara (Foghorn Flattery Series)

Foghorn Flattery and the Vanishing Rhinos. Avon, 1991

Foghorn Flattery and the Dancing Horses. Avon, 1991

Foghorn got his name because of his husky voice. He and his sister C.C. travel the world with their journalist father (like the Arrow boys) and become involved with several adventures. In the first, while in Kenya, they track down killers of the endangered rhinoceros; in the second, set in Vienna, they search for a horse stolen from the Spanish Riding School. Grades 4-6.

STEINER, Barbara (Oliver Dibbs Series)
Oliver Dibbs to the Rescue! Avon, 1988
Oliver Dibbs and the Dinosaur Case. Avon, 1988
These books are acceptable. The writing does sound like an adult thinking rather than a youngster, but the plots are interesting, with Ollie trying to raise funds for wildlife conservation and get the stegosaurus named the state lizard. Grades 5 and up.

STEPPING STONE BOOKS (Series)
BERENDS, Polly Berrien
The Case of the Elevator Duck. Random, 1973
BULLA, Clyde Robert
The Chalk Box Kid. Random, 1987
White Bird. Random, 1990
CAMERON, Ann
Julian, Dream Doctor. Random, 1990
Julian, Secret Agent. Random, 1988
Julian's Glorious Summer. Random, 1987
CHANG, Heidi
Elaine and the Flying Frog. Random, 1991
ETRA, Jonathan, and **Stephanie SPINNER**
Aliens for Breakfast. Random, 1988
Aliens for Lunch. Random, 1991
GONDOSCH, Linda
Brutus the Wonder Poodle. Random, 1990
HOOKS, William H.
Pioneer Cat. Random, 1988
MARZOLLO, Jean
The Pizza Pie Slugger. Random, 1989
Red Ribbon Rosie. Random, 1988
O'CONNOR, Jim, and **Jane O'CONNOR**
The Ghost in Tent 19. Random, 1988
Slime Time. Random, 1990
SACHS, Betsy
The Boy Who Ate Dog Biscuits. Random, 1991
The Trouble with Santa. Random, 1990
SAUNDERS, Susan
The Daring Rescue of Marlon the Swimming Pig. Random, 1987
The Mystery of the Hard Luck Rodeo. Random, 1989
SHREVE, Susan
Lily and the Runaway Baby. Random, 1987
SIMON, Jo Ann
Star. Random, 1989
SKURZYNSKI, Gloria
The Minstrel in the Tower. Random, 1988
STEVENSON, Jocelyn
O'Diddy. Random, 1988
WEISS, Ellen, and **Mel FRIEDMAN**
The Adventures of Ratman. Random, 1990
WHELAN, Gloria
Next Spring An Oriole. Random, 1987
Silver. Random, 1988

YEP, Laurence

The Curse of the Squirrel. Random, 1987

Aimed at ages 7-9, the simple vocabulary and sentence construction will be a boon to novice readers. There are occasional illustrations to perk up the text. The authors are good quality, which makes their offerings a step above what one usually finds written with these kinds of restrictions.

STEVENSON, Drew

The Case of the Horrible Swamp Monster. Putnam, 1984
The Case of the Visiting Vampire. Putnam, 1986
The Case of the Wandering Werewolf. Putnam, 1987

Each of these cases is a mystery involving a group of youngsters with what appears to be a monster. Although they do not always get along very well, the kids act well enough as a team to solve the mystery of what (or Who) the monster really is. These are acceptable fare for mystery lovers 8-12.

STINE, Megan, and **H. William STINE** (Jeffrey and the Third Grade Ghost)

1—*Mysterious Max*. Fawcett, 1988
2—*Haunted Halloween*. Fawcett, 1988
3—*Christmas Visitors*. Fawcett, 1988
4—*Pet Day Surprises*. Fawcett, 1989
5—*Max on Stage*. Fawcett, 1989
6—*Max Saves the Day*. Fawcett, 1989
"Jeffrey and the Fourth Grade Ghost"
1—*Max Is Back*. Fawcett, 1989
2—*Baseball Card Fever*. Fawcett, 1989
3—*Max's Secret Formula*. Fawcett, 1989
4—*Mad Science*. Fawcett, 1990
5—*Camp Duck Down*. Fawcett, 1990
6—*Big Brother Blues*. Fawcett, 1990

Jeffrey and his ghost friend Max tackle the usual school problems, including coming up with a science fair project and locating a missing baseball card collection. These are easy reading fun for grades 3-6.

STINE, R. L. (Fear Street)

1—*Missing*. Pocket, 1990
2—*The Overnight*. Pocket, 1990
3—*The New Girl*. Pocket, 1989
4—*Surprise Party*. Pocket, 1989
5—*The Stepsister*. Pocket, 1990
6—*Halloween Party*. Pocket, 1990
7—*Haunted*. Pocket, 1990
8—*Sleepwalker*. Pocket, 1990
9—*The Wrong Number*. Pocket, 1990
10—*Ski Weekend*. Pocket, 1990
11—*The Fire Game*. Pocket, 1991
12—*The Secret Bedroom*. Pocket, 1991

Stine specializes in horror fiction for teens—a really popular genre. For pre-Stephen King and Christopher Pike fans.

STOLZ, Mary (*Barkham Street Series)

3—*Explorer of Barkham Street*. Harper, 1985

Martin Hastings is an unusual hero; feared as a bully, through the course of this perceptive series, the reader has come to discover why he acts the way he does and to pull for him as he tries to change his ways. In this last book, he makes friends with an elderly lady and learns that exploring can mean finding yourself as well as new places. Excellent choice for grades 4-7.

STOLZ, Mary
Ferris Wheel. Harper, 1977
Cider Days. Harper, 1978

Kate and Polly are as close as friends can be, ever since the first day of kindergarten when Kate had comforted a crying Polly. But when friends are so close they are not easy to replace, and expectations and needs based on that past friendship can often get in the way of new relationships. Very well written, with an easy-to-identify-with heroine for grades 4-6.

STOLZ, Mary
Go Catch a Flying Fish. Harper, 1979
What Time of Night Is It? Harper, 1981

Rather like Cynthia Voigt's Tillerman family, Stolz's Reddicks must face life without their mother, who has deserted them. Unlike the Tillermans, the Reddicks still have their father, but he is a loner too filled with his own pain to help the children with theirs. The two older children try to pretend nothing has happened, but the youngest cannot hide his feelings. In the second book the advent of their grandmother once again alters the family structure. Very good choices for teens.

STOVER, Marjorie
Midnight in the Dollhouse. Whitman, 1989
When the Dolls Woke. Whitman, 1985

There is a classic appeal in stories of small dolls or people who coexist together and the adventures they experience together. One of the more recent entries in this genre are these books by Stover. They combine fantasy and mystery in an appealing way. These are not on a level with the Borrowers or the Indian series by Banks, but will definitely appeal to grades 3-6.

STRASSER, Todd
Rock 'n' Roll Nights. Delacorte, 1982
Turn It Up! Delacorte, 1985
Wildlife. Delacorte, 1987

Gary Specter has a dream. One day his band will be recognized as the best band in New York City. But that dream will not be an easy one to fulfill. Strasser vividly captures the New York club scene and the feelings experienced by aspiring musicians. Through the series we see Gary and his friends go through good times and bad until, in the final book, they achieve success. The first entry is an ALA Best Book for Young Adults. All three are enjoyable and worth reading. Grades 7 and up.

SUNFIRE (Series)
GORDON, Jeffie Ross
Jacquelyn. Scholastic, 1985
Nora. Scholastic, 1987
MINER, Jane Claypool
Corey. Scholastic, 1987
Jennie. Scholastic, 1989
Joanna. Scholastic, 1984
Margaret. Scholastic, 1988
Roxanne. Scholastic, 1985
Veronica. Scholastic, 1986
RANSOM, Candice
Amanda. Scholastic, 1984
Emily. Scholastic, 1985
Kathleen. Scholastic, 1985
Nicole. Scholastic, 1986
Sabrina. Scholastic, 1986
Susannah. Scholastic, 1984

ROBERTS, Willo Davis
Caroline. Scholastic, 1984
Elizabeth. Scholastic, 1984
Victoria. Scholastic, 1985
SCHURFRANZ, Vivian
Cassie. Scholastic, 1985
Danielle. Scholastic, 1984
Heather. Scholastic, 1987
Josie. Scholastic, 1988
Julie. Scholastic, 1986
Laura. Scholastic, 1985
Megan. Scholastic, 1986
Merrie. Scholastic, 1987
Rachel. Scholastic, 1986
Renee. Scholastic, 1989
SHURA, Mary Francis
Darcy. Scholastic, 1989
Diana. Scholastic, 1988
Gabrielle. Scholastic, 1987
Jessica. Scholastic, 1984
Marilee. Scholastic, 1985

Different young women from many periods of American history are the protagonists in these books, a series of historical fiction novels. Each book contains romance, suspense, mystery and some factual information. From Texas in 1835, to a trip on the Mayflower, to the blazing sun on the Oregon Trail, these young women are interesting reading. Grades 8 and up.

SUTCLIFF, Rosemary
The Light beyond the Forest. Dutton, 1980
The Sword and the Circle. Dutton, 1981
The Road to Camlann. Dutton, 1982

Veteran historical novelist Sutcliff here tackles the Arthurian legends. These are beautifully retold, with no sugar coating over the sins of Arthur and Guinevere, so that the tragic end of Camelot can be foreseen and understood by young readers. At the beginning of each book, the reader is brought up to date on events so far. The first two books concentrate mostly on the magic and growth of the Round Table, while the last shows the sorrowful end. Grades 4-7.

SWEET DREAMS (Series)
CONKLIN, Barbara
1–*P.S. I Love You*. Bantam, 1981
VERNON, Rosemary
2–*Popularity Plan*. Bantam, 1981
RAND, Suzanne
3–*Laurie's Song*. Bantam, 1981
POLLOWITZ, Melinda
4–*Princess Anne*. Bantam, 1981
GREENE, Yvonne
5–*Little Sister*. Bantam, 1981
QUIN-HARKIN, Janet
6–*California Girl*. Bantam, 1981
RAND, Suzanne
7–*Green Eyes*. Bantam, 1981
CAMPBELL, Joanna
8–*Thoroughbred*. Bantam, 1981
GREENE, Yvonne
9–*Cover Girl*. Bantam, 1982

QUIN-HARKIN, Janet
10—*Love Match*. Bantam, 1981
VERNON, Rosemary
11—*The Problem with Love*. Bantam, 1982
SPECTOR, Debra
12—*Night of the Prom*. Bantam, 1982
CONKLIN, Barbara
13—*The Summer Jenny Fell in Love*. Bantam, 1982
SAAL, Jocelyn
14—*Dance of Love*. Bantam, 1982
NOBILE, Jeanett
15—*Thinking of You*. Bantam, 1982
BURMAN, Margaret
16—*How Do You Say Goodbye?* Bantam, 1982
RAND, Suzanne
17—*Ask Annie*. Bantam, 1982
QUIN-HARKIN, Janet
18—*Ten-Boy Summer*. Bantam, 1982
PARK, Anne
19—*Love Song*. Bantam, 1982
VERNON, Rosemary
20—*Popularity Summer*. Bantam, 1982
ANDREWS, Jeanne
21—*All's Fair in Love*. Bantam, 1982
CAMPBELL, Joanna
22—*Secret Identity*. Bantam, 1982
CONKLIN, Barbara
23—*Falling in Love Again*. Bantam, 1985
ELLEN, Jaye
24—*The Trouble with Charlie*. Bantam, 1982
VILOTT, Rhondi
25—*Her Secret Self*. Bantam, 1982
WOODRUFF, Marian
26—*It Must Be Magic*. Bantam, 1982
MARAVEL, Gailanne
27—*Too Young for Love*. Bantam, 1982
SAAL, Jocelyn
28—*Trusting Hearts*. Bantam, 1982
DUKORE, Jesse
29—*Never Love a Cowboy*. Bantam, 1982
FISHER, Lois
30—*Little White Lies*. Bantam, 1983
SPECTOR, Debra
31—*Close to You*. Bantam, 1983
QUIN-HARKIN, Janet
32—*Daydreamer*. Bantam, 1983
VERNON, Rosemary
33—*Dear Amanda*. Bantam, 1983
WOODRUFF, Marian
35—*Forbidden Love*. Bantam, 1983
CONKLIN, Barbara
36—*Summer Dreams*. Bantam, 1983
NOBILE, Jeanett
37—*Portrait of Love*. Bantam, 1983

SAAL, Jocelyn
38–*Running Mates*. Bantam, 1983
SPECTOR, Debra
39–*First Love*. Bantam, 1983
AARON, Anna
40–*Secrets*. Bantam, 1983
JOHNS, Janetta
41–*The Truth about Me and Bobby V*. Bantam, 1983
WOODRUFF, Marian
42–*The Perfect Match*. Bantam, 1983
PARK, Anne
43–*Tender Loving Care*. Bantam, 1983
DUKORE, Jesse
44–*Long Distance Love*. Bantam, 1983
BURMAN, Margaret
45–*Dream Prom*. Bantam, 1983
SAAL, Jocelyn
46–*On Thin Ice*. Bantam, 1983
KENT, Deborah
47–*Te Amo Means I Love You*. Bantam, 1983
WOODRUFF, Marian
48–*Dial "L" for Love*. Bantam, 1983
RAND, Suzanne
49–*Too Much Too Lose*. Bantam, 1983
MARAVEL, Gailanne
50–*Lights, Camera, Love*. Bantam, 1984
SPECTOR, Debra
51–*Magic Moments*. Bantam, 1984
CAMPBELL, Joanna
52–*Love Notes*. Bantam, 1984
QUIN-HARKIN, Janet
53–*Ghost of a Chance*. Bantam, 1984
FISHER, Lois
54–*I Can't Forget You*. Bantam, 1984
PINES, Nancy
55–*Spotlight on Love*. Bantam, 1984
COWAN, Dale
56–*Campfire Nights*. Bantam, 1984
RAND, Suzanne
57–*On Her Own*. Bantam, 1984
FOSTER, Stephanie
58–*Rhythm of Love*. Bantam, 1984
CRAWFORD, Alice
59–*Please Say Yes*. Bantam, 1984
BLAKE, Susan
60–*Summer Breezes*. Bantam, 1984
QUIN-HARKIN, Janet
61–*Exchange of Hearts*. Bantam, 1984
RAND, Suzanne
62–*Just Like the Movies*. Bantam, 1984
WOODRUFF, Marian
63–*Kiss Me, Creep*. Bantam, 1984
VERNON, Rosemary
64–*Love in the Fast Lane*. Bantam, 1984

QUIN-HARKIN, Janet
65—*The Two of Us*. Bantam, 1984
FOSTER, Stephanie
66—*Love Times Two*. Bantam, 1984
QUIN-HARKIN, Janet
67—*Lovebirds*. Bantam, 1984
CONKLIN, Barbara
68—*I Believe in You*. Bantam, 1984
BLAIR, Shannon
69—*Call Me Beautiful*. Bantam, 1984
FIELDS, Terri
70—*Special Someone*. Bantam, 1984
DICKENSON, Celia
71—*Too Many Boys*. Bantam, 1984
CONKLIN, Barbara
72—*Goodbye Forever*. Bantam, 1984
VERNON, Rosemary
73—*The Language of Love*. Bantam, 1984
GREGORY, Diana
74—*Don't Forget Me*. Bantam, 1984
FOSTER, Stephanie
75—*First Summer Love*. Bantam, 1984
RAND, Suzanne
76—*Three Cheers for Love*. Bantam, 1984
KENT, Deborah
77—*Ten-Speed Summer*. Bantam, 1985
CAPRON, Jean
78—*Never Say No*. Bantam, 1985
BLAIR, Shannon
79—*Star Struck*. Bantam, 1985
JARNOW, Jill
80—*A Shot at Love*. Bantam, 1985
SPECTOR, Debra
81—*Secret Admirer*. Bantam, 1985
POLCOVAR, Jane
82—*Hey, Good Looking*. Bantam, 1985
PARK, Anne
83—*Love by the Book*. Bantam, 1985
BLAKE, Susan
84—*The Last Word*. Bantam, 1985
RAND, Suzanne
85—*The Boy She Left Behind*. Bantam, 1985
VERNON, Rosemary
86—*Questions of Love*. Bantam, 1985
CRANE, Marion
87—*Programmed for Love*. Bantam, 1985
BLAIR, Shannon
88—*Wrong Kind of Boy*. Bantam, 1985
QUIN-HARKIN, Janet
89—*101 Ways to Meet Mr. Right*. Bantam, 1985
GREGORY, Diana
90—*Two's a Crowd*. Bantam, 1985
GREENE, Yvonne
91—*The Love Hunt*. Bantam, 1985

BLAIR, Shannon
92—*Kiss and Tell*. Bantam, 1985
QUIN-HARKIN, Janet
93—*The Great Boy Chase*. Bantam, 1985
LEVINSON, Nancy
94—*Second Chances*. Bantam, 1985
HEHL, Eileen
95—*No Strings Attached*. Bantam, 1985
CONKLIN, Barbara
96—*First, Last, and Always*. Bantam, 1985
ROSS, Carolyn
97—*Dancing in the Dark*. Bantam, 1985
GREGORY, Diana
98—*Love Is in the Air*. Bantam, 1985
CAUDELL, Marian
99—*One Boy Too Many*. Bantam, 1985
QUIN-HARKIN, Janet
100—*Follow That Boy*. Bantam, 1985
SPECTOR, Debra
101—*Wrong for Each Other*. Bantam, 1986
FIELDS, Terri
102—*Hearts Don't Lie*. Bantam, 1986
GREGORY, Diana
103—*Cross My Heart*. Bantam, 1986
STEVENS, JANICE
104—*Playing for Keeps*. Bantam, 1986
REYNOLDS, Elizabeth
105—*The Perfect Boy*. Bantam, 1986
MAKRIS, Kathryn
106—*Mission Love*. Bantam, 1986
STEINER, Barbara
107—*If You Love Me*. Bantam, 1986
JARNOW, Jill
108—*One of the Boys*. Bantam, 1986
WHITE, Charlotte
109—*No More Boys*. Bantam, 1986
HEHL, Eileen
110—*Playing Games*. Bantam, 1986
REYNOLDS, Elizabeth
111—*Stolen Kisses*. Bantam, 1986
CAUDELL, Marian
112—*Listen to Your Heart*. Bantam, 1986
WINFIELD, Julia
113—*Private Eyes*. Bantam, 1989
BOIES, Janice
114—*Just the Way You Are*. Bantam, 1986
REDISH, Jane
115—*Promise Me Love*. Bantam, 1986
MACBAIN, Carol
116—*Heartbreak Hill*. Bantam, 1986
FIELDS, Terri
117—*The Other Me*. Bantam, 1987
CURTIS, Stefanie
118—*Heart to Heart*. Bantam, 1987

CADWALLADER, Sharon
119–*Star Crossed Love*. Bantam, 1987
MICHAELS, Fran
120–*Mr. Wonderful*. Bantam, 1987
WINFIELD, Julia
121–*Only Make-Believe*. Bantam, 1987
PALEY, Dee
122–*Stars in Her Eyes*. Bantam, 1987
SMILEY, Virginia
123–*Love in the Wings*. Bantam, 1987
BOIES, Janice
124–*More Than Friends*. Bantam, 1987
BEECHAM, Jahnna
125–*Parade of Hearts*. Bantam, 1987
CURTIS, Stefanie
126–*Here's My Heart*. Bantam, 1987
QUIN-HARKIN, Janet
127–*My Best Enemy*. Bantam, 1987
FIELDS, Terri
128–*One Boy at a Time*. Bantam, 1987
GREGORY, Diana
129–*A Vote for Love*. Bantam, 1987
BEECHAM, Jahnna
130–*Dance with Me*. Bantam, 1987
SCHULTZ, Mary
131–*Hand-Me-Down Heart*. Bantam, 1987
LYKKEN, Laune
132–*Winner Takes All*. Bantam, 1987
HEHL, Eileen
133–*Playing the Field*. Bantam, 1987
MICHAELS, Fran
134–*Past Perfect*. Bantam, 1987
FINNEY, Shan
135–*Geared for Romance*. Bantam, 1987
MACBAIN, Carol
136–*Stand by for Love*. Bantam, 1987
WYETH, Sharon
137–*Rocky Romance*. Bantam, 1988
BOIES, Janice
138–*Heart and Soul*. Bantam, 1988
BEECHAM, Jahnna
139–*The Right Combination*. Bantam, 1988
CURTIS, Stefanie
140–*Love Detour*. Bantam, 1988
141–*Winter Dreams*. Bantam, 1988
JARNOW, Jill
142–*Lifeguard Summer*. Bantam, 1988
BEECHAM, Jahnna
143–*Crazy for You*. Bantam, 1988
LYKKEN, Laune
144–*Princess Love*. Bantam, 1988
GORMAN, Susan
145–*This Time for Real*. Bantam, 1988
SIMBAL, Joanne
146–*Gifts from the Heart*. Bantam, 1988

FINNEY, Shan
147—*Trust in Love*. Bantam, 1988
BAER, Judy
148—*Riddles of Love*. Bantam, 1988
BEECHAM, Jahnna
149—*Practice Makes Perfect*. Bantam, 1988
BLAKE, Susan
150—*Summer Secrets*. Bantam, 1988
SCHULTZ, Mary
151—*Fortunes of Love*. Bantam, 1988
RICHARDS, Ann
152—*Cross-Country Match*. Bantam, 1988
LYKKEN, Laune
153—*Perfect Catch*. Bantam, 1988
GRIMES, Frances
154—*Love Lines*. Bantam, 1988
GORMAN, Susan
155—*The Game of Love*. Bantam, 1988
BLOSS, Janet
156—*Two Boys Too Many*. Bantam, 1988
CURTIS, Stefanie
157—*Mr. Perfect*. Bantam, 1988
BOIES, Janice
158—*Crossed Signals*. Bantam, 1988
SIMBAL, Joanne
159—*Long Shot*. Bantam, 1988
SMILEY, Virginia
160—*Blue Ribbon Romance*. Bantam, 1989
BAER, Judy
161—*My Perfect Valentine*. Bantam, 1989
BLAKE, Susan
162—*Trading Hearts*. Bantam, 1989
BRACALE, Carla
163—*My Dream Guy*. Bantam, 1989
BOIES, Janice
164—*Playing to Win*. Bantam, 1989
ST. PIERRE, Stephanie
165—*Brush with Love*. Bantam, 1990
DALE, Allison
166—*Three's a Crowd*. Bantam, 1990
167—*Working at Love*. Bantam, 1990
BRACALE, Carla
168—*Dream Date*. Bantam, 1988
BALLARD, Jane
169—*Golden Girl*. Bantam, 1990
LYKKEN, Laune
170—*Rock 'n' Roll Sweetheart*. Bantam, 1990
WALLACH, Susan
171—*Acting on Impulse*. Bantam, 1990
ST. PIERRE, Stephanie
172—*Sun-Kissed*. Bantam, 1990
LASKIN, Pamela
173—*Music from the Heart*. Bantam, 1990
BOIES, Janice
174—*Love on Strike*. Bantam, 1990

BRACALE, Carla
175–*Puppy Love*. Bantam, 1991
SOUTH, Sheri Cobb
176–*Wrong-Way Romance*. Bantam, 1991
LYKKEN, Laune
177–*The Truth about Love*. Bantam, 1991
ST. PIERRE, Stephanie
178–*Project Boyfriend*. Bantam, 1991
SLOATE, Susan
179–*Racing Hearts*. Bantam, 1991
SINGLETON, Linda
180–*Opposites Attract*. Bantam, 1991
O'CONNELL, June
181–*Time Out for Love*. Bantam, 1991
BRACALE, Carla
182–*Down with Love*. Bantam, 1991
MCHUGH, Elisabet
183–*The Real Thing*. Bantam, 1991

Sweet Dreams is one of the oldest young adult original paperbacks series in existence. There are over 27 million copies in print. Each book has different characters but all of the situations revolve around the relationships between boyfriend and girlfriend. These are popular books as evidenced by their longevity. Grades 7-9.

SYPHER, Lucy
4– **Turnabout Year*. Atheneum, 1976

Lucy and her large, loving family face the outbreak of World War I in their small village of Wales, South Dakota. Other events are in the offing as well, with mother expecting a new baby late in life and Lucy hoping desperately to go to the big city high school rather than at home. This historical series is based on Lucy Sypher's growing up experiences. Grades 4-7.

TANNEN, Mary
Wizard Culdren of Finn. Knopf, 1981
Lost Legend of Finn. Knopf, 1982

The McCool children travel in time to try to find out about their unknown father. They make friends with an Irish warrior named Finn, and later seek to return to his time, only to find themselves in the wrong era. Eventually they come to learn that they really are from the earlier time, and that their mother has brought them forward in time to protect them. An interesting fantasy adventure for grades 4-6.

TAPP, Kathy Kennedy (Moth-Kin Books)
Moth-Kin Magic. McElderry, 1983
Flight of the Moth-Kin. McElderry, 1987

Ripple is a member of the Moth-Kin, a tiny race of people with some magical properties. They have some frightening run-ins with the Giants (who are really humans). There are similar themes in the Borrowers books as well as others, but these have a more serious tone, with the Moth-Kin facing real dangers. Grades 4-7.

TAYLOR, Mildred D. (Logan Family Series)
1–*Song of the Trees*. Dial, 1975
2–*Roll of Thunder, Hear My Cry*. Dial, 1976
3–*Let the Circle Be Unbroken*. Dial, 1981
4–*The Friendship*. Dial, 1987
5–*The Road to Memphis*. Dial, 1990
6–*Mississippi Bridge*. Dial, 1990

Taylor has written an award-winning series about the Logans, a black family growing up in the South during the Depression. The Logans own their own land, which allows them a pride many of their friends cannot afford. They survive the Klan, public humiliation, and the tensions of growing up gifted and black in pre-World War II America. *Song of the Trees* and *The Friendship* are novelettes that the 8-10 year olds can read; the others are for the more mature readers, grades 5 and up. Outstanding choices.

TAYLOR, Sydney (*All-of-a-Kind Family Series)
5 – *Ella of All-of-a-Kind Family*. Dutton, 1978
Ella, the oldest in the All-of-a-Kind Family, is now eighteen. Jules, her almost-sweetheart has just returned from World War I. They need some time and privacy to discover what their feelings are, plus Ella must deal with her theatrical aspirations. Fans of this series will enjoy seeing how all the children develop. Grades 4-6.

TAYLOR, Theodore (Hatteras Banks Trilogy)
3 – **Odyssey of Ben O'Neal*. Doubleday, 1977
Taylor ends his trilogy with this book. Teetoncey has left for England, and at long last Ben leaves the Hatteras Banks for the seafaring life he has longed for. There are lots of local color and strong characterizations to add depth to this tale of two turn-of-the-century youngsters. Grades 5-9.

TAYLOR, Theodore (Tuck the Dog Series)
The Trouble with Tuck. Doubleday, 1981
Tuck Triumphant. Doubleday, 1990
Tuck is a golden Labrador who is going blind. Helen decides she must help him remain independent by getting him a seeing-eye companion. This is a heartwarming story for dog lovers ages 11-14.

THESMAN, Jean (The Whitney Cousins Trilogy)
Amelia. Avon, 1990
Erin. Avon, 1990
Heather. Avon, 1990
The Whitney Cousins know they can always count on each other. Although cousins by birth, they are friends by choice and they couldn't be happier with that decision. These three companion editions will be enjoyed by young adults from 14 years and up. The plots range from beginning a new life in a new town to what happens when you date the wrong boy.

THOMAS, Jane Resh
Comeback Dog. Houghton, 1981
Fox in a Trap. Houghton, 1987
Daniel is a child of today, growing up on his family's farm in Michigan. He finds the farm life increasingly stifling, as he dreams of wilderness adventure like his Uncle Pete. He does learn that excitement exacts a high price, and that all of life does not have to be lived "all or nothing." The illustrations indicate that Daniel may be eight or nine, but the underlying message is really more suitable for older readers, grades 5-8.

THOMAS, Joyce Carol
Marked by Fire. Avon, 1982
Bright Shadow. Avon, 1983
Water Girl. Avon, 1986
Readers are introduced to Abyssinia Jackson, Abby for short, in these three novels. She was born under a vast Oklahoma sky, but she and her family are all but destroyed when a tornado hits and drives her family apart. Abby must then stand up to the vengeful terror of her neighbors. In *Water Girl*, the saga continues through Amber Westbrook as she searches for the secret of her family's past. *Marked by Fire* received the American Book Award. These are three good books for teens.

THRASHER, Crystal

1—*The Dark Didn't Catch Me*. Atheneum, 1975
2—*Between Dark and Daylight*. Atheneum, 1979
3—*End of a Dark Road*. Atheneum, 1982
4—*Julie's Summer*. Atheneum, 1981
5—*A Taste of Daylight*. Atheneum, 1984

This series centers around the Robinson family and their life and trials during the Depression as they share trials and troubles as they cope to survive. In *Julie's Summer*, Seely's sister Julie decides to stay in her small town as her family moves on to find work. She wants to finish her last year of high school and go on to college to become a teacher. The final work in this series tells the reader of their father's death and their final move to the city. Grades 7 and up.

***THREE INVESTIGATORS** (Series)

ARDEN, William

24—*The Mystery of the Dancing Devil*. Random, 1976
25—*The Mystery of the Headless Horse*. Random, 1977
26—*The Mystery of the Deadly Double*. Random, 1978

CAREY, M. V.

27—*The Mystery of the Magic Circle*. Random, 1978
28—*The Mystery of the Sinister Scarecrow*. Random, 1979

ARDEN, William

29—*The Secret of Shark Reef*. Random, 1979

CAREY, M. V.

30—*The Mystery of the Death Trap Mine*. Random, 1980
31—*The Mystery of the Blazing Cliffs*. Random, 1981
32—*The Mystery of the Scar-Faced Beggar*. Random, 1981

ARDEN, William

33—*The Mystery of the Purple Pirate*. Random, 1982

CAREY, M. V.

34—*The Mystery of the Wandering Cave Man*. Random, 1982

BRANDEL, Marc

35—*The Mystery of the Kidnapped Whale*. Random, 1983

CAREY, M. V.

36—*The Mystery of the Missing Mermaid*. Random, 1983

BRANDEL, Marc

37—*The Mystery of the Two-Toed Pigeon*. Random, 1984

ARDEN, William

38—*The Mystery of the Smashing Glass*. Random, 1984

CAREY, M. V.

39—*The Mystery of the Trail of Terror*. Random, 1984

BRANDEL, Marc

40—*The Mystery of the Rogues' Reunion*. Random, 1985

CAREY, M. V.

41—*The Mystery of the Creep-Show Crooks*. Random, 1985

ARDEN, William

42—*The Mystery of Wreckers' Rock*. Random, 1986

CAREY, M. V.

43—*The Mystery of the Cranky Collector*. Random, 1987

Continuing with this popular series, the authors present plots that are simple, straightforward, easy to read, and far less exciting than the titles would lead one to believe. Readers are hooked, however, and these do appeal to reluctant readers. Grades 3-8.

THREE INVESTIGATORS CRIMEBUSTERS (Series)

ARDEN, William

1—*Hot Wheels*. Random, 1989

STINE, Megan, and **H. William STINE**

2—*Murder to Go*. Random, 1989

STONE, G. H.

3—*Rough Stuff*. Random, 1989

MCKAY, William

4—*Funny Business*. Random, 1989

BRANDEL, Marc

5—*An Ear for Danger*. Random, 1989

STINE, Megan, and **H. William STINE**

6—*Thriller Diller*. Random, 1989

STONE, G. H.

7—*Reel Trouble*. Random, 1989

MCKAY, William

8—*Shoot the Works*. Random, 1990

LERANGIS, Peter

9—*Foul Play*. Random, 1990

STINE, Megan, and **H. William STINE**

10—*Long Shot*. Random, 1990

STONE, G. H.

11—*Fatal Error*. Random, 1990

Intended for older readers than the original Three Investigator series, this one has the gang dealing with car thieves, rock bands, and drugs. They are easy reading, with a built-in audience. Readers of the Hardy Boys Case Files will also enjoy them. Ages 12 and up.

THREE INVESTIGATORS FIND YOUR FATE MYSTERIES (Series)

STINE, Megan, and **H. William STINE**

1—*The Case of the Weeping Coffin*. Random, 1985

ESTES, Rose

2—*The Case of the Dancing Dinosaur*. Random, 1985

STINE, Megan, and **H. William STINE**

3—*The Thundercats and the Ghost Warrior*. Random, 1985

4—*The Thundercats and the Snowmen of Hook Mountain*. Random, 1985

ESTES, Rose

5—*The Trail of Death*. Random, 1985

6—*The Mystery of the Turkish Tattoo*. Random, 1986

STINE, Megan, and **H. William STINE**

7—*The Case of the House of Horrors*. Random, 1986

CAREY, M. V.

8—*The Case of the Savage Statue*. Random, 1987

In order to jump on the popular Choose Your Own Adventure bandwagon, Random took their popular Three Investigators and put them in a series of adventures that allow the reader to participate in the plot development. Once again, these will prove popular to fans of both series and reluctant readers grades 4-7.

TIME TOURS (Series)

WU, William

1—*Robinhood Ambush*. Harper, 1991

BARON, Nick

2—*Glory's End*. Harper, 1991

DOYLE, Debra

3—*Time Crime, Inc.* Harper, 1991

SHADWELL, Thomas

4—*Dinosaur Trackers*. Harper, 1991

COX, Greg
5—*Pirate Paradise*. Harper, 1991
Written under the supervision of Robert Silverberg, this series is aimed at the 10-14 year old age group. It is filled with excitement, history and adventure. The setting is in the future when time travel has become possible. The teen characters travel back and forth through history on dates, vacations and errands. This is an original paperback series.

TOLAN, Stephanie S. (Skinner Family Series)
1—*The Great Skinner Strike*. Macmillan, 1983
2—*The Great Skinner Enterprise*. Puffin, 1988
3—*The Great Skinner Getaway*. Puffin, 1988
4—*The Great Skinner Homestead*. Four Winds, 1988
It all started when Mrs. Skinner decided that she had carried the family workload alone for too long. She went on strike, and the event caught not only neighborhood but also media attention. This adventure is followed by others, such as Mr. Skinner's foray into private enterprise after he loses his job. Entertainingly written, YAs will find themselves laughing in recognition of the Skinner children's activities and relationship with their parents.

TOLLES, Martha (Katie Series)
Katie for President. Scholastic, 1976
Katie's Babysitting Job. Scholastic, 1985
Katie and Those Boys. Scholastic, 1988
Katie is a middle schooler who deals with the usual problems: love, running for school office, and being accused of theft on her first sitting job. Nothing special, but paperback readers ages 8-12 will still read them.

TOLLES, Martha (Darci Series)
Who's Reading Darci's Diary? Scholastic, 1985
Darci and the Dance Contest. Scholastic, 1987
Darci in Cabin 13. Scholastic, 1989
This is a typical paperback series for girls: predictable plot, superficial characterizations, and easy-to-read text. Grades 4-6.

TRAVERS, P. L. (*Mary Poppins Series)
5—*Mary Poppins in Cherry Tree Lane*. Delacorte, 1982
6—*Mary Poppins and the House Next Door*. Delacorte, 1989
These latest additions to the classic Mary Poppins series lack some of the charm of the originals. The earlier books are meatier, with many charming stories; these are more like an extended short story. Only where patron demand exists. Grades 3-6.

UCHIDA, Yoshiko
Jar of Dreams. Atheneum, 1981
The Best Bad Thing. Atheneum, 1983
The Happiest Ending. Atheneum, 1985
Rinko's story begins with she and her family living in California. They face prejudice, but also have many good times, including Rinko's attempt to interfere in an arranged marriage between a Japanese girl and a Japanese-American older man. Grades 4-7.

UCHIDA, Yoshiko
Journey to Topaz. Scribner, 1971
Journey Home. Atheneum, 1978
Japanese-American author Uchida draws on her own childhood experiences when she and her family were removed to a Relocation Center in Utah. She describes how Yuki's family loses their property, their money, and their dignity in the forced move. Their return home is equally hard because they find distrust and prejudice awaiting them. These excellent books show readers what impact a little-discussed, shameful episode in American history had on a minority. Grades 4-7.

URE, Jean

See You Thursday. Delacorte, 1981
After Thursday. Delacorte, 1985

Mariann is a feisty and independent teen, so when her mother announces that she has rented the upstairs room to a blind man, she doesn't like the idea. Abe turns out to be an attractive and talented musician, and eventually she falls in love. He wants to be independent and pursue his music career so he leaves for a concert tour. Mariann is not interest in Peter, a friend who is interested in her, but she doesn't know if Abe will be back. These books are well done and are for grades 6-10.

VAIL, Virginia (Animal Inn)

1—*Pets Are for Keeps*. Scholastic, 1986
2—*A Kid's Best Friend*. Scholastic, 1986
3—*Monkey Business*. Scholastic, 1987
4—*Scaredy Cat*. Scholastic, 1987
5—*Adopt-a-Pet*. Scholastic, 1987
6—*All the Way Home*. Scholastic, 1987
7—*The Pet Makeover*. Scholastic, 1990
8—*Petnapped*. Scholastic, 1990
9—*One Dog Too Many*. Scholastic, 1990
10—*Parrot Fever*. Scholastic, 1990
11—*Oh Deer!* Scholastic, 1990
12—*Gift Horse*. Scholastic, 1991

As in other Scholastic series, a group of pre-teens have easy to read adventures centered around a theme, this one being the kennel run by Valentine Taylor and family, including her veterinarian father. Fun for animal lovers grades 4-6.

VANDER ELS, Betty

The Bomber's Moon. Farrar, 1985
Leaving Point. Farrar, 1987

Ruth and Simeon are the children of missionaries in China when the Japanese invade. They are shipped off to a boarding school where they stay for years. They are finally forced to leave China, but Ruth's friendship with a young revolutionary may jeopardize everything. Written more from an adult point of view than a child's. Grades 5-9.

VAN DE WETERING, Jan (Hugh Pine Series)

Hugh Pine. Houghton, 1980
Hugh Pine and the Good Place. Houghton, 1986
Hugh Pine and Something Else. Houghton, 1989

Hugh Pine is a large porcupine (4 feet tall) who lives with a small (5 feet tall) mailman named Mr. McTosh. The two whiskered fellows resemble one another, particularly since Hugh stands erect, wears clothes, and can speak quite a bit of human. These books chronicle their low-key adventures together. The Dr. Doolittle crowd will enjoy these. Grades 3-6.

VAN LEEUWEN, Jean (Benjy Series)

Benjy and the Power of Zingies. Dial, 1982
Benjy in Business. Dial, 1983
Benjy, the Football Hero. Dial, 1985

Benjy is an average third grader and his low-key adventures, like trying to earn enough money for a coveted baseball mitt, will have a mild appeal. Grades 3-6.

VAN LEEUWEN, Jean (*Marvin the Magnificent Series)

3—*The Great Rescue Operation*. Dial, 1982

Marvin and friends Fats and Raymond continue to live at Macy's in the toy department—a perfect home for mice. In this humorous series addition, trouble arises when the doll carriage Fats is napping in is sold and the others must rescue him. Good fun for fans 8-12.

VAN STEENWYCK, Elizabeth (Sports Mysteries)
1—*The Ghost in the Gym*. Childrens, 1983
2—*The Secret of the Spotted Horse*. Childrens, 1983
3—*The Southpaw from Sonora Mystery*. Childrens, 1983
4—*Terror on the Rebound*. Childrens, 1983
These are moderately entertaining mysteries with a sports setting. Team work and dedication are emphasized, and girls are presented in active sports roles in two of the books. Grades 3-6.

VARSITY COACH
HALLOWELL, Tommy
1—*Fourth and Goal*. Bantam, 1986
FRANKLIN, Lance
2—*Takedown*. Bantam, 1986
HALLOWELL, Tommy
3—*Out of Bounds*. Bantam, 1987
FRANKLIN, Lance
4—*Double Play*. Bantam, 1987
Dan Cronin is a busy man; he is the varsity coach for football, basketball, baseball, and wrestling at Kenmore High. In each of these books he helps a different star athlete cope with their problems (anything from injuries to divorcing parents). These are useful for the reluctant reader. Grades 7-10.

VIVELO, Jackie
Super Sleuth. Putnam, 1985
Beagle in Trouble. Putnam, 1986
Super Sleuth and the Bare Bones. Putnam, 1988
Much like Encyclopedia Brown, each book in this series contains 12 solve-it-yourself mysteries. The mysteries are short and readable, with a built-in clientele. Because the characters are seventh graders, older reluctant readers as well as readers ages 8-12 could enjoy them.

VOGEL, Ilse-Marget
1—*Dodo Every Day*. Harper, 1977
2—*Farewell, Aunt Isabell*. Harper, 1979
3—*My Twin Sister Erika*. Harper, 1976
4—*My Summer Brother*. Harper, 1981
5—*Tikhon*. Harper, 1984
These books are set in post-World War I Germany. Inge's world is full of uncertainty, although her warm family life shields her from some of it. There are serious themes here, as Inge must cope with the death of her twin, and faces another loss as her Russian soldier friend tries to find a way home. Grades 4-6.

VOIGT, Cynthia
Jackaroo. Atheneum, 1985
On Fortune's Wheel. Atheneum, 1990
Newbery Medal winner Voigt introduces her readers to the myth of the masked outlaw Jackaroo, a Robin Hood-like man. A young girl coming of age must overcome shock and betrayal to discover the truth behind the legend. Two generations later the reader meets Birle, an innkeeper's daughter, who would agree that Lady Fortune has a wheel and all men rise and fall with the turn of the wheel. She leaves her kingdom for the southern lands where fortune's wheel turns swiftly and dangerously. Both books are full of adventure and are well done. Ages 11 and up.

VOIGT, Cynthia (Tillerman Saga)
1—*Homecoming*. Atheneum, 1981
2—*Dicey's Song*. Atheneum, 1984

3—*Solitary Blue*. Atheneum, 1983
4—*Come a Stranger*. Atheneum, 1986
5—*Sons from Afar*. Atheneum, 1987
6—*17 Against the Dealer*. Atheneum, 1989

Dicey Tillerman, her sister and brothers have a problem. Their mother has abandoned them at a mall miles from home. The Tillerman Saga tells their moving story of survival and coming-of-age. These favorites are well written. *Dicey's Song* received the 1983 Newbery Medal. The series just needs to be visible to be read by young people in grades 6 and up.

WADDELL, Martin (Harriet Series)
Harriet and the Crocodiles. Minstrel, 1986
Harriet and the Haunted School. Minstrel, 1986
Harriet and the Robot. Minstrel, 1988

Harriet's bright ideas lead to plenty of trouble, like the time she decides to adopt a croc for a pet, or the time she hides a horse at school so her friend Anthea can learn to ride, or the time she creates a robot (and havoc) by building a robot for Anthea's birthday. These are funny choices for grades 2-4.

WALKER, Diana
The Year of the Horse. Abelard, 1975
Mother Wants a Horse. Abelard, 1978

Joanna eats, sleeps, and thinks horses continually. Over the course of a year she learns to ride well enough to qualify for a major competition. All her plans seem lost when she fails English and her father insists she spend the summer being tutored. A foolish ride leads to a serious fall and a major change in her life. Horse-lovers grades 5-9 will find these a plus with their mix of horse lore and romance.

WALLACE, Barbara (Claudia Series)
Hello, Claudia. Follett, 1982
Claudia and Duffy. Follett, 1982
Claudia. Follett, 1969

Claudia is a likeable tomboy who faces various growing up problems with her best friend, Duffy. Sometimes he is the problem, though, because he is so much younger and a boy. Claudia's mother keeps thinking he is not a proper playmate for her. Acceptable for grades 4-6.

WALLACE, Barbara (Hawkins Series)
The Contest Kid Strikes Again. Abingdon, 1980
Hawkins and the Soccer Solution. Abingdon, 1981

Harvey is the kind of kid who goes for anything free, regardless of what it is. That is how he acquires Hawkins, a valet. Hawkins turns out to be a great asset, for he is a man of many talents. There is lots of action here as the two get into and out of a number of scrapes. Grades 4-6.

WALLACE, Barbara (Miss Switch Series)
The Trouble with Miss Switch. Archway, 1981
Miss Switch to the Rescue. Abingdon, 1981

Kids may already be familiar with Miss Switch since she has become the star of two TV shows. She is supposed to be a teacher, but really turns out to be a good witch. There are lighthearted adventures aplenty for grades 4-6.

WALSH, Jill Paton
Goldengrove. Farrar, 1985
Unleaving. Avon, 1986

These excellent novels have been widely praised. Both center on Madge Fielding. The first finds her as a girl becoming involved with reading to a blind professor. The result is a loss of innocence for her. The second brings her as the heir to her grandmother's seaside home, first as a teenager, then returning many years later. She must once again deal with unsettling events as she learns to exercise her intellect with her peers, and yet must cope with the possibility that one of her new friends may have caused the death of his retarded sibling. For YAs.

WALTER, Mildred Pitts (Mariah Series)
Mariah Loves Rock. Bradbury, 1988
Mariah Keeps Cool. Bradbury, 1990

Mariah lives in the city. She is 11 and has the usual low-level problems: bossy big sister, making the team, half-sister coming to live with the family. More importantly she faces prejudice. Mariah is both likeable and believable, so readers grades 3-6 will care what happens to her.

WARNER, Gertrude Chandler (*Boxcar Children Series)
19—*Benny Uncovers a Mystery*. Whitman, 1976

The last of Warner's Alden Family series continues the mystery adventures of the children. Certainly ordinary enough fare, the easy vocabulary and straightforward plots, along with an attractive paperback format have combined to keep this series popular with a new generation of readers. Good for grades 3-6 and reluctant readers.

WEBB, Sharon (Earthsong Trilogy)
Earthchild. Atheneum, 1982
Earth Song. Atheneum, 1983
Ram Song. Atheneum, 1984

Kurt becomes a leader of the earth children after a scientific process makes them immortal. He is their minister of culture, but because of the immortality process, all creative thinking has ended. In order to change that effect the creative children must make a commitment to end their immortality. Finally, Kurt and his Starship Ram are called to help on the planet Aulos. A threat has developed at the edge of the universe. These are well written and enjoyable fantasy books. Grades 7-12.

WERSBA, Barbara
Fat: A Love Story. Harper, 1987
Love Is the Crooked Thing. Harper, 1987
Beautiful Losers. Harper, 1988

Rita is sixteen and weighs 200. She takes a job delivering cheesecakes for Arnold Bromberg. She begins to confide in him and discovers that he is intelligent, passionate, twice her age and in love with her. The feeling is mutual. When he moves to Europe she needs to come up with enough money to find him. When she does, she realizes he is a confirmed bachelor and returns home. Arnold returns to Rita to marry her. She is torn between her comfortable life with her family and her love for Arnold. Filled with humor, these will appeal to junior high and up.

WERSBA, Barbara
Just Be Gorgeous. Harper, 1988
Wonderful Me. Dell, 1991

Heidi Rosenbloom is a heroine a lot of teens can identify with: she is overweight, untalented, not particularly bright—and a disappointment to her parents. In the first book she is challenged by a dancer friend filled with ambition. In the second she gets her first job, and is the recipient of increasingly disturbing mash letters. These are well written, perceptive books for YAs.

WESTALL, Robert
The Machine Gunners. Greenwillow, 1976
Fathom Five. Greenwillow, 1979
The Haunting of Charles McGill. Greenwillow, 1983

In 1941 teenager Chas McGill comes across a German pilot that has been shot down in the woods near his town. The dead man is still holding his machine gun, a novelty for Chas who has been collecting bits and pieces of the war. He and his friends build an emplacement for the gun with the hopes of using it to shoot down German planes that are bombing his town. *Fathom Five* has Chas and his friends convinced that a Nazi spy is hiding in their village. The teens race against time to unmask the spy. The third has to do with the ghost of a World War I deserter. The first book won the Carnegie Medal in 1976 and its sequel was an SLJ Best Book of the Year. For 12 year olds and up.

WEYN, Suzanne (Bakers' Dozen)
Make Room for Patty. Scholastic, 1991
Hilary and the Rich Girl. Scholastic, 1991
This new series centers around the Baker family who have adopted eleven children of a variety of ages and ethnic backgrounds. The opener deals with the arrival of child #12, Patty, who finds that at least one of her possible siblings resents her arrival. This is a complex topic that is treated very superficially. For grades 2-4.

WEYN, Suzanne (Makeover Series)
The Makeover Club. Avon, 1986
The Makeover Summer. Avon, 1988
The Makeover Campaign. Avon, 1990
The makeover club was started to transform its members into the pretty, popular types they always wanted to be. Well, they succeed but are later "stuck" with the weird foreign exchange student, and they get involved with the "de-glamorizing" of a fellow friend who is running for class president. These are less than impressive: they advocate the stereotype that you must be pretty to be popular and successful in school. Grades 7-10.

WHITE, Ellen Emerson
Life without Friends. Scholastic, 1987
Friends for Life. Scholastic, 1983
The first entry is a tale of drugs, murder, and destruction wrought by Tim. In the second book we find out about Tim's girlfriend who also became a victim. She must come to terms with her involvement in Tim's murder spree. She receives understanding from Derek, but not without problems. Poignant and believable, these are for students in grades 7-10.

WHITE, Ellen Emerson
The President's Daughter. Avon, 1984
White House Autumn. Avon, 1985
Long Live the Queen. Scholastic, 1989
Meg happens to be the President's daughter. Not just any President, either. Her mother is the first female President of the United States. For that reason the pressures on Meg are strong to be a good role model and try to carry on a real life with a Secret Service bodyguard. Meg is an appealing heroine whose adventures will give readers some perspective on how troublesome life in the spotlight can be. Ages 12 and up.

WHITEHEAD, Victoria (Chimney Witches Series)
The Chimney Witches. Orchard, 1987
Chimney Witch Chase. Orchard, 1988
Set in England (and using silhouettes for illustration), this series follow two children on a series of adventures with the witches who live in their chimney. These are acceptable, but nothing special, for grades 4-6.

WIBBERLY, Leonard (*Treegate Family Saga)
7—*The Last Battle*. Farrar, 1976
This brings to an end the story that began during the Revolutionary War. The final book is set at the battle of Tippecanoe. Good historical fiction for YAs.

WILKINSON, Brenda (Ludell Series)
Ludell. Harper, 1975
Ludell and Willie. Harper, 1977
Ludell's New York Time. Harper, 1980
Ludell is a young black girl growing up in Georgia in the mid-50s. The first book was an ALA Best of the Best for YAs. She is experiencing events with her family that are going to have an affect on the plans that she and beau Willie have made for the future. The relationship between those two is believable and well written. In the end Ludell's grandmother has died and so she moves to Harlem to plan her wedding. Meanwhile, Willie is busy with family problems in Georgia. Good for YAs.

WILLARD, Nancy
Sailing to Cythera. Harcourt, 1974
The Island of the Grass King. Harcourt, 1979
Uncle Terrible. Harcourt, 1982
Veteran fantasy writer Willard has concocted a special treat. This trilogy follows the adventures of young Anatole, who eventually winds up involved in a struggle against the power of an evil wizard. For fantasy lovers grades 5-8.

WILLIAMS, Barbara (Mitzi Series)
Mitzi and the Terrible Tyrannosaurus Rex. Dutton, 1982
Mitzi's Honeymoon with Nana Potts. Dutton, 1983
Mitzi and Frederick the Great. Dutton, 1984
Mitzi and the Elephants. Dutton, 1985
Eight year old Mitzi is not at all sure she wants to be part of a blended family that includes a brainy older stepbrother and a three year old who thinks he is a dinosaur. Among her easy to enjoy adventures are a summer on an archaeological dig and trying to convince her parents that a St. Bernard puppy is *the* perfect addition to their family. Grades 4-6.

WILLIAMS, Jay, and **Raymond ABRASHKIN** (*Danny Dunn Series)
15—*Danny Dunn and the Universal Glue*. McGraw, 1977
Danny's last adventure finds the boy inventor and his friends trying out his latest creation: a superglue. He winds up using it to combat nearby water pollution. Like the others, this one has a resourceful hero with a scientific (and earth-conscious) bent that could make using intelligence an appealing proposition. Grades 3-6.

WINTHROP, Elizabeth (Miranda Series)
Marathon Miranda. Puffin, 1990
Miranda in the Middle. Puffin, 1990
Miranda meets her friend Phoebe while both of them train to run a marathon. She even acts as cupid between her grandfather and a neighbor. All of this catches up with her when she finds herself caught in the middle of these relationships, acting as go-between. She is a conscientious girl, with all the uncertainties that twelve year olds face. For ages 8-12.

WISLER, G. Clifton
The Antrian Messenger. Lodestar, 1986
The Seer. Lodestar, 1989
The Mind Trap. Lodestar, 1990
Scott Childers thinks he is just unusually bright until the day he sees an exploding star through a telescope that no one else sees and hears a whispered message that no one else does. When his dreams begin to come true, he gets really frightened. His further adventures find him fighting a doctor doing mind experiments. This sci-fi/fantasy series will appeal to YAs.

WISLER, G. Clifton

Buffalo Moon. Lodestar, 1984

Thunder on the Tennessee. Lodestar, 1983

Set around the time of the Civil War, a fourteen year old leaves his Texas ranch to spend some time with the Comanche Indians. Two years later he joins the Second Texas Regiment along with his father to fight the Yankees. He thinks war is glamorous until he sees its brutal reality. These books bring the reality of the Civil War home to the young reader. These are wonderfully written. Grades 6-10.

WOJCIECHOWSKI, Susan

Patty Dillman of Hot Dog Fame. Orchard, 1989

And the Other, Gold. Orchard, 1987

In the first of these two related books, thirteen year old Patty is assigned a project to perform a work of mercy; so, she tags along with her mother to a soup kitchen. Wojciechowski nicely handles the homeless issue in this book which ends up with Patty having performed a heartfelt work of mercy. In the companion novel Patty enters St. Ignatius High School and finds her first love. Judy Blume fans will enjoy these two books about friendship and families that were written for junior high school students.

WOLFE, L. E. (Jack B. Quick, Sports Detective)

1—*The Case of the Basketball Joker*. Sports Illustrated, 1990

2—*The Case of the Missing Playbook*. Sports Illustrated, 1990

3—*The Tour de Tricks*. Sports Illustrated, 1991

4—*The Case of the Sneaker Snatcher*. Sports Illustrated, 1991

Jack is a detective who limits his investigations to sports mysteries. There is a lot of sports byplay here—these read like a newspaper replay of a game. This quality may attract sports fans—or turn them off. Grades 4-6.

WRIGHT, Betty Ren

The Secret Window. Holiday, 1982

A Ghost in the Window. Holiday, 1987

Meg is troubled by dreams. Sometimes they are pleasant, sometimes they are nightmares. But whatever form they take, they always come true. Meg is afraid of her gift and afraid of being different from her friends. She has family problems as well with the breakup of her parents' marriage. Wright is a popular author in paranormal fiction. For grades 4-7.

WRIGHTSON, Patricia

1—*Nargun and the Stars*. Atheneum, 1974

2—*Ice Is Coming*. Atheneum, 1977

3—*Dark Bright Water*. Atheneum, 1978

4—*Journey behind the Wind*. Atheneum, 1981

Set in Australia, Simon Brett and his cousins are trying to save their family from the Nargun, a creature that is almost indistinguishable from the earth. It is killing the local wildlife and is threatening humans. Wirrun is a young aborigine who also battles the Nargun and its people. He also helps save Australia from other strange events and creatures. Grades 6-10.

WYETH, Sharon Dennis (Annie K's Theater)

Dinosaur Tooth. Bantam, 1990

Ghost Show. Bantam, 1990

Chicken Pox Party. Bantam, 1990

In this series aimed at grades 2-4, Annie K and her friends run into problems as they plan and rehearse plays. An added bonus is the script for the play in question, which is included at the end of each book, in case readers would like to perform it as well.

WYETH, Sharon Dennis (Pen Pals Series)
1–*Boys Wanted*. Dell, 1989
2–*Too Cute for Words*. Dell, 1989
3–*P.S. Forget It*. Dell, 1989
4–*No Creeps Need Apply*. Dell, 1989
5–*Sam the Sham*. Dell, 1989
6–*Amy's Song*. Dell, 1990
7–*Handle with Care*. Dell, 1990
8–*Sealed with a Kiss*. Dell, 1990
9–*Stolen Pen Pals*. Dell, 1990
10–*Palmer at Your Service*. Dell, 1990
11–*Roommate Trouble*. Dell, 1990
12–*Lisa's Secret*. Dell, 1990
13–*Lisa, We Miss You*. Dell, 1990
14–*The Mystery about Maxie*. Dell, 1990
15–*The Heartbreak Guy*. Dell, 1991
16–*Boy Crazy*. Dell, 1991
17–*The Boy Project*. Dell, 1991
18–*Double Date*. Dell, 1991
Another group of girlfriends, paperback style. This bunch shares a suite at a boarding school and their problems are the usual: boys and friends. Grades 4-6.

YEP, Laurence
Dragon of the Lost Sea. Harper, 1982
Dragon Steel. Harper, 1985
These two books weave Chinese legend into a tapestry of myth and folklore. Shimmer is a renegade dragon princess and in order to redeem herself she must capture an evil witch. However she can't do it alone so she must, despite her feelings towards humans, have help from a young boy she rescued. In the follow up, she and Thorn must continue their quest in order to restore Skimmer's clan to their ancestral home. The first book was an ALA Notable. Grades 7-10.

YEP, Laurence
The Serpent's Children. Harper, 1984
Mountain Light. Harper, 1985
Set in 19th century China, Cassia must fight against famine and poverty while her father trains her and her brother to fight for freedom from Manchu and British occupation. In the sequel Cassia falls in love with Squeaky Lau during their flight from a failed rebellion. But Squeaky needs to prove himself a man so he leaves for California to make his fortune. An interesting look at the culture of the mid-1800s Chinese. Junior high and up.

YOLEN, Jane (Pit Dragon Trilogy)
Dragon's Blood. Delacorte, 1982
Heart's Blood. Delacorte, 1984
Sending of Dragons. Delacorte, 1987
This trilogy focuses on Jaklah who has few choices in life: he can spend his life in bondage as a dragon trainer or he can get his own dragon and become free. In order to ensure his freedom he must steal a dragon hatchling and secretly train it in the desert, using his telepathic powers to communicate with it. He is successful, so he and the dragon, Heart's Blood, set off on their own adventures. Later he is accused of sabotage and is exiled to a distant planet. These are highly recommended fantasy novels for YAs.

ZINDEL, Paul (Pigman Series)
The Pigman. Harper, 1968
The Pigman's Legacy. Harper, 1980
These two books are musts for any library collection. The classic, *The Pigman*, was an ALA Best for Young Adults in 1975. It makes an excellent choice for a book discussion group. In the sequel, John and Lorraine discover the essence of the Pigman and his legacy. Readers ages 13 and up will enjoy these.

Non-Fiction Series

ACHIEVERS (Series)
AASENG, Nathan
Bob Dylan: Spellbinding Songwriter. Lerner, 1987
AYRES, Carter M.
Chuck Yeager: Fighter Pilot. Lerner, 1988
CHADWICK, Roxane
Amelia Earhart: Aviation Pioneer. Lerner, 1987
Anne Morrow Lindbergh: Pilot and Poet. Lerner, 1987
ERLANGER, Ellen
Isaac Asimov: Scientist and Storyteller. Lerner, 1986
Jane Fonda: More Than a Movie Star. Lerner, 1984
WESTMAN, Paul
Neil Armstrong: Space Pioneer. Lerner, 1980

A lot of the emphasis here seems to be on biographies of flight-oriented people, with a few entertainment figures thrown in. They are very well done, with good, easy to read background information that tries to explain the personality as well as the exploits. Good photos add to the appeal. Grades 4-7. No index.

ADVENTURE SPORTS
HALL, Jackie, and **David JEFFERIS**
Skiing and Snow Sports. Watts, 1990
JAY, Michael
Camping and Orienteering. Watts, 1990
Swimming and Scuba Diving. Watts, 1990
JEFFERIS, David
Trail Bikes and Motocross. Watts, 1990

Each of these high appeal sports gets the once-over with colorful illustrations that will beguile enthusiasts and ensnare neophytes. The background of each sport is presented, along with information on training, equipment maintenance, competition, and related skills. There is a glossary and an index. The authors emphasize sport safety. Grades 4-8.

ALL ABOUT
LAMBERT, David
The Age of Dinosaurs. Random, 1987
MAYNARD, Christopher
The Great Ice Age. Random, 1987
ROWLAND-ENTWISTLE, Theodore
Animal Homes. Random, 1987
Animal Journeys. Random, 1987

RUTLAND, Jonathan

The Age of Steam. Random, 1987
Built to Speed. Random, 1987
Knights and Castles. Random, 1987
The Planets. Random, 1987
UFO's. Random, 1987
The Violent Earth. Random, 1987

TUNNEY, Christopher

Midnight Animals. Random, 1987

WILLIAMS, Brian

War and Weapons. Random, 1987

These books are brief overviews of the subjects for grades 2-5. One topic is covered in a boxed format on each page, accompanied by illustrations that take as much room as the text. These books are fine for introductory or pleasure reading, but do not really provide enough material for school assignments.

ALTERNATIVES TO COLLEGE

ABRAMS, Kathleen S.

Guide to Careers without College. Watts, 1988

DUBROVIN, Vivian

Guide to Alternative Education and Training. Watts, 1988

PERRY, Robert L.

Guide to Self-Employment. Watts, 1989

"Should I go to college?", "Can I have a career without going to college?", "What else is available?" These questions and more are discussed in the three books in this series. Simply written, they provide a great deal of information about careers, job training and other choices for students who are not planning to attend college. The books are illustrated, indexed, and offer suggested readings for those needing more information. Grades 9-12.

ALVIN JOSEPHY'S BIOGRAPHY SERIES OF AMERICAN INDIANS

BLACK, Sheila

Sitting Bull. Silver, 1989

CWIKLIK, Robert

King Philip. Silver, 1989
Sequoyah. Silver, 1989

MCCLARD, Megan

Hiawatha. Silver, 1989

SHORTO, Russell

Geronimo. Silver, 1989
Tecumseh. Silver, 1989

Students can certainly use more information on Indians and this paperback series with line drawings and occasional photo reproductions could prove a boon. These are written for grades 5-9, and there is little available on this age level. A big caveat, however: the texts refer to emotional responses and conversations without any source material cited as a basis for these interpretations. Bibliography, no index.

AMAZING ANIMAL FACTS

MCDONNELL, Janet

Animal Builders. Childrens, 1989
Animal Camouflage. Childrens, 1989
Animal Communication. Childrens, 1989
Animal Migration. Childrens, 1989

For those budding young scientists who would like to find out more about how various species of animals communicate, migrate, etc., this series could hit the spot. There is not, however, enough information on individual animals to serve as a basis for school assignments. For collections with science browsers grades 2-5.

AMAZING SCIENCE

PEARCE, Q. L.

Armadillos and Other Unusual Animals. Messner, 1989
Killer Whales and Other Frozen World Wonders. Messner, 1991
Lightning and Other Wonders of the Sky. Messner, 1989
Piranhas and Other Wonders of the Jungle. Messner, 1990
Quicksand and Other Earthly Wonders. Messner, 1989
Saber-Toothed Cats and Other Prehistoric Wonders. Messner, 1991
Tidal Waves and Other Ocean Wonders. Messner, 1989
Tyrannosaurus Rex and Other Dinosaur Wonders. Messner, 1990

The titles in this series are a bit misleading. The books actually begin by describing how the planet may have evolved. Then a page is spent on each of a variety of related topics, with a color illustration on the opposite page. The misleading part is the "other wonders," which may include animal life, plant life, natural phenomenon, weather, pollution, and alien life! So do not buy these expecting a compendium of information on lightning and storms, for example. There will be many other loosely related, lightly covered topics. The books would be better served with photos than the unrealistic drawings that are used. Bibliography, index. Ages 9-12.

AMERICA THE BEAUTIFUL

CARSON, Robert

Mississippi. Childrens, 1988

GREEN, Carl, and **William SANFORD**

Missouri. Childrens, 1989

HARGROVE, James

Nebraska. Childrens, 1988

HARRINGTON, Ty

Maine. Childrens, 1989

HEINRICHS, Ann

Alaska. Childrens, 1990
Arizona. Childrens, 1991
Arkansas. Childrens, 1989
Montana. Childrens, 1991
Oklahoma. Childrens, 1988
Rhode Island. Childrens, 1990

HERGUTH, Margaret S.

North Dakota. Childrens, 1990

KENT, Deborah

Colorado. Childrens, 1988
Connecticut. Childrens, 1989
Delaware. Childrens, 1991
Iowa. Childrens, 1991
Louisiana. Childrens, 1988
Maryland. Childrens, 1990
Massachusetts. Childrens, 1987
New Jersey. Childrens, 1987
Ohio. Childrens, 1989
Pennsylvania. Childrens, 1988
South Carolina. Childrens, 1989
Washington, D.C. Childrens, 1990

KENT, Zachary

Georgia. Childrens, 1988
Idaho. Childrens, 1990
Kansas. Childrens, 1990

LEPTHIEN, Emilie U.

South Dakota. Childrens, 1991

LILLEGARD, Dee
Nevada. Childrens, 1990
MCCARTHY, Betty
Utah. Childrens, 1989
MCNAIR, Sylvia
Alabama. Childrens, 1988
Hawaii. Childrens, 1989
Kentucky. Childrens, 1988
Tennessee. Childrens, 1990
Vermont. Childrens, 1991
Virginia. Childrens, 1989
STEIN, R. Conrad
California. Childrens, 1988
Illinois. Childrens, 1987
Indiana. Childrens, 1990
Michigan. Childrens, 1987
Minnesota. Childrens, 1990
New Mexico. Childrens, 1988
New York. Childrens, 1988
North Carolina. Childrens, 1989
Oregon. Childrens, 1989
Texas. Childrens, 1989
West Virginia. Childrens, 1990
Wisconsin. Childrens, 1987
STONE, Lynn M.
Florida. Childrens, 1987

Although it resembles Childrens' Enchantment of America Series, there are some major differences. To begin with, it is more up to date than the Carpenter books. The photos are in color, and half of the text is devoted to the history of each state. The other half handles the basics on current government, economy, etc. Major cities and regional areas are described and the "Facts at a Glance" section cumulates all the important data in one spot for students. An excellent choice for grades 4-12.

AMERICAN DREAM
BARNES, Jeremy
Samuel Goldwyn. Silver, 1989
BOWMAN, John S.
Andrew Carnegie. Silver, 1989
FRAZIER, Nancy
William Randolph Hearst. Silver, 1989
GLASSMAN, Bruce
J. P. Getty. Silver, 1989
SOUKER, Nancy
Elizabeth Arden. Silver, 1989
John D. Rockefeller. Silver, 1989

This is a series of biographies of important American entrepreneurs. Each book takes a look at the subject's life from childhood through their later years. Each book discusses major historical events and the economics of the time that allowed these people to live the American dream from rags-to-riches. The series is well researched and includes many illustrations as well as a bibliography and index. Grades 7-10.

AMERICAN HISTORY SERIES FOR YOUNG PEOPLE

BRADY, Philip
Reluctant Hero. Walker, 1990
COSNER, Shaaron
War Nurses. Walker, 1990
COOPER, Kay
Where Did You Get Those Eyes? Walker, 1988
FLEMING, Thomas
Band of Brothers. Walker, 1987
Behind the Headlines. Walker, 1989
GREENE, Jacqueline Dembar
The Leveller. Walker, 1984
HANSEN, Joyce
Out from This Place. Walker, 1988
Which Way Freedom. Walker, 1986
MCCALL, Edith
Better Than a Brother. Walker, 1988
Message from the Mountains. Walker, 1985
Mississippi Steamboatman. Walker, 1986
MCKISSACK, Patricia, and **Fredrick MCKISSACK**
A Long Hard Journey. Walker, 1989
MARKO, Katherine McGlade
Away to Fundy Bay. Walker, 1985
MARSTON, Elsa
Mysteries in American Archaeology. Walker, 1986
SIEGEL, Beatrice
A New Look at the Pilgrims. Walker, 1977
WARMSER, Richard
Allan Pinkerton, America's First Private Eye. Walker, 1990

Walker's series studies little-known stories in American history. One book examines the labor history of Pullman porters, while another describes what motivated the Pilgrims to emigrate; still another, unexplained mysteries in American archaeology. There are many photos and a generous, almost oversize format that makes the books visually appealing. The subjects covered are not usually in the curriculum, so these books would be supplementary additions to history collections for grades 5-12.

AMERICAN HISTORY TOPIC BOOKS

MORRIS, Richard B.
The American Revolution. Lerner, 1985
The Constitution. Lerner, 1985
The Founding of the Republic. Lerner, 1985
The Indian Wars. Lerner, 1985
The War of 1812. Lerner, 1985

Morris is an outstanding historian who manages in a conversational tone to relate the underlying causes of these important events, then describe the event itself, ending with a discussion of its importance both then and now. The only drawback is the rather unappealing blue-and-black illustrations, which are neither realistic, impressionistic nor of the period. Grades 4-8. Index.

AMERICAN WOMEN OF ACHIEVEMENT

BERGMAN, Carol
Mae West. Chelsea, 1988

BERRY, Michael
Georgia O'Keeffe. Chelsea, 1989

BIRACREE, Tom
Althea Gibson. Chelsea, 1989
Wilma Rudolph. Chelsea, 1988

BLAU, Justine
Betty Friedan. Chelsea, 1990

BROWN, Jordan
Elizabeth Blackwell. Chelsea, 1989

CAIN, Michael
Louise Nevelson. Chelsea, 1989
Mary Cassatt. Chelsea, 1989

DAFFRON, Caroline
Edna St. Vincent Millay. Chelsea, 1990
Gloria Steinem. Chelsea, 1987
Margaret Bourke-White. Chelsea, 1988

EHRLICH, Elizabeth
Nellie Bly. Chelsea, 1989

HAMILTON, Leni
Clara Barton. Chelsea, 1989

HUBER, Peter
Sandra Day O'Connor. Chelsea, 1990

ILGENFRITZ, Elizabeth
Anne Hutchinson. Chelsea, 1991

JACKOUBEK, Robert
Harriet Beecher Stowe. Chelsea, 1989

JAMES, Cary
Julia Morgan. Chelsea, 1990

JEZER, Marty
Rachel Carson. Chelsea, 1988

JONES, Constance
Karen Horney. Chelsea, 1989

KENT, Charlotte
Barbara McClintock. Chelsea, 1991

KITTREDGE, Mary
Helen Hayes. Chelsea, 1990
Jane Addams. Chelsea, 1988

KOZODAY, Ruth
Isadora Duncan. Chelsea, 1988

KRONSTADT, Janet
Florence Sabin. Chelsea, 1990

LAFARGE, Ann
Gertrude Stein. Chelsea, 1988
Pearl Buck. Chelsea, 1988

LATHAM, Caroline
Katharine Hepburn. Chelsea, 1987

LEACH, William
Edith Wharton. Chelsea, 1988

LEFER, Diane
Emma Lazarus. Chelsea, 1988

LYNN, Elizabeth
Babe Didrikson Zaharias. Chelsea, 1988

LYONS, Joseph
Clare Booth Luce. Chelsea, 1988
PAOLUCCI, Bridget
Beverly Sills. Chelsea, 1990
OLSEN, Victoria
Emily Dickinson. Chelsea, 1990
OSBORNE, Angela
Abigail Adams. Chelsea, 1989
RICHMOND, M. A.
Phillis Wheatley. Chelsea, 1988
SHORE, Nancy
Amelia Earhart. Chelsea, 1987
SMITH, Louise
Mary Baker Eddy. Chelsea, 1990
TEDARDS, Anne
Marian Anderson. Chelsea, 1989
THORLIEFSON, Alex
Ethel Barrymore. Chelsea, 1990
TOMPKINS, Nancy
Grandma Moses. Chelsea, 1989
TOOR, Rachel
Eleanor Roosevelt. Chelsea, 1989
TOWNS, Saundra
Lillian Hellman. Chelsea, 1989
WALDSTREICHER, David
Emma Goldman. Chelsea, 1990
WEISBERG, Barbara
Susan B. Anthony. Chelsea, 1988
WEPMAN, Dennis
Helen Keller. Chelsea, 1987
WOLFE, Charles
Mahalia Jackson. Chelsea, 1990
YUAN, Margaret S.
Agnes de Mille. Chelsea, 1990
ZIESK, Edra
Margaret Mead. Chelsea, 1990

A number of these titles have won awards for their content, research and approach to the individual's life and impact on American society. All are well illustrated and include a bibliography and index. While many of these people have already been written about, these clear, concise, well documented books make an excellent choice. They are well written and would be an excellent addition to a library's biography collection. Grades 6 and up.

AMES DRAWING BOOKS

AMES, Lee J.
Draw 50 Airplanes, Aircraft & Spacecraft. Doubleday, 1977
Draw 50 Animals. Doubleday, 1974
Draw 50 Athletes. Doubleday, 1985
Draw 50 Beasties. Doubleday, 1990
Draw 50 Boats, Ships, Trucks & Trains. Doubleday, 1976
Draw 50 Buildings & Other Structures. Doubleday, 1980
Draw 50 Cars, Trucks & Motorcycles. Doubleday, 1986
Draw 50 Cats. Doubleday, 1986
Draw 50 Creepy Crawlies. Doubleday, 1991
Draw 50 Dinosaurs & Other Prehistoric Animals. Doubleday, 1985
Draw 50 Dogs. Doubleday, 1981
Draw 50 Famous Cartoons. Doubleday, 1979

Draw 50 Famous Faces. Doubleday, 1978
Draw 50 Famous Stars. Doubleday, 1982
Draw 50 Holiday Decorations. Doubleday, 1990
Draw 50 Horses. Doubleday, 1984
Draw 50 Monsters, Creeps, Superheroes, Demons, Dragons, Nerds, Dirts, Ghouls, Giants, Vampires, Zombies, & Other Curiosa. Doubleday, 1983
Draw 50 Vehicles. Doubleday, 1978
How to Draw Star Heroes, Creatures, Spaceships & Other Fantastic Things. Doubleday, 1984

Available in both paperback and hardback, this outstanding series shows how to draw a wide variey of subjects step-by-step. Drawing books are highly popular and these are excellent choices for grades 2 and up

ANCIENT WORLD

ODIJK, Pamela

The Aztecs. Silver, 1990
The Egyptians. Silver, 1990
The Greeks. Silver, 1990
The Incas. Silver, 1990
The Israelites. Silver, 1990
The Mayas. Silver, 1990
The Phoenicians. Silver, 1990
The Romans. Silver, 1990
The Sumerians. Silver, 1990
The Vikings. Silver, 1990

These attractively produced oversize books will fill requests for information on ancient civilizations. Beginning with a timeline, she discusses the impact of landforms and climate on the development of each group. The economy, family life, culture, and ultimate decline are also examined. A section of brief biographies of famous people is appended. Grades 4-9. Glossary, index.

ANIMAL FRIENDS

ANDERS, Rebecca

Ali Desert Fox. Carolrhoda, 1977
Clover the Calf. Carolrhoda, 1977
Dolly the Donkey. Carolrhoda, 1976
Lorito the Parrot. Carolrhoda, 1976

JOHNSON, Sylvia A.

Downy the Duckling. Carolrhoda, 1976
The Lions of Africa. Carolrhoda, 1977
Penelope the Tortoise. Carolrhoda, 1976

OVERBECK, Cynthia

Curly the Piglet. Carolrhoda, 1976
Rusty the Irish Setter. Carolrhoda, 1977
Tanya the Turtledove. Carolrhoda, 1977
Tippy the Fox Terrier. Carolrhoda, 1976

PURSELL, Margaret Sanford

Jessie the Chicken. Carolrhoda, 1977
Polly the Guinea Pig. Carolrhoda, 1977
Shelley the Seagull. Carolrhoda, 1977
Sprig the Tree Frog. Carolrhoda, 1976

Written in a conversational style, this series introduces children to animals from the day they are born. These animals are pets, so their young owners are told how to handle them. The books also tell how the animals develop. There are two pages of animal facts at the end. These will be a nice introduction for preschool to grade 3.

ANIMAL KINGDOM

PENNY, Malcolm

Animal Adaptations. Watts, 1989
Animal Camouflage. Watts, 1988
Animal Defenses. Watts, 1988
Animal Evolution. Watts, 1987
Animal Homes. Watts, 1987
Animal Migration. Watts, 1987
Animal Movement. Watts, 1988
Animal Partnerships. Watts, 1989
Animal Reproduction. Watts, 1988
Animal Signals. Watts, 1989
Endangered Animals. Watts, 1988
The Food Chain. Watts, 1988
Hunting and Stalking. Watts, 1988

A wide variety of animal behaviors are explored in this series. Each book shows how different animals accomplish migration, signaling, etc. Watts's usual excellent illustrations add to the value, and the authors provide bibliographies and glossaries. For student purposes, however, these titles do not go into much detail on individual creatures; these will be helpful primarily where assignments relate to general animal behavior. Grades 5-8.

ANIMAL LIVES

FEDER, Jan

The Life of a Cat. Childrens, 1982
The Life of a Dog. Childrens, 1982
The Life of a Hamster. Childrens, 1982
The Life of a Rabbit. Childrens, 1982

Each book begins with a story about the animal, complete with color illustrations. The plot follows the animal's habits right down to the rearing of the young. The second half of the book is nonfiction, with facts including a brief history, anatomy, species, habits, and interesting facts. While the stories are bland, the informational section will capture pet lovers grades 2-4. These will best be used as nonfiction.

ANIMAL WORLD

BAILEY, Donna

Bears. Steck, 1990
Butterflies. Steck, 1990
Snakes. Steck, 1990

BUTTERWORTH, Christine

Eagles. Steck, 1990
Frogs. Steck, 1990
Kangaroos. Steck, 1990

BUTTERWORTH, Christine, and **Donna BAILEY**

Alligators. Steck, 1990
Chimpanzees. Steck, 1990
Crabs. Steck, 1990
Deer. Steck, 1990
Foxes. Steck, 1990
Owls. Steck, 1990

POTTER, Tessa

Cows. Steck, 1990
Donkeys. Steck, 1990
Ducks and Geese. Steck, 1990
Goats. Steck, 1990
Hens. Steck, 1990
Sheep. Steck, 1990

Like the New True Books, these introduce the youngest readers to basics about animals. Each page features a color photo, along with two or three sentences of explanation. Grades K-3. Index.

ANIMALS IN THE WILD

HOFFMAN, Mary

Antelope. Raintree, 1987
Bear. Raintree, 1986
Bird of Prey. Raintree, 1987
Elephant. Raintree, 1984
Giraffe. Raintree, 1986
Gorilla. Raintree, 1985
Hippopotamus. Raintree, 1985
Lion. Raintree, 1985
Monkey. Raintree, 1984
Panda. Raintree, 1985
Penguin. Raintree, 1985
Seal. Raintree, 1987
Snake. Raintree, 1988
Tiger. Raintree, 1984
Wild Cat. Raintree, 1986
Zebra. Raintree, 1985

SERVENTY, Vincent

Crocodile and Alligator. Raintree, 1985
Kangaroo. Raintree, 1985
Koala. Raintree, 1975
Kookaburra. Raintree, 1985
Lizard. Raintree, 1986
Parrot. Raintree, 1986
Shark and Ray. Raintree, 1985
Turtle and Tortoise. Raintree, 1985
Whale and Dolphin. Raintree, 1985
Wild Dog. Raintree, 1986

Like the New True Books, this series is aimed at the youngest readers, K-3, and furnish the basics about each animal in easy to read sentences. A color photo decorates each page. No glossary or index.

ARNOLD, Caroline

Cheetah. Morrow, 1989
Giraffe. Morrow, 1987
Hippo. Morrow, 1989
Kangaroo. Morrow, 1987
Koala. Morrow, 1987
Llama. Morrow, 1988
Orangutan. Morrow, 1990
Penguin. Morrow, 1988
Wild Goat. Morrow, 1990
Zebra. Morrow, 1987

These charming books tell all about each animal: its origin, physical and mating characteristics, and behavior. Each animal profiled has been observed in a zoo, and so there is a personal touch with information shared about specific residents. The color photos by Richard Hewitt add a lot. Excellent choices for grades 4-7. Index.

ARNOSKY, Jim
Sketching Outdoors in Autumn. Lothrop, 1988
Sketching Outdoors in Spring. Lothrop, 1987
Sketching Outdoors in Summer. Lothrop, 1988
Sketching Outdoors in Winter. Lothrop, 1988
These four books from well-known artist Jim Arnosky are wonderful. He encourages artists, beginners, and the more experienced to explore outdoors throughout the year. Included in the books are many of his illustrations and he explains how to do what he did. He also offers advice on how to sketch outdoors in all types of weather and conditions. These books are great to just look at but are written for grades 5 and up and attempt to inspire an appreciation of nature.

AROUND THE YEAR
DELLINGER, Annetta
Creative Games for Young Children. Childrens, 1986
FOSTER, Betty
Creative Science for Young Children. Childrens, 1988
HOLZBAUER, Beth
Creative Crafts for Young Children. Childrens, 1986
TOWNSEND, Lucy, and **Jane Belk MONCURE**
Creative Dramatics for Young Children. Childrens, 1986
Although the publisher lists these as teacher resource books, the crafts, experiments, skits, and games included could certainly be used by parents, day care providers, and youngsters themselves on their own. For this reason the series is included. They are usable for children on the elementary level.

ARTS
BLACKWOOD, Alan
Music. Steck-Vaughn, 1990
CUMMING, David
Photography. Steck-Vaughn, 1990
HUNTER, Nigel
The Movies. Steck-Vaughn, 1990
LOXTON, Howard
Theater. Steck-Vaughn, 1990
MCDERMOTT, Catherine
Design. Steck-Vaughn, 1990
POWELL, Jillian
Painting and Sculpture. Steck-Vaughn, 1990
VAN ZANDT, Eleanor
Architecture. Steck-Vaughn, 1990
Dance. Steck-Vaughn, 1990
WILLIAMS, Brian
Literature. Steck-Vaughn, 1990
The authors trace the development of various art forms through history and world-wide variations. Famous practitioners and current developments are touched upon. Glossary, bibliography, index. Grades 5-12.

ASIMOV, Isaac (Isaac Asimov's Library of the Universe)
Ancient Astronomy. Dell, 1988
Did Comets Kill the Dinosaurs? Dell, 1987
Is There Life on Other Planets? Dell, 1989
Quasars, Pulsars, and Black Holes. Dell, 1988
Rockets, Probes, and Satellites. Dell, 1988
Science Fiction, Science Fact. Dell, 1989

The Space Spotter's Guide. Dell, 1988
Unidentified Flying Objects. Dell, 1988
These books are simplistic "what if..." explorations of various aspects of space. Less than a page of large print in each slender volume is spent on each topic, with large color illustrations accompanying. There is very little information here; additional purchase only. Grades 3-5. Bibliography, glossary, index.

AT RISK
DICK, Jean
Bomb Squads and SWAT Teams. Crestwood, 1988
DUDEN, Jane
Animal Handlers and Trainers. Crestwood, 1989
GOODMAN, Michael
Astronauts. Crestwood, 1989
HARRIS, Jack C.
Test Pilots. Crestwood, 1989
KERAN, Shirley
Underwater Specialists. Crestwood, 1988
LORD, Suzanne
Drug Enforcement Agents. Crestwood, 1989
NIELSEN, Nancy
Helicopter Pilots. Crestwood, 1988
STEWART, Gail
Coal Miners. Crestwood, 1988
Off-Shore Oil Rig Workers. Crestwood, 1988
Smokejumpers and Forest Firefighters. Crestwood, 1988
Stunt People. Crestwood, 1988
WHITE, Dana
High-Rise Workers. Crestwood, 1988
This series could be used a number of ways. Dangerous jobs appeal to youngsters, so curiosity alone will draw readers in. They are certainly a different approach for a career-study unit, and reluctant readers may also be interested. Background about the job is interspersed with stories and quotes about real people in the profession. Grades 3-8. Glossary, index.

BARRON'S BOOK NOTES
The Aeneid, Virgil. Barron's, 1984
All Quiet on the Western Front, Remarque. Barron's, 1984
All the King's Men, Warren. Barron's, 1985
Animal Farm, Orwell. Barron's, 1984
Anna Karenina, Tolstoy. Barron's, 1985
As I Lay Dying, Faulkner. Barron's, 1985
As You Like It, Shakespeare. Barron's, 1985
Babbitt, Lewis. Barron's, 1985
Beowulf. Barron's, 1984
Billy Budd & Typee, Melville. Barron's, 1984
Brave New World, Huxley. Barron's, 1984
Candide, Voltaire. Barron's, 1985
Canterbury Tales, Chaucer. Barron's, 1984
Catch-22, Heller. Barron's, 1985
The Catcher in the Rye, Salinger. Barron's, 1984
Crime and Punishment, Dostoevski. Barron's, 1984
The Crucible, Miller. Barron's, 1984
Cry, the Beloved Country, Paton. Barron's, 1985
Daisy Miller & Turn of the Screw, James. Barron's, 1985
David Copperfield, Dickens. Barron's, 1985

Death of a Salesman, Miller. Barron's, 1984
The Divine Comedy: The Inferno, Dante. Barron's, 1984
Dr. Faustus, Marlowe. Barron's, 1985
A Doll's House & Hedda Gabler, Ibsen. Barron's, 1985
Don Quixote, Cervantes. Barron's, 1985
Ethan Frome, Wharton. Barron's, 1985
A Farewell to Arms, Hemingway. Barron's, 1984
Faust: Parts I and II, Goethe. Barron's, 1985
For Whom the Bell Tolls, Hemingway. Barron's, 1986
The Glass Menagerie & A Streetcar Named Desire, Williams. Barron's, 1985
The Good Earth, Buck. Barron's, 1985
The Grapes of Wrath, Steinbeck. Barron's, 1984
Great Expectations, Dickens. Barron's, 1984
The Great Gatsby, Fitzgerald. Barron's, 1984
Gulliver's Travels, Swift. Barron's, 1984
Hamlet, Shakespeare. Barron's, 1984
Hard Times, Dickens. Barron's, 1985
Heart of Darkness & The Secret Sharer, Conrad. Barron's, 1984
Henry IV: Part I, Shakespeare. Barron's, 1984
The House of Seven Gables, Hawthorne. Barron's, 1985
Huckleberry Finn, Twain. Barron's, 1984
The Iliad, Homer. Barron's, 1984
Invisible Man, Ellison. Barron's, 1985
Jane Eyre, Bronte. Barron's, 1984
Julius Caesar, Shakespeare. Barron's, 1984
The Jungle, Sinclair. Barron's, 1984
King Lear, Shakespeare. Barron's, 1984
Light in August, Faulkner. Barron's, 1985
Lord Jim, Conrad. Barron's, 1985
Lord of the Flies, Golding. Barron's, 1984
The Lord of the Rings & The Hobbit, Tolkien. Barron's, 1985
Macbeth, Shakespeare. Barron's, 1984
Madame Bovary, Flaubert. Barron's, 1985
The Mayor of Casterbridge, Hardy. Barron's, 1985
The Merchant of Venice, Shakespeare. Barron's, 1985
A Midsummer Night's Dream, Shakespeare. Barron's, 1985
Moby Dick, Melville. Barron's, 1984
My Antonia, Cather. Barron's, 1985
Native Son & Black Boy, Wright. Barron's, 1985
New Testament. Barron's, 1985
1984, Orwell. Barron's, 1984
The Odyssey, Homer. Barron's, 1984
Oedipus Trilogy, Sophocles. Barron's, 1984
Of Mice and Men, Steinbeck. Barron's, 1984
The Old Man and the Sea, Hemingway. Barron's, 1984
Old Testament. Barron's, 1985
Oliver Twist, Dickens. Barron's, 1985
One Flew Over the Cuckoo's Nest, Kesey. Barron's, 1984
Othello, Shakespeare. Barron's, 1984
Our Town, Wilder. Barron's, 1985
Paradise Lost, Milton. Barron's, 1984
The Pearl, Steinbeck. Barron's, 1985
Portrait of the Artist as a Young Man, Joyce. Barron's, 1985
Pride and Prejudice, Austen. Barron's, 1984
The Prince, Machiavelli. Barron's, 1985

The Red Badge of Courage, Crane. Barron's, 1984
The Republic, Plato. Barron's, 1984
The Return of the Native, Hardy. Barron's, 1984
Richard III, Shakespeare. Barron's, 1985
Romeo and Juliet, Shakespeare. Barron's, 1984
The Scarlet Letter, Hawthorne. Barron's, 1984
A Separate Peace, Knowles. Barron's, 1984
Silas Marner, Eliot. Barron's, 1985
Slaughterhouse Five, Vonnegut. Barron's, 1985
Sons and Lovers, Lawrence. Barron's, 1985
The Sound and the Fury, Faulkner. Barron's, 1985
Steppenwolf & Siddhartha, Hesse. Barron's, 1985
The Stranger, Camus. Barron's, 1985
The Sun Also Rises, Hemingway. Barron's, 1984
A Tale of Two Cities, Dickens. Barron's, 1984
The Taming of the Shrew, Shakespeare. Barron's, 1985
The Tempest, Shakespeare. Barron's, 1985
Tess of the D'Urbervilles, Hardy. Barron's, 1984
To Kill a Mockingbird, Lee. Barron's, 1984
Tom Jones, Fielding. Barron's, 1985
Tom Sawyer, Twain. Barron's, 1985
Twelfth Night, Shakespeare. Barron's, 1985
Uncle Tom's Cabin, Stowe. Barron's, 1985
Walden, Thoreau. Barron's, 1984
Who's Afraid of Virginia Wolfe, Albee. Barron's, 1985
Wuthering Heights, Bronte. Barron's, 1984

Similar to the popular Cliff's Notes, Barron's Book Notes is published by the leader in educational study aids. Guided by an advisory board of educators, each book offers a plot summary, character analysis and a discussion of the book's themes. There is also a short biography of the author which helps to give the student some background on the book. Barron's includes sample tests, answers and term paper ideas, which should thrill high school English teachers. Students will not need to be led to these, just have them accessible, but remind them, as Barron's does a number of times, that reading Book Notes is not a substitute for the real thing.

BASEBALL LEGENDS

APPEL, Martin
Joe Dimaggio. Chelsea, 1990

BJARKMAN, Peter
Roberto Clemente. Chelsea, 1991

ECKHOUSE, Morris
Bob Feller. Chelsea, 1990

GRABOWSKI, John
Jackie Robinson. Chelsea, 1991
Sandy Koufax. Chelsea, 1991
Willie Mays. Chelsea, 1990

KAVANAGH, Jack
Dizzy Dean. Chelsea, 1990
Grover Cleveland Alexander. Chelsea, 1990
Rogers Hornsby. Chelsea, 1991

MACHT, Norm
Babe Ruth. Chelsea, 1991
Christy Mathewson. Chelsea, 1991
Frank Robinson. Chelsea, 1991
Jimmie Foxx. Chelsea, 1990
Satchel Paige. Chelsea, 1991

SHANNON, Mike
Johnny Bench. Chelsea, 1990
TACKACH, James
Hank Aaron. Chelsea, 1991
Roy Campanella. Chelsea, 1990
WOLFF, Rick
Brooks Robinson. Chelsea, 1990
Mickey Mantle. Chelsea, 1991

The greatest athletes in the history of baseball are chronicled or will be, in this new series (more books are expected). The biographies pay a great deal of attention to the important games of the players' careers, as well as their life in general. Extensive statistics, a chronology, bibliography, and index are included. There are also a good number of illustrations in each book. Grades 5 and up.

BASIC INVESTOR'S LIBRARY
EPSTEIN, Rachel
Alternative Investments. Chelsea, 1987
Careers in the Investment World. Chelsea, 1987
Investment Banking. Chelsea, 1987
Investments and the Law. Chelsea, 1987
KAUFMAN, Jo
Mutual Funds. Chelsea, 1987
LITTLE, Jeffrey B.
Bonds, Preferred Stocks and the Money Market. Chelsea, 1987
Growth Stocks. Chelsea, 1987
Investing and Trading. Chelsea, 1987
Principles of Technical Analysis. Chelsea, 1987
Reading the Financial Pages. Chelsea, 1987
Stock Options. Chelsea, 1987
Understanding a Company. Chelsea, 1987
Wall Street—How It Works. Chelsea, 1987
What Is a Share of Stock? Chelsea, 1988

The complexities of the business world is the subject of this well written and easy to understand series. Each book is written by experienced business journalists and is at a level that junior high school students can understand. There are many illustrations in each volume along with a glossary, an index and bibliography. A good asset to a library's (school or public) collection. Grades 7 and up.

BASICS
FOX, Ron
Wrestling Basics. Simon & Schuster, 1986
GOLDBERG, Bob
Diving Basics. Simon & Schuster, 1986
LIPTAK, Karen
Robotics Basics. Simon & Schuster, 1984
MACCLEAN, Norman
Hockey Basics. Simon & Schuster, 1983
NARDI, Thomas
Karate Basics. Simon & Schuster, 1984
PEZZANO, Chuck
Bowling Basics. Simon & Schuster, 1984
SCHIFFMAN, Roger
Golf Basics. Simon & Schuster, 1986
WALLACE, Don
Water Sports Basics. Simon & Schuster, 1985

These slim volumes touch on the history of each sport, mentioning a few famous practitioners, but the primary emphasis is a presentation of the basic moves and rules. A combination of drawings and photos helps readers. Interestingly, these discuss the pros and cons of each sport. Glossary, index. Ages 9-12.

BEGINNING HISTORY

BLACKWOOD, Alan

The Age of Exploration. Watts, 1990

COOTE, Roger

Roman Cities. Watts, 1990

JESSOP, Joanne

Crusaders. Watts, 1990

MATTHEWS, Rupert

Roman Soldiers. Watts, 1990

Viking Explorers. Watts, 1990

RICKARD, Graham

Norman Castles. Watts, 1990

STEEL, Anne

Egyptian Pyramids. Watts, 1990

STEEL, Barry

Greek Cities. Watts, 1990

Younger readers will get a colorful, interesting introduction to history with this new series. Buildings and how they were constructed, ways of life, and religious rites are all described and illustrated in appealing color. Vocabulary is simplified, with glossary terms in boldface. There is also an index and bibliography. Excellent choices for grades 2-5.

BERGER, Melvin

Atoms, Molecules and Quarks. Putnam, 1986

Bright Stars, Red Giants and White Dwarfs. Putnam, 1983

Comets, Meteors and Asteroids. Putnam, 1981

Lights, Lenses and Lasers. Putnam, 1987

Solids, Liquids and Gases. Putnam, 1989

Space Shots, Shuttles and Satellites. Putnam, 1983

Star Gazing, Comet Watching and Sky Mapping. Putnam, 1984

UFOs, ETs and Visitors from Space. Putnam, 1988

Berger is a veteran author on scientific subjects for young people. This series focuses on aspects of space, ranging from astronomy, to rockets, to extraterrestrials. He discusses their origins, what they are like now, and what the future may bring. Black and white photos and glossaries are included.

BETTER SPORTS BOOKS

SULLIVAN, George

Better Basketball for Girls. Putnam, 1978

Better BMX Riding and Racing for Boys and Girls. Putnam, 1984

Better Cross-Country Running for Boys and Girls. Putnam, 1983

Better Field Events for Girls. Putnam, 1982

Better Field Hockey for Girls. Putnam, 1981

Better Gymnastics for Girls. Putnam, 1977

Better Ice Skating for Boys and Girls. Putnam, 1976

Better Karate for Boys. Putnam, 1972

Better Roller Skating for Boys and Girls. Putnam, 1978

Better Soccer for Boys and Girls. Putnam, 1978

Better Synchronized Swimming for Boys and Girls. Putnam, 1981

Better Track for Boys. Putnam, 1985

Better Track for Girls. Putnam, 1981

Better Volleyball for Girls. Putnam, 1979
Better Wrestling for Boys. Putnam, 1986

These entries continue a long-running series. Basic how-to's are provided for playing each sport, starting with descriptions of equipment and rules, and moving on to techniques of play. Photos, illustrations, and glossaries of terms are provided. Some books specify that they are for boys or girls because the rules and techniques may differ for each sex in competition. This is the best all-around series of its kind for ages 8 and up.

BLACK AMERICANS OF ACHIEVEMENT

ADAIR, Gene
George Washington Carver. Chelsea, 1989

ALDRED, Lisa
Thurgood Marshall. Chelsea, 1990

BERGMAN, Carol
Sidney Poitier. Chelsea, 1989

BISHOP, Jack
Ralph Ellison. Chelsea, 1989

BISSON, Terry
Harriet Tubman. Chelsea, 1989
Nat Turner. Chelsea, 1989

BORZENDOWSKI, Janice
John Russwurm. Chelsea, 1989

CONLEY, Kevin
Benjamin Banneker. Chelsea, 1989
Charles Waddell Chesnutt. Chelsea, 1989

DIAMOND, Arthur
Paul Cuffe. Chelsea, 1989

EDWARDS, Lillie J.
Denmark Vesey. Chelsea, 1990

FRANKL, Ron
Duke Ellington. Chelsea, 1989

GENTRY, Tony
Jesse Owens. Chelsea, 1989
Paul Laurence Dunbar. Chelsea, 1989

GILMAN, Michael
Matthew Henson. Chelsea, 1988

GRANT, Dell
Booker T. Washington. Chelsea, 1989

HALASA, Malu
Elijah Muhammad. Chelsea, 1989
Mary McLeod Bethune. Chelsea, 1989

HANLEY, Sally
A. Philip Randolph. Chelsea, 1989

HUGGINS, Nathan I. (Editor)
Madame C. J. Walker. Chelsea, 1989

JAKOUBEK, Bob
Adam Clayton Powell. Chelsea, 1988
Joe Louis. Chelsea, 1989
Martin Luther King Jr. Chelsea, 1989
Ralph Bunche. Chelsea, 1989

KING, Perry
Prince Hall. Chelsea, 1989

KLIMENT, Bud
Ella Fitzgerald. Chelsea, 1989

KRASS, Peter
Sojourner Truth. Chelsea, 1989
LARKIN, Russell
John Hope. Chelsea, 1989
LAWLER, Mary
Marcus Garvey. Chelsea, 1989
MAHONE-LONESOME, Robyn
Charles R. Drew. Chelsea, 1989
PALMER, Leslie
Gordon Parks. Chelsea, 1989
Lena Horne. Chelsea, 1988
PIETSCH, Michael
Billie Holliday. Chelsea, 1990
PRESTON, Kitty
Scott Joplin. Chelsea, 1989
ROSSET, Lisa
James Baldwin. Chelsea, 1989
RUMMEL, Jack
Langston Hughes. Chelsea, 1989
Malcolm X. Chelsea, 1989
Muhammad Ali. Chelsea, 1989
RUSSELL, Sharman
Frederick Douglass. Chelsea, 1989
SAMUELS, Steven
Chester Himes. Chelsea, 1989
Paul Robeson. Chelsea, 1989
SCOTT, Richard
Jackie Robinson. Chelsea, 1989
STAFFORD, Mark
W. E. B. DuBois. Chelsea, 1989
SWAIN, Charles
Blanche K. Bruce. Chelsea, 1989
TANENHAUS, Sam
Louis Armstrong. Chelsea, 1989
Walter White. Chelsea, 1989
TOLBERT-ROUCHALEAU, Jane
James Weldon Johnson. Chelsea, 1989
URBAN, Joan
Richard Wright. Chelsea, 1989
WASHINGTON, Jerome
William Hastie. Chelsea, 1989
WILLIAMSON, Mel
Richard Allen. Chelsea, 1990

Chelsea House has distinguished itself as a leader in young adult reference materials and this series is another example of their fine work. Seventy-five titles are included and range the broad spectrum of Black Americans in U.S. history. The books begin with an introductory essay from Coretta Scott King and are filled with photographs and other illustrations. All contain an index, bibliography, and chronology of the subject's life. An excellent series for students in 6th grade and up.

BOSTON CHILDREN'S MUSEUM ACTIVITY BOOKS
ZUBROWSKI, Bernie
Balloons. Lothrop, 1990
Clocks. Lothrop, 1988
Raceways. Lothrop, 1985

Tops. Lothrop, 1989
Wheels at Work. Lothrop, 1986

Beginning with the history of each object under study, the author provides a number of experiments (good for home or classroom) illustrating how and why they worked at each stage of their evolution. Grades 5-9. No index or glossary.

BROWN PAPER SCHOOL BOOKS

ALLISON, Linda
Reasons for Seasons. Little, 1975

BELL, Neill
Only Human. Little, 1983

BURNS, Marilyn
Good for Me. Little, 1978
I Am Not a Short Adult. Little, 1977
Math for Smarty Pants. Little, 1982
This Book Is about Time. Little, 1978

JOBB, Jamie
Night Sky Book. Little, 1977

RIGHTS, Mollie
Beastly Neighbors. Little, 1981

SCHNEIDER, Tom
Everybody's a Winner. Little, 1976

WALTHER, Tom
Make Mine Music. Little, 1981

WEITZMAN, David
My Backyard History Book. Little, 1975

So-called because their jackets resemble brown paper bags and the inside pages are also brown, these books are loaded with highly readable information accompanied with illustrative experiments. The only drawback is the lack of indexing, which severely limits their research usefulness. Grades 5-9.

CAMBRIDGE INTRODUCTION TO HISTORY

Barbarians, Christians, and Muslims. Lerner, 1975
The Birth of Modern Europe. Lerner, 1975
Europe around the World. Lerner, 1975
The Middle Ages. Lerner, 1975
The Old Regime and the Revolution. Lerner, 1980
People Become Civilized. Lerner, 1975
Power for the People. Lerner, 1980
The Twentieth Century. Lerner, 1984

These books cover world history from ancient times to the 20th century. Events and peoples on various continents at each time period are discussed: their culture, religion, economy and, in many cases, the spread of their empires. There are maps and illustrations. Grades 6 and up. Index.

CAMBRIDGE TOPIC BOOKS

BOYD, Anne
Life in a Fifteenth-Century Monastery. Lerner, 1979

CAIRNS, Conrad
Medieval Castles. Lerner, 1989

CORFE, Tom
The Murder of Archbishop Thomas. Lerner, 1977

DUNSTER, Jack
China and Mao Zedong. Lerner, 1983

EVANS, Arthur N.
The Automobile. Lerner, 1985

HIGHAM, Charles
The Maoris. Lerner, 1983
MORGAN, Gwynneth
Life in a Medieval Village. Lerner, 1982
REGAN, Geoffrey
Israel and the Arabs. Lerner, 1986
VIALLS, Christine
The Industrial Revolution Begins. Lerner, 1982
WATSON, Percy
Building the Medieval Cathedrals. Lerner, 1976
WILKES, John
The Roman Army. Lerner, 1973

While not much to look at, these books nonetheless give a good basic introduction to life at assorted periods of history. The era is described along with the importance of the subject under discussion. How buildings developed, lifestyles adapted, and disintegrated are all covered. There are illustrations, but they are small and in black and white. Color would have added immensely to eye appeal, but the text is detailed. Grades 5 and up. Glossary, index.

CAREER CHOICES FOR THE 90'S
Art. Walker, 1990
Business. Walker, 1990
Communications and Journalism. Walker, 1990
Computer Science. Walker, 1990
Economics. Walker, 1990
English. Walker, 1990
History. Walker, 1990
Mathematics. Walker, 1990
Political Science and Government. Walker, 1990
Psychology. Walker, 1990
Law. Walker, 1990
MBA. Walker, 1990

This new series of career guides is arranged by the student's field of interest and study. Each book reviews a number of career options that are available to students with a degree in that particular field. Each career path is discussed and important companies in the field are listed. Job qualifications, responsibilities, salaries, working conditions and a list of recommended reading are also included. The most interesting aspect is the interviews of current professionals. The interviews discuss relative information and offer suggestions for the aspiring student. This series is for high school students.

CAREERS
ALLMAN, Paul
Exploring Careers in Video. Rosen, 1989
BLEICH, Alan R.
Exploring Careers in Medicine. Rosen, 1990
BROWN, Margaret F.
Careers in Occupational Therapy. Rosen, 1989
CARTER, Sharon
Careers in Aviation. Rosen, 1990
COHEN, Paul, and **Shari COHEN**
Careers in Law Enforcement and Security. Rosen, 1990
DUNCAN, Jane Caryl
Careers in Veterinary Medicine. Rosen, 1988
EDWARDS, E. W.
Exploring Careers Using Foreign Languages. Rosen, 1990

EPSTEIN, Lawrence
Exploring Careers in Computer Sales. Rosen, 1990
FIELDS, Carl
Exploring Careers in Tool and Die Making. Rosen, 1985
GRANT, Edgar
Exploring Careers in the Travel Industry. Rosen, 1989
HADDOCK, Patricia
Careers in Banking and Finance. Rosen, 1990
HERON, Jackie
Careers in Health and Fitness. Rosen, 1990
Exploring Careers in Nursing. Rosen, 1990
IPSA, Jean
Exploring Careers in Child Care Services. Rosen, 1990
JOHNSON, Barbara L.
Careers in Beauty Culture. Rosen, 1989
JONES, Marilyn
Exploring Careers as an Electrician. Rosen, 1987
KOESTER, Pat
Careers in Fashion Retailing. Rosen, 1990
LEE, Richard S., and **Mary PRICE**
Careers for Women in Politics. Rosen, 1989
Careers in the Restaurant Industry. Rosen, 1990
MASTERSON, Richard
Exploring Careers in Computer Graphics. Rosen, 1990
NELSON, Cordner
Careers in Pro Sports. Rosen, 1990
NEUFELD, Rose
Exploring Nontraditional Jobs for Women. Rosen, 1989
RICKERT, Jessica A.
Exploring Careers in Dentistry. Rosen, 1988
ROBERSON, Virginia Lee
Careers in the Graphic Arts. Rosen, 1988
ROSENTHAL, Lawrence
Exploring Careers in Accounting. Rosen, 1988
SCHAUER, Donald D.
Careers in Trucking. Rosen, 1987
SHAPIRO, Stanley J.
Exploring Careers in Science. Rosen, 1989
SHOCKLEY, Robert
Careers in Teaching. Rosen, 1990
SIGEL, Lois S.
New Careers in Hospitals. Rosen, 1990
SOUTHWORTH, Scott
Exploring High-Tech Careers. Rosen, 1988
SPENCER, Jean
Careers in Word Processing and Desktop Publishing. Rosen, 1990
Exploring Careers as a Computer Technician. Rosen, 1989
Exploring Careers in the Electronic Office. Rosen, 1989
STROMBOTNE, James
Exploring Careers in the Fine Arts. Rosen, 1984
WEINTRAUB, Joseph
Exploring Careers in the Computer Field. Rosen, 1990

This is an excellent career series for teens. The authors present an overview of each career that is spiced with comments and interviews with people active in the career. Salaries and job responsibilities are given and illustrated with real life examples. Personal and educational characteristics that are helpful for each job are also mentioned. Samples of course offerings, resumes, job interest surveys, and addresses for further information add to the usefulness of this series.

CAREERS FOR TODAY

SCHULZ, Marjorie R.

Community Services. Watts, 1990
Hospitality and Recreation. Watts, 1990
Transportation. Watts, 1990
Travel and Tourism. Watts, 1990

Schulz has written these career books for teens with low reading skills. They focus on entry-level positions in different occupational areas than the norm for students of this type. This series gives information on training possibilities, how to conduct a job search and a personal essay from people who have jobs in the positions described. Illustrated with color photographs and charts. High school students with learning difficulties should appreciate these.

CENTER STAGE

KOENIG, Teresa

Bruce Springsteen. Crestwood, 1986
Lionel Richie. Crestwood, 1986
Tina Turner. Crestwood, 1986

SANFORD, William, and **Carl GREEN**

Alabama. Crestwood, 1986
Beach Boys. Crestwood, 1986
Bill Cosby. Crestwood, 1986
Cyndi Lauper. Crestwood, 1986
Hulk Hogan. Crestwood, 1986
Julian Lennon. Crestwood, 1986
Michael J. Fox. Crestwood, 1986
Sylvester Stallone. Crestwood, 1986
Stevie Wonder. Crestwood, 1986

Entertainers are the focus of this series for grades 3-6. Easy to read, these biographies tell about early life, then emphasize their accomplishments. There are many photos and these should appeal to reluctant readers. Some of these stars are not as popular as they once were, but those that are still "big" will find a ready audience. No index.

CHILD ABUSE

ANDERSON, Deborah, and **Martha FINNE**

Jason's Story: Going to a Foster Home. Dillon, 1986
Liza's Story: Neglect and the Police. Dillon, 1986
Margaret's Story: Sexual Abuse and Working with a Counselor. Dillon, 1986
Michael's Story: Emotional Abuse and Working with a Counselor. Dillon, 1986
Robin's Story: Physical Abuse and Seeing the Doctor. Dillon, 1986

Told in the first person, these stories are a kind of biblio-therapy that can be used with children faced with these kinds of traumatizing situations. Teachers, counselors, and medical personnel could use them with youngsters from first grade on up. The reading level is grades 2-4. After the story, there is a section that explains important aspects of the story that can be discussed with kids, along with a list of people and places to go to for help if they are suffering this kind of abuse. There are also two sections of hints for adults when dealing with children who may be abused. Glossary.

CHILDHOOD OF FAMOUS AMERICANS

AIRD, Hazel B., and **Catherine RUDDIMAN**

Henry Ford: Young Man with Ideas. Macmillan, 1986

BORLAND, Kathryn

Harry Houdini: Young Magician. Macmillan, 1991

FRISBEE, Lucy P.

John Fitzgerald Kennedy: America's Youngest President. Macmillan, 1986

HAMMONTREE, Marie

Albert Einstein: Young Thinker. Macmillan, 1986

MASON, Miriam E.

Mark Twain: Young Writer. Macmillan, 1991

MILLENDER, Dharathula H.

Crispus Attucks: Black Leader of Colonial Patriots. Macmillan, 1986

MONSELL, Helen A.

Robert E. Lee: Young Confederate. Macmillan, 1983

Susan B. Anthony: Champion of Women's Rights. Macmillan, 1986

SEYMOUR, Flora Warren

Sacagawea: American Pathfinder. Macmillan, 1991

STEVENSON, Augusta

Buffalo Bill: Frontier Daredevil. Macmillan, 1991

WAGONER, Jean B.

Martha Washington: America's First, First Lady. Macmillan, 1983

WEIL, Ann

Betsy Ross: Designer of Our Flag. Macmillan, 1983

This veteran series has a new updated look. The titles have also changed slightly, but essentially this is still the same old series. Gone are the black silhouette illustrations, replaced by line drawings. Many are available in paperback as well as hardcover. As before, however, the books cover only the childhood of the famous person, so that their feats are not discussed. The other major flaw is the continuing tendency of the authors to write imaginary conversations. There are no indexes. Only where nothing else is available. Grades 3-6.

CITY LIFE

EINHORN, Barbara

Living in Berlin. Silver, 1986

MOORE, Robert

Living in Sidney. Silver, 1986

SHANG, Anthony

Living in Hong Kong. Silver, 1986

SPROULE, Anna

Living in London. Silver, 1986

By taking an in-depth look at the ordinary citizens of these major cities, the authors have attempted to present an understanding of different ways of life. Each book reviews the history, past times, economy and religions of the city's inhabitants. There are numerous photographs and maps in each book along with an index. Grades 5-8.

CLOSER LOOK AT...

HUGHES, Jill

A Closer Look at Arctic Lands. Watts, 1987

POPE, Joyce

A Closer Look at Horses. Watts, 1987

ROBSON, Denny

A Closer Look at Butterflies and Moths. Watts, 1986

All aspects of these animals' lives are pictured in these English imports. Each animal's physical characteristics, life cycle, and life style is briefly examined. Grades 5-7.

COLE, Joanna

A Bird's Body. Morrow, 1982
A Cat's Body. Morrow, 1982
A Dog's Body. Morrow, 1986
A Frog's Body. Morrow, 1980
A Horse's Body. Morrow, 1981
An Insect's Body. Morrow, 1984
A Snake's Body. Morrow, 1981

Cole teaches youngsters about animals by showing how the animal's body works: how it evolved, how its characteristics help it survive, how it reproduces. The excellent photos and illustrations make these an outstanding teaching tool. Recommended for grades 3-7.

COMMUNITY HELPERS A TO Z

JOHNSON, Jean

Firefighters A to Z. Walker, 1985
Librarians A to Z. Walker, 1989
Police Officers A to Z. Walker, 1986
Postal Workers A to Z. Walker, 1987
Sanitation Workers A to Z. Walker, 1988
Teachers A to Z. Walker, 1987

This early career series quite literally takes various aspects of each job and examines them alphabetically. Tasks are clarified in several short sentences, accompanied by large, illustrative photos of the activities. At the end of the A-Z portion there is a more detailed discussion of the different responsibilities practitioners of the career might have. A nice introduction for ages 5-8.

CONCEPT BOOKS

ADORJAN, Carol

I Can! Can You? Whitman, 1990

AMADEO, Diana

There's a Little Bit of Me in Jamey. Whitman, 1989

ASELTINE, Lorraine

I'm Deaf and It's Okay. Whitman, 1986
First Grade Can Wait. Whitman, 1987

AYLESWORTH, Jim

The Bad Dream. Whitman, 1985

BERNSTEIN, Joanne, and **Bryna FIRESIDE**

Special Parents, Special Children. Whitman, 1990

COLLINS, Pat Lowery

Waiting for Baby Joe. Whitman, 1990

DELTON, Judy

I'll Never Love Anything Ever Again. Whitman, 1985
My Mom Hates Me in January. Whitman, 1977

DELTON, Judy, and **Dorothy TUCKER**

My Grandma's in a Nursing Home. Whitman, 1986

EMMERT, Michelle

I'm the Big Sister Now. Whitman, 1989

FASSLER, Joan

Howie Helps Himself. Whitman, 1975

GIRARD, Linda Walvoord

Adoption Is for Always. Whitman, 1986
Alex, the Kid with AIDS. Whitman, 1990
At Daddy's on Saturdays. Whitman, 1987
My Body Is Private. Whitman, 1984
We Adopted You, Benjamin Koo. Whitman, 1989

Who Is a Stranger and What Should I Do? Whitman, 1985
You Were Born on Your Very First Birthday. Whitman, 1983

HAMM, Diane Johnston
Grandma Drives a Motor Bed. Whitman, 1987

HENRIOD, Lorraine
Grandma's Wheelchair. Whitman, 1982

HOOKER, Ruth
Sara Loves Her Brother. Whitman, 1987

JORDAN, Mary Kate
Losing Uncle Tim. Whitman, 1989

LASKER, Joe
He's My Brother. Whitman, 1974
Nick Joins In. Whitman, 1980

LITCHFIELD, Ada B.
A Button in Her Ear. Whitman, 1976
Cane in Her Hand. Whitman, 1977
Making Room for Uncle Joe. Whitman, 1984
Words in Our Hands. Whitman, 1980

MULDOON, Kathleen M.
Princess Pooh. Whitman, 1989

NEWTON, Laura
Me and My Aunts. Whitman, 1986

OSTROW, William, and **Vivian OSTROW**
All about Asthma. Whitman, 1989

PIRNER, Connie
Even Little Kids Get Diabetes. Whitman, 1990

POWERS, Mary Ellen
Our Teacher's in a Wheelchair. Whitman, 1986

RABE, Berniece
Where's Chimpy? Whitman, 1988
A Smooth Move. Whitman, 1978

SCHLEIN, Miriam
The Way Mothers Are. Whitman, 1963

SHARMAT, Marjorie Weinman
My Mother Never Listens to Me. Whitman, 1984

SIMON, Norma
All Kinds of Families. Whitman, 1975
How Do I Feel? Whitman, 1970
I Am Not *a Crybaby!* Whitman, 1989
I Was So Mad. Whitman, 1974
I'm Busy, Too. Whitman, 1988
I Wish I Had My Father. Whitman, 1983
Nobody's Perfect, Not Even My Mother. Whitman, 1981
The Saddest Time. Whitman, 1986
Wedding Days. Whitman, 1987
Why Am I Different? Whitman, 1976

STANEK, Muriel
Don't Hurt Me, Mama. Whitman, 1983
I Won't Go without a Father. Whitman, 1972
I Speak English for My Mom. Whitman, 1989
My Mom Can't Read. Whitman, 1986
All Alone after School. Whitman, 1985

STANTON, Elizabeth, and **Henry STANTON**
Sometimes I Like to Cry. Whitman, 1978

TOMPERT, Ann
Will You Come Back for Me? Whitman, 1988
VIGNA, Judith
Grandma without Me. Whitman, 1984
I Wish Daddy Didn't Drink So Much. Whitman, 1988
Mommy and Me by Ourselves Again. Whitman, 1987
My Big Sister Takes Drugs. Whitman, 1990
Nobody Wants a Nuclear War. Whitman, 1986
Saying Goodbye to Daddy. Whitman, 1990
She's Not My Real Mother. Whitman, 1980
WILLIAMS, Barbara
Donna Jean's Disaster. Whitman, 1986

This series covers a variety of social topics for the younger reader, ranging from illiteracy to child abuse to family illness. Some of the books, for example the Stanek entries, are written as fictional problem representations that could be used in bibliotherapy. Others are definitely informational, with a recent entry by William Ostrow, a youngster himself, writing about what asthma is and how to live with it—particularly outstanding. These can be used with ages 5-10.

CONFLICT IN THE 20th CENTURY
BAYNHAM, Simon
Africa: From 1945. Watts, 1987
DELEE, Nigel
The Rise of the Asian Superpowers. Watts, 1987
PIMLOTT, John
The Cold War. Watts, 1987
South and Central America. Watts, 1988

Areas that are or have been the center of trouble are examined here. Their problem history is tracked clear up to the present time. Because of the size of the areas involved only a brief overview can be presented; nonetheless, the student will get a general idea of the situation. There is a chronology, and important people are highlighted. Grades 5-12.

CONSERVING OUR WORLD
BAINES, John D.
Acid Rain. Steck, 1990
Atmosphere. Steck, 1990
Protecting the Oceans. Steck, 1990
BANKS, Martin
Conserving Rain Forests. Steck, 1990
JAMES, Barbara
Waste and Recycling. Steck, 1990
LAMBERT, Mark
Farming and the Environment. Steck, 1990
MCLEISH, Ewan
Spread of Deserts. Steck, 1990
PENNY, Malcolm
Protecting Wildlife. Steck, 1990

Like several other series, including Green Issues, this one focuses on environmental issues in a colorful oversize format with plenty of illustrations. The major difference here is that the emphasis is more international in scope. The authors discuss the problem worldwide: how and why it occurs, what its impact has been and will be, and what is and can be done about it worldwide. Several experiments are included, along with a list of addresses, bibliography, glossary, and index. Good choices for grades 5 and up.

CONTEMPORARY CONCERNS

HIRSCH, Karen

Becky. Carolrhoda, 1981

KIBBEY, Marsha

My Grammy. Carolrhoda, 1988

PAYNE, Sherry Neuwirth

A Contest. Carolrhoda, 1982

POWELL, E. Sandy

Geranium Morning. Carolrhoda, 1990

SCHUCHMAN, Joan

Two Places to Sleep. Carolrhoda, 1979

Like Whitman's Concept books, this series uses a story format to sensitize readers to various social problems. Plots involve deafness, parental death, divorce, cerebral palsy, and Alzheimer's. The characters face these difficulties with the help of friends and family. Sorrow, anger, lack of understanding, and need for acceptance are emphasized. Grades 1-4.

CONTRIBUTIONS OF WOMEN

DILLON, Ann, and **Cynthia BIX**

Theater. Dillon, 1978

FOWLER, Carol

Dance. Dillon, 1979

LEVINSON, Nancy Smiler

Business. Dillon, 1981

The First Women Who Spoke Out. Dillon, 1983

This series of collective biographies will be most useful where women's studies are emphasized. The biographees are from the modern era and did contribute to society; many, however, will be unknown names, and unless there is a related assignment, they will find little use. Grades 5-12.

COPING WITH MODERN PROBLEMS

BOWE-GUTMAN, Sonia

Teen Pregnancy. Lerner, 1987

ERLANGER, Ellen

Eating Disorders. Lerner, 1988

JOHNSON, Julie Tallard

Understanding Mental Illness. Lerner, 1989

KOLEHMAINEN, Janet, and **Sandra HANDWERK**

Teen Suicide. Lerner, 1986

LERNER, Ethan A.

Understanding AIDS. Lerner, 1987

RENCH, Janice E.

Teen Sexuality. Lerner, 1988

TERKEL, Susan Neiburg

Feeling Safe, Feeling Strong. Lerner, 1984

Hot topics for teens are the order of the day with this series. The primary emphasis is on how a youngster can recognize and deal with these problems in their own lives, but they can also be used for report material. Some case studies are related but primarily the discussion centers on the problem, how it can manifest itself, statistics, and possible treatments. A list of helpful agencies is appended, along with a bibliography and index.

CORNERSTONES OF FREEDOM

ASH, Maureen

Harriet Beecher Stowe. Childrens, 1990

The Story of the Women's Movement. Childrens, 1989

CLINTON, Patrick
The Story of the Empire State Building. Childrens, 1987
CLINTON, Susan
The Story of the Green Mountain Boys. Childrens, 1987
The Story of Seward's Folly. Childrens, 1987
The Story of Susan B. Anthony. Childrens, 1986
FOSTER, Leila M.
The Cold War. Childrens, 1990
Rachel Carson and the Environmental Movement. Childrens, 1990
The Story of the Great Society. Childrens, 1991
FOX, Mary Virginia
The Story of Women Who Shaped the West. Childrens, 1991
HARGROVE, James
Jonas Salk and the Discovery of the Polio Vaccine. Childrens, 1990
The Story of the Black Hawk War. Childrens, 1986
The Story of the FBI. Childrens, 1988
The Story of Presidential Elections. Childrens, 1988
The Story of the Teapot Dome Scandal. Childrens, 1989
The Story of Watergate. Childrens, 1988
KENT, Zachary
Henry Ford and the Automobile. Childrens, 1990
The New York Stock Exchange. Childrens, 1990
The Peace Corps. Childrens, 1990
The Story of Admiral Peary of the North Pole. Childrens, 1988
The Story of the Battle of Bull Run. Childrens, 1986
The Story of the Battle of Shiloh. Childrens, 1991
The Story of the Brooklyn Bridge. Childrens, 1988
The Story of the Challenger *Disaster*. Childrens, 1986
The Story of Cara Barton. Childrens, 1987
The Story of the Election of Abraham Lincoln. Childrens, 1986
The Story of Ford's Theater and the Death of Lincoln. Childrens, 1987
The Story of Geronimo. Childrens, 1989
The Story of John Brown's Raid on Harper's Ferry. Childrens, 1988
The Story of the Rough Riders. Childrens, 1991
The Story of the Salem Witch Trials. Childrens, 1986
The Story of Sherman's March to the Sea. Childrens, 1987
The Story of the Sinking of the Battleship Maine. Childrens, 1988
The Story of the Surrender at Appomattox Court House. Childrens, 1987
The Story of the Surrender at Yorktown. Childrens, 1989
The Story of the Triangle Factory Fire. Childrens, 1989
Television. Childrens, 1990
RICHARDS, Norman
The Story of Apollo 11. Childrens, 1985
SIMON, Charnan
The Story of the Haymarket Riot. Childrens, 1988
STEIN, R. Conrad
The Story of Arlington National Cemetery. Childrens, 1979
The Story of the Assassination of John F. Kennedy. Childrens, 1985
The Story of the Barbary Pirates. Childrens, 1982
The Story of the Battle of the Bulge. Childrens, 1977
The Story of the Battle for Iwo Jima. Childrens, 1977
The Story of the Boston Tea Party. Childrens, 1984
The Story of the Burning of Washington. Childrens, 1985
The Story of the Chicago Fire. Childrens, 1982
The Story of Child Labor Laws. Childrens, 1984

The Story of the Clipper Ships. Childrens, 1981
The Story of D-Day. Childrens, 1977
The Story of Ellis Island. Childrens, 1979
The Story of the Erie Canal. Childrens, 1985
The Story of the Flight at Kitty Hawk. Childrens, 1981
The Story of the Gold at Sutter's Mill. Childrens, 1981
The Story of the Golden Spike. Childrens, 1978
The Story of the Great Depression. Childrens, 1985
The Story of the Homestead Act. Childrens, 1978
The Story of the Johnstown Flood. Childrens, 1985
The Story of the Lafayette Escadrille. Childrens, 1983
The Story of the Lewis and Clark Expedition. Childrens, 1978
The Story of Lexington and Concord. Childrens, 1983
The Story of the Little Bighorn. Childrens, 1983
The Story of the Lone Star Republic. Childrens, 1988
The Story of Marquette and Joliet. Childrens, 1981
The Story of Mississippi Steamboats. Childrens, 1987
The Story of the Monitor *and the* Merrimac. Childrens, 1983
The Story of the Montgomery Bus Boycott. Childrens, 1986
The Story of the New England Whalers. Childrens, 1982
The Story of the Nineteenth Amendment. Childrens, 1982
The Story of the Oregon Trail. Childrens, 1984
The Story of the Panama Canal. Childrens, 1982
The Story of the Pony Express. Childrens, 1981
The Story of the Powers of Congress. Childrens, 1985
The Story of the Powers of the President. Childrens, 1985
The Story of the Powers of the Supreme Court. Childrens, 1989
The Story of the Pullman Strike. Childrens, 1982
The Story of the San Francisco Earthquake. Childrens, 1983
The Story of the Smithsonian Institution. Childrens, 1979
The Story of The Spirit of St. Louis. Childrens, 1984
The Story of the Trail of Tears. Childrens, 1985
The Story of the Underground Railroad. Childrens, 1981
The Story of the United Nations. Childrens, 1986
The Story of the U.S.S. Arizona. Childrens, 1977
The Story of Valley Forge. Childrens, 1985
The Story of Wounded Knee. Childrens, 1983

WRIGHT, David K.

The Story of the Vietnam Memorial. Childrens, 1989

The publishers undoubtedly hoped to make history come alive to young readers with these brief, story-like presentations of important events. Unfortunately the illustrations are drab and unappealing. Although texts are readable, the authors take liberties while describing people's thoughts and feelings, and there are no indexes for those who might use these for school assignments. Marginal purchases for those with history buffs grades 2-4.

COULD YOU EVER?

DARLING, David

Could You Ever Build a Time Machine? Dillon, 1991
Could You Ever Dig a Hole to China? Dillon, 1990
Could You Ever Fly to the Stars? Dillon, 1990
Could You Ever Live Forever? Dillon, 1991
Could You Ever Meet an Alien? Dillon, 1990
Could You Ever Speak Chimpanzee? Dillon, 1990

With these catchy titles science author Darling may well attract the interest of browsers, and they will be surprised to find a lot of detailed information here. The current scientific knowledge is presented, then the author talks about how and whether the "could you ever..." will ever be possible. Glossary, index.

COUNT YOUR WAY

HASKINS, Jim

Count Your Way through Africa. Carolrhoda, 1989
Count Your Way through Canada. Carolrhoda, 1989
Count Your Way through China. Carolrhoda, 1987
Count Your Way through Germany. Carolrhoda, 1990
Count Your Way through Italy. Carolrhoda, 1990
Count Your Way through Japan. Carolrhoda, 1987
Count Your Way through Korea. Carolrhoda, 1989
Count Your Way through Mexico. Carolrhoda, 1989
Count Your Way through Russia. Carolrhoda, 1987
Count Your Way through the Arab World. Carolrhoda, 1987

The simple text and watercolor illustrations make these excellent choices for introducing young children to other countries. Even though they seem like picture books, the amount of information they contain justifies their use with grades K-2 for school assignments. The author uses the numbers 1-10, each number (written in the language of the country) presenting a set of facts. A pronunciation guide is appended. Where a non-Roman alphabet is used in the country, author Haskins uses it in the book, which is helpful when kids need to show examples of foreign alphabets.

COUNTRIES OF THE WORLD

ALVARADO, Manuel
Spain. Watts, 1990

ARMITAGE, Ronda
New Zealand. Watts, 1988

BLACKWOOD, Alan
France. Watts, 1988

BRICKENDEN, Jack
Canada. Watts, 1989

CARY, Pam
The United States. Watts, 1989

CUMMING, David
India. Watts, 1989
Pakistan. Watts, 1989

DOWNER, Leslie
Japan. Watts, 1990

EINHORN, Barbara
West Germany. Watts, 1988

GRIFFITHS, John
The Caribbean. Watts, 1989

HOLLINGER, Peggy
Greece. Watts, 1990

KELLY, Andrew
Australia. Watts, 1989

OSBORNE, Christine
The Netherlands. Watts, 1990

POWELL, Julian
Italy. Watts, 1990

SPROULE, Anna
Great Britain. Watts, 1988

WATERLOW, Julia
China. Watts, 1990

Not as detailed as Childrens' Enchantment of the World nor as thorough as Lippincott's new Lands and Peoples books, these still give a quick overview that will be useful for many students grades 5-8. The oversize format, with plentiful illustrations, certainly have an eye appeal not matched by the other series. There is a glossary, bibliography, and index.

COUNTRY MUSIC LIBRARY

KRISHEF, Robert K.

Dolly Parton. Lerner, 1980
The Grand Ole Opry. Lerner, 1978
Jimmie Rodgers. Lerner, 1978
The New Breed. Lerner, 1978

KRISHEF, Robert K., and **Bonnie LAKE**

Western Stars of Country Music. Lerner, 1978

In many parts of the U.S. country music is the main staple. It is surprising that more is not available for kids on these stars, because this series does not come up to snuff. It needs to be updated: the books here are more than ten years old and many of the people profiled are no longer popular and may even be largely unknown to kids. Lerner needs to revamp and focus on today's stars. Not a necessary purchase.

CRAFT BOOKS

LOHF, Sabine

Building Your Own Toys. Childrens, 1989
Christmas Crafts. Childrens, 1989
I Made It Myself. Childrens, 1989
Making Things for Easter. Childrens, 1989
Nature Crafts. Childrens, 1990

LOHF, Sabine, and **Hannelore SCHAEL**

Making Things with Yarn. Childrens, 1989

MICHALSKI, Ute, and **Tilman MICHALSKI**

Wind Crafts. Childrens, 1990

SCHAEL, Hannelore, **Ulla ABDALLA**, and **Angela WIESNER**

Toys Made of Clay. Childrens, 1990

Kids are always looking for things to create, and this series presents loads of ideas. Clear color illustrations and instructions will help children, teachers, and parents make the crafts. Materials should be readily available at home. Grades 3 and up.

CREATIVE MINDS BIOGRAPHIES

COLLINS, David R.

The Country Artist: A Story about Beatrix Potter. Carolrhoda, 1989
To the Point: A Story about E. B. White. Carolrhoda, 1989

CROFFORD, Emily

Frontier Surgeons: A Story about the Mayo Brothers. Carolrhoda, 1990
Healing Warrior: A Story about Sister Elizabeth Kenny. Carolrhoda, 1989

FERRIS, Jeri

Go Free or Die: A Story about Harriet Tubman. Carolrhoda, 1988
Walking the Road to Freedom: A Story about Sojourner Truth. Carolrhoda, 1989
What Are You Figuring Now? A Story about Benjamin Banneker. Carolrhoda, 1988
What Do You Mean? A Story about Noah Webster. Carolrhoda, 1988

MCPHERSON, Stephanie

Rooftop Astronomer: A Story about Maria Mitchell. Carolrhoda, 1990

MITCHELL, Barbara

America, I Hear You: A Story about George Gershwin. Carolrhoda, 1987
Between Two Worlds: A Story about Pearl Buck. Carolrhoda, 1988
Click! A Story about George Eastman. Carolrhoda, 1986
Good Morning, Mr. President: A Story about Carl Sandburg. Carolrhoda, 1988

A Pocketful of Goobers: A Story about George Washington Carver. Carolrhoda, 1986
Raggin': A Story about Scott Joplin. Carolrhoda, 1987
Shoes for Everyone: A Story about Jan Matzeliger. Carolrhoda, 1986
We'll Race You, Henry: A Story about Henry Ford. Carolrhoda, 1986

WEIDT, Maryann N.
Mr. Blue Jeans: A Story about Levi Strauss. Carolrhoda, 1990

Intermediate readers are the targets of this quality series from Carolrhoda. The coverage is nicely detailed within the limited vocabulary used. One of the best aspects to this series is that the biographees are unusual ... many are not written about elsewhere and it is nice to have these as a resource for grades 3-6.

CREATURES FROM THE PAST

STIDWORTHY, John
The Day of the Dinosaurs. Silver, 1986
Life Begins. Silver, 1986
Mighty Mammals of the Past. Silver, 1986
When Humans Began. Silver, 1986

This paperback series is a catch-all for a brief overview of aspects of prehistoric life. Both drawings and descriptions show how creatures evolved, fought, and died. It may be a case of too much attempted in too little space, however. Interesting puzzles are brought up only to be glossed over (often with no explanatory illustration). These books may prove more frustrating than tantalizing. Grades 4-6. Index.

CULTURAL GEOGRAPHY

HANMER, Trudy J.
Living in Mountains. Watts, 1988

HINTZ, Martin
Living in the Tropics. Watts, 1987

MARKL, Lise
Living in Maritime Regions. Watts, 1988
Living on Islands. Watts, 1987

ROBERT, Leo
Living in Grasslands. Watts, 1988

Looking at the major geographical regions of the world, this series describes the cultural life and activities experienced by the inhabitants. Each book compares three towns from three different parts of the world that share the same geographical features. Each book is illustrated with photographs and contains a glossary, index and bibliography. For YAs.

DECADES

GARRETT, Michael
The Seventies. Steck, 1990

GREY, Edward
The Eighties. Steck, 1990
The Sixties. Steck, 1990

STACY, Tom
The Fifties. Steck, 1990

Like the Timeline series, this one explores the highlights of each decade of modern history. Leisure, fashion, music/media, and youth are covered. A scant ten pages of "images" hits the political/historical high spots. There is a glossary, bibliography, and index. Grades 5-12.

DELL YEARLING BIOGRAPHIES

ADAMS, Patricia
The Story of Pocahontas. Dell, 1987

DAVIDSON, Margaret
The Story of Alexander Graham Bell. Dell, 1989
The Story of Benjamin Franklin. Dell, 1988
The Story of Jackie Robinson. Dell, 1988
DENENBERG, Barry
The Story of Muhammad Ali. Dell, 1990
DUBOWSKI, Cathy East
The Story of Squanto. Dell, 1990
EISENBERG, Lisa
The Story of Babe Ruth. Dell, 1990
FIORI, Carlo
The Story of Shirley Temple Black. Dell, 1990
GRAFF, Stewart, and **Polly Anne GRAFF**
Helen Keller: Crusader for the Blind and Deaf. Dell, 1991
MCGILL, Marcy Ridlon
The Story of Louisa May Alcott. Dell, 1988
MCMULLEN, Kate
The Story of Harriet Tubman. Dell, 1991
MILTON, Joyce
Marching to Freedom: The Story of Martin Luther King, Jr. Dell, 1987
The Story of Thomas Jefferson. Dell, 1990
The Story of Paul Revere. Dell, 1990
O'CONNOR, Jim
The Story of Roberto Clemente. Dell, 1989
OSBORNE, Mary Pope
The Story of Christopher Columbus. Dell, 1987
ROWLAND, Della
The Story of Sacajawea. Dell, 1989
ST. PIERRE, Stephanie
The Story of Jim Henson. Dell, 1991
SELDEN, Bernice
The Story of Walt Disney. Dell, 1989
SUFRIN, Mark
George Bush. Dell, 1989
WEINBERG, Larry
The Story of Abraham Lincoln. Dell, 1991
WHITE, Florence Meiman
The Story of Junipero Serra. Dell, 1987

Written for grades 4-6, these books give a balanced, factual picture of the biographee. There is a section of photos and illustrations in the center. Glossary, no index.

DINOSAURS

RIEHECKY, Janet
Allosaurus. Childrens, 1988
Anatosaurus. Childrens, 1989
Apatosaurus. Childrens, 1988
Brachiosaurus. Childrens, 1989
Iguanodon. Childrens, 1989
Maiasaura. Childrens, 1989
Stegosaurus. Childrens, 1988
Triceratops. Childrens, 1988
Tyrannosaurus. Childrens, 1988

Very often dinosaur books have terrific pictures, but the texts are too difficult for the youngest readers. In this series, the vocabulary is accessible for beginning readers, with all of the basic information intact, accompanied by color drawings. For ages 6-9.

DISASTER!

FRADIN, Dennis

Disaster! Blizzards and Winter Weather. Childrens, 1983
Disaster! Droughts. Childrens, 1983
Disaster! Earthquakes. Childrens, 1982
Disaster! Famines. Childrens, 1986
Disaster! Fires. Childrens, 1982
Disaster! Floods. Childrens, 1982
Disaster! Hurricanes. Childrens, 1982
Disaster! Tornadoes. Childrens, 1982
Disaster! Volcanoes. Childrens, 1982

Natural disasters often fascinate youngsters, and some disasters, like earthquakes and volcanoes, are studied in schools. This series will prove helpful as needed for students grades 4 and up. Each book features many photos, interviews with survivors, descriptions of famous disasters throughout history, scientific background on how and why they occur, and what people can do to minimize their possible injuries and losses.

DISCOVERING NATURE

BAILEY, Jill

Discovering Deer. Watts, 1988
Discovering Rats and Mice. Watts, 1987
Discovering Shrews, Moles, and Voles. Watts, 1989
Discovering Trees. Watts, 1989

BANKS, Martin

Discovering Badgers. Watts, 1988
Discovering Otters. Watts, 1988

BREWSTER, Bernice

Discovering Freshwater Fish. Watts, 1988

BURTON, Robert

Discovering Owls. Watts, 1990

COLDREY, Jennifer

Discovering Flowering Plants. Watts, 1987
Discovering Fungi. Watts, 1988
Discovering Slugs and Snails. Watts, 1987

DAVIES, Adrian

Discovering Squirrels. Watts, 1987

LOSITO, Linda

Discovering Damselflies and Dragonflies. Watts, 1988

MCGAVIN, George

Discovering Bugs. Watts, 1989

MACQUITTY, Miranda

Discovering Foxes. Watts, 1988
Discovering Jellyfish. Watts, 1989
Discovering Weasels. Watts, 1989

MILKINS, Colin S.

Discovering Pond Life. Watts, 1990
Discovering Songbirds. Watts, 1990

MULLENEUX, Jane

Discovering Bats. Watts, 1989

O'TOOLE, Christopher

Discovering Ants. Watts, 1986
Discovering Flies. Watts, 1987

PENNY, Malcolm

Discovering Beetles. Watts, 1987

PORTER, Keith
Discovering Crickets and Grasshoppers. Watts, 1987
PRESTON-MAFHAM, Ken
Discovering Centipedes and Millipedes. Watts, 1990
WHARTON, Anthony
Discovering Ducks, Geese and Swans. Watts, 1987
Discovering Sea Birds. Watts, 1987
WHEELER, Alwyne
Discovering Saltwater Fish. Watts, 1988

This English import introduces readers to all aspects of the animal's natural life, from anatomy to food to reproduction. Color photos and diagrams supplement the text. New terms are in boldface and defined in the glossary. These will prove to be solid introductory fare for grades 3-8. A word of warning, however. Some of the subjects, like freshwater fish and songbirds are covered in general terms, since there are less than 50 pages, and could not be used for reports on specific species.

DISCOVERING OUR HERITAGE
ADAMS, Faith
El Salvador: Beauty among the Ashes. Dillon, 1986
Nicaragua: Struggling with Change. Dillon, 1987
BALERDI, Susan
France: The Crossroads of Europe. Dillon, 1984
BRYANT, Adam
Canada: Good Neighbor to the World. Dillon, 1987
CARPENTER, Mark
Brazil: An Awakening Giant. Dillon, 1987
GALVIN, Irene Flum
Chile: Land of Poets and Patriots. Dillon, 1990
GARLAND, Sherry
Vietnam: Rebuilding a Nation. Dillon, 1990
GILLIES, John
The Soviet Union: The World's Largest Country. Dillon, 1985
JACOBS, Judy
Indonesia: A Nation of Islands. Dillon, 1990
KEYWORTH, Valerie
New Zealand: Land of the Long White Cloud. Dillon, 1990
MCCARTHY, Kevin
Saudi Arabia: A Desert Kingdom. Dillon, 1986
MCCLURE, Vimala
Bangladesh: Rivers in a Crowded Land. Dillon, 1989
PETERSON, Marge, and **Rob PETERSON**
Argentina: A Wild West Heritage. Dillon, 1989
PFEIFFER, Christine
Germany: Two Nations, One Heritage. Dillon, 1987
Poland: Land of Freedom Fighters. Dillon, 1984
SCHREPFER, Margaret
Switzerland: The Summit of Europe. Dillon, 1989
SCHWABACH, Karen
Thailand: Land of Smiles. Dillon, 1990
SPYROPULOS, Diana
Greece: A Spirited Independence. Dillon, 1990
STARK, Al
Australia: A Lucky Land. Dillon, 1987
Zimbabwe: A Treasure of Africa. Dillon, 1986

TAITZ, Emily, and **Sondra HENRY**
Israel: A Sacred Land. Dillon, 1987
WOODS, Geraldine
Spain: A Shining New Democracy. Dillon, 1987
YUSUFALI, Jabeen
Pakistan: An Islamic Treasure. Dillon, 1990

Like other series about foreign countries, this one covers the usual bases of geography, economy, religion, people, and culture. What sets this one apart is the frank discussions of the political ramifications pro and con of each country and its relationship with the United States. Historical background is not limited to early days, but a sound coverage of recent history is emphasized. Citizens' lifestyles are clearly portrayed. A few recipes are provided, along with addresses of the consulates, some foreign phrases, a glossary, index, and bibliography. Excellent choices for grades 5 and up.

DISCOVERING OUR UNIVERSE
DARLING, David
Comets, Meteors, and Asteroids: Rocks in Space. Dillon, 1984
The Galaxies: Cities of Stars. Dillon, 1985
The Moon: A Spaceflight Away. Dillon, 1984
The New Astronomy: An Ever-Changing Universe. Dillon, 1985
Other Worlds: Is There Life Out There? Dillon, 1985
The Planets: The Next Frontier. Dillon, 1984
The Stars: From Birth to Black Hole. Dillon, 1985
The Sun: Our Neighborhood Star. Dillon, 1984
The Universe: Past, Present, and Future. Dillon, 1985
Where Are We Going in Space? Dillon, 1984

This series is rather a mixed bag. The author begins with a page of facts, then several pages of questions and answers related to the topic. *Then* he moves on to an examination of the subject, suggesting that readers imagine themselves visiting the planet. This approach is dropped for more hard information, with new words in boldface. At the end the "visit" motif is picked up again, followed by appendices of observation suggestions, a list of amateur astronomy groups, a list of space missions, and a list of robot missions. This disjointed approach could prove confusing to the age group it is intended for—ages 7-10.

DISCOVERING SCIENCE
BERGER, Melvin
As Old as the Hills. Watts, 1989
PATENT, Dorothy Hinshaw
Grandfather's Nose: Why We Look Alike or Different. Watts, 1989
Singing Birds and Flashing Fireflies: How Animals Talk to Each Other. Watts, 1989
ZASLAVSKY, Claudia
Zero! Is It Something? Is It Nothing? Watts, 1989

Second and third graders are the target group of these books. The authors explain various phenomena of natural science, math, and heredity in a simple manner, with color illustrations. The text is conversational, there is a glossary, but no index. Fine for introductory material.

DISCOVERY
FRANK, Julia
Alzheimer's Disease: The Silent Epidemic. Lerner, 1985
GROSS, Cynthia S.
The New Biotechnology: Putting Microbes to Work. Lerner, 1988
JOHNSON, Rebecca L.
The Secret Language: Pheromones in the Animal World. Lerner, 1989
JOHNSON, Sylvia A., and **Alice AAMODT**
Wolf Pack: Tracking Wolves in the Wild. Lerner, 1985

WILCOX, Frank H.

DNA: The Thread of Life. Lerner, 1988

Scientific topics ranging from biotechnology to biology to oceanography are studied here. The authors are experts in their field and examine their subjects with considerable depth. They examine past and current knowledge, as well as future possibilities. There are some illustrations. Grades 5 and up. Glossary, index.

DISCOVERY BIOGRAPHIES

ANDERSON, LaVere

Martha Washington. Chelsea, 1991
Mary McLeod Bethune. Chelsea, 1991
Mary Todd Lincoln. Chelsea, 1991

BEACH, James C.

Theodore Roosevelt. Chelsea, 1991

BLASSINGAME, Wyatt

Jim Beckwourth. Chelsea, 1991

COLLINS, David R.

Harry S. Truman. Chelsea, 1991

COLLINS, David R.

Charles Lindbergh. Chelsea, 1991

GLENDINNING, Richard, and **Sally GLENDINNING**

The Ringling Brothers. Chelsea, 1991

GRAVES, Charles P.

Annie Oakley. Chelsea, 1991
Paul Revere. Chelsea, 1991
Robert E. Lee. Chelsea, 1991

HENRY, Joanne L.

Robert Fulton. Chelsea, 1991

LATHAM, Jean

David Farragut. Chelsea, 1991

LATHAM, Jean L.

Eli Whitney. Chelsea, 1991
Elizabeth Blackwell. Chelsea, 1991
George W. Goethals. Chelsea, 1991
Rachel Carson. Chelsea, 1991
Sam Houston. Chelsea, 1991
Samuel F. B. Morse. Chelsea, 1991

LUCE, Williard

Jim Bridger. Chelsea, 1991

MALONE, Mary

Dorothea Dix. Chelsea, 1991

MOSELEY, Elizabeth R.

Davy Crockett. Chelsea, 1991

PARLIN, John

Andrew Jackson. Chelsea, 1991

PATTERSON, Lillie

Booker T. Washington. Chelsea, 1991
Francis Scott Key. Chelsea, 1991
Frederick Douglass. Chelsea, 1991

PETERSON, Helen S.

Abigail Adams. Chelsea, 1987
Henry Clay. Chelsea, 1991

ROSE, Mary C.
Clara Barton. Chelsea, 1991
WILKIE, Katharine E.
Daniel Boone. Chelsea, 1991

This series is a reprint of a series published almost thirty years ago by Garrard. The cover art is updated and there are a lot of drawings sprinkled throughout, but the text is unchanged. There is an overabundance of "conversations," alleged emotions, and no index. There are so many other good biographical series, this one is a marginal choice. Grades 3-6.

DOWNTOWN AMERICA

ADAMS, Barbara Johnston
New York City. Dillon, 1988
AYRES, Becky
Salt Lake City. Dillon, 1990
BALCER, Bernadette, and **Fran O'BYRNE-PELHAM**
Philadelphia. Dillon, 1989
BERRY, S. L.
Indianapolis. Dillon, 1990
FISCHER, Marsha
Miami. Dillon, 1990
FORD, Barbara
St. Louis. Dillon, 1989
HADDOCK, Patricia
San Francisco. Dillon, 1989
LYNCH, Amy
Nashville. Dillon, 1991
MONKE, Ingrid
Boston. Dillon, 1988
NICHOLS, Joan Kane
New Orleans. Dillon, 1989
OBERLE, Joseph G.
Anchorage. Dillon, 1990
O'CONNOR, Karen
San Diego. Dillon, 1990
PEIFER, Charles, Jr.
Houston. Dillon, 1988
PENISTEN, John
Honolulu. Dillon, 1989
PFEIFFER, Christine
Chicago. Dillon, 1988
REEF, Catherine
Baltimore. Dillon, 1990
Washington, D.C. Dillon, 1989
SNOW, Pegeen
Atlanta. Dillon, 1988
SPIES, Karen
Denver. Dillon, 1988
STURMAN, Susan
Kansas City. Dillon, 1990
ZACH, Cheryl
Los Angeles. Dillon, 1989
ZIMMERMAN, Chanda K.
Detroit. Dillon, 1989

While information on states is plentiful, there is little available on large cities. This series fills the void. Each book begins with a list of important facts, then a map of the city itself. At the end, the authors provide a list of places to visit and a time line. In between comes the portrait of the city, its rhythm, lifestyle, and the people who live there. Grades 5-12.

DRUG-ALERT SERIES

BECKATE, Danielle J.
Focus on Hallucinogens. Childrens, 1990
DESTEFANO, Susan
Focus on Opiates. Childrens, 1990
FRIEDMAN, David
Focus on Drugs and the Brain. Childrens, 1990
O'NEILL, Catherine
Focus on Alcohol. Childrens, 1990
PERRY, Robert
Focus on Nicotine and Caffeine. Childrens, 1990
SHULMAN, Jeffrey
The Drug-Alert Dictionary and Resource Guide. Childrens, 1990
Focus on Cocaine and Crack. Childrens, 1990
TALMADGE, Katherine
Focus on Steroids. Childrens, 1990
WEST, Elizabeth
Focus on Medicines. Childrens, 1990
ZELLER, Paula Klevan
Focus on Marijuana. Childrens, 1990

Introductory material on various kinds of often-abused drugs is provided in this new series. The basics are covered in a simple, straightforward way. Repercussions of drug use on babies is included, as well as sample statements of denial and enabling which may help youngsters recognize similar responses in their own lives. Grades 4-6.

EARLY CAREER BOOKS

BELL, Rivian, and **Teresa KOENIG**
Careers with a Record Company. Lerner, 1983
BLUMENFELD, Milton J.
Careers in Photography. Lerner, 1979
FRICKE, Pam
Careers with an Electric Company. Lerner, 1984
LERNER, Mark
Careers with a Radio Station. Lerner, 1983
Careers in Auto Racing. Lerner, 1980
STORMS, Laura
Careers with an Advertising Agency. Lerner, 1984
Careers with an Orchestra. Lerner, 1983

To whet a youngster's appetite or give a *very* brief overview of a career, these books could prove useful. One small page, with a facing color photo, is spent on one variant of a job: i.e., industrial photographer, colorist, etc. Grades 2-4. No index or glossary.

EARLY NATURE PICTURE BOOKS

AASENG, Nathan
Animal Specialists. Lerner, 1987
Horned Animals. Lerner, 1987
Meat-Eating Animals. Lerner, 1987
Prey Animals. Lerner, 1987
ORANGE, Anne
The Flower Book. Lerner, 1975
The Leaf Book. Lerner, 1975

OVERBECK, Cynthia

The Butterfly Book. Lerner, 1978
The Fish Book. Lerner, 1978
The Fruit Book. Lerner, 1977
The Vegetable Book. Lerner, 1975

These small books begin by describing the general characteristics of the subject. Individual species members then are allowed about four pages of coverage, including a color drawing. These can be good sources for material on hard-to-find animals. Maps indicate where they are found and are accompanied by vital statistics. A chart at the end compares the sizes of the animals under discussion. Grades 2-5. No glossary or index.

EARTH ALERT

DUDEN, Jane
The Ozone Layer. Crestwood, 1990
DUGGLEBY, John
Pesticides. Crestwood, 1990
GOLD, Susan Dudley
Toxic Waste. Crestwood, 1990
HARRIS, Jack C.
The Greenhouse Effect. Crestwood, 1990
LAZO, Caroline Evensen
Endangered Species. Crestwood, 1990
PHILLIPS, Anne W.
The Ocean. Crestwood, 1990
STEWART, Gail B.
Drought. Crestwood, 1990
TURCK, Mary
Acid Rain. Crestwood, 1990

Like Green Issues (and several other series), this one examines environmental issues. The authors describe the problems, discuss how they came to be, future implications, and possible solutions. The emphasis is on the global aspects. There are some color photos, addresses to write for more information, bibliography, glossary, index. Grades 4-7.

EARTH SCIENCE LIBRARY

BRAMWELL, Martyn
Deserts. Watts, 1988
Glaciers and Ice Caps. Watts, 1987
Mountains. Watts, 1987
The Oceans. Watts, 1987
Planet Earth. Watts, 1987
Rivers and Lakes. Watts, 1986
Volcanoes and Earthquakes. Watts, 1987
Weather. Watts, 1988

Bramwell has written this series for junior high school students, to whom he explains the forces that have shaped the earth. Each book is filled with color photographs, maps and diagrams. A glossary and index are included. This series should be a welcome addition to the science collection in a library.

EARTH WATCH

BANNAN, Jan Gumprecht
Sand Dunes. Carolrhoda, 1989
JACOBS, Linda
Letting Off Steam: The Story of Geothermal Energy. Carolrhoda, 1987
WALKER, Sally M.
Glaciers: Ice on the Move. Carolrhoda, 1990

Like the Nature Watch series, this one accents the study of earth science for grades 4-8 by thorough discussions of each topic accompanied by excellent color photos. There is a glossary and index. The history, natural development, and importance to man is examined.

EASY MENU ETHNIC COOKBOOKS

AMARI, Suad
Cooking the Lebanese Way. Lerner, 1986

BACON, Josephine
Cooking the Israeli Way. Lerner, 1986

BISIGNANO, Alphonse
Cooking the Italian Way. Lerner, 1982

CHRISTIAN, Rebecca
Cooking the Spanish Way. Lerner, 1982

CHUNG, Okwha, and **Judy MONROE**
Cooking the Korean Way. Lerner, 1988

CORONADO, Rosa
Cooking the Mexican Way. Lerner, 1982

GERMAINE, Elizabeth, and **Ann L. BURCKHARDT**
Cooking the Australian Way. Lerner, 1990

HARGITTAI, Magdolna
Cooking the Hungarian Way. Lerner, 1986

HARRISON, Supenn, and **Judy MONROE**
Cooking the Thai Way. Lerner, 1986

HILL, Barbara W.
Cooking the English Way. Lerner, 1982

KAUFMAN, Cheryl
Cooking the Caribbean Way. Lerner, 1988

MADAVAN, Vijay
Cooking the Indian Way. Lerner, 1985

MUNSEN, Sylvia
Cooking the Norwegian Way. Lerner, 1982

NABWIRE, Constance, and **Bertha Vining MONTGOMERY**
Cooking the African Way. Lerner, 1988

NGUYEN, Chi, and **Judy MONROE**
Cooking the Vietnamese Way. Lerner, 1983

PARNELL, Helga
Cooking the German Way. Lerner, 1988

PLOTKIN, Gregory, and **Rita PLOTKIN**
Cooking the Russian Way. Lerner, 1986

VILLIOS, Lynne W.
Cooking the Greek Way. Lerner, 1984

WALDEE, Lynne Marie
Cooking the French Way. Lerner, 1982

WESTON, Reiko
Cooking the Japanese Way. Lerner, 1983

YU, Ling
Cooking the Chinese Way. Lerner, 1982

ZAMOJSKA-HUTCHINS, Danuta
Cooking the Polish Way. Lerner, 1984

Many readers will use this eye appealing series. Cooks young and not so young will find representative recipes for all three meals plus dessert here. Ingredients are common ones, and a section with metric conversion charts and safety hints will benefit beginners. The authors also list necessary utensils, special ingredients, and cooking terms. Several pages of information on each land precede the recipes. Students and Scouts can also utilize these for studying other cultures. Grades 4 and up.

EASY-READ FACT BOOKS

HAMER, Martyn

Comets. Watts, 1984

JAY, Michael

Planets. Watts, 1987

Tanks. Watts, 1987

JEFFERIS, David

Flags. Watts, 1985

Helicopters. Watts, 1987

Lasers. Watts, 1986

Military Planes. Watts, 1985

Satellites. Watts, 1987

JEFFERIS, David, and **Kenneth GATLAND**

Robots. Watts, 1982

LAMBERT, David

Rocks and Minerals. Watts, 1986

Snakes. Watts, 1986

Introductory material on assorted topics is provided by these books on the early reading level. Each volume provides background information, a glossary, index, and facts about the subject. Color illustrations accompany the text. Grades K-4.

ECONOMICS FOR TODAY

FLAGLER, John J.

The Labor Movement in the United States. Lerner, 1990

KILLEN, M. Barbara

Economics and the Consumer. Lerner, 1990

LUBOV, Andrea

Taxes and Government Spending. Lerner, 1990

O'TOOLE, Thomas

Economic History of the United States. Lerner, 1990

There is next to nothing available to teach young readers about economics: how and why it works the way it does, and how it affects them. This series does an excellent job of it by examining individual aspects of economic life. The high spots are briefly explained, with adequate graphs and diagrams to clarify the topics. New words are in boldface and defined in the glossary. Grades 5 and up. Glossary, index.

ENCHANTMENT OF AMERICA

CARPENTER, Allan

Alabama. Childrens, 1978

Alaska. Childrens, 1979

Arizona. Childrens, 1979

Arkansas. Childrens, 1978

California. Childrens, 1978

Colorado. Childrens, 1978

Connecticut. Childrens, 1979

Delaware. Childrens, 1979

District of Columbia. Childrens, 1979

Far-Flung America. Childrens, 1979

Florida. Childrens, 1979

Georgia. Childrens, 1979

Hawaii. Childrens, 1979

Idaho. Childrens, 1979

Illinois. Childrens, 1979

Indiana. Childrens, 1979

Iowa. Childrens, 1979

Kansas. Childrens, 1979
Kentucky. Childrens, 1979
Louisiana. Childrens, 1978
Maine. Childrens, 1979
Maryland. Childrens, 1979
Massachusetts. Childrens, 1978
Michigan. Childrens, 1978
Minnesota. Childrens, 1978
Mississippi. Childrens, 1978
Missouri. Childrens, 1978
Montana. Childrens, 1979
Nebraska. Childrens, 1979
Nevada. Childrens, 1979
New Hampshire. Childrens, 1979
New Jersey. Childrens, 1979
New Mexico. Childrens, 1978
New York. Childrens, 1978
North Carolina. Childrens, 1979
North Dakota. Childrens, 1979
Ohio. Childrens, 1979
Oklahoma. Childrens, 1979
Oregon. Childrens, 1979
Pennsylvania. Childrens, 1978
Rhode Island. Childrens, 1979
South Carolina. Childrens, 1979
South Dakota. Childrens, 1978
Tennessee. Childrens, 1979
Texas. Childrens, 1979
Utah. Childrens, 1979
Vermont. Childrens, 1979
Virginia. Childrens, 1978
Washington. Childrens, 1979
West Virginia. Childrens, 1979
Wisconsin. Childrens, 1978
Wyoming. Childrens, 1979

Similar to the same publisher's America the Beautiful series, this one places a little more emphasis on current state information rather than historical. Otherwise the coverage is much the same. This series is ten years old and there are not as many photos, nor are the production values as high. The reference section is only 3 pages long, compared to at least twice that number in the other series. Grades 4-8.

ENCHANTMENT OF THE WORLD

BACHELIS, Faren
El Salvador. Childrens, 1990

BEATON, Margaret
Syria. Childrens, 1988

BRILL, Marlene Targ
Algeria. Childrens, 1990
Libya. Childrens, 1987

BROWN, Marion Marsh
Singapore. Childrens, 1989

CARRAN, Betty B.
Romania. Childrens, 1988

CASAS, Rosa E., and **Ana Maria B. VAZQUEZ**
Cuba. Childrens, 1987

CROSS, Esther, and **Wilbur CROSS**
Portugal. Childrens, 1986
Spain. Childrens, 1985
CROSS, Wilbur
Brazil. Childrens, 1984
Egypt. Childrens, 1982
DIAMOND, Judith
Laos. Childrens, 1989
FOSTER, Leila M.
Bhutan. Childrens, 1989
Iraq. Childrens, 1991
FOX, Mary Virginia
Iran. Childrens, 1991
New Zealand. Childrens, 1991
Tunisia. Childrens, 1990
FRADIN, Dennis
Ethiopia. Childrens, 1988
Netherlands. Childrens, 1983
Republic of Ireland. Childrens, 1984
GREENE, Carol
Austria. Childrens, 1986
England. Childrens, 1982
Japan. Childrens, 1983
Poland. Childrens, 1983
Yugoslavia. Childrens, 1984
HARGROVE, James
Belgium. Childrens, 1988
HINTZ, Martin
Argentina. Childrens, 1985
Chile. Childrens, 1985
Finland. Childrens, 1983
Ghana. Childrens, 1987
Hungary. Childrens, 1988
Morocco. Childrens, 1985
Norway. Childrens, 1982
Sweden. Childrens, 1985
Switzerland. Childrens, 1986
West Germany. Childrens, 1983
JONES, Helen Hinckley
Israel. Childrens, 1986
LANE, Martha S. B.
Malawi. Childrens, 1990
LAURE, Jason
Angola. Childrens, 1990
Zambia. Childrens, 1989
Zimbabwe. Childrens, 1988
LEPTHIEN, Emilie U.
Australia. Childrens, 1982
Ecuador. Childrens, 1986
Greenland. Childrens, 1989
Iceland. Childrens, 1987
Luxembourg. Childrens, 1989
Philippines. Childrens, 1986
MCLENIGHAN, Valjean
China: A History to 1949. Childrens, 1983
People's Republic of China. Childrens, 1984

MCNAIR, Sylvia
India. Childrens, 1990
Korea. Childrens, 1986
Thailand. Childrens, 1987
MORRISON, Marion
Bolivia. Childrens, 1988
Colombia. Childrens, 1990
Venezuela. Childrens, 1989
MOSS, Peter, and **Thelma PALMER**
France. Childrens, 1986
RESNICK, Abraham
Russia: A History to 1917. Childrens, 1983
Union of Soviet Socialist Republics. Childrens, 1984
SHEPHERD, Jenifer
Canada. Childrens, 1987
STEIN, R. Conrad
Greece. Childrens, 1987
Hong Kong. Childrens, 1985
Italy. Childrens, 1984
Kenya. Childrens, 1985
Mexico. Childrens, 1984
South Africa. Childrens, 1986
SUTHERLAND, Dorothy
Scotland. Childrens, 1985
Wales. Childrens, 1987
WRIGHT, David K.
Burma. Childrens, 1991
Malaysia. Childrens, 1988
Vietnam. Childrens, 1989

The highlights of this series are the color photos and clear, easily accessible text. They are simply enough written to be usable to grades 3-8, and cover history and socio-political-economic aspects, winding up with a section of mini-facts for researchers. The coverage is cursory, however, so these are best used by younger readers, for short reports, or in conjunction with other sources.

ENCYCLOPEDIA BROWN'S BOOKS
SOBOL, Donald J.
Encyclopedia Brown's Book of the Wacky Outdoors. Morrow, 1987
Encyclopedia Brown's Book of Wacky Animals. Morrow, 1985
Encyclopedia Brown's Book of Wacky Cars. Morrow, 1987
Encyclopedia Brown's Book of Wacky Spies. Morrow, 1984
Encyclopedia Brown's Book of Wacky Sports. Morrow, 1984
Encyclopedia Brown's 3rd Record Book of Weird and Wonderful Facts. Morrow, 1985

This series uses the popular character Encyclopedia Brown to introduce youngsters to brief factual anecdotes on a variety of subjects. The trivia is fun for those interested, but it is purely trivia. There is no index and the information is not in-depth enough to use for school assignments. Grades 3-7.

ENCYCLOPEDIA OF DISCOVERY AND INVENTION
BIEL, Timothy Levi
Atoms: Building Blocks of Matter. Greenhaven, 1990
GANO, Lila
Television: Electronic Pictures. Greenhaven, 1990

HIZEROTH, Deborah
Radar: The Silent Detector. Greenhaven, 1990
NARDO, Don
Computers: Mechanical Minds. Greenhaven, 1990
Gravity: The Universal Force. Greenhaven, 1990
Lasers: Humanity's Magic Light. Greenhaven, 1990
STACEY, Tom
Airplanes: The Lure of Flight. Greenhaven, 1990
STEFFENS, Bradley
Printing Press: Ideas into Type. Greenhaven, 1990

Each volume examines an invention or discovery and the concepts that preceded it. The people who had a hand in the particular invention are also discussed and their contributions are outlined. Photographs and numerous appendices. Grades 5-8.

ENCYCLOPEDIA OF HEALTH
AVARAHAM, Regina
The Circulatory System. Chelsea, 1989
The Digestive System. Chelsea, 1989
The Reproductive System. Chelsea, 1991
CHECK, William
AIDS. Chelsea, 1988
Alzheimer's Disease. Chelsea, 1989
Child Abuse. Chelsea, 1989
The Mind-Body Connection. Chelsea, 1989
EDELSON, Edward
Aging. Chelsea, 1989
Allergies. Chelsea, 1989
Genetics and Heredity. Chelsea, 1990
The Immune System. Chelsea, 1989
Sports Medicine. Chelsea, 1988
EPSTEIN, Rachel
Careers in Health Care. Chelsea, 1989
Eating Habits and Disorders. Chelsea, 1989
FRIEDLAND, Bruce
Personality Disorders. Chelsea, 1991
GALPERIN, Ann
Gynecological Disorders. Chelsea, 1989
Stroke and Heart Disease. Chelsea, 1991
GILBERT, Susan
Medical Fakes and Frauds. Chelsea, 1989
GORDON, James
Holistic Medicine. Chelsea, 1988
Stress Management. Chelsea, 1990
GRAUER, Neil
Medicine and the Law. Chelsea, 1989
GRINNEY, Ellen
The Hospital. Chelsea, 1989
HALES, Diane
Depression. Chelsea, 1989
Pregnancy and Birth. Chelsea, 1989
KITTREDGE, Mary
The Common Cold. Chelsea, 1989
Headaches. Chelsea, 1989
The Human Body: An Overview. Chelsea, 1990
Organ Transplants. Chelsea, 1989

Prescription and Over-the-Counter Drugs. Chelsea, 1989
The Respiratory System. Chelsea, 1989
The Senses. Chelsea, 1990

KNOX, Jean
Death and Dying. Chelsea, 1989
Learning Disabilities. Chelsea, 1989

KUSINITZ, Marc
Tropical Medicine. Chelsea, 1989

LAMBERG, Lynne
Skin Disorders. Chelsea, 1990

LITTLE, Marjorie
Diabetes. Chelsea, 1989
The Endocrine System. Chelsea, 1990

LUNDY, Allan
Diagnosing and Treating Mental Illness. Chelsea, 1990

MARSHALL, Eliot
Medical Ethics. Chelsea, 1989

RODGERS, Joanne
Cancer. Chelsea, 1990

SAMZ, Jane
Vision. Chelsea, 1990

SHADER, Laurel
Mononucleosis and Other Infectious Diseases. Chelsea, 1989

STEFOFF, Rebecca
Adolescence. Chelsea, 1988
Friendship and Love. Chelsea, 1989

YOUNG, Patrick
Schizophrenia. Chelsea, 1988

This series examines a number of health and related issues. Each book gives comprehensive, but coherent, information relating to that particular field. Illustrated with graphs, charts, and pictures. Each book includes an index, bibliography, and appendices. The names and addresses of places where the reader can turn to for more information are also included. For those students who have a health class or are just interested in learning about any of these topics, this series is a good start. Written for students ages 12 and up.

ENCYCLOPEDIA OF PRESIDENTS

BRILL, Marlene Targ
James Buchanan. Childrens, 1988
John Adams. Childrens, 1986

CASEY, Jane Clark
Millard Fillmore. Childrens, 1988
William Howard Taft. Childrens, 1989

CLINTON, Susan
Benjamin Harrison. Childrens, 1989
Herbert Hoover. Childrens, 1988
James Madison. Childrens, 1986

FITZ-GERALD, Christine Maloney
James Monroe. Childrens, 1987
William Henry Harrison. Childrens, 1987

HARGROVE, Jim
Abraham Lincoln. Childrens, 1988
Dwight D. Eisenhower. Childrens, 1987
Harry S. Truman. Childrens, 1987
Lyndon B. Johnson. Childrens, 1987
Martin Van Buren. Childrens, 1987
Thomas Jefferson. Childrens, 1986

KENT, Zachary
Andrew Johnson. Childrens, 1989
Calvin Coolidge. Childrens, 1988
George Bush. Childrens, 1989
George Washington. Childrens, 1986
Grover Cleveland. Childrens, 1988
John F. Kennedy. Childrens, 1987
John Quincy Adams. Childrens, 1987
Ronald Reagan. Childrens, 1989
Rutherford B. Hayes. Childrens, 1989
Theodore Roosevelt. Childrens, 1988
Ulysses S. Grant. Childrens, 1989
William McKinley. Childrens, 1988
Zachary Taylor. Childrens, 1988

LILLEGARD, Dee
James A. Garfield. Childrens, 1987
James K. Polk. Childrens, 1988
John Tyler. Childrens, 1987
Richard Nixon. Childrens, 1988

OSINSKI, Alice
Andrew Jackson. Childrens, 1987
Franklin D. Roosevelt. Childrens, 1987
Woodrow Wilson. Childrens, 1989

SIMON, Charnan
Chester A. Arthur. Childrens, 1989
Franklin Pierce. Childrens, 1988

SIPIERA, Paul
Gerald Ford. Childrens, 1989

WADE, Linda R.
James Carter. Childrens, 1989
Warren G. Harding. Childrens, 1989

This outstanding series profiles each president in great detail. Photos and drawings from the period add to the interest. Each subject is treated from birth to death, with considerable explanation of the times each lived in and why he was important. A chronology of American history is appended, with the president's time frame shaded in—a feature most helpful in creating time lines. Excellent coverage for grades 5-12.

ENCYCLOPEDIA OF PSYCHOACTIVE DRUGS

AUGUST, Paul
Brain Function. Chelsea, 1986
Drugs and Women. Chelsea, 1987

AVRAHAM, Regina
The Downside of Drugs. Chelsea, 1987
Substance Abuse: Prevention and Treatment. Chelsea, 1988

BABOR, Thomas
Alcohol: Customs and Rituals. Chelsea, 1986

BYCK, Robert
Treating Mental Illness. Chelsea, 1986

CARROLL, Marilyn
PCP: The Dangerous Angel. Chelsea, 1985
Quaaludes: The Quest for Oblivion. Chelsea, 1985

CHECK, William
Drugs and Perception. Chelsea, 1987
Drugs of the Future. Chelsea, 1987

CHILES, John
Teenage Depression and Suicide. Chelsea, 1986
COHEN, Miriam
Marijuana: Its Effects on Mind and Body. Chelsea, 1985
COX, W. Miles
Addictive Personality. Chelsea, 1986
EDELSON, Edward
Drugs and the Brain. Chelsea, 1987
Nutrition and the Brain. Chelsea, 1987
FISHMAN, Ross
Alcohol and Alcoholism. Chelsea, 1987
FREEMAN, Sally
Drugs and Civilization. Chelsea, 1987
FRIEDLAND, Bruce
Emotions and Thoughts. Chelsea, 1987
FURST, Peter E.
Mushrooms: Psychedelic Fungi. Chelsea, 1986
GILBERT, Richard J.
Caffeine: The Most Popular Stimulant. Chelsea, 1986
GLOWA, John R.
Inhalants: The Toxic Fumes. Chelsea, 1986
GOODMAN, Paula
Designer Drugs. Chelsea, 1988
GRAUER, Neil A.
Drugs and the Law. Chelsea, 1988
GWYNNE, Peter
Who Uses Drugs? Chelsea, 1988
HALES, Dianne P.
Case Histories. Chelsea, 1987
HENNINGFIELD, Jack E.
Barbiturates: Sleeping Potion or Intoxicant. Chelsea, 1986
Nicotine: An Old-fashioned Addiction. Chelsea, 1985
HOOBLER, Thomas
Drugs and Crime. Chelsea, 1987
HUTCHINGS, Donald
Methadone: Treatment for Addiction. Chelsea, 1985
JOHANSON, Chris E.
Cocaine: A New Epidemic. Chelsea, 1986
KNOX, Jean McBee
Drinking, Driving and Drugs. Chelsea, 1987
Drugs through the Ages. Chelsea, 1987
KUSINITZ, Marc
Celebrity Drug Use. Chelsea, 1987
Drug Use around the World. Chelsea, 1988
Drugs and the Arts. Chelsea, 1987
LAMBERG, Lynne
Drugs and Sleep. Chelsea, 1988
LANG, Alan R.
Alcohol: Teenage Drinking. Chelsea, 1985
LUKAS, Scott E.
Amphetamines: Danger in the Fast Lane. Chelsea, 1985
MCLELLAN, Tom
Escape from Anxiety and Stress. Chelsea, 1986
MARSHALL, Eliot
Legalization: A Debate. Chelsea, 1987

MARTIN, Jo
Drugs and the Family. Chelsea, 1987
MEER, Jeff
Drugs and Sports. Chelsea, 1987
MILLER, Mark S.
Bad Trips. Chelsea, 1986
RICHARDSON, P. Mick
Flowering Plants: Magic in Bloom. Chelsea, 1986
RODGERS, Joann Ellison
Drugs and Pain. Chelsea, 1987
Drugs and Sexual Behavior. Chelsea, 1987
SAMZ, Jane
Drugs and Diet. Chelsea, 1987
SANBERG, Paul
Over-the-counter Drugs: Harmless or Hazardous? Chelsea, 1986
Prescription Narcotics: The Addictive Painkillers. Chelsea, 1986
SCHNOLL, Sidney H.
Getting Help: Treatments for Drug Abuse. Chelsea, 1986
SHADER, Laurel
Drugs and Disease. Chelsea, 1987
THEODORE, Alan
Origins and Sources of Drugs. Chelsea, 1988
TRULSON, Michael
LSD: Visions or Nightmares? Chelsea, 1985
WINGER, Gail
Valium and Other Tranquilizers. Chelsea, 1986
YOUNG, Patrick
Drugs and Pregnancy. Chelsea, 1987
Mental Disturbances. Chelsea, 1987
ZACKON, Fred
Heroin: The Street Narcotic. Chelsea, 1986

High school students love the type of book that concentrates on a single subject—it makes writing term papers easier. Well, this series is a hit. Each book contains a glossary, bibliography, index and a directory of drug treatment agencies. Well written and illustrated, the books are straightforward and easy to comprehend. Although written in the mid to late 80s, some titles may be slightly dated (i.e., *Cocaine: A New Epidemic* does not mention "crack" cocaine). This series is a must for school libraries.

ENGINEERS AT WORK

BENDER, Lionel
Eurotunnel. Watts, 1990
CAWTHORNE, Nigel
Airliner. Watts, 1988
FURNISS, Tim
Space Rocket. Watts, 1988
GRAHAM, Ian
Attack Submarine. Watts, 1989
Salvage at Sea. Watts, 1990
IRVINE, Mat
Telesatellite. Watts, 1989
OSTLER, Tim
Skyscraper. Watts, 1988
TRIER, Mike
Super Car. Watts, 1988

A variety of engineering feats are examined in this excellent series. The design, construction, the engineers themselves, even *why* something is built the way it is, is explained. There are even a couple of pages of experiments that illustrate appropriate engineering principles for readers. Grades 5-8.

ENTERTAINMENT WORLD

AASENG, Nathan

Jim Henson: Muppet Master. Lerner, 1988

GREENBERG, Keith Elliot

Bruce Springsteen. Lerner, 1986
Cyndi Lauper. Lerner, 1985
Madonna. Lerner, 1986
Michael J. Fox. Lerner, 1986
Ralph Macchio. Lerner, 1987
Rap. Lerner, 1988
Whitney Houston. Lerner, 1988

HASKINS, Jim

Break Dancing. Lerner, 1985

KOENIG, Teresa, and **Rivian BELL**

Eddie Murphy. Lerner, 1985

MABERY, D. L.

George Lucas. Lerner, 1987
Janet Jackson. Lerner, 1988
Julian Lennon. Lerner, 1986
Prince. Lerner, 1985
This Is Michael Jackson. Lerner, 1984
Tina Turner. Lerner, 1986

Stars with name-appeal to youngsters are targeted in this series. These books emphasize the career rather than the entire personal background of the star, although there are some biographical details provided. There are many photos. While the format will attract younger readers, the vocabulary really is aimed at those 10 and up. Needless to say, some of these stars are no longer as popular, and some biographies will be out of date, like the one on Jim Henson, who has died since its publication. But these are otherwise fine choices as needed. No index.

EQUINOX GUIDES

DICKINSON, Terence

Exploring the Night Sky. Firefly, 1989
Exploring the Sky by Day. Firefly, 1988
Nightwatch. Firefly, 1989

FORSYTHE, Adrian (editor)

Architecture of Animals. Firefly, 1989

Parents and teachers will appreciate the clear explanations of these subjects that appeal to young people. Weather, astronomy, the universe and animal life are all described using dozens of color illustrations. The text is easily understood and written for seventh graders and up.

ETHNIC AND TRADITIONAL HOLIDAYS

BEHRENS, June

Fiesta! Childrens, 1978
Gung Hay Fat Choy. Childrens, 1982
Hanukkah. Childrens, 1983
Passover. Childrens, 1987
Powwow. Childrens, 1983
Samoans! Childrens, 1986

Introductory material on an unusual assortment of holidays for early readers is provided by this series. Celebrations of Mexican, Jewish, Chinese, Samoan, and Native American holidays are described, complete with color photos. The purpose of the holiday is mentioned, traditional foods, costumes, and games are discussed. These will prove useful in areas with ethnic populations or where other cultures are studied. Grades preschool-3.

EVERYDAY LIFE

CHAMBERLIN, Russell

Everyday Life in the 19th Century. Silver, 1983

GRANT, Neil

Everyday Life in the 18th Century. Silver, 1983

MACDONALD, Fiona

Everyday Life in the Middle Ages. Silver, 1984

MIDDLETON, Hadyn

Everyday Life in the 16th Century. Silver, 1983

TAYLOR, Laurence

Everyday Life in the 17th Century. Silver, 1983

These cover much the same territory as the two Cambridge series, but are far more attractive and written more approachably. A page or two of text with color illustration is devoted to various subjects, from agriculture to religion to culture to politics. A time line of famous events and people is provided. For grades 5 and up. Glossary, index.

EXPERIMENTAL SCIENCE

GARDNER, Robert

Famous Experiments You Can Do. Watts, 1990

Ideas for Science Fair Projects. Watts, 1989

More Ideas for Science Fair Projects. Watts, 1989

TOCCI, Salvatore

How to Do a Science Fair Project. Watts, 1989

WALLACE, Diane A., and **Philip L. HERSHEY**

How to Master Science Labs. Watts, 1989

Really good science fair project books are always welcome, and these deserve to be added to that list. Students are instructed in the scientific method; how to decide on and set up a project; safety factors are given; and a variety of experiments that feature materials usually found at home are presented. Excellent choices for grades 5 and up.

EXPLORATION AND DISCOVERY

BECKLAKE, Sue

The Mysterious Universe. Silver, 1981

The Solar System. Silver, 1981

GRIFFITHS, John

Lasers and Holograms. Silver, 1983

JEREMIAH, David

The Computer Revolution. Silver, 1983

Yet another science series that gives a quick going-over to these topics. There are color illustrations and explanations of the basics. With subjects as timely as these, however, it is important that titles be updated due to the many changes that occur, and these titles may already be slightly outdated. Grades 4-7. Glossary, index.

EXPLORATION THROUGH THE AGES

HUMBLE, Richard

The Age of Leif Eriksson. Watts, 1989

The Travels of Marco Polo. Watts, 1990

The Voyage of Magellan. Watts, 1989

The Voyages of Captain Cook. Watts, 1990

World exploration remains a perennial "hot topic" for elementary school students. This handsome series will prove a fine collection builder. The volumes are oversize, with a combination of full-color illustrations, maps, and reproductions of historical art and texts. The author also furnishes a glossary, index, and timechart. Excellent choices for grades 4-8.

EXPLORING NATURE AROUND THE YEAR
WEBSTER, David
Fall. Messner, 1990
Spring. Messner, 1990
Summer. Messner, 1990
Winter. Messner, 1990
These books study the seasons through a program of observation and experiments of plants, animals, and even the sky. Although these are written at the third to sixth grade level, a teacher could easily use the projects with children as young as preschool age.

EXPLORING SCIENCE
CATHERALL, Ed
Energy Sources. Steck, 1990
Exploring Electricity. Steck, 1990
Exploring Light. Steck, 1989
Exploring Magnets. Steck, 1990
Exploring Sound. Steck, 1990
Soil and Rocks. Steck, 1990
Uses of Energy. Steck, 1990
Weather. Steck, 1990
Students in search of science fair projects as well as teachers in need of classroom activities will find this series useful. Various aspects of science are explained in 2-page chapters, each complete with an illustrative project. Necessary items are highlighted in a box, as are safety warnings. The end of each section includes a self-test. Glossary, index. Grades 4-9.

EXTRAORDINARY ANIMALS
TAYLOR, David
Animal Attackers. Lerner, 1989
Animal Magicians. Lerner, 1989
Animal Monsters. Lerner, 1989
Animal Olympians. Lerner, 1989
The author is a zoo veterinarian who brings considerable expertise to this series, as well as a flair for making these animals fascinating. The *Animal Magicians* book, for example, talks about chameleons and other creatures that can perform "tricks," while the *Monsters* book explores legendary creatures and discusses their possible real origins. Each animal receives several pages of coverage, including illustrations. Grades 4-6. Glossary, index.

EYEWITNESS BOOKS
ARDLEY, Neil
Music. Knopf, 1989
ARTHUR, Alex
Shell. Knopf, 1989
BENDER, Lionel
Invention. Knopf, 1991
BURNIE, David
Bird. Knopf, 1988
Plant. Knopf, 1989
Tree. Knopf, 1988
BYAM, Michele
Arms and Armor. Knopf, 1988

COSGROVE, Brian
Weather. Knopf, 1991
CRAMPTON, William
Flag. Knopf, 1989
CRIBB, Joe
Money. Knopf, 1990
HAMMOND, Tim
Sports. Knopf, 1988
HART, George
Ancient Egypt. Knopf, 1990
JAMES, Simon
Ancient Rome. Knopf, 1990
MCCARTHY, Colin, and **Nick ARNOLD**
Reptile. Knopf, 1991
MERRIMAN, Nick
Early Humans. Knopf, 1989
MOUND, Laurence
Insect. Knopf, 1990
NAHUM, Andrew
Flying Machine. Knopf, 1990
NORMAN, David, and **Angela MILNER**
Dinosaur. Knopf, 1989
PARKER, Steve
Fish. Knopf, 1990
Mammal. Knopf, 1989
Pond and River. Knopf, 1988
Seashore. Knopf, 1989
Skeleton. Knopf, 1988
SUTTON, Richard
Car. Knopf, 1990
SYMES, R. F.
Rocks and Minerals. Knopf, 1988
SYMES, R. F., and **Roger HARDING**
Crystal and Gem. Knopf, 1991
TAYLOR, Paul
Fossil. Knopf, 1990
WHALLEY, Paul
Butterfly and Moth. Knopf, 1988

This is the most appealing science series to emerge in a long time. Each volume is oversize, with a two-page spread on each topic. Numerous color photos of various sizes dot each page, completely annotated to describe the subject at hand. Interesting tidbits are interspersed with more detailed information. Useful for school assignments, this series will also arouse the interest of the browser and amateur scientist.

EYEWITNESS JUNIORS
CLARKE, Barry
Amazing Frogs and Toads. Knopf, 1990
LING, Mary
Amazing Crocodiles and Reptiles. Knopf, 1991
Amazing Fish. Knopf, 1991
PARSONS, Alexandra
Amazing Birds. Knopf, 1990
Amazing Cats. Knopf, 1990
Amazing Mammals. Knopf, 1990
Amazing Poisonous Animals. Knopf, 1990
Amazing Snakes. Knopf, 1990
Amazing Spiders. Knopf, 1990

SMITH, Trevor
Amazing Lizards. Knopf, 1990
STEEDMAN, Scott
Amazing Monkeys. Knopf, 1991
STILL, John
Amazing Butterflies and Moths. Knopf, 1991

Intended for a younger audience (ages 7-10) than its companion series, Eyewitness Books, this one also features glorious color photos and drawings that accompany a fact filled text. Each animal has a two-page spread, with topics explained in a half-dozen short paragraphs. These books are about half the size of the originals. Sure to pique the interest. Index.

FACT OR FICTION FILES
CANADEO, Anne
Fact or Fiction Files: Ghosts. Walker, 1990
Fact or Fiction Files: UFO's. Walker, 1990
HOOBLER, Dorothy, and **Tom HOOBLER**
Fact or Fiction Files: Vanished. Walker, 1991

This new series explores hotly debated paranormal topics. Half of the book relates factual cases—unfortunately without photos of the apparitions. The reader must then flip the book over to read the other section. One section presents one point of view—pro or con the reality of the phenomenon, while the other details the opposing viewpoint. Both sections have indexes; there is a bibliography and list of addresses for organizations involved in psychic research. These are hot demand subjects that will appeal to grades 5-9; the only drawback is the lack of illustrative material.

FACTS ABOUT
ALMONTE, Paul, and **Theresa DESMOND**
Diabetes. Crestwood, 1991
BAILEY, Marilyn
Single-Parent Families. Crestwood, 1989
Stepfamilies. Crestwood, 1990
BARDEN, Renardo
Fears and Phobias. Crestwood, 1989
Gangs. Crestwood, 1989
BARMAT, Jeanne
Foster Families. Crestwood, 1991
BARON, Connie
The Physically Disabled. Crestwood, 1988
BECKELMAN, Laurie
Alzheimer's Disease. Crestwood, 1989
The Homeless. Crestwood, 1989
Transplants. Crestwood, 1990
CRISFIELD, Deborah
Gambling. Crestwood, 1991
DICK, Jean
Mental and Emotional Disabilities. Crestwood, 1988
GUERNSEY, JoAnn Bren
Animal Rights. Crestwood, 1990
Missing Children. Crestwood, 1990
Rape. Crestwood, 1990
Teen Pregnancy. Crestwood, 1989
HARRIS, Jack C.
Gun Control. Crestwood, 1990
HJELMELAND, Andy
Drinking and Driving. Crestwood, 1990

LAZO, Caroline Evenson
Divorce. Crestwood, 1989
MONROE, Judy
Censorship. Crestwood, 1990
Drug Testing. Crestwood, 1990
Latchkey Children. Crestwood, 1989
Leukemia. Crestwood, 1990
Prescription Drugs. Crestwood, 1988
Stimulants and Hallucinogens. Crestwood, 1988
STEVENS, Sarah
Steroids. Crestwood, 1991
STEWART, Gail B.
Adoption. Crestwood, 1989
Child Abuse. Crestwood, 1989
Death. Crestwood, 1989
Discrimination. Crestwood, 1989
Peer Pressure. Crestwood, 1989
Teen Suicide. Crestwood, 1988
TURCK, Mary C.
AIDS. Crestwood, 1988
Alcohol and Tobacco. Crestwood, 1988
Crack and Cocaine. Crestwood, 1990
WOLHART, Dayna
Anorexia and Bulimia. Crestwood, 1988

This series mixes books on diseases with social and other topical problems. Historical backgrounds are given along with facts and personal stories. Written for 8 to 11 year olds. Glossary, index.

FACTS ABOUT...
BAILEY, Donna
Birds. Steck-Vaughn, 1990
Cars, Trucks, and Trains. Steck-Vaughn, 1990
Cities. Steck-Vaughn, 1990
Deserts. Steck-Vaughn, 1990
Energy All around Us. Steck-Vaughn, 1990
Energy for Our Bodies. Steck-Vaughn, 1990
Energy from Oil and Gas. Steck-Vaughn, 1990
Energy from Wind and Water. Steck-Vaughn, 1990
Families. Steck-Vaughn, 1990
Farmers. Steck-Vaughn, 1990
Far Planets. Steck-Vaughn, 1990
Fish. Steck-Vaughn, 1990
Forests. Steck-Vaughn, 1990
Insects. Steck-Vaughn, 1990
Looking at Stars. Steck-Vaughn, 1990
Mountains. Steck-Vaughn, 1990
Near Planets. Steck-Vaughn, 1990
Nomads. Steck-Vaughn, 1990
Planes. Steck-Vaughn, 1990
Reptiles. Steck-Vaughn, 1990
Rivers. Steck-Vaughn, 1990
Ships. Steck-Vaughn, 1990
Space. Steck-Vaughn, 1988

Early readers will benefit from this colorful science series. Simple, general presentation of information with vocabulary at the second through fourth grade range will be a boon at report time. Color photos and illustrations add to usability. Glossary, index.

FACTS ON...

ARNOLD, Guy

Facts on Nuclear Energy. Watts, 1990
Facts on Water, Wind and Solar Power. Watts, 1990

JOHNSTONE, Hugh

Facts on Domestic Waste and Industrial Pollutants. Watts, 1990
Facts on Future Energy Possibilities. Watts, 1990
Facts on Nuclear Waste and Radioactivity. Watts, 1990

SHAPIRO, Harry

Facts on Drugs in Sports. Watts, 1989
Facts on Inhalants. Watts, 1989

TAYLOR, Ron

Facts on Pesticides and Fertilizers in Farming. Watts, 1990
Facts on Radon and Asbestos. Watts, 1990

TWIST, Clint

Facts on Alcohol. Watts, 1989
Facts on Fossil Fuels. Watts, 1990
Facts on the Crack and Cocaine Epidemic. Watts, 1989

This series focuses on both ecological concerns and substance abuse problems. Like other Watts entries, these are oversize, with plentiful illustrations, glossary, and index. The history of the problem, current practices, and the results are all dealt with. Grades 5-8.

FACTS/STORIES/GAMES

BAKER, Lucy

Chimpanzees. Puffin, 1991
Eagles. Puffin, 1990
Elephants. Puffin, 1991
Pandas. Puffin, 1991
Polar Bears. Puffin, 1990
Seals. Puffin, 1990
Snakes. Puffin, 1990
Tigers. Puffin, 1990

The slim volumes in this series are loaded with interesting facts that are taught in a variety of ways. The first 2/3 of the book is factual, then several reinforcing games are presented, along with a brief story that includes details of animal life, and a true/false test ends the proceedings. Teachers and parents will find these most useful with grades 2-4. Index.

FAMILIES THE WORLD OVER

ADLER, Ann

A Family in West Germany. Lerner, 1985

ALEXANDER, Bryan, and **Cherry ALEXANDER**

An Eskimo Family. Lerner, 1985

ASHBY, Gwynneth

A Family in South Korea. Lerner, 1987

BARKER, Carol

A Family in Nigeria. Lerner, 1985

BENNETT, Gay

A Family in Sri Lanka. Lerner, 1985

BENNETT, Olivia

A Family in Brazil. Lerner, 1986
A Family in Egypt. Lerner, 1985

BROWNE, Rollo

An Aboriginal Family. Lerner, 1985
A Family in Australia. Lerner, 1987

DUTTON, Roderic

An Arab Family. Lerner, 1985

ELKIN, Judith
A Family in Japan. Lerner, 1987
FYSON, Nance Lui, and **Richard GREENHILL**
A Family in China. Lerner, 1985
GOOM, Bridget
A Family in Singapore. Lerner, 1986
GRIFFIN, Michael
A Family in Kenya. Lerner, 1988
HUBLEY, John, and **Penny HUBLEY**
A Family in Italy. Lerner, 1987
A Family in Jamaica. Lerner, 1985
HUMPHREY, Sally
A Family in Liberia. Lerner, 1987
MCKENNA, Nancy Durrell
A Family in Hong Kong. Lerner, 1987
A Zulu Family. Lerner, 1986
MORAN, Tom
A Family in Ireland. Lerner, 1986
A Family in Mexico. Lerner, 1987
REGAN, Mary
A Family in France. Lerner, 1985
ST. JOHN, Jetty
A Family in Bolivia. Lerner, 1986
A Family in Chile. Lerner, 1986
A Family in England. Lerner, 1988
A Family in Hungary. Lerner, 1988
A Family in Norway. Lerner, 1988
A Family in Peru. Lerner, 1987
SCARSBROOK, Ailsa, and **Alan SCARSBROOK**
A Family in Pakistan. Lerner, 1985
STEWART, Judy
A Family in Morocco. Lerner, 1986
A Family in Sudan. Lerner, 1988
TAYLOR, Allegra
A Kibbutz in Israel. Lerner, 1987
THOMSON, Ruth, and **Neil THOMSON**
A Family in Thailand. Lerner, 1988
TIGWELL, Tony
A Family in India. Lerner, 1985

To increase familiarity with people in other lands, Lerner provides this series. The reader follows a child and their family through various activities at home and school. A page of fast facts is appended. While there is information here on each country, there are other series that fill that gap in a more accessible and usable format. These could be used as an introduction with younger children, grades 2-5. No index.

FAMOUS WOMEN

BALL, Jacqueline
Georgia O'Keeffe. Rosen, 1990
BOUCHARD, Elizabeth
Benazir Bhutto. Rosen, 1990
BROWN, Gene
Bette Davis. Rosen, 1990
JOHNSON, Linda C.
Barbara Jordan. Rosen, 1990
Mother Teresa. Rosen, 1990

KAHANER, Ellen

Marion Wright Edelman. Rosen, 1990

Wilma Mankiller: Chief of the Cherokee Nation. Rosen, 1990

Written for the reluctant reader, Famous Women gives a description of some of the most influential women in the world. The books are short and are filled with color illustrations. An index and bibliography are also included. Interest level grades 7-12.

FIELD TRIP BOOKS

HANNUM, Dottie

A Visit to the Fire Station. Childrens, 1985

A Visit to the Police Station. Childrens, 1985

TESTER, Sylvia Root

A Visit to the Library. Childrens, 1985

A Visit to the Zoo. Childrens, 1987

ZIEGLER, Sandra

A Visit to the Airport. Childrens, 1988

A Visit to the Bakery. Childrens, 1987

A Visit to the Dairy Farm. Childrens, 1987

A Visit to the Natural History Museum. Childrens, 1988

A Visit to the Post Office. Childrens, 1989

Children might visit these places on field trips, but they might also go for other reasons. Parents and teachers will find the color photos and simple vocabulary a plus with preschool through 3rd grade. They could be used to prepare a child for a trip or to answer questions about what a fireman does, etc. Good introductory material.

FIGHTING SHIPS

HUMBLE, Richard

U-Boat. Watts, 1990

World War I Battleship. Watts, 1989

World War II Aircraft Carrier. Watts, 1989

These brief books provide a historical look at the various fighting ships during the twentieth century. The books are colorfully illustrated and include a chronological time chart, glossary and index. An average introductory look for junior high schoolers.

FIRST BIOGRAPHIES

ADLER, David A.

George Washington: Father of Our Country. Holiday, 1988

Martin Luther King, Jr.: Free at Last. Holiday, 1986

Thomas Alva Edison: Great Inventor. Holiday, 1990

Thomas Jefferson: Father of Our Democracy. Holiday, 1987

These are introductory biographies aimed at readers in grades 3-5. Highlights of each life, as well as background on why their work was important, is simply presented. For example, in the book on Dr. King, some explanation of Jim Crow laws and Gandhi's teachings is provided. There is an index and a list of important dates. Attractive black-and-white drawings add to the charm.

FIRST BOOKS

ANDERSON, Madelyn Klein

Environmental Diseases. Watts, 1987

APFEL, Necia H.

Space Law. Watts, 1988

Space Station. Watts, 1987

ARNOLD, Caroline

Australia Today. Watts, 1987

Genetics: From Mendel to Gene Splicing. Watts, 1986

BERKE, Art
Gymnastics. Watts, 1988
BESHORE, George
Science in Ancient China. Watts, 1988
Science in Early Islamic Culture. Watts, 1988
BRANDT, Sue R.
Facts about the 50 States. Watts, 1988
How to Write a Report. Watts, 1986
BRIMNER, Larry Dane
BMX Freestyle. Watts, 1987
Karate. Watts, 1988
BROWN, Fern G.
Hereditary Diseases. Watts, 1987
CARTER, Alden R.
The American Revolution: Colonies in Revolt. Watts, 1988
The American Revolution: Darkest Hours. Watts, 1988
The American Revolution: At the Forge of Liberty. Watts, 1988
The American Revolution: Birth of the Republic. Watts, 1988
Radio: From Marconi to the Space Age. Watts, 1987
COOPER, Carolyn E.
VCRS. Watts, 1987
EAGLES, Douglas A.
The Menace of AIDS. Watts, 1988
Nutritional Diseases. Watts, 1987
FICHTER, George S.
Cells. Watts, 1986
FISHER, Maxine P.
The Walt Disney Story. Watts, 1988
FORCE, Eden
Theodore Roosevelt. Watts, 1987
GALLANT, Roy A.
From Living Cells to Dinosaurs. Watts, 1986
Our Restless Earth. Watts, 1986
The Rise of Mammals. Watts, 1986
GARDNER, Robert
Science Experiments. Watts, 1988
GAY, Kathlyn
Science in Ancient Greece. Watts, 1988
GREENE, Laura, and **Eva Barash DICKER**
Sign Language. Watts, 1981
GRIGOLI, Valorie
Service Industries. Watts, 1984
GUTNIK, Martin J.
Electricity: From Faraday to Solar Generators. Watts, 1986
Simple Electrical Devices. Watts, 1986
HANMER, Trudy J.
Nicaragua. Watts, 1986
HARRIS, Jacqueline L.
Science in Ancient Rome. Watts, 1988
HUGHES, Barbara
Drug-Related Diseases. Watts, 1987
KLEEBERG, Irene Cumming
Ethiopia. Watts, 1986
KOLANDA, Jo, and **Judge Patricia CURLEY**
Trial by Jury. Watts, 1988

LAMPTON, Christopher
Astronomy: From Copernicus to the Space Telescope. Watts, 1987
Rocketry: From Goddard to Space Travel. Watts, 1988
The Space Telescope. Watts, 1987
Star Wars. Watts, 1987
Thomas Alva Edison. Watts, 1988
Undersea Archaeology. Watts, 1988
LANDAU, Elaine
Alzheimer's Disease. Watts, 1987
LAWSON, Don
The War in Vietnam. Watts, 1981
LEE, Martin
Paul Revere. Watts, 1987
LEE, Sally
Donor Banks: Saving Lives with Organ and Tissue Transplants. Watts, 1988
MCGOWEN, Tom
The Circulatory System: From Harvey to the Artificial Heart. Watts, 1988
Radioactivity: From the Curies to the Atomic Age. Watts, 1986
War Gaming. Watts, 1985
MANETTI, Lisa
Equality. Watts, 1985
MANGO, Karin N.
Codes, Ciphers and Other Secrets. Watts, 1988
METOS, Thomas H.
Communicable Diseases. Watts, 1987
METZGER, Larry
Abraham Lincoln. Watts, 1987
MISCHEL, Florence D.
How to Write a Letter. Watts, 1988
MOSS, Carol
Science in Ancient Mesopotamia. Watts, 1988
NOURSE, Alan E.
Menstruation. Watts, 1987
Your Immune System. Watts, 1983
PATTERSON, Charles
Thomas Jefferson. Watts, 1987
REISCHE, Diana
Patrick Henry. Watts, 1987
RYAN, Margaret
Figure Skating. Watts, 1987
SANDAK, Cass R.
Explorers and Discovery. Watts, 1983
SGROI, Peter
...This Constitution. Watts, 1986
SLOAN, Frank
Titanic. Watts, 1987
SMITH, Beth
Castles. Watts, 1988
SONNETT, Sherry
Smoking. Watts, 1988
SOULE, Gardner
Antarctica. Watts, 1985

STWERTKA, Albert, and **Eve STWERTKA**
Marijuana. Watts, 1986
Physics: From Newton to the Big Bang. Watts, 1986
STWERTKA, Eve
Psychoanalysis: From Freud to the Age of Therapy. Watts, 1988
TANNENBAUM, Beulah, and **Harold E. TANNENBAUM**
Science of the Early American Indians. Watts, 1988
VOGT, Gregory
Electricity and Magnetism. Watts, 1985
WEBSTER, David
How to Do a Science Project. Watts, 1974
WEHMEYER, Lillian Biermann
Futuristics. Watts, 1986
WHITE, Laurence B., and **Ray BROEKEL**
Optical Illusions. Watts, 1986
WOODS, Geraldine
Drug Use and Drug Abuse. Watts, 1986
Science in Ancient Egypt. Watts, 1988
WOODS, Geraldine, and **Harold WOODS**
Cocaine. Watts, 1985
The Right to Bear Arms. Watts, 1986
The United Nations. Watts, 1985

Any library in need of this wide assortment of non-fiction topics will find these books outstanding. The texts are detailed with ample illustrations. Super choices as needed for grades 5-8.

FIRST LIBRARY
PETTY, Kate
Crocodiles and Alligators. Watts, 1986
Dinosaurs. Watts, 1984
Frogs and Toads. Watts, 1986
Sharks. Watts, 1985
Snakes. Watts, 1985
Spiders. Watts, 1985

Beginning readers will find these informative; two or three informational sentences per page in easily accessible vocabulary are accompanied by color illustrations. At the end is a "Look Back and Find" section, which asks review questions. These will be especially useful in conjunction with classroom teaching for grades K-3.

FIRST LOOK AT
SELSAM, Millicent E., and **Joyce HUNT**
A First Look at Animals That Eat Other Animals. Walker, 1989
A First Look at Animals with Horns. Walker, 1989
A First Look at Bats. Walker, 1991
A First Look at Birds. Walker, 1973
A First Look at Caterpillars. Walker, 1987
A First Look at Cats. Walker, 1981
A First Look at Dinosaurs. Walker, 1982
A First Look at Ducks, Geese and Swans. Walker, 1990
A First Look at Frogs, Toads, and Salamanders. Walker, 1976
A First Look at Horses. Walker, 1981
A First Look at Insects. Walker, 1974
A First Look at Kangaroos. Walker, 1985
A First Look at Leaves. Walker, 1972
A First Look at Owls, Eagles, and Other Hunters of the Sky. Walker, 1986

A First Look at Poisonous Snakes. Walker, 1987
A First Look at Rocks. Walker, 1984
A First Look at Seals, Sea Lions, and Walruses. Walker, 1988
A First Look at Sharks. Walker, 1979
A First Look at Snakes, Lizards, and Other Reptiles. Walker, 1975
A First Look at Spiders. Walker, 1983

Selsam is a veteran author of many juvenile science books. These are aimed at ages 5-9, and cover a wide range of biological topics. The information is very basic with pronunciations of difficult words given in parentheses and scientific classifications given at the end. Attractive black and white drawings add to the appeal. Good choices for younger readers.

FIRST PETS

PETTY, Kate

Cats. Watts, 1989
Dogs. Watts, 1989
Gerbils. Watts, 1989
Guinea Pigs. Watts, 1989
Hamsters. Watts, 1989
Rabbits. Watts, 1989

This series informs the youngest readers about pets: different types, body characteristics, and the importance of gentle care. The color photos are appealing. There is a little introductory information but not enough to guide a youngster in terms of day-to-day care. These are acceptable for starters for grades K-2.

FIRST SIGHT

BENDER, Lionel

Animals of the Night. Watts, 1989
Creatures of the Deep. Watts, 1989
Crocodiles and Alligators. Watts, 1988
Kangaroos and Other Marsupials. Watts, 1988
Life on a Coral Reef. Watts, 1989
Lions and Tigers. Watts, 1988
Lizards and Dragons. Watts, 1988
Poisonous Insects. Watts, 1988
Polar Animals. Watts, 1989
Pythons and Boas. Watts, 1988
Spiders. Watts, 1988
Whales. Watts, 1988

CHIVERS, David

Gorillas and Chimpanzees. Watts, 1987

MCCARTHY, Colin

Poisonous Snakes. Watts, 1987

PETTY, Kate

Birds of Prey. Watts, 1987

WHEELER, Alwyne

Sharks. Watts, 1987

Various species of animals comprise the subjects of this series. The usual ground is covered: anatomy, life style, life cycle. These British imports are more graphically illustrated than American counterparts: some photos show animals violently attacking others; some show orphan animals; others show bloody animal carcasses. The intent may be to increase awareness of endangered species, but the animals pictured are *not* endangered. Grades 5-7.

FOCUS ON SCIENCE

ALTER, Anna
Destination: Outer Space. Barron, 1988
AVEROUS, Pierre
The Atom. Barron, 1988
BALIBAR, Francoise, and **Jean-Pierre MAURY**
How Things Fly. Barron, 1989
BARLOY, Jean-Jacques
Prehistory. Barron, 1987
BEAUFAY, Gabriel
Dinosaurs and Other Extinct Animals. Barron, 1987
CHENEL, Pascale
Life and Death of Dinosaurs. Barron, 1987
CHEVALLIER-LE GUYADER, Marie-Francoise
Biology's Building Blocks. Barron, 1989
HAGENE, Bernard, and **Charles LENAY**
The Origin of Life. Barron, 1987
KOHLER, Pierre
Earth and the Conquest of Space. Barron, 1988
Weather. Barron, 1988
MAURY, Jean-Pierre
Atmosphere. Barron, 1989
Heat and Cold. Barron, 1989
TORDJMAN, Nathalie
Climates: Past, Present and Future. Barron, 1988

Originally published in France, these pocket-size books are colorful collections of scientific nuggets. There is a lot of introductory information provided, along with many illustrations. Grades 4-8. Glossary, index.

FOOD AND DRINK

ALVARADO, Manuel
Mexican Food and Drink. Watts, 1988
BIUCCHI, Edwina
Italian Food and Drink. Watts, 1987
DOWNER, Lesley
Japanese Food and Drink. Watts, 1988
EINHORN, Barbara
West German Food and Drink. Watts, 1989
GIBRILL, Martin
African Food and Drink. Watts, 1989
OSBORNE, Christine
Australian and New Zealand Food and Drink. Watts, 1989
Middle Eastern Food and Drink. Watts, 1988
Southeast Asian Food and Drink. Watts, 1989
PARAISO, Aviva
Caribbean Food and Drink. Watts, 1989
Jewish Food and Drink. Watts, 1989
SPROULE, Anna
British Food and Drink. Watts, 1988

This series aims to teach youngsters about a country by examining the food it eats. The first chapter gives background on the country, then comes a section on agriculture and what foods are available. The remainder of the book examines the staple diet and regional specialties, complete with menus. Glossary, bibliography, and index are included. Grades 4-8.

FOODS WE EAT

CLARK, Elizabeth

Fish. Carolrhoda, 1990

Meat. Carolrhoda, 1990

MERRISON, Lynne

Rice. Carolrhoda, 1990

MILLER, Susanna

Beans and Peas. Carolrhoda, 1990

NOTTRIDGE, Rhoda

Sugar. Carolrhoda, 1990

TURNER, Dorothy

Bread. Carolrhoda, 1989

Eggs. Carolrhoda, 1989

Milk. Carolrhoda, 1990

Potatoes. Carolrhoda, 1989

WAKE, Susan

Butter. Carolrhoda, 1990

Citrus Fruits. Carolrhoda, 1990

Vegetables. Carolrhoda, 1990

Preschool and early education students often study nutrition and food groups. This series fills an important void. Large, colorful illustrations and photos accompany a simple, basic text. While these youngsters could not read the text on their own, parent or teacher can understandably read it to them. New terms are in boldface, then defined in a glossary. The food source, processing, and related products are discussed. Several easy recipes are included. Good choices for grades preschool-grade 3.

FRED NEFF'S SELF-DEFENSE LIBRARY

NEFF, Fred

Basic Jujitsu Handbook. Lerner, 1976

Basic Karate Handbook. Lerner, 1976

Basic Self-Defense Manual. Lerner, 1976

Foot-Fighting Manual for Self-Defense and Sport Karate. Lerner, 1977

Hand-Fighting Manual for Self-Defense and Sport Karate. Lerner, 1977

Keeping Fit Handbook for Physical Conditioning and Better Health. Lerner, 1977

Manual of Throws for Sport Judo and Self-Defense. Lerner, 1976

Self-Protection Guidebook for Girls and Women. Lerner, 1977

The martial arts are always a heavily requested subject area, and this excellent series will fit the bill for any young user. Neff is a long time student and instructor who begins by explaining when martial arts should be used then moves on to warming up exercises. Individual stances are discussed, with clear photos and step-by-step instructions. Safety rules are appended. For readers 10 and up. Index.

FRESH START

CALDECOTT, Barry

Kites. Watts, 1990

DEVONSHIRE, Hilary

Collage. Watts, 1988

Drawing. Watts, 1990

Moving Art. Watts, 1990

Printing. Watts, 1988

DEVONSHIRE, Hilary, Lyndie WRIGHT, and **John LANCASTER**

Christmas Crafts. Watts, 1990

HULL, Jean

Clay. Watts, 1989

LANCASTER, John
Cardboard. Watts, 1989
Decorated Lettering. Watts, 1990
Lettering. Watts, 1988
Paper Sculpture. Watts, 1989
PLUCKROSE, Henry
Crayons. Watts, 1988
Paints. Watts, 1988
WRIGHT, Lyndie
Masks. Watts, 1990
Puppets. Watts, 1989

What can you do with these various craft supplies? The authors show the reader plenty of alternatives in this colorful series that talks about the properties and history of the craft, useful techniques, and craft ideas. The supplies are common household items and the projects are simple; there is a bibliography, index, and listing of famous museums where examples of these crafts can be found. Grades 4-9.

FRITZ, Jean
And Then What Happened, Paul Revere? Coward, 1973
Can't You Make Them Behave, King George? Coward, 1977
George Washington's Breakfast. Coward, 1969
Shh! We're Writing the Constitution. Coward, 1987
What's the Big Idea, Ben Franklin? Coward, 1976
Where Do You Think You're Going, Christopher Columbus? Coward, 1981
Where Was Patrick Henry on the 29th of May? Coward, 1975
Who's That Stepping on Plymouth Rock? Coward, 1975
Why Don't You Get a Horse, Sam Adams? Coward, 1974
Will You Sign Here, John Hancock? Coward, 1976

In a very folksy way Jean Fritz introduces young readers to famous early American heroes and events. All the statistical information is here along with fascinating anecdotes, background on the period, and a perspective on why these people and events were and are important – and all in less than 50 pages! All are illustrated, and the reading level is aimed at grades 3-5. An excellent choice.

FULL-COLOR FIRST BOOKS
ABRAMOWSKI, Dwain
Mountain Bikes. Watts, 1990
ALTER, Judith
Eli Whitney. Watts, 1990
Growing up in the Old West. Watts, 1989
Women of the Old West. Watts, 1989
ANDERSON, Madelyn Klein
Oil Spills. Watts, 1990
ARMBRUSTER, Ann, and **Elizabeth A. TAYLOR**
Astronaut Training. Watts, 1990
Tornadoes. Watts, 1989
BASKIN-SALZBERG, Anita, and **Allen SALZBERG**
Predators! Watts, 1991
BENDICK, Jeanne
Egyptian Tombs. Watts, 1989
BERGER, Melvin
Our Atomic World. Watts, 1989
BRIMNER, Larry Dane
Snowboarding. Watts, 1989

BROWN, Fern G.
Owls. Watts, 1991
CARTER, Alden R.
The Battle of Gettysburg. Watts, 1990
Last Stand at the Alamo. Watts, 1990
The Shoshoni. Watts, 1989
COIL, Suzanne M.
George Washington Carver. Watts, 1990
Poisonous Plants. Watts, 1991
COLLINS, James L.
Exploring the American West. Watts, 1989
Lawmen of the Old West. Watts, 1990
CORBIN, Carole Lynn
Knights. Watts, 1989
COSNER, Shaaron
Dinosaurs Dinners. Watts, 1991
Lunar Bases. Watts, 1990
DEWITT, Lynda
Eagles, Hawks, and Other Birds of Prey. Watts, 1989
DICERTO, Joseph J.
The Pony Express: Hoofbeats in the Wilderness. Watts, 1989
DOHERTY, Craig A., and **Katherine M. DOHERTY**
The Apaches and Navajos. Watts, 1989
The Iroquois. Watts, 1989
EVITTS, William J.
Early Immigration in the United States. Watts, 1989
FELDMAN, Eve B.
Benjamin Franklin: Scientist and Inventor. Watts, 1990
FERRELL, Nancy Warren
Camouflage: Nature's Defense. Watts, 1989
FICHTER, George S.
The Space Shuttle. Watts, 1990
FLATLEY, Dennis R.
The Railroads: Opening the West. Watts, 1989
FOSTER, Leila Merrell
The Sumerians. Watts, 1990
GUTFREUND, Geraldine Marshall
Animals Have Cousins Too. Watts, 1990
HALLIBURTON, Warren J.
The Tragedy of Little Big Horn. Watts, 1989
HERDA, D. J.
Operation Rescue: Satellite Maintenance and Repair. Watts, 1990
HUMPHREY, Kathryn Long
Pompeii: Nightmare at Midday. Watts, 1990
KATZ, Phyllis
Exploring Science through Art. Watts, 1990
KERBY, Mona
Cockroaches. Watts, 1989
Samuel Morse. Watts, 1991
KORAL, April
In the Newsroom. Watts, 1989
Our Global Greenhouse. Watts, 1989

LANDAU, Elaine
Cowboys. Watts, 1990
Jupiter. Watts, 1991
Lyme Disease. Watts, 1990
Mars. Watts, 1991
Neptune. Watts, 1991
Robert Fulton. Watts, 1991
Saturn. Watts, 1991
The Sioux. Watts, 1989
Tropical Rain Forests around the World. Watts, 1990
Venus. Watts, 1991
Wildflowers around the World. Watts, 1991
LEE, Martin
The Seminoles. Watts, 1989
LIPTAK, Karen
North American Indian Medicine People. Watts, 1990
North American Indian Sign Language. Watts, 1990
North American Indian Survival Skills. Watts, 1990
LUCAS, Eileen
Vincent Van Gogh. Watts, 1991
MCWILLIAMS, Karen
Pirates. Watts, 1989
MARKO, Katherine McGlade
Animals in Orbit. Watts, 1991
NEWMAN, Gerald
Happy Birthday, Little League. Watts, 1989
NOURSE, Alan E.
Lumps, Bumps, and Rashes: A Look at Kids' Diseases. Watts, 1990
PATRICK, Diane
Martin Luther King, Jr. Watts, 1990
POOLE, Frederick King
Early Exploration of North America. Watts, 1989
SHEBAR, Sharon Sigmond, and **Susan E. SHEBAR**
Bats. Watts, 1990
QUIRI, Patricia Ryon
Alexander Graham Bell. Watts, 1991
REISCHE, Diana
Founding the American Colonies. Watts, 1989
ROBINSON, Nancy
Buffalo Bill. Watts, 1991
SCHORSCH, Nancy
Saving the Condor. Watts, 1991
SLOAN, Frank
Bismarck! Watts, 1991
STANGL, Jean
Crystals and Crystal Gardens You Can Grow. Watts, 1990
STWERTKA, Eve
Rachel Carson. Watts, 1991
TAYLOR, Richard L.
The First Flight: The Story of the Wright Brothers. Watts, 1990
WIGGERS, Raymond
Picture Guide to Tree Leaves. Watts, 1991
WOLFE, Rinna Evelyn
Charles Richard Drew, M.D. Watts, 1991
ZITER, Cary B.
When Turtles Come to Town. Watts, 1989

Like Watts's First Books, these cover a variety of topics in a thorough, well researched manner. There are plentiful (color) illustrations, as well as bibliographies. Outstanding choices for grades 5-8.

FUNSEEKERS

NENTL, Jerolyn

Freestyle Skiing. Crestwood, 1978
Marathon Running. Crestwood, 1980
Mountain Climbing. Crestwood, 1978
Roller Skating. Crestwood, 1980
Skydiving. Crestwood, 1978
Surfing. Crestwood, 1978

SCHMITZ, Dorothy Childers

Fabulous Frisbee. Crestwood, 1978
Kite Flying. Crestwood, 1978
Skateboarding. Crestwood, 1978

These books provide a brief overview of a high profile sport: a little history, a little on current trends, a little on how-to, and a little on safety. The color photos and simple vocabulary will make these appealing both to younger and reluctant readers, but there is not much meat here. Grades 3-6. No index.

FUN WITH SCIENCE

CASH, Terry

Electricity and Magnets. Watts, 1989
Sound. Watts, 1989

PARKER, Steve

Chemistry. Watts, 1990
Weather. Watts, 1990

WALPOLE, Brenda

Air. Watts, 1987
Light. Watts, 1987
Water. Watts, 1987

These books contain many science projects and experiments that can be used in the classroom or for science fair projects. There are one or two projects on each page, with large color illustrations showing how to proceed, and outlining the principles learned. Excellent sources for grades 5-8.

GARDNER'S SCIENCE ACTIVITIES

GARDNER, Robert

Kitchen Chemistry. Messner, 1982
Projects in Space Science. Messner, 1988
Science around the House. Messner, 1985
Science in Your Backyard. Messner, 1987

These books combine science information with experiments, with the accent on the information. There are occasional illustrations, a list of supply sources, bibliography, and index. Grades 5 and up.

GENIUS

BROWN, Gene

Duke Ellington. Silver, 1990

GLASSMAN, Bruce

Arthur Miller. Silver, 1990
Mikhail Baryshnikov. Silver, 1990

MACDONALD, Patricia

Pablo Picasso. Silver, 1990

MURPHY, Wendy
Frank Lloyd Wright. Silver, 1990
SHUKER, Nancy
Maya Angelou. Silver, 1990

These biographies explore the lives and works of famous 20th century artists, from music, to art, to writers. The individual's life is reviewed along with what training and inspiration helped them turn their dreams into reality. Each book contains a timeline, index and bibliography. There are also a number of illustrations in each book. Grades 7-9.

GEO BOOKS
RADLAUER, Ed, and **Ruth RADLAUER**
Earthquakes. Childrens, 1987
RADLAUER, Ruth
Volcanoes. Childrens, 1981
RADLAUER, Ruth, and **Henry M. ANDERSON**
Reefs. Childrens, 1983
RADLAUER, Ruth, and **Lisa Sue GITKIN**
The Power of Ice. Childrens, 1985
RADLAUER, Ruth, and **Charles H. STEMBRIDGE**
Comets. Childrens, 1984
Planets. Childrens, 1984
RADLAUER, Ruth, and **Carolynn YOUNG**
Voyagers 1 & 2: *Robots in Space*. Childrens, 1987

These books serve as simple introductions to young students of various scientific phenomenon. One concept is discussed on each page. A color photo accompanies on the other page; new terms are in boldface in the text, then defined at the foot of the page. This resembles the Disaster Series, in that scientific causes and famous examples are provided, but the reading level is much simpler. Grades 3-6.

GETTING TO KNOW THE WORLD'S GREATEST ARTISTS
VENEZIA, Mike
Botticelli. Childrens, 1991
Da Vinci. Childrens, 1989
Edward Hopper. Childrens, 1990
Francisco Goya. Childrens, 1991
Mary Cassatt. Childrens, 1990
Monet. Childrens, 1990
Picasso. Childrens, 1988
Rembrandt. Childrens, 1988
Van Gogh. Childrens, 1988

Like exposing a child to books, exposing them to great art can begin very young. This series is aimed at 2nd to 4th graders. The author uses large print and simple vocabulary to communicate information about the artist's life and work. Art reproductions in color abound on every page. Art teachers and interested parents will rejoice at the availability of something on this level.

GLENN, Mel
Class Dismissed! Clarion, 1982
Class Dismissed II. Clarion, 1986
Back to Class. Clarion, 1988

English teacher Mel Glenn has written books of poetry for and about high school students. The poems deal with the many aspects of adolescence: cars, sports, acne, dating and growing up. They are entertaining, straightforward and humorous. The first book is an ALA Best Book for Young Adults and if YAs can get past the genre, they will love them.

GODS AND HEROES OF THE NEW WORLD

BIERHORST, John

The Mythology of North America. Morrow, 1985
The Mythology of South America. Morrow, 1988
The Mythology of Mexico and Central America. Morrow, 1990

Bierhorst, a noted editor and translator of Indian myths and tales, has written this collection detailing the myths of our ancestors. The books detail the background and history of the myths, as well as provide a glimpse of the views and beliefs held by the people living in different regions of the Americas. Included in each book are maps, other illustrations and indexes. Good books for high school students, especially those who want an alternative to European mythology.

GOLDEN FIELD GUIDES

ABBOTT, R. Tucker
Seashells of North America. Golden, 1968

AUSTIN, Oliver L.
Families of Birds. Golden, 1985

BROCKMAN, C. Frank
Trees of North America. Golden, 1979

CHARTRAND, Mark R.
Skyguide. Golden, 1982

GABRIELSON, Ira H., and **Herbert S. ZIM**
Birds. Golden, 1987

LEVI, Herbert W., and **Lorna R. LEVI**
Spiders and Their Kin. Golden, 1990

ROBBINS, Chandler S., **Bertel BRUUN**, and **Herbert S. ZIM**
Birds of North America. Golden, 1984

SMITH, Hobart M.
Amphibians of North America. Golden, 1978
Reptiles of North America. Golden, 1982

VENNING, Frank D.
Wildflowers of North America. Golden, 1984

These books are essential for every collection—they are excellent identification tools with good color illustrations and a paragraph of information on each example. Scientific names are provided. All ages. Index.

GONE FOREVER

CROFFORD, Emily
The Great Auk. Crestwood, 1989

DUGGLEBY, John
The Sabertooth Cat. Crestwood, 1989

DUNNAHOO, Terry
The Lost Parrots of America. Crestwood, 1989

HORN, Gabriel
Steller's Sea Cow. Crestwood, 1989

MELL, Jan
The Atlantic Grey Whale. Crestwood, 1989

MORRISON, Susan
The Passenger Pigeon. Crestwood, 1989

SANFORD, William, and **Carl GREEN**
The Dodo. Crestwood, 1989
The Woolly Mammoth. Crestwood, 1989

Most of the current batch of books on the endangered planet topic concentrate on species currently in jeopardy. This one instead studies extinct species. A few pages are spent on the overall development over time of the animal and how it adapted, or failed to adapt, to a changing environment. Their appearance, habitat and habits are described. A final plea for animal conservation is appended. There is a glossary/index. Grades 3-6.

GREAT AMERICANS

SMITH, Kathy Billingslea

Abraham Lincoln. Messner, 1986
Albert Einstein. Messner, 1989
George Washington. Messner, 1986
Harriet Tubman. Messner, 1990
John F. Kennedy. Messner, 1986
Martin Luther King, Jr. Messner, 1986
Men of the Constitution. Messner, 1986
Sitting Bull. Messner, 1989
Thomas Jefferson. Messner, 1990

These easy biographies are aimed at beginning readers grades 2-4. The texts are simple but readable with photos and drawings. No table of contents or index.

GREAT BATTLES OF WORLD WAR II

TAYLOR, Theodore

The Battle in the English Channel. Avon, 1983
The Battle off Midway Island. Avon, 1981
H.M.S. Hood *vs.* Bismarck*: The Battleship Battle*. Avon, 1982

These are well written accounts of World War II battles. Written for young people 12 and up, and in a format they enjoy—paperback—these books present history in a dramatic, breathtaking manner. Photographs and maps are included along with an index and bibliography.

GREAT CITIES OF THE WORLD

AYLESWORTH, Thomas, and **Virginia AYLESWORTH**

Chicago. Rosen, 1990

DUNNAN, Nancy

Barcelona. Rosen, 1990

GLASSMAN, Bruce

New York. Rosen, 1990

MARKER, Sherry

London. Rosen, 1990

MURPHY, Wendy, and **Jack MURPHY**

Hong Kong. Rosen, 1990
Toronto. Rosen, 1990

STEINS, Richard

Berlin. Rosen, 1990

ZANGER, Walter

Jerusalem. Rosen, 1990

These geography guides are written for the reluctant reader in grades 7-12. Each is indexed, contains maps, and lists a chronology of the history of the city. The peoples living in each city are discussed along with their backgrounds. These books help give an understanding of the world in relation to where the reader lives.

GREAT CIVILIZATIONS

BATEMAN, Penny

Aztecs and Incas. Watts, 1988

JAMES, Simon

Rome. Watts, 1987

MCKILLOP, Beth
China. Watts, 1988
MILLARD, Anne
Egypt. Watts, 1988
PILBEAM, Mavis
Japan. Watts, 1988
POWELL, Anton
Greece 1600-30 B.C. Watts, 1987

In these books the authors study the beginnings, development, peak, and disintegration of important ancient civilizations. Timelines, maps, and color illustrations add to the usefulness. Various aspects of how life was lived including religion, food, education, and housing are described. Excellent sources for grades 5-8.

GREAT DISASTERS
DAY, James
The Black Death. Watts, 1989
The Hindenburg *Tragedy*. Watts, 1989
DUDMAN, John
The San Francisco Earthquake. Watts, 1988
The Sinking of the Titanic. Watts, 1988
MCCARTER, James
The Space Shuttle Disaster. Watts, 1988
MATTHEWS, Rupert
The Attack on the Lusitania. Watts, 1989
The Eruption of Krakatoa. Watts, 1989
The Fire of London. Watts, 1989
RICKARD, Graham
The Chernobyl Catastrophe. Watts, 1989
ROSEN, Mike
The Destruction of Pompeii. Watts, 1988

Human disasters, whether natural or man made, are the focus of these books. They are written in a conversational tone to interest the 8-11 year old set. Life before the disaster, the factors behind the disaster, and the aftermath of it are all outlined. Glossary words are in boldface, plus there are indexes and bibliographies.

GREAT JOURNEYS
COOTE, Roger
The First Voyage around the World. Watts, 1990
FURNISS, Tim
The First Men on the Moon. Watts, 1989
HOOK, Jason
The Voyages of Captain Cook. Watts, 1990
HUNTER, Nigel
The Expeditions of Cortes. Watts, 1990
HYNDLEY, Kate
The Voyage of the Beagle. Watts, 1989
MATTHEWS, Rupert
The Race to the South Pole. Watts, 1989
The Voyage of Columbus. Watts, 1989
ROSEN, Mike
The Conquest of Everest. Watts, 1990
The First Transatlantic Flight. Watts, 1989
The Journey to the North Pole. Watts, 1990
The Journeys of Hannibal. Watts, 1990
The Travels of Marco Polo. Watts, 1989

Various explorations are detailed in this excellent series. Not only are the achievers and achievements examined, so are the competitors and near misses. Each title is replete with maps, drawings, and photos. There is a nice mix here between ancient and modern explorers. There is a glossary, bibliography, and list of agencies to contact for more information in each volume. Grades 5-8.

GREAT LIVES

BLACKWOOD, Alan

Beethoven. Bookwright, 1987
Captain Cook. Bookwright, 1987
Ferdinand Magellan. Bookwright, 1986
Napolean. Bookwright, 1987

CLARK, Elizabeth

Tchaikovsky. Bookwright, 1988

CONNER, Edwina

Marie Curie. Bookwright, 1987

HOOK, Jason

Sir Francis Drake. Bookwright, 1988
Wright Brothers. Bookwright, 1989

HUNTER, Nigel

Charles Dickens. Bookwright, 1989
Einstein. Bookwright, 1987
Gandhi. Bookwright, 1987
Helen Keller. Bookwright, 1986
Karl Marx. Bookwright, 1987
Martin Luther King, Jr. Bookwright, 1985

JESSOP, Joanne

Richard the Lionhearted. Bookwright, 1989

KEELER, Stephen

Louis Braille. Bookwright, 1986

LANGLEY, Andrew

John F. Kennedy. Bookwright, 1986

LEIGH, Vanora

Elvis Presley. Bookwright, 1986
John Lennon. Bookwright, 1986
Mother Teresa. Bookwright, 1986

MATTHEWS, Rupert

Julius Caesar. Bookwright, 1989
Winston Churchill. Bookwright, 1989

NOTTRIDGE, Harold

Joan of Arc. Bookwright, 1988

TURNER, Dorothy

Florence Nightingale. Bookwright, 1986
Henry VIII. Bookwright, 1988
Mary Queen of Scots. Bookwright, 1988
Queen Elizabeth I. Bookwright, 1987
Queen Victoria. Bookwright, 1989
William Shakespeare. Bookwright, 1985

YOUNG, Percy

Mozart. Bookwright, 1988

Originally published in England, this series of slim volumes (32 p.) hits the highlights of many famous lives. There are many illustrations and photos, a list of important dates, glossary, and list of further readings. The vocabulary is simple, so that readers as young as 8 can use these.

GREAT LIVES

CARLSON, Judy

Harriet Tubman: Call to Freedom. Fawcett, 1989

DOLAN, Sean J.

Christopher Columbus: The Intrepid Mariner. Fawcett, 1989

HURWITZ, Jane

Sally Ride: Shooting for the Stars. Fawcett, 1989

OTFINOSKI, Steven

Mikhail Gorbachev: The Soviet Innovator. Fawcett, 1989

SELFRIDGE, John W.

John F. Kennedy: Courage in Crisis. Fawcett, 1989

SLOATE, Susan

Abraham Lincoln: The Freedom President. Fawcett, 1989

STEFOFF, Rebecca

Nelson Mandela: A Voice Set Free. Fawcett, 1990

Intended for middle school students, these biographies are in an attractive paperback format with occasional illustrations and photos. The text is the important thing here though. There are some liberties taken, with imaginary conversations sprinkled throughout. While this may be more readable than straight facts, it is still inaccurate. There are also no indexes. With these caveats these are decent choices where longer biographies are needed.

GREAT LIVES

FABER, Doris, and **Harold FABER**

Great Lives: American Government. Scribner, 1988

Great Lives: Nature and the Environment. Scribner, 1991

LOMASK, Milton

Great Lives: Exploration. Scribner, 1988

SULLIVAN, George

Great Lives: Sports. Scribner, 1988

This is an excellent series of collective biographies for readers grades 5 and up. There is a nice mix of newer subjects with old standbys, with each receiving at least 4 pages of treatment, accompanied by reproductions of maps, portraits, and photos. A list of important dates is appended. Bibliography, index.

GREAT MYSTERIES

ALDEN, Laura

Houdini. Childrens, 1989

ODOR, Ruth Shannon

Bigfoot. Childrens, 1989

RIEHECKY, Janet

Haunted Houses. Childrens, 1989

UFO's. Childrens, 1989

Kids (and many adults) are often intrigued by the paranormal. These books examine various phenomena in a thorough, rational manner. The authors do examine hoaxes and the irrational fringe element, but also go into detail about those occurrences that cannot be easily explained away. The use of actual photos is effective, but the additional illustrations are unappealing and detract from the serious tone of the text. Even so, there is very little for this age group on this popular subject, so they definitely merit attention. Grades 5 and up.

GREAT MYSTERIES

CRAWFORD, Sue

Lands of Legend. Watts, 1989

MATTHEWS, Rupert

Ancient Mysteries. Watts, 1989

Ghosts. Watts, 1989

Monster Mysteries. Watts, 1989
The Supernatural. Watts, 1989
WILSON, Ben
Sea Mysteries. Watts, 1989
UFO's. Watts, 1989
WRIGHT, John
Lost Treasures. Watts, 1989

This series takes a look at the world's most intriguing phenomena. Introducing the reader to lost civilizations, mysteries, and tales, this series should interest readers in grades seven and up. Lots of illustrations, an index, and bibliography are also included.

GREAT MYSTERIES OPPOSING VIEWPOINTS
BACHRACH, Deborah
Custer's Last Stand. Greenhaven, 1990
BELGUM, Erik
Artificial Intelligence. Greenhaven, 1990
COLE, Jacci
Animal Communication. Greenhaven, 1989
GAFFRON, Norma
The Bermuda Triangle. Greenhaven, 1989
Bigfoot. Greenhaven, 1989
LEDER, Jane
Amelia Earhart. Greenhaven, 1989
MCGUIRE, Leslie
Anastasia, Czarina or Fake. Greenhaven, 1989
ROOP, Peter, and **Connie ROOP**
Dinosaurs. Greenhaven, 1989
STEIN, Wendy
Atlantis. Greenhaven, 1989
STEWART, Gail
Alternative Healing. Greenhaven, 1990
SWISHER, Clarice
The Beginning of Language. Greenhaven, 1989
WAGGONER, Jeffrey
The Assassination of President Kennedy. Greenhaven, 1989

An opposing viewpoints series that reviews investigations into the mysteries of science, history and philosophy. The controversies are explained and the pro/con issues are detailed. Easy to read and interesting. Grades 6-9.

GREEN ISSUES
BECKLAKE, John
Pollution. Watts, 1990
The Population Explosion. Watts, 1990
GARDINER, Brian
Energy Demands. Watts, 1990
PECKHAM, Alexander
Resources Control. Watts, 1990

Like other Watts series (Issues & Save Our Earth), this one explores important issues facing the world. The books are oversize, with large color illustrations and texts that examine the problems by describing how they have occurred, what the current and potential future impact could be, and possible solutions. Very good choices for ages 11-15.

GREEN WORLD
COCHRANE, Jennifer
Food Plants. Steck, 1990
Trees of the Tropics. Steck, 1990

GREENAWAY, Theresa
Fir Trees. Steck, 1990
First Plants. Steck, 1990
Grasses and Grains. Steck, 1990
Woodland Trees. Steck, 1990
MADGWICK, Wendy
Flowering Plants. Steck, 1990
Fungi and Lichens. Steck, 1990
Investigating various forms of plant life, including their biology, ecology, and economic and environmental importance is the aim of this series. The plant life explored is international, not the usual American-only slant. Plentiful color illustrations, glossary, index, list of scientific names of plants discussed and bibliography complete the picture. Grades 3-6.

HANDS ON SCIENCE
ARDLEY, Neil
Muscles to Machines: Projects with Movement. Watts, 1990
Sound Waves to Music: Projects with Sound. Watts, 1990
LAFFERTY, Peter
Burning and Melting: Projects with Heat. Watts, 1990
Magnets to Generators: Projects with Magnetism. Watts, 1989
Wind to Flight: Projects with the Wind. Watts, 1989
TWIST, Clint
Rain to Dams: Projects with Water. Watts, 1990
WHYMAN, Kathryn
Rainbows to Lasers: Projects with Light. Watts, 1989
Sparks to Power Stations: Projects with Electricity. Watts, 1989
Teachers will appreciate this excellent series that explains, illustrates, and provides projects illuminating a number of scientific principles. Two pages are devoted to each subject, with an experiment in each section. The projects involve easily obtained materials, and can be done in the classroom, or for science fairs. Grades 5-8.

HEALTH FACTS
BAILEY, Donna
All about Birth and Growth. Steck, 1991
All about Digestion. Steck, 1991
All about Heart and Blood. Steck, 1991
All about Your Senses. Steck, 1991
All about Skin, Hair, and Teeth. Steck, 1991
All about Your Brain. Steck, 1991
All about Your Lungs. Steck, 1991
All about Your Skeleton. Steck, 1991
This series is intended for a much younger reader than Watts' Human Body series. The simple vocabulary, large print, and few sentences all combine to make these good choices for grades 2-4. Glossary words are in boldface, plus there are plentiful color photos and an index.

HISTORIC COMMUNITIES SERIES
KALMAN, Bobbie
The Gristmill. Dillon, 1990
Home Crafts. Dillon, 1990
The Kitchen. Dillon, 1990
Visiting a Village. Dillon, 1990
This series has several potential uses: to back up social studies and history units on colonial and pioneer times, and to prepare youngsters for visits to historic communities. Author Kalman gives background on the development and operation of these important aspects of early American life, accompanied by color photos taken at real historical sites. Grades 3-6. Glossary, index.

HISTORY HIGHLIGHTS

ADAMS, Brian

Medieval Castles. Watts, 1989

MILLARD, Anne

Pyramids. Watts, 1989

MULVIHILL, Margaret

The French Revolution. Watts, 1989

Roman Forts. Watts, 1990

Viking Longboats. Watts, 1989

ROBERTS, Jenny

Samurai Warriors. Watts, 1990

Another in Watts' historical entries, this one has the same oversize format with plentiful color illustrations as the others. These books concentrate on showing a way of life: the people's religion, ways at war, home life, economy, and government. The authors also examine what happened to these cultures as they spread outside their own borders. There are date charts and indexes. Good coverage for grades 4-9.

HISTORY OF THE CIVIL RIGHTS MOVEMENT

DALLARD, Shyrlee

Ella Baker. Silver, 1990

DAVIES, Mark

Malcolm X. Silver, 1990

FRIESE, Kai Jabir

Rosa Parks. Silver, 1990

HESS, Debra

Thurgood Marshall. Silver, 1990

JOHNSON, Jacqueline

Stokely Carmichael. Silver, 1990

ROWLAND, Della

Martin Luther King, Jr. Silver, 1990

RUBEL, David

Fannie Lou Hamer. Silver, 1990

WILKINSON, Brenda

Jesse Jackson. Silver, 1990

WRIGHT, Sarah E.

A. Philip Randolph. Silver, 1990

This excellent series is aimed at older readers, from grades 5 through high school. Leaders of the civil rights movement are profiled in some detail. How early experiences shaped their later actions, as well as their role in the movement are the primary focuses of these works. No punches are pulled about racism or some of the negative aspects of these people's lives. There are photos, a time line of important events in civil rights history, a timetable, bibliography, and index.

HISTORY OF THE WORLD

Africa and the Origin of Humans. Raintree, 1989

Civilizations of Asia. Raintree, 1989

Civilizations of the Americas. Raintree, 1989

Civilizations of the Middle East. Raintree, 1989

The Early Middle Ages. Raintree, 1989

Europe at the Time of Greece and Rome. Raintree, 1989

The Late Middle Ages. Raintree, 1989

Prehistoric and Ancient Europe. Raintree, 1989

This is an ambitious title for a series. The books are oversize, with an abundance of illustrations, but basically, they present an overview of various historical periods as they occurred worldwide. A page of text alternates with a page of illustration, so while a reader gets a feel for the basic information and look of the time, there is no in-depth treatment. A timeline prefaces each book. Grades 5 and up. Glossary, index.

HI-TECH CAREERS

ESKOWE, Dennis

Laser Careers. Watts, 1988

LAURANCE, Robert

Electronic Service Careers. Watts, 1987

SCHEFTER, James L.

Aerospace Careers. Watts, 1987

Telecommunication Careers. Watts, 1988

Careers in the highly technical fields covered in these books are among the fastest growing job opportunities available. These books offer an interesting viewpoint in the discussion of these careers. Each title offers interviews with current high-tech professionals and covers opportunities and drawbacks. This is a good series offering straightforward information. Grades 9-12.

HOLIDAY MAGIC

BAKER, James W.

April Fool's Day Magic. Lerner, 1989

Arbor Day Magic. Lerner, 1990

Birthday Magic. Lerner, 1988

Christmas Magic. Lerner, 1988

Columbus Day Magic. Lerner, 1989

Halloween Magic. Lerner, 1988

Independence Day Magic. Lerner, 1989

New Year's Magic. Lerner, 1989

President's Day Magic. Lerner, 1989

St. Patrick's Day Magic. Lerner, 1990

Thanksgiving Magic. Lerner, 1988

Valentine Magic. Lerner, 1988

In an unusual turn on holiday books, these feature only magic tricks that have been adapted to entertain seasonally. Wanna-be magicians enjoy any source for tricks, but limited library budgets might require tricks that can be used more than one season a year.

HOLIDAY SYMBOL BOOKS

BARTH, Edna

Hearts, Cupids, and Red Roses. Clarion, 1974

Holly, Reindeer, and Colored Lights. Clarion, 1971

Lilies, Rabbits, and Painted Eggs. Clarion, 1970

Shamrocks, Harps, and Shillelaghs. Clarion, 1977

Turkeys, Pilgrims, and Indian Corn. Clarion, 1975

Witches, Pumpkins, and Grinning Ghosts. Clarion, 1972

GIBLIN, James C.

Fireworks, Picnics, and Flags. Clarion, 1983

PERL, Lila

Candles, Cakes, and Donkey Tails. Clarion, 1984

Teachers will be delighted with this series exploring the historical background to holiday customs. What various symbols mean and why is also included. Bibliography, index.

HOLIDAYS

DUDEN, Jane

Christmas. Crestwood, 1990

Thanksgiving. Crestwood, 1990

SANDAK, Cass
Columbus Day. Crestwood, 1990
Easter. Crestwood, 1980
Halloween. Crestwood, 1977
Patriotic Holidays. Crestwood, 1990
Valentine's Day. Crestwood, 1980
TURCK, Mary
Jewish Holidays. Crestwood, 1990

These books are in season all year long. Each book begins with a story relating to current holiday happenings and then reviews the history of each holiday. Some craft ideas are included as well as an index. HOLIDAYS was written for the reluctant reader in grades 6-9.

HORSES
NENTL, Jerolyn
Draft Horses. Crestwood, 1983
PHILP, Candice Tillis
Rodeo Horses. Crestwood, 1983
ROBISON, Nancy
Hunters and Jumpers. Crestwood, 1983
The Ponies. Crestwood, 1983

Horse lovers will read their fill with these books. Most of the information here is on the animals themselves: history, breeds, skills—even training is described. These are somewhat detailed; although a glossary is provided, non-aficionados may find these too specialized. Grades 4-8.

HOTSPOTS
BRADLEY, John
China: A New Revolution? Watts, 1990
Eastern Europe: The Road to Democracy. Watts, 1990
Soviet Union: Will Perestroika Work? Watts, 1989
LEWIS, John
Ireland: A Divided Country. Watts, 1989
PEARCE, Jenny
Colombia: The Drug War. Watts, 1990
ROBERTS, Elizabeth
Europe, 1992: The United States of Europe? Watts, 1990

Very timely indeed is this new series, focusing on current international areas of change. Historical background on the area is provided, followed by a description of present-day developments and future possibilities. There is a chronology, glossary, and index. Grades 5-9.

HOUSES AND HOMES
JAMES, Alan
Castles and Mansions. Lerner, 1989
Homes in Cold Places. Lerner, 1989
Homes in Hot Places. Lerner, 1989
Homes on Water. Lerner, 1989
LAMBERT, Mark
Homes in the Future. Lerner, 1989
RICKARD, Graham
Building Homes. Lerner, 1989
Homes in Space. Lerner, 1989
Mobile Homes. Lerner, 1989

Younger children may be intrigued by this series, which examines a wide variety of homes. How (and out of what materials) homes are built is explored in one title; others show how people adapt their housing to the climate and geography of their locale. Geared to the 6-10 year old set, these have two color photos per page, glossary words in boldface, and a controlled vocabulary. Bibliography, index.

HOW DID WE FIND OUT ABOUT

ASIMOV, Isaac

How Did We Find out about Atoms? Walker, 1976
How Did We Find out about Black Holes? Walker, 1978
How Did We Find out about Blood? Walker, 1986
How Did We Find out about Comets? Walker, 1975
How Did We Find out about Computers? Walker, 1984
How Did We Find out about DNA? Walker, 1985
How Did We Find out about Earthquakes? Walker, 1981
How Did We Find out about Energy? Walker, 1981
How Did We Find out about Germs? Walker, 1973
How Did We Find out about Lasers? Walker, 1990
How Did We Find out about Microwaves? Walker, 1989
How Did We Find out about Neptune? Walker, 1990
How Did We Find out about Nuclear Power? Walker, 1976
How Did We Find out about Photosynthesis? Walker, 1989
How Did We Find out about Pluto? Walker, 1991
How Did We Find out about Solar Power? Walker, 1981
How Did We Find out about Sunshine? Walker, 1987
How Did We Find out about Superconductivity? Walker, 1988
How Did We Find out about the Brain? Walker, 1987
How Did We Find out about the Speed of Light? Walker, 1986
How Did We Find out about the Universe? Walker, 1983
How Did We Find out about Vitamins? Walker, 1974
How Did We Find out about Volcanoes? Walker, 1982

Each topic examined here deals primarily with the scientific developments historically. How it was discovered, experimented with, and used throughout time. The basic principles are mentioned, as are future possibilities. The text sometimes moves into other areas (for example, the volume on solar energy spends a chapter on nuclear and petroleum power), that are only marginally related. The drawings are more decorative than useful for report purposes. Unless the collection requires books with primarily an historical perspective, these should be considered marginal purchases for grades 4-8.

HOW IT FEELS

KREMENTZ, Jill

How It Feels to Be Adopted. Random, 1982
How It Feels When a Parent Dies. Random, 1981
How It Feels When Parents Divorce. Random, 1984

Author Krementz has interviewed a variety of youngsters about their feelings and advice on how to handle these kinds of personal problems. Accompanying the text are many large black and white photos. These can be used with grades 4-12.

HOW IT WORKS

GRAHAM, Ian

Battle Tanks. Watts, 1990
Combat Aircraft. Watts, 1990
Helicopters. Watts, 1989
Racing Cars. Watts, 1990
Space Shuttles. Watts, 1989
Submarines. Watts, 1989
Trucks. Watts, 1990

KERROD, Robin

Motorcycles. Watts, 1989

Children are often fascinated by various vehicles, and these books will be just the ticket. Large, clear color drawings and photos show how each vehicle is put together, different kinds of models, engines that power them, facts and figures, glossary, and index. Grades 3-8.

HOW OUR BODIES WORK

ARDLEY, Bridget, and **Neil ARDLEY**

Skin, Hair, and Teeth. Silver Burdette, 1988

BURGESS, Jan

Birth and Growth. Silver Burdette, 1988

Food and Digestion. Silver Burdette, 1988

Heart and Blood. Silver Burdette, 1988

DINEEN, Jacqueline

The Five Senses. Silver Burdette, 1988

Skeleton and Movement. Silver Burdette, 1988

LAMBERT, Mark

Brain and Nervous System. Silver Burdette, 1988

Lungs and Breathing. Silver Burdette, 1988

This series about the human body covers a great deal of territory. Some brief historical background is given, then anatomical information about the structure of the body. Each system's uses in everyday functions are both discussed and illustrated. In addition to this standard information, the authors discuss injuries and diseases that can affect the body, how the body can be repaired, first aid, and how to stay in shape. And all in less than 50 pages! The information is brief and concise; it could fill assignments for grades 3-6, but certainly not in any depth.

HOW PEOPLE LIVE

The Crowded Cities. Silver, 1989

Families around the World. Silver, 1989

Farming. Silver, 1989

Life in the Tropics. Silver, 1989

Living by the Water. Silver, 1989

On the Move. Silver, 1989

This is one of several series originally published by Schoolhouse Press that has been reissued by Silver Burdette. This one relates the way people live to their climates. Crops, housing, animals and other wildlife are all covered. Then examples of people in various cultures are discussed and compared. Social studies teachers will find these fine supplements to classroom learning. Grades 4-8. Glossary, index.

HUMAN BODY

PARKER, Steve

The Brain and Nervous System. Watts, 1990

The Ear and Hearing. Watts, 1989

The Eye and Seeing. Watts, 1989

The Food and Digestion. Watts, 1990

The Heart and Blood. Watts, 1989

The Lungs and Breathing. Watts, 1989

The Skeleton and Movement. Watts, 1989

Touch, Taste and Smell. Watts, 1989

This excellent series will provide a super source for young students with reports on the human body and its functions. There are numerous diagrams and photos. Author Parker relates the body to various machines that students are familiar with, tells how they work, and also discusses problems that can occur when the body is not working correctly. There is a glossary and index. Grades 4-9.

HUMAN STORY

Asian Civilizations. Silver, 1988
The Earliest Cities. Silver, 1987
Europe in the Middle Ages. Silver, 1988
The First Empires. Silver, 1988
The First People. Silver, 1986
The First Settlements. Silver, 1987
Mediterranean Civilizations. Silver, 1987
The Rise of the Religions. Silver, 1988

This is a very good series of books that takes a look at human history from the dawn of the earth. There are color photographs, charts, and maps. Young adults in seventh grade and above.

KNOW ABOUT SERIES

HYDE, Margaret O.
Know about AIDS. Walker, 1990
Know about Drugs. Walker, 1990
Know about Smoking. Walker, 1990

Hyde has successfully explained the dangers and risks associated with the topics of these three books. Written in a clear, steady tone, she tells teens that those risks can happen to them. Included in the books are illustrations, an index, and suggestions for further reading. Most importantly, she tells the reader that it is up to them to make their own decisions, that young people should not bend to peer pressure because it can end up hurting them.

I CAN BE BOOKS

BECKMAN, Beatrice
I Can Be President. Childrens, 1984
I Can Be a Teacher. Childrens, 1985

BEHRENS, June
I Can Be an Astronaut. Childrens, 1984
I Can Be a Nurse. Childrens, 1986
I Can Be a Pilot. Childrens, 1985
I Can Be a Truck Driver. Childrens, 1985

BRILL, Marlene Targ
I Can Be a Lawyer. Childrens, 1987

BROEKEL, Ray
I Can Be an Author. Childrens, 1986
I Can Be an Auto Mechanic. Childrens, 1985

CLINTON, Patrick
I Can Be a Father. Childrens, 1988

CLINTON, Susan
I Can Be an Architect. Childrens, 1986

FITZ-GERALD, C.
I Can Be a Mother. Childrens, 1988
I Can Be a Reporter. Childrens, 1986
I Can Be a Textile Worker. Childrens, 1987

GREENE, Carol
I Can Be a Baseball Player. Childrens, 1985
I Can Be a Football Player. Childrens, 1984
I Can Be a Forest Ranger. Childrens, 1989
I Can Be a Librarian. Childrens, 1988
I Can Be a Model. Childrens, 1985
I Can Be a Salesperson. Childrens, 1989

HALLENSTEIN, Kathryn
I Can Be a TV Camera Operator. Childrens, 1984

HANKIN, Rebecca
I Can Be a Doctor. Childrens, 1985
I Can Be a Firefighter. Childrens, 1985
I Can Be a Musician. Childrens, 1984
HENDERSON, Kathy
I Can Be a Farmer. Childrens, 1989
I Can Be a Horse Trainer. Childrens, 1990
I Can Be a Rancher. Childrens, 1990
LILLEGARD, Dee
I Can Be a Baker. Childrens, 1986
I Can Be a Beautician. Childrens, 1987
I Can Be a Carpenter. Childrens, 1986
I Can Be a Secretary. Childrens, 1987
LILLEGARD, Dee, and **Wayne STOKER**
I Can Be an Electrician. Childrens, 1986
I Can Be a Plumber. Childrens, 1987
I Can Be a Welder. Childrens, 1986
LUMLEY, Kay
I Can Be an Animal Doctor. Childrens, 1985
MARTIN, Claire
I Can Be a Weather Forecaster. Childrens, 1987
MATTHIAS, Catherine
I Can Be a Computer Operator. Childrens, 1985
I Can Be a Police Officer. Childrens, 1984
OSINSKI, Christine
I Can Be a Photographer. Childrens, 1986
PICKERING, Robert
I Can Be an Archaeologist. Childrens, 1987
ROWAN, Jim
I Can Be a Zoo Keeper. Childrens, 1985
SIPIERA, Paul
I Can Be an Astronomer. Childrens, 1986
I Can Be a Geographer. Childrens, 1990
I Can Be a Geologist. Childrens, 1986
I Can Be an Oceanographer. Childrens, 1987
I Can Be a Physicist. Childrens, 1991
STORM, Betsy
I Can Be an Interior Designer. Childrens, 1989
TOMCHEK, Ann
I Can Be a Chef. Childrens, 1985
WILKINSON, Sylvia
I Can Be a Race Car Driver. Childrens, 1986

Career units begin very early in school, and these books can be used with the youngest readers. The format is usable with grades 1-3, with large print and simple vocabulary, with just a few sentences on each page. Color photos add spice to the text, along with a glossary and index.

IDEAS IN CONFLICT
FANNING, Beverly J.
Workfare vs. Welfare. McCuen, 1989
MCCUEN, Gary E.
The AIDS Crisis: Conflicting Social Values. McCuen, 1987
The Apartheid Reader. McCuen, 1986
Children Having Children. McCuen, 1988
Hi-Tech Babies. McCuen, 1990
Illiteracy in America. McCuen, 1988

Inner-City Violence. McCuen, 1990
The International Drug Trade. McCuen, 1989
The Iran-Iraq War. McCuen, 1987
Manipulating Life: Debating the Genetic Revolution. McCuen, 1985
Militarizing Space. McCuen, 1989
Nicaragua Revolution. McCuen, 1986
Nuclear Waste. McCuen, 1990
Nuclear Winter. McCuen, 1987
Our Endangered Atmosphere. McCuen, 1987
Political Murder in Central America. McCuen, 1985
Poor and Minority Health Care. McCuen, 1988
Pornography and Sexual Violence. McCuen, 1985
Protecting Water Quality. McCuen, 1986
Religion and Politics. McCuen, 1989
The Religious Right. McCuen, 1989
Reviving the Death Penalty. McCuen, 1985
Secret Democracy. McCuen, 1990
Terminating Life: Conflicting Values in Health Care. McCuen, 1985
Treating the Mentally Disabled. McCuen, 1988
World Hunger and Social Justice. McCuen, 1986

A well used set of books in the public library. Clear and factual, they present both sides of their particular topic in an easy-to-read manner. Each book includes study guides and discussion activities that make it a good resource for high school libraries. These are comparable to the Opposing Viewpoints series. For YAs.

IF YOU...

GROSS, Ruth Belov

If You Grew up with George Washington. Scholastic, 1985

LEVINE, Ellen

If You Lived at the Time of Martin Luther King. Scholastic, 1990
If You Were an Animal Doctor. Scholastic, 1988
If You Lived at the Time of the Great San Francisco Earthquake. Scholastic, 1987
If You Traveled on the Underground Railroad. Scholastic, 1988
If You Traveled West in a Covered Wagon. Scholastic, 1986

LEVY, Elizabeth

If You Were There When They Signed the Constitution. Scholastic, 1987

MCGOVERN, Ann

If You Grew up with Abraham Lincoln. Scholastic, 1985
If You Lived with the Sioux Indians. Scholastic, 1976
If You Sailed on the Mayflower. Scholastic, 1969

With a question-and-answer format, this series tries to show younger readers (grades 3-5) what life was really like for people involved in famous historical events. There is no index, but the table of contents will help readers reach specific topics. New terms are explained within the text.

ILLUSTRATED SCIENCE ALBUMS

MCGOWEN, Tom

Album of Astronomy. Childrens, 1984
Album of Dinosaurs. Childrens, 1989
Album of Prehistoric Man. Childrens, 1987
Album of Sharks. Childrens, 1987
Album of Whales. Childrens, 1989
Dinosaurs and Other Prehistoric Animals. Childrens, 1984

Originally published by Rand McNally and called Animal Albums, this oversize series has large color illustrations and adequate subject information. There are a number of other series that offer equally good coverage with more eye appeal and better illustrations. Grades 5-9.

IMAGINE LIVING HERE

COBB, Vickie

This Place Is Cold. Walker, 1990
This Place Is Dry. Walker, 1989
This Place Is High. Walker, 1989
This Place Is Lonely. Walker, 1991
This Place Is Wet. Walker, 1989

This series takes an imaginative approach to showing readers ages 7-9 what life is like in countries with different climates. Types of wildlife, geography, transportation, and how the climates were adapted to by people are all covered in readable text. The accompanying color illustrations give the aura of a picture book, rather than a science book, and add greatly to the reader appeal. Recommended for pleasure and supplemental school material.

IMPACT BIOGRAPHIES

BENTLEY, Judith
Harriet Tubman. Watts, 1990

BERKE, Art
Babe Ruth. Watts, 1988

CANNON, Marian G.
Dwight David Eisenhower. Watts, 1990

CAULKINS, Janet
Joseph Stalin. Watts, 1990

DOHERTY, Katherine M., and **Craig A. DOHERTY**
Benazir Bhutto. Watts, 1990

HARRIS, Jacqueline L.
Martin Luther King, Jr. Watts, 1983

HOOBLER, Dorothy, and **Thomas HOOBLER**
Nelson and Winnie Mandela. Watts, 1987

HUMPHREY, Kathryn L.
Satchel Paige. Watts, 1988

KORT, Michael
Mikhail Gorbachev. Watts, 1990
Nikita Khrushchev. Watts, 1989

LAMPTON, Christopher
Werner Von Braun. Watts, 1988

LOVE, Robert
Elvis Presley. Watts, 1986

MCKISSACK, Patricia, and **Frederick MCKISSACK**
W.E.B. Dubois. Watts, 1990

PATTERSON, Charles
Marian Anderson. Watts, 1988

RANDOLPH, Blythe
Amelia Earhart. Watts, 1987

THAYER, Bonita E.
Emily Dickinson. Watts, 1989

WEPMAN, Dennis
Desmond Tutu. Watts, 1989

People who have had an impact on world history are the subjects of this series. Beginning with their childhood through their present day lives, these titles use illustrations and easy to understand text to give the reader a view of the person in history. An index and bibliography are included in these books written for high school students.

IMPACT BOOKS

ANDREWS, Elaine K.
Civil Defense in the Nuclear Age. Watts, 1985
BERGER, Gilda
Crack: The New Epidemic. Watts, 1987
Drug Testing. Watts, 1987
National Debt. Watts, 1987
BERGER, Melvin
Artificial Heart. Watts, 1987
CARROLL, Raymond
Future of the United Nations. Watts, 1985
CHENY, Glenn Alan
El Salvador. Watts, 1990
CLAYPOOL, Jane
Alcohol and You. Watts, 1988
CORRICK, James A.
Recent Revolutions in Biology. Watts, 1987
Recent Revolutions in Chemistry. Watts, 1986
DAVIS, Bertha
America's Housing Crisis. Watts, 1990
Crisis in Industry. Watts, 1989
Instead of Prison. Watts, 1986
DOLAN, Edward F., and **Margaret M. SCARIANO**
Cuba and the United States. Watts, 1987
FEINBERG, Barbara S.
Marx and Marxism. Watts, 1985
FERRARA, Peter L.
NATO: An Entangled Alliance. Watts, 1984
FISHER, Maxine P.
Recent Revolutions in Anthropology. Watts, 1986
GAY, Kathlyn
Greenhouse Effect. Watts, 1986
Ozone. Watts, 1989
Silent Killers. Watts, 1988
Water Pollution. Watts, 1990
HEINTZE, Carl
Medical Ethics. Watts, 1987
HELGERSON, Joel
Nuclear Accidents. Watts, 1988
KELSEY, Larry, and **Darrel HOFF**
Recent Revolutions in Astronomy. Watts, 1987
KRONENWETTER, Michael
Capitalism vs. Socialism. Watts, 1986
Journalism Ethics. Watts, 1988
LAMPTON, Christopher
Endangered Species. Watts, 1988
Flying Safe? Watts, 1986
Supernova! Watts, 1988
LANDAU, Elaine
Black Market Adoption and the Sale of Children. Watts, 1990
LAWSON, Don
New Philippines. Watts, 1986
LEE, Sally
Throwaway Society. Watts, 1990

LOEB, Robert H., Jr.
Crime and Capital Punishment. Watts, 1986
MCCORMICK, Michele
Designer-Drug Abuse. Watts, 1989
MCCOY, J. J.
How Safe Is Our Food Supply? Watts, 1990
Plight of the Whales. Watts, 1989
NEWTON, David
Science Ethics. Watts, 1987
NUWER, Hank
Steroids. Watts, 1990
RIERDEN, Anne B.
Reshaping the Supreme Court. Watts, 1988
ROSSBACHER, Lisa A.
Recent Revolutions in Geology. Watts, 1986
STERN, Alan
U.S. Space Program after Challenger. Watts, 1987
STWERTKA, Albert
Recent Revolutions in Mathematics. Watts, 1987
STWERTKA, Eve, and **Albert STWERTKA**
Genetic Engineering. Watts, 1989
TAYLOR, L. B., Jr.
Hostage! Kidnapping and Terrorism in Our Time. Watts, 1989
Space? Battleground of the Future. Watts, 1988
TERKEL, Susan Neiburg
Abortion: Facing the Issues. Watts, 1988
VOGT, Gregory
Forests on Fire. Watts, 1990
WILLIAMS, Gene B.
Nuclear War, Nuclear Winter. Watts, 1987
WOODS, Geraldine
Affirmative Action. Watts, 1989

This critically acclaimed series offers objective viewpoints of a number of current topics that have an impact on people's lives. The books are carefully researched and written by knowledgeable authors. The series is wide ranging, including books that deal with health and personal growth, science, nature and technology, and social studies and geography. These are written for students in grades 9-12. Bibliography, index.

***IN AMERICA BOOKS**
AVAKIAN, Arra S.
Armenians in America. Lerner, 1977
ENGLE, Eloise
Finns in America. Lerner, 1977
HARIK, Elsa Marston
Lebanese in America. Lerner, 1987
HARTMANN, Edward G.
American Immigration. Lerner, 1979
PATTERSON, Wayne
Koreans in America. Lerner, 1977
PETERSEN, Peter L.
Danes in America. Lerner, 1987
RUTLEDGE, Paul
Vietnamese in America. Lerner, 1987
WINTER, Frank H.
Filipinos in America. Lerner, 1988

These are the latest entries in this series dedicated to describing the many peoples who emigrated to this country. The country of origin is described and the authors go into some detail as to why so many people felt they had to leave. What happened when they reached America is also touched on, including details of discrimination. How American culture has impacted on them and vice versa is another subject; their culture is described, and there are brief biographies of famous immigrants. These will prove helpful both with assignments on immigration, and also to promote understanding within communities where people from other lands have settled. Grades 4 and up. Index.

INSIDE BUSINESS

AASENG, Nathan

Better Mousetraps. Lerner, 1990
Close Calls. Lerner, 1990
Fortunate Fortunes. Lerner, 1989
From Rags to Riches. Lerner, 1990
Midstream Changes. Lerner, 1990
Problem Solvers. Lerner, 1989
Rejects. Lerner, 1989
Unsung Heroes. Lerner, 1989

With an increasing emphasis on the importance of business in modern life and to the economic well being of America, this series fills a large gap in most children's collections. Important inventions, products that brought companies into prominence, and successful entrepreneurs are among the subjects of these books. Grades 5 and up. Bibliography, index.

IN THE SPOTLIGHT

BEIRNE, Barbara

Under the Lights: A Child Model at Work. Carolrhoda, 1988

HUBERMAN, Caryn, and **Jo Anne WETZEL**

Onstage/Backstage. Carolrhoda, 1987

ZECK, Gerry

I Love to Dance. Carolrhoda, 1982

Similar to Jill Krementz's Very Young Series, this one profiles youngsters who are involved professionally in various kinds of performing. The numerous black-and-white photos give a strong sense of the experience. The text emphasizes how the child began, what they learned, and what they are currently involved in. Any child who is involved in the arts or thinking of taking lessons will find these inspiring. Grades 3-6.

INCREDIBLE HISTORIES

DUGGLEBY, John

Doomed Expeditions. Crestwood, 1990
Impossible Quests. Crestwood, 1990

GOLD, Susan Dudley

The Pharaoh's Curse. Crestwood, 1990

LAZO, Caroline Evensen

Missing Treasure. Crestwood, 1990

LORD, Suzanne

Superstitions. Crestwood, 1990

ROM, Christine

Creepy Castles. Crestwood, 1990

SOTNAK, Lewann

Haunted Houses. Crestwood, 1990

STEWART, Gail B.

Famous Hoaxes. Crestwood, 1990

Both regular and reluctant readers will be drawn to these books because of their high-interest subjects. Historical background is given, along with discussions about why people choose to believe in the supernatural and what the underlying explanations may be. The black and white drawings are not particularly appealing—photos definitely make these subjects more realistic! Grades 4-7. Bibliography, index.

INDIANS OF NORTH AMERICA

AIGNER, Jean S.
Eskimo. Chelsea, 1989

ARMITAGE, Peter
Montagnais. Chelsea, 1989

BAIRD, W. D.
Quapaws. Chelsea, 1989

BEAN, Lowell J., and **Lisa BOURGEAULT**
Cahuilla. Chelsea, 1989

BEE, Robert L.
Yuma. Chelsea, 1989

BERDAN, Frances F.
Aztecs. Chelsea, 1989

BLU, Karen
Lumbee. Chelsea, 1989

BONVILLAIN, Nancy
Huron. Chelsea, 1989

BRAIN, Jeffrey
Tunica-Biloxi. Chelsea, 1989

BUNTE, Pamela A., and **Robert J. FRANKLIN**
Paiute. Chelsea, 1989

CALLOWAY, Colin G.
Abenaki. Chelsea, 1988

CLIFTON, James A.
Potawatomi. Chelsea, 1988

DOBYNS, Henry F.
Pima-Maricopa. Chelsea, 1989

FAULK, Odie B., and **Laura E. FAULK**
Modoc. Chelsea, 1988

FIXICO, Donald L.
Urban Indians. Chelsea, 1989

FOWLER, Loretta
Arapaho. Chelsea, 1989

GARBARINO, Merwin S.
Seminole. Chelsea, 1989

GIBSON, Robert O.
Chumash. Chelsea, 1989

GRAYMOUNT, Barbara
Iroquois. Chelsea, 1989

GREEN, Michael D.
Creek. Chelsea, 1989

GREEN, Rayna
Women in American Indian Society. Chelsea, 1989

GRUMET, Robert S.
Lenapes. Chelsea, 1989

HAIG, Stanley
Cheyenne. Chelsea, 1989

HALE, Duane
Chickasaw. Chelsea, 1989

HOOVER, Herbert
Yankton Sioux. Chelsea, 1988
HOZIE, Frederick E.
Crow. Chelsea, 1989
IVERSON, Peter J.
Navajo. Chelsea, 1989
KELLY, Lawrence C.
Federal Indian Policy. Chelsea, 1989
KENNEDY, John
Tarahumara. Chelsea, 1989
MCKEE, Jesse O.
Choctaw. Chelsea, 1989
MELODY, Michael E.
Apache. Chelsea, 1988
MERRELL, James H.
Catawbas. Chelsea, 1989
NABAKOV, Peter
Nez Perce. Chelsea, 1989
ORTIZ, Alfonso
Pueblo. Chelsea, 1989
OVRADA, Patricia
Menominee. Chelsea, 1989
PERDUE, Theda
Cherokee. Chelsea, 1989
PORTER, Frank W.
Coast Salish People. Chelsea, 1989
Nanticoke. Chelsea, 1987
RAWLINGS, Willard
Comanche. Chelsea, 1989
RUOFF, A. Lavonne
American Indian Literature. Chelsea, 1989
SCHNEIDER, Mary J.
Hidatsa. Chelsea, 1989
SCHUSTER, Helen H.
Yakima. Chelsea, 1989
SIMMONS, William S.
Narragansett. Chelsea, 1989
SMITH, James G.
Chipewyan. Chelsea, 1989
SNOW, Dean R.
Archaeology of North America. Chelsea, 1989
TRAFZER, Clifford
Chinook. Chelsea, 1990
TROUT, Lawana
Maya. Chelsea, 1989
TURNER, Helen H.
Ojibwa. Chelsea, 1989
WALENS, Stanley
Kwak. Chelsea, 1989
WEINSTEIN-FARSON, Laurie
Wampanoag. Chelsea, 1988
WILSON, Terry P.
Osage. Chelsea, 1988
WUNDER, John R.
Kiowa. Chelsea, 1989

American Indians have played a significant and often tarnished role in our history. This series of books gives a clear and accurate description of American Indians and places them in the proper perspective for students 12 and up. The books describe Indian culture, give tribal history and discuss the relationship each tribe has had with our government. Excellent photographs, a glossary, maps and an index make each of these books an excellent addition to any library.

IN-FOCUS BIOGRAPHIES

BENTLEY, Judith

Fidel Castro. Messner, 1991

MOSKIN, Marietta

Margaret Thatcher. Messner, 1990

PATTERSON, Charles

Hafiz al-Asad. Messner, 1991

WORTH, Richard

Robert Mugabe. Messner, 1990

Diverse, modern political leaders are the focus of this series. Each book looks at a world leader and the personal philosophies and governmental policies that shape the roles they play. This series also examines the leaders from the viewpoint of the world arena. Grades 9-12.

INSIDE

DAS, Prodeepta

India. Watts, 1990

JAMES, Ian

Australia. Watts, 1989
China. Watts, 1989
France. Watts, 1989
Great Britain. Watts, 1988
Israel. Watts, 1990
Italy. Watts, 1988
Japan. Watts, 1989
Mexico. Watts, 1989
Netherlands. Watts, 1990
Spain. Watts, 1989
United States. Watts, 1990
West Germany. Watts, 1989

LYE, Keith

Soviet Union. Watts, 1989

Coverage is very similar to that of Watts's Passport series. Both are oversize with lots of color illustrations, with information on geography, religion, the people, etc. These are for a younger reading level, however. There is a fact section. Grades 3-6.

INSIDE TRACK LIBRARY

DUNNAN, Nancy

Banking. Silver Burdette, 1990
Collectibles. Silver Burdette, 1990
Entrepreneurship. Silver Burdette, 1990
Stock Market. Silver Burdette, 1990

Nancy Dunnan, a nationally known author and security analyst, turns her attention to aspiring business professionals in grades 7 and up with this series. She focuses on familiar examples from the reader's world to explain and illustrate the concepts of economics. She uses simulations (for example, "buying" Reebok stock) to entice the reader to explore the finance world. Each book includes an index, illustration and appendices.

INTO THE THIRD CENTURY

BERNSTEIN, Richard B., and **Jerome AGEL**

Congress. Walker, 1989

President. Walker, 1989

Supreme Court. Walker, 1989

These volumes provide a detailed study of our three arms of government. Their historical beginnings are studied and important developments and personalities are highlighted. Recent history is included as well as a chapter on how each institution actually operates today. Possibilities for future developments give the series its title. Although there are few photos, these will prove excellent resources for grades 5 and up.

INVENTIONS THAT CHANGED OUR LIVES

COSNER, Shaaron

Light Bulb. Walker, 1984

Rubber. Walker, 1986

FORD, Barbara

Automobile. Walker, 1987

Keeping Things Cool. Walker, 1985

GLEASNER, Diana

Movies. Walker, 1983

SIEGEL, Beatrice

Sewing Machine. Walker, 1984

SMITH, Elizabeth Simpson

Cloth. Walker, 1985

Paper. Walker, 1984

Each invention in this series is examined from its development internationally to what the early models were like. A chapter is also included on present day life with the invention. Each slim volume (about 60 pages) is simply written with historical photos that may be of interest, but much the same information is available at the same reading level in encyclopedias and books that cover a variety of inventions. An additional purchase for grades 4-6.

ISSUES

BECKLAKE, John

Climate Crisis: Greenhouse Effect and the Ozone Layer. Watts, 1989

BOSE, Mihir

Crash! A New Money Crisis? Watts, 1989

BRADLEY, John

Human Rights. Watts, 1987

BROWN, David

Crack and Cocaine. Watts, 1987

CAMPBELL, Duncan

Secret Service. Watts, 1988

CONDON, Judith

Smoking. Watts, 1989

EVANS, Michael

Gulf Crisis. Watts, 1988

South Africa. Watts, 1988

HAWKES, Nigel

AIDS. Watts, 1987

Gun Control. Watts, 1988

Nuclear Arms Race. Watts, 1986

Safety in the Sky. Watts, 1990

Space Shuttle: A New Era? Watts, 1989

Toxic Waste and Recycling. Watts, 1988

HITCHCOX, Linda

Refugees. Watts, 1990

LOBSTEIN, Tim
Poisoned Food? Watts, 1990
MCCORMICK, John
Acid Rain. Watts, 1986
MCDOWELL, David
Palestinians. Watts, 1986
PARKER, Steve
Drug War. Watts, 1990
TIMBERLAKE, Lloyd
Famine in Africa. Watts, 1986
WRIGHT, Pearce
Space Race. Watts, 1987

Watts is going gangbusters in producing series about "earth consciousness," like this one, Green Issues, and Save Our Planet. This one is oversize, with the standard Watts format of a page of text alternating with a page of color illustration. Each topic is very clearly explained, including causes of the problems, potential results, and suggestions for saving the situation. Grades 5-8.

ISSUES FOR THE 1990's
COIL, Suzanne
The Poor in America. Messner, 1989
JUSSIN, Daniel
Medical Ethics. Messner, 1990
KRONENWETTER, Michael
Drugs in America. Messner, 1990
Managing Toxic Waste. Messner, 1989
The War on Terrorism. Messner, 1989
SHERROW, Victoria
Challenges in Education. Messner, 1991

Well written and readable, the titles in this series present a number of the problems that will need to be faced in the 1990s. The contents cover current points of view and try to predict what the future may bring. For young adults.

ISSUES IN AMERICAN HISTORY
CORBIN, Carole L.
Right to Vote. Watts, 1985
HANMER, Trudy J.
Advancing Frontier. Watts, 1986
KRONENWETTER, Michael
Politics and the Press. Watts, 1987
PASCOE, Elaine
Racial Prejudice. Watts, 1985
SAPINSLEY, Barbara
Taxes. Watts, 1986

The themes presented in this series have at one time or another been important throughout the course of American history. These books discuss the background and beginnings of those themes in a way that students in grades 8-12 should easily understand. Included are illustrations, suggested reading lists, and indexes. Also included are expalanations of how things evolved to the way they are today.

JANE GOODALL'S ANIMAL WORLD
GOODALL, Jane
Chimps. Atheneum, 1989
Elephants. Atheneum, 1990
Gorillas. Atheneum, 1990
Hippos. Atheneum, 1989

Lions. Atheneum, 1989
Pandas. Atheneum, 1989
Sea Otters. Atheneum, 1990
Tigers. Atheneum, 1990

Renowned animal behaviorist Goodall has compiled a series about animals that she has studied in the wild. There are color photos and 2-3 pages on each topic. The author presents both facts and comments on her own personal observations in the wild. While this certainly adds interest and validity, the lack of indexing is a large handicap for students, especially when combined with her personal stories. It makes it more difficult to dig out the basic facts for report writers. Grades 4 and up.

JEWISH HOLIDAYS

CHAIKIN, Miriam

Ask Another Question: The Story and Meaning of Passover. Clarion, 1985
Light Another Candle: The Story and Meaning of Hanukkah. Clarion, 1981
Make Noise, Make Merry: The Story and Meaning of Purim. Clarion, 1983
Shake a Palm Branch: The Story and Meaning of Sukkot. Clarion, 1984
Sound the Shofar: The Story and Meaning of Rosh Hashanah and Yom Kippur. Clarion, 1986

Each holiday is introduced with a description of the historical background of the time. The Biblical story behind it is retold, along with information on how the holiday has evolved. Traditional foods and rituals are described. Bibliography, glossary, index. Grades 4-8.

JOURNEY THROUGH HISTORY

RIUS, Maria, Gloria VERGES, and **Oriol VERGES**

The Contemporary Age. Childrens, 1988
The Greek and Roman Eras. Childrens, 1988
The Middle Ages. Childrens, 1988
Modern Times. Childrens, 1988
Prehistory to Egypt. Childrens, 1988
The Renaissance. Childrens, 1988

This series attempts to introduce readers grades 2-4 to what life was like during various periods in history. The format is story-like, with color drawings and characters taken from all levels of society commenting on their lives. Although there is no index, the end of the book contains a guide for parents and teachers. These could serve as a painless introduction to history for the younger set.

JUNIOR SCIENCE

JENNINGS, Terry

Balancing. Watts, 1989
Bouncing and Rolling. Watts, 1990
Colors. Watts, 1989
Earthworms. Watts, 1990
Electricity. Watts, 1990
Floating and Sinking. Watts, 1990
Hot and Cold. Watts, 1989
Insects. Watts, 1991
Light and Dark. Watts, 1991
Magnets. Watts, 1990
Making Sounds. Watts, 1990
Seeds. Watts, 1990
Sliding and Rolling. Watts, 1989
Slugs and Snails. Watts, 1989
Spiders. Watts, 1989
Time. Watts, 1990

Trees. Watts, 1991
Weather. Watts, 1990

To introduce young readers to science by using simple experiments, teachers and parents will find this series handy. One simple statement is made on each page, which is followed by an illustration and brief explanation. The text is easy enough for grades 1-3 to read on their own; they could also easily duplicate the experiments with an adult's help. For collections that need early childhood science materials.

JUNIOR WORLD EXPLORERS
BLASSINGAME, Wyatt
Ponce de Leon. Chelsea, 1991
BRISTOW, Jean
Robert F. Scott. Chelsea, 1991
GRAVES, Charles P.
Henry Morton Stanley. Chelsea, 1991
John Smith. Chelsea, 1991
Marco Polo. Chelsea, 1991

These were originally published by Garrard as World Explorer Books. Little has changed except the cover art. There are still unattractive drawings throughout the text, instead of illustrations of the period, and conversations and emotions are attributed to the biographees. Not a first choice where anything else is available. Grades 3-6.

KAUFMAN, Joe
About the Big Sky, About the High Hills, About the Rich Earth ... and the Deep Sea. Golden, 1978
How We Are Born, How We Grow, How Our Bodies Work ... and How We Learn. Golden, 1975
Slimy, Creepy Crawly Creatures. Golden, 1985
What Makes It Go? What Makes It Work? What Makes It Fly? What Makes It Float? Golden, 1971
Wings, Paws, Hoofs, and Flippers: A Book about Animals. Golden, 1981

These oversize books are loaded with color illustrations. The subjects under discussion range from human biology to earth science to animal biology. The coverage is cursory: readable for the browser, but not detailed or specific enough for report material. Grades 3-6. No index.

KEEPING MINIBEASTS
HENWOOD, Chris
Beetles. Watts, 1989
Caterpillars. Watts, 1989
Earthworms. Watts, 1988
Frogs. Watts, 1989
Slugs and Snails. Watts, 1988
Spiders. Watts, 1989
WATTS, Barrie
Ants. Watts, 1990
Ladybugs. Watts, 1990

Potential owners of creepy crawly pets will be delighted with this terrific series. Although simply written (grades 2-4), these books clearly cover pet care, and it is hard to find such good information on these particular animals. Readers learn where to find the animals, how to house them, about their anatomy and other physical characteristics, reproduction, care, and unusual facts. Excellent choices.

KNOW YOUR GOVERNMENT

BARNES-SVARNEY, Patricia
National Science Foundation. Chelsea, 1989

BARTY, Carl
Department of State. Chelsea, 1989

BROBERG, Merle
Department of Health. Chelsea, 1989

BURKHARDT, Robert
Federal Aviation Administration. Chelsea, 1989

CLEMENT, Fred
Department of the Interior. Chelsea, 1989
Nuclear Regulatory Commission. Chelsea, 1988

CROUCH, T.
National Aeronautics and Space Administration. Chelsea, 1989

CUTRONA, Cheryl
Department of Labor. Chelsea, 1988

DOGGETT, Clinton L.
Equal Employment Opportunities Commission. Chelsea, 1989

DOGGETT, Clinton L., and **Arthur M. SCHLESINGER**
U.S. Information Agency. Chelsea, 1990

DOLIN, Eric J.
U.S. Fish and Wildlife Service. Chelsea, 1989

DUNN, Lynne
Department of Justice. Chelsea, 1989

ELLIS, Rafaela
Central Intelligence Agency. Chelsea, 1987

FISCH, Arnold G., Jr.
Department of the Army. Chelsea, 1988

FRIEDMAN, Leon
Surpreme Court. Chelsea, 1986

GILBO, Patrick F.
American Red Cross. Chelsea, 1987

HEINSOHN, Beth, and **Andrew COHEN**
Department of Defense. Chelsea, 1989

HIGHLAND, Jean
Federal Communications Commission. Chelsea, 1989

HOPSON, Glover E.
Veterans Administration. Chelsea, 1988

HURT, R. Douglas
Department of Agriculture. Chelsea, 1989

ISRAEL, Fred L.
Department of Housing and Urban Development. Chelsea, 1990
Federal Bureau of Investigation. Chelsea, 1986
U.S. Arms Control and Disarmament Agency. Chelsea, 1990

KOSLOW, Philip
Securities and Exchange Commission. Chelsea, 1989

KRAUSE, Theresa
Department of the Navy. Chelsea, 1989

LAW, Kevin J.
Environmental Protection Agency. Chelsea, 1988

MCAFFEE, Cheryl W.
United States Postal Service. Chelsea, 1987

MACKINTOSH, Barry
National Park Service. Chelsea, 1988

MATUSKY, Gregory, and **John P. HAYES**
U.S. Secret Service. Chelsea, 1988
PATRICK, Bill
Food and Drug Administration. Chelsea, 1988
PORTER, Frank W.
Bureau of Indian Affairs. Chelsea, 1988
RAGSDALE, Bruce A.
House of Representatives. Chelsea, 1989
RHEA, John
Department of the Air Force. Chelsea, 1989
RICHIE, Donald A.
Senate. Chelsea, 1988
U.S. Constitution. Chelsea, 1989
RUDYSMITH, Christina
National Archives and Records Administration. Chelsea, 1989
RUMMEL, Jack
U.S. Marine Corps. Chelsea, 1989
SAMUELS, Michael
Public Health Service. Chelsea, 1989
SAWYER, Kem K.
National Foundation on the Arts and Humanities. Chelsea, 1989
SCHLESINGER, Arthur M. (editor)
Commission on Civil Rights. Chelsea, 1989
Department of Commerce. Chelsea, 1989
Federal Government: How It Works. Chelsea, 1989
Forest Service. Chelsea, 1989
Small Business Administration. Chelsea, 1989
SCIABINE, Christine
Presidency. Chelsea, 1988
SIMPSON, Andrew L.
Library of Congress. Chelsea, 1989
SNEIGOSKI, Stephen
Department of Education. Chelsea, 1988
STEFOFF, Rebecca
Drug Enforcement Administration. Chelsea, 1989
U.S. Coast Guard. Chelsea, 1990
STEPHANY, Wallace C.
Department of Transportation. Chelsea, 1988
STOKES, Michael D.
Federal Trade Commission. Chelsea, 1989
TAYLOR, Gary
Federal Reserve System. Chelsea, 1989
TUGGLE, Catherine, and **Gary WEIS**
Department of Energy. Chelsea, 1989
TURNER, Ellis
Immigration and Naturalization Service. Chelsea, 1989
VAN FLEET, Alanson
Tennessee Valley Authority. Chelsea, 1987
WALSTON, Mark
Department of the Treasury. Chelsea, 1989
WATTS, James
Smithsonian. Chelsea, 1986
WEITSMAN, Madeline
Peace Corps. Chelsea, 1989
WOLMAN, Paul
U.S. Mint. Chelsea, 1987

The clearly written texts in these books are interesting and factual. The books are generously illustrated and include indexes and bibliographies. Each title includes a specific history of a department as well as an overview and case studies of how it operates today. This series can be very helpful in a junior high or high school government studies class.

KNOW YOUR PETS

PALMER, Joan

Aquarium Fish. Watts, 1989
Ponies. Watts, 1989

SPROULE, Anna, and **Michael SPROULE**

Cats. Watts, 1988
Dogs. Watts, 1988
Gerbils. Watts, 1988
Guinea Pigs. Watts, 1989
Hamsters. Watts, 1988
Mice and Rats. Watts, 1989
Parakeets. Watts, 1989
Rabbits. Watts, 1988

Young pet owners will find lots to like in these books. Color photos and drawings help to clearly explain how to care for each pet: how to choose, house, feed, mate, rear the young, and even show them. A glossary and bibliography are provided. Grades 4-8.

LANDS, PEOPLES, AND CULTURES SERIES

KALMAN, Bobbie

China: The Culture. Dillon, 1989
China: The Land. Dillon, 1989
China: The People. Dillon, 1989
India: The Culture. Dillon, 1990
India: The Land. Dillon, 1990
India: The People. Dillon, 1990
Japan: The Culture. Dillon, 1989
Japan: The Land. Dillon, 1989
Japan: The People. Dillon, 1989
Tibet. Dillon, 1990

Anyone wishing to study these aspects of a country in more detail than is usually present in children's books will gravitate to these. Oversize, full of color photos, with subjects clearly headlined and marked into a paragraph or two, the information is readily accessible. In the book on "people," for instance, one learns about the many ethnic groups, age groups, homes, school, economy, and leisure activities. There is a glossary and index. Grades 4-8.

LANGUAGE POWER

DUNBAR, Robert E.

How to Debate. Watts, 1987
Making Your Point. Watts, 1990

EVERHART, Nancy

So You Have to Write a Term Paper. Watts, 1987

NEWMAN, Gerald, and **Eleanor WEINTRAUB**

Writing Your College Admissions Essay. Watts, 1987

Being able to speak and use the English language effectively is an extremely important skill for young adults. This collection of books explores the power of words and focuses on hands-on information that they are able to use. Includes term paper topics, index, and bibliography.

LEARNING ABOUT...

ALDEN, Laura

Learning about Fairies. Childrens, 1982
Learning about Mummies. Childrens, 1988
Learning about Unicorns. Childrens, 1985

ANDERSON, Leone Castell

Learning about Towers and Dungeons. Childrens, 1982

GILLEO, Alma

Learning about Monsters. Childrens, 1982

ODOR, Ruth Shannon

Learning about Castles and Palaces. Childrens, 1982
Learning about Giants. Childrens, 1981

STALLMAN, Birdie

Learning about Dragons. Childrens, 1981
Learning about Witches. Childrens, 1981

TESTER, Sylvia

Learning about Ghosts. Childrens, 1981

TOWNSEND, Lucy

Learning about Hidden Treasure. Childrens, 1987

This series is an odd mixture of factual and mythical subjects. The factual books give background on each topic: how they are made, who practiced the art, famous examples and legends and modern examples. The mythical ones talk about the legends, how and why they evolved, and why people are still interested in them today. There are appealing drawings, simple text, and popular subjects that will draw readers ages 7-11.

LERNER NATURAL SCIENCE BOOKS

DALINGER, Jane

Frogs and Toads. Lerner, 1982
Grasshoppers. Lerner, 1981
Spiders. Lerner, 1981

JOHNSON, Sylvia A.

Apple Trees. Lerner, 1983
Bats. Lerner, 1985
Beetles. Lerner, 1982
Chirping Insects. Lerner, 1986
Coral Reefs. Lerner, 1984
Crabs. Lerner, 1982
Elephant Seals. Lerner, 1989
Fireflies. Lerner, 1986
Hermit Crabs. Lerner, 1990
How Leaves Change. Lerner, 1986
Inside an Egg. Lerner, 1982
Ladybugs. Lerner, 1983
Morning Glories. Lerner, 1985
Mosses. Lerner, 1983
Mushrooms. Lerner, 1982
Penguins. Lerner, 1981
Potatoes. Lerner, 1984
Rice. Lerner, 1985
Silkworms. Lerner, 1982
Snails. Lerner, 1982
Snakes. Lerner, 1986
Tree Frogs. Lerner, 1986
Wasps. Lerner, 1984
Water Insects. Lerner, 1990
Wheat. Lerner, 1990

OVERBECK, Cynthia

Ants. Lerner, 1982
Cactus. Lerner, 1982
Carnivorous Plants. Lerner, 1982
Cats. Lerner, 1983
Dragonflies. Lerner, 1982
Elephants. Lerner, 1981
How Seeds Travel. Lerner, 1982
Monkeys. Lerner, 1981
Sunflowers. Lerner, 1981

This is a good, basic series covering a variety of living things. The language is clear, with pronunciation provided for new terms, and color illustrations. The authors discuss the biology of each life form, including anatomy, behavior, and reproduction. Grades 4-6. Glossary, index.

LET'S CELEBRATE

BARKAN, Joanne
Abraham Lincoln and President's Day. Silver, 1990

BOYNTON, Alice Benjamin
Priscilla Alden and the First Thanksgiving. Silver, 1990

CARTER, Polly
Harriet Tubman and Black History Month. Silver, 1990

HOOBLER, Dorothy, and **Thomas HOOBLER**
George Washington and President's Day. Silver, 1990

WOODSON, Jacqueline
Martin Luther King, Jr. and His Birthday. Silver, 1990

YOUNG, Robert
Christopher Columbus and His Voyage to America. Silver, 1990

Readers grades 2-4 will find this biographical series easy to like. The color illustrations and simple text, which often quotes from the person's own speeches and writings, make a good beginning offering. The titles are somewhat misleading, however. These are strictly biographies, and no mention or correlation is made between the individual and their holiday. The only drawback is the lack of index, glossary, or bibliography.

LET'S DISCOVER CANADA

LEVERT, Suzanne

Alberta. Chelsea, 1991
British Columbia. Chelsea, 1991
Manitoba. Chelsea, 1991
Ontario. Chelsea, 1991
Prince Edward Island. Chelsea, 1991
Quebec. Chelsea, 1991
Saskatchewan. Chelsea, 1991

Much like several series on the U.S., this one profiles Canada by examining each province. Each book provides a quick fact sheet, complete with color pictures of the flag, bird, etc. Geography, history, the economy, people, major cities, tourist attractions and festivals, (very) brief facts about the province and famous people, along with a chronology, bibliography, and index are provided. There are lots of color photos. This well produced series fills a major gap in information on our cousins to the north. A must for grades 5-12.

LET'S DISCOVER THE STATES

AYLESWORTH, Thomas G., and **Virginia L. AYLESWORTH**

Atlantic: Virginia, West Virginia, District of Columbia. Chelsea, 1988
Eastern Great Lakes: Ohio, Indiana, Michigan. Chelsea, 1988
The Great Plains: Montana, North Dakota, South Dakota, Wyoming, Nebraska. Chelsea, 1988

Lower Atlantic: North Carolina, South Carolina. Chelsea, 1987
Mid-Atlantic: Pennsylvania, Delaware, Maryland. Chelsea, 1988
Northern New England: Maine, Vermont, New Hampshire. Chelsea, 1988
The Northwest: Washington, Oregon, Alaska, Idaho. Chelsea, 1988
The Pacific: California, Hawaii. Chelsea, 1987
The South: Mississippi, Alabama, Florida. Chelsea, 1987
South Central: Louisiana, Arkansas, Missouri, Kansas, Oklahoma. Chelsea, 1988
The Southeast: Kentucky, Tennessee, Georgia. Chelsea, 1987
Southern New England: Connecticut, Massachusetts, Rhode Island. Chelsea, 1988
The Southwest: Texas, New Mexico, Colorado. Chelsea, 1988
Territories and Possessions: Guam, Puerto Rico, U.S. Virgin Islands, American Samoa, North Mariana Islands. Chelsea, 1988
Upper Atlantic: New York, New Jersey. Chelsea, 1987
The West: Arizona, Nevada, Utah. Chelsea, 1988
Western Great Lakes: Illinois, Iowa, Wisconsin, Minnesota. Chelsea, 1987

Each volume in this series looks at several states linked by geographical location. Some history is discussed, as well as economy, important cities, government, and the usual statistics. Enchantment of America provides better coverage of the states individually, but where there are budget restrictions, these will make good choices. Index and illustrations. Grades 3-9.

LET'S LOOK AT...

DINEEN, Jacqueline
Let's Look at Rain. Watts, 1989

FURNISS, Tim
Let's Look at Outer Space. Watts, 1987

LANGLEY, Andrew
Let's Look at Aircraft. Watts, 1989
Let's Look at Bikes and Motorcycles. Watts, 1989
Let's Look at Monster Machines. Watts, 1990
Let's Look at Racing Cars. Watts, 1990
Let's Look at Trains. Watts, 1989
Let's Look at Trucks. Watts, 1989

MATTHEWS, Rupert
Let's Look at Castles. Watts, 1988
Let's Look at Ships and Boats. Watts, 1990

MEADWAY, Wendy
Let's Look at Birds. Watts, 1990

MILBURN, Constance
Let's Look at Colors. Watts, 1988
Let's Look at Dinosaurs. Watts, 1987
Let's Look at Sunshine. Watts, 1988
Let's Look at the Seasons. Watts, 1988

NOTTRIDGE, Rhoda
Let's Look at Big Cats. Watts, 1990

PANKHURST, Sylvia
Let's Look at Farming. Watts, 1988

PENNY, Malcolm
Let's Look at Bears. Watts, 1990
Let's Look at Sharks. Watts, 1990
Let's Look at Whales. Watts, 1990

QUICKE, Kenneth
Let's Look at Horses. Watts, 1988

RICKARD, Graham
Let's Look at Tractors. Watts, 1989
Let's Look at Volcanoes. Watts, 1989

Told in simple language, with simple vocabulary, these books introduce young readers to natural and mechanical sciences. They are basic enough to be shared with nonreading kids as well as readers grades 2-3. There are color illustrations throughout, with a glossary, index, and bibliography.

LET'S TALK ABOUT...

BARTON, Miles

Why Do People Harm Animals? Watts, 1989

FARQUHAR, Clare, and **Pete SANDERS**

Problem of AIDS. Watts, 1989

GRUNSELL, Angela

Bullying. Watts, 1990
Divorce. Watts, 1990
Racism. Watts, 1991
Stepfamilies. Watts, 1990

HEMMING, Judith

Why Do People Take Drugs? Watts, 1988

SANDERS, Pete

Death and Dying. Watts, 1991
Food and Hygiene. Watts, 1990
Why Do People Drink Alcohol? Watts, 1989
Why Do People Smoke? Watts, 1989

For young readers grades 3-5, this series examines various social problems that youngsters must deal with. The texts deal step-by-step, in nonjudgmental fashion, with the realities of each situation. One page of text alternates with a color photo. There is a glossary and index. Very good choice for this age group.

LET'S VISIT PLACES AND PEOPLES OF THE WORLD

Angola. Chelsea, 1988

ANTHONY, Suzanne

Haiti. Chelsea, 1989

BALL, John

Fiji. Chelsea, 1988
Bangladesh. Chelsea, 1988

BARNES-SVARNEY, Patricia

Zimbabwe. Chelsea, 1989

BARNETT, Jennie

Ghana. Chelsea, 1989

BEATTY, Noelle B.

Suriname. Chelsea, 1988
Belize. Chelsea, 1988

BENDER, Evelyn

Brazil. Chelsea, 1990

BENOIT, Marie

Mauritius. Chelsea, 1988

BLACK, Lorraine

Monaco. Chelsea, 1988

BONOMI, Kathryn

Italy. Chelsea, 1988

BOYETTE, William

Soviet Georgia. Chelsea, 1989

BROBERG, Merle

Barbados. Chelsea, 1989

BROTHERS, Don

South Africa. Chelsea, 1989
West Indies. Chelsea, 1989

BRUNS, Roger A.
Bermuda. Chelsea, 1986
CAHILL, Mary J.
Israel. Chelsea, 1988
Lebanon. Chelsea, 1988
Northern Ireland. Chelsea, 1987
CALDWELL, John C.
India. Chelsea, 1988
New Zealand. Chelsea, 1988
Pakistan. Chelsea, 1988
Cameroon. Chelsea, 1990
CANESSO, Claudia
Cambodia. Chelsea, 1989
CARRICK, Noel
Andorra. Chelsea, 1988
Belgium. Chelsea, 1988
Luxembourg. Chelsea, 1988
New Guinea. Chelsea, 1989
COLE, Cathy
Turkey. Chelsea, 1988
COLE, Wendy M.
Congo. Chelsea, 1990
Vietnam. Chelsea, 1989
CONRY, Kieran
Vatican. Chelsea, 1988
CONWAY, Mike
Swaziland. Chelsea, 1989
CROUCH, Clifford
Cuba. Chelsea, 1988
DOAK, Claude
Gibraltar. Chelsea, 1988
DOLAN, Sean
West Germany. Chelsea, 1988
DOLCE, Laura
Australia. Chelsea, 1990
DWYER, Chris
Chile. Chelsea, 1990
EISENBERG, Joyce
Grenada. Chelsea, 1988
EVANS, J. O.
Iceland. Chelsea, 1988
GESS, Denise
Puerto Rico. Chelsea, 1986
Togo. Chelsea, 1988
GHAZARIAN, S. H.
Armenia. Chelsea, 1990
GOULD, Dennis
Botswana. Chelsea, 1988
Comores. Chelsea, 1988
GREVETTE, A. Gerard
Guyana. Chelsea, 1989
Guatemala. Chelsea, 1988
HAINES, George
Wales. Chelsea, 1988

HARTSEN, Betty
England. Chelsea, 1988
HASSEL, S., and P. HASSEL
Brunei. Chelsea, 1988
HAYNES, Tricia
Colombia. Chelsea, 1988
Costa Rica. Chelsea, 1988
Honduras. Chelsea, 1988
HOLLMES, Timothy
Zambia. Chelsea, 1988
HOOPER, Neil
Maldive Islands. Chelsea, 1989
HOPE, Constance M.
Liberia. Chelsea, 1987
Iraq. Chelsea, 1988
HOWARTH, Michael
Afghanistan. Chelsea, 1988
ISRAEL, Fred
Albania. Chelsea, 1987
Ivory Coast. Chelsea, 1989
JAMES, Alan
Austria. Chelsea, 1988
Denmark. Chelsea, 1988
Finland. Chelsea, 1988
JAMES, R. S.
Mozambique. Chelsea, 1988
JOHNSON, Julia
Jordan. Chelsea, 1988
United Arab Emirate. Chelsea, 1988
KENDALL, Sarita
Ecuador. Chelsea, 1987
KOBLER, Evelyn
United Kingdom Dependencies. Chelsea, 1987
LAW, Kevin J.
Canada. Chelsea, 1988
Rwanda. Chelsea, 1988
St. Lucia. Chelsea, 1988
LEAR, Aaron
Burkina Faso. Chelsea, 1986
Lesotho. Chelsea, 1988
LEVINE, Charlotte
Danish Dependencies. Chelsea, 1989
LIEBOWITZ, Sol
Argentina. Chelsea, 1988
Liechtenstein. Chelsea, 1988
LISICKY, Paul
Dominican Republic. Chelsea, 1987
Uganda. Chelsea, 1988
LUTZ, William
Guam. Chelsea, 1987
Netherlands Antilles. Chelsea, 1986
LYLE, Garry
Cyprus. Chelsea, 1988
Greece. Chelsea, 1988
Hong Kong. Chelsea, 1988

Indonesia. Chelsea, 1988
Pacific Islands. Chelsea, 1988

MCCULLEN, Patricia E.
Bahamas. Chelsea, 1988
Tanzania. Chelsea, 1989

MCDOWELL, David
Algeria. Chelsea, 1988

MCKENNA, David
East Germany. Chelsea, 1988

MACVICAR, Angus
Scotland. Chelsea, 1988

MILLER, Arthur
Spain. Chelsea, 1989

MOORE, James
Switzerland. Chelsea, 1988

MORRISON, Marion
Uruguay. Chelsea, 1988

MULLOY, Martin
Kuwait. Chelsea, 1988
Namibia. Chelsea, 1988
North Yemen. Chelsea, 1988
Saudi Arabia. Chelsea, 1988

NAVAZELSKIS, Ina
Union of Soviet Socialist Republics. Chelsea, 1988

NAYLOR, Kim
Mali. Chelsea, 1988

NEWMAN, Bernard
Malaysia. Chelsea, 1988
Nicaragua. Chelsea, 1988
Niger. Chelsea, 1989
Nigeria. Chelsea, 1988
North Korea. Chelsea, 1988

OPARENKO, Christine
Ukraine. Chelsea, 1988

OZER, Steven
Netherlands. Chelsea, 1988
Panama. Chelsea, 1988

PANKHURST, Richard
Ethiopia. Chelsea, 1988
Paraguay. Chelsea, 1988

PERRYMAN, Andrew
Gabon. Chelsea, 1988
Peru. Chelsea, 1988
Philippines. Chelsea, 1988

POMERAY, J. K.
Ireland. Chelsea, 1988

POPESCU, Julian
Bulgaria. Chelsea, 1988
Czechoslovakia. Chelsea, 1988
Hungary. Chelsea, 1988
Poland. Chelsea, 1988
Romania. Chelsea, 1988

RICKMAN, Maureen
Qatar. Chelsea, 1988

RODDIS, Ingrid
Sudan. Chelsea, 1988
RUMMEL, Jack
Mexico. Chelsea, 1989
Russia. Chelsea, 1989
San Marino. Chelsea, 1988
SANDERS, Reinfeld
El Salvador. Chelsea, 1988
Libya. Chelsea, 1987
Malawi. Chelsea, 1988
SCHIMMEL, Karen
Bolivia. Chelsea, 1990
SELFRIDGE, John
Portugal. Chelsea, 1990
SETH, Ronald
Antarctica. Chelsea, 1988
Malta. Chelsea, 1988
Seychelles. Chelsea, 1988
Sierra Leone. Chelsea, 1988
Somalia. Chelsea, 1988
SOOKRAM, Brian
France. Chelsea, 1990
South Korea. Chelsea, 1988
Sri Lanka. Chelsea, 1988
STEFOFF, Rebecca
Iran. Chelsea, 1989
Japan. Chelsea, 1988
Mongolia. Chelsea, 1986
West Bank/Gaza Strip. Chelsea, 1988
Zaire. Chelsea, 1987
STEVENS, RITA
French Overseas Departments and Territories. Chelsea, 1988
Madagascar. Chelsea, 1988
Venda. Chelsea, 1989
SUNG, San uu Kyi
Bhutan. Chelsea, 1988
Burma. Chelsea, 1988
Nepal. Chelsea, 1988
Syria. Chelsea, 1988
Taiwan. Chelsea, 1988
Thailand. Chelsea, 1988
TILLEY, P. F.
Oman. Chelsea, 1988
Tunisia. Chelsea, 1988
TWOIBERS, Marion
Burundi. Chelsea, 1989
UROSEVICH, Patricia R.
Trinidad and Tobago. Chelsea, 1988
Venezuela. Chelsea, 1988
WEE, Jessie
Singapore. Chelsea, 1988
WILKINS, Francis
Egypt. Chelsea, 1988
Gambia. Chelsea, 1988
Jamaica. Chelsea, 1988

Morocco. Chelsea, 1988
Uzbekistan. Chelsea, 1988
WILLIAMS, Jeff T.
Macao. Chelsea, 1988
WINSLOW, Zachary
Kenya. Chelsea, 1987
Yugoslavia. Chelsea, 1988
ZICKGRAF, Ralph
Laos. Chelsea, 1989
Norway. Chelsea, 1988
Sweden. Chelsea, 1988

Every country, territory, occupied land, etc. is covered in this collection of 171 titles. Each individual book is a comprehensive study of the country's people, history, culture, government, economy, and more. Along with an easy-to-read, well written text, there are numerous illustrations and a glossary and index. Excellent books for high school students.

LIFE AND TIMES
GIBB, Christopher
Richard the Lionhearted and the Crusades. Watts, 1985
HARRIS, Nathaniel
Alexander the Great and the Greeks. Watts, 1986
Leonardo and the Renaissance. Watts, 1987
MAY, Robin
Daniel Boone and the American West. Watts, 1986
ROWLAND-ENTWISTLE, Theodore
Confucius and Ancient China. Watts, 1987

Coverage emphasizes the times more than the lives. Only the first section of the book is biographical, and that information is short and superficial. The remaining sections give a (very) quick overview of the times in which the individual lived. Important people and events are mentioned in a sentence or two. They seem to be listed merely because they cannot be overlooked, rather than to really tell something meaningful about them. There is a chronology, glossary, bibliography, and suggestions of places to visit. Grades 4-6.

LIFE CYCLES SERIES
BAILEY, Jill
Life Cycle of a Bee. Watts, 1990
Life Cycle of a Crab. Watts, 1990
Life Cycle of a Duck. Watts, 1989
Life Cycle of a Grasshopper. Watts, 1990
Life Cycle of a Ladybug. Watts, 1989
Life Cycle of a Spider. Watts, 1989
Life Cycle of an Owl. Watts, 1990
COLDREY, Jennifer
Life Cycle of a Snail. Watts, 1989
PARKER, Philip
Life Cycle of a Stickleback. Watts, 1988
Life Cycle of a Sunflower. Watts, 1988
TERRY, Trevor, and **Margaret LINTON**
Life Cycle of a Butterfly. Watts, 1988
Life Cycle of an Ant. Watts, 1988
WILLIAMS, John
Life Cycle of a Frog. Watts, 1988
Life Cycle of a Rabbit. Watts, 1988
Life Cycle of a Swallow. Watts, 1989
Life Cycle of a Tree. Watts, 1989

The Life Cycle books begin with some basic information on the animal: where they live, how they look, what they eat. Then, beginning with mating, the life cycle is described. Easy vocabulary in short paragraphs alternates with color drawings. These are good introductory books for the earliest readers, K-3. One small drawback: the bibliography is limited only to Watts publications.

LIFE GUIDES

WARD, Brian R.

Alcohol Abuse. Watts, 1988
Dental Care. Watts, 1986
Diet and Nutrition. Watts, 1987
Drugs and Drug Abuse. Watts, 1988
Environment and Health. Watts, 1989
Exercise and Fitness. Watts, 1988
First Aid. Watts, 1987
Health and Hygiene. Watts, 1988
Overcoming Disability. Watts, 1989
Smoking and Health. Watts, 1986

This series is a companion piece to the Human Body series, with the same type of cover and illustrations. One page of text is devoted to each subject. Historical background, scientific information and statistics, and health concerns are the topics. Good overview for grades 4-8.

LIFE IN...

BAKER, Lucy

Life in the Deserts. Watts, 1990
Life in the Oceans. Watts, 1990
Life in the Rainforests. Watts, 1990

BYLES, Monica

Life in the Polar Lands. Watts, 1990

These slim, oversize volumes are intended to introduce early elementary audiences to what life is like in various climates. Weather, animals and plant life, people, and curious facts are touched on. After the facual information, a "creation" folk tale relating to the origin of the area is retold. Glossary, index.

LIFETIMES

TAMES, Richard

Alexander Fleming. Watts, 1990
Alexander Graham Bell. Watts, 1990
Amelia Earhart. Watts, 1990
Anne Frank. Watts, 1989
Florence Nightingale. Watts, 1990
Guglielmo Marconi. Watts, 1990
Helen Keller. Watts, 1989
Louis Pasteur. Watts, 1990
Marie Curie. Watts, 1990
Mother Teresa. Watts, 1990
Thomas Edison. Watts, 1990
The Wright Brothers. Watts, 1990

Famous people and their times are treated in this series. The highlights of their lives are touched on (with plentiful photos), their importance for their era as well as their importance for future generations is explored. All of the subjects have been written about before, but the treatment makes it easy for readers to see *why* they are important and is more accessible than other series for this age group (11-14).

LIVING HERE

DE SKALON, Anna, and Christa STADTLER

We Live in Portugal. Watts, 1987

FAIRCLOUGH, Chris

We Live in Indonesia. Watts, 1986

FERNANDO, Gilda Cordero

We Live in the Philippines. Watts, 1986

GRIFFITHS, John

We Live in the Caribbean. Watts, 1985

HOAD, Abdul Latif Al

We Live in Saudi Arabia. Watts, 1987

HUBER, Alex

We Live in Chile. Watts, 1986

KRISTENSEN, Preben, and Fiona CAMERON

We Live in Belgium and Luxembourg. Watts, 1986
We Live in Egypt. Watts, 1987
We Live in South Africa. Watts, 1985
We Live in Switzerland. Watts, 1987
We Live in the Netherlands. Watts, 1985

SHARMAN, Tim

We Live in East Germany. Watts, 1986

These are "up close and personal" views of each country as seen through the eyes of their inhabitants. Interviews with individuals occupy 2 pages, complete with photos. While there is an index, this personal approach will not help the student who has to write a report. Grades 5-8.

LIVING IN ANOTHER TIME

The Days of Charlemagne. Silver, 1985
The Days of the Cave People. Silver, 1985
The Days of the Pharaoh. Silver, 1986
Working in the First Factories. Silver, 1986

This series takes a little different approach to teaching history: each chapter of the book revolves around the activities of several fictional characters during that time period. The reader sees them at home, school, work, and worship. All the basic information is provided, but without an index to help, these are more difficult for students to use than books with a standard format. Each chapter ends with a fact section and the color illustrations add appeal. There is a chronology and a list of museums where artifacts can be viewed. Grades 3-6.

LIVING WITH...

PARKER, Steve

Living with Blindness. Watts, 1989
Living with Heart Disease. Watts, 1989

SHENKMAN, John

Living with Arthritis. Watts, 1990
Living with Physical Handicap. Watts, 1990

SMAIL, Simon

Living with Cancer. Watts, 1990

TAYLOR, Barbara

Living with Deafness. Watts, 1989
Living with Diabetes. Watts, 1989

WHITE, Tony

Living with Allergies. Watts, 1990

Various physical problems and diseases are examined in this excellent series. Possible causes of the problem are explored, then the various types of the illness are described, along with possible diagnostic procedures and treatments. Illustrations are plentiful; there is an index, glossary, and list of useful addresses. Grades 5-8.

MACAULEY, David

Castle. Houghton, 1977
Cathedral: The Story of Its Construction. Houghton, 1973
City: A Story of Roman Planning and Construction. Houghton, 1974
Mill. Houghton, 1983
Pyramid. Houghton, 1975
Unbuilding. Houghton, 1980
Underground. Houghton, 1976

A best-selling author with *The Way Things Work*, Macauley began enchanting children with his oversize books a long time ago. His works show step-by-step how various kinds of historical buildings were built. He even illustrates the tools and materials that were used, as well as methods of construction. In *Unbuilding*, he shows how a skyscraper is demolished. Really fascinating fare for anyone interested in history and/or architecture.

MAKE THE TEAM

CARSON, Charles Jr.
Swimming/Diving. Sports Illustrated, 1991
CROSE, Mark
Baseball. Sports Illustrated, 1991
BRENNER, Richard J.
Basketball. Sports Illustrated, 1990
Soccer. Sports Illustrated, 1990

These are good skill teaching books for young athletes. After a brief history of the game, the author discusses necessary equipment, the field of play, and basic rules. Practice drills that a player can do on their own are provided and game tactics are discussed. The line drawings are clear and feature players of both sexes. Grades 5 and up. Glossary.

IDEAS IN CONFLICT

FANNING, Beverly J.
Workfare vs. Welfare. McCuen, 1989
MCCUEN, Gary E.
AIDS Crisis: Conflicting Social Values. McCuen, 1987
Apartheid Reader. McCuen, 1986
Children Having Children. McCuen, 1988
Hi-Tech Babies. McCuen, 1990
Illiteracy in America. McCuen, 1988
Inner-City Violence. McCuen, 1990
International Drug Trade. McCuen, 1989
Iran-Iraq War. McCuen, 1987
Manipulating Life: Debating the Genetic Revolution. McCuen, 1985
Militarizing Space. McCuen, 1989
Nicaragua Revolution. McCuen, 1986
Nuclear Waste. McCuen, 1990
Nuclear Winter. McCuen, 1987
Our Endangered Atmosphere. McCuen, 1987
Political Murder in Central America. McCuen, 1985
Poor and Minority Health Care. McCuen, 1988
Pornography and Sexual Violence. McCuen, 1985
Protecting Water Quality. McCuen, 1986
Religion and Politics. McCuen, 1989
Religious Right. McCuen, 1989
Reviving the Death Penalty. McCuen, 1985
Secret Democracy. McCuen, 1990
Terminating Life: Conflicting Values in Health Care. McCuen, 1985
Treating the Mentally Disabled. McCuen, 1988
World Hunger and Social Justice. McCuen, 1986

A well used set of books in the public library. Clear and factual, they present both sides of their particular topic in an easy-to-read manner. Each book includes study guides and discussion activities that make it a good resource for high school libraries.

MESSNER HOLIDAY LIBRARY

CORWIN, Judith Hoffman

Birthday Fun. Messner, 1986
Christmas Fun. Messner, 1983
Cookie Fun. Messner, 1985
Easter Fun. Messner, 1984
Halloween Fun. Messner, 1983
Jewish Holiday Fun. Messner, 1987
Patriotic Fun. Messner, 1986
Thanksgiving Fun. Messner, 1984
Valentine Fun. Messner, 1983

Youngsters and teachers alike will benefit from these easy craft books with a holiday orientation. Reading level is for ages 7-11. Large patterns and step-by-step instructions using easily obtainable materials make these very usable. Index.

MILITARY OPPORTUNITIES

COLLINS, Robert F.

America at its Best: Opportunities in the National Guard. Rosen, 1989
Basic Training: What to Expect and How to Prepare. Rosen, 1988
Reserve Officers Training Corps. Rosen, 1986
Qualifying for Admission to the Service Academy. Rosen, 1987

MACDONALD, Robert

Exploring Careers in the Military Services. Rosen, 1987
Transitions: Military Pathways to Civilian Careers. Rosen, 1988

SLAPPEY, Mary McGowan

Exploring Military Service for Women. Rosen, 1989

STREMLOW, Mary

Coping with Sexism in the Military. Rosen, 1990

WHITE, Carl P.

Citizen Soldier: Opportunities in the Reserves. Rosen, 1990

All the authors of this YA career series are Armed Forces officers. Because of this, the series seems like a recruitment exercise. The information provided is detailed, complete with pie charts and statistics and information on transitional careers in civilian life. Nowhere are the down sides of military life and their impact on the human psyche really explained. With the preceding proviso, this series may be useful for YAs who are interested in a military career.

MODERN MILITARY TECHNIQUES

GANDER, Terry

Artillery. Lerner, 1987

GIBBONS, Tony

Submarines. Lerner, 1987

HOGG, Ian V.

Tanks. Lerner, 1985

LADD, James D.

Amphibious Techniques. Lerner, 1985
Military Helicopters. Lerner, 1987

LOWE, Malcolm V.

Bombers. Lerner, 1987
Fighters. Lerner, 1985

MARTIN, Laurence W.

Nuclear Warfare. Lerner, 1989

PRESTON, Anthony

Aircraft Carriers. Lerner, 1985

Many kids are fascinated with the machineries of war. This series, complete with color drawings, will find a built-in audience there. The early development of each weapon is shown, then applications through history, clear up to modern technology. Grades 5 and up. Glossary, index.

MOMENTS IN AMERICAN HISTORY

Brighter Tomorrows. Steck, 1990
Clouds of War. Steck, 1990
Creative Days. Steck, 1990
A Cry for Action. Steck, 1990
Flying High. Steck, 1990
Larger Than Life. Steck, 1990
Racing to the West. Steck, 1990
Rebellion's Song. Steck, 1990
Risking It All. Steck, 1990
You Don't Own Me. Steck, 1990

These collective biographies concentrate on people, male and female, of importance at various periods of U.S. history. Unfortunately, the paper is poor quality, easily torn, and the text is full of fictionalized dialogue. No index. Not recommended.

MONSTERS

SANFORD, William, and **Carl GREEN**

The Invisible Man. Crestwood, 1987
The Murders in the Rue Morgue. Crestwood, 1987
The Phantom of the Opera. Crestwood, 1987

THORNE, Ian

The Blob. Crestwood, 1982
Creature from the Black Lagoon. Crestwood, 1981
The Deadly Mantis. Crestwood, 1982
Dracula. Crestwood, 1977
Frankenstein. Crestwood, 1977
Frankenstein Meets Wolf Man. Crestwood, 1981
Godzilla. Crestwood, 1977
It Came from Outer Space. Crestwood, 1982
King Kong. Crestwood, 1977
Mad Scientists. Crestwood, 1977
The Mummy. Crestwood, 1981
The Wolf Man. Crestwood, 1977

This series is a twin of Crestwood's Movie Monsters. Even the black cover with orange trim is alike. These also retell the plot, accompanied by photo stills from the movie. The major difference is that these include a section on how the makeup was done. Horror film fans and reluctant readers will go for these. Grades 3-6.

MONSTERS OF MYTHOLOGY

EVSLIN, Bernard

Amycus. Chelsea, 1989
Anteus. Chelsea, 1988
The Calydonian Boar. Chelsea, 1989
Cerberus. Chelsea, 1987
Chimaera. Chelsea, 1988
The Cyclopes. Chelsea, 1987
Drabne of Dole. Chelsea, 1990
The Dragon of Boeotia. Chelsea, 1987

Fafnir. Chelsea, 1989
Fenris. Chelsea, 1991
The Furies. Chelsea, 1989
Geryon. Chelsea, 1987
Harpalyce. Chelsea, 1991
Hecate. Chelsea, 1987
The Hydra. Chelsea, 1989
Ladon. Chelsea, 1990
Medusa. Chelsea, 1987
The Minotaur. Chelsea, 1987
The Nemean Lion. Chelsea, 1990
Pig's Ploughman. Chelsea, 1990
Procrustes. Chelsea, 1987
Scylla and Charybdis. Chelsea, 1989
The Sirens. Chelsea, 1988
The Spear-birds. Chelsea, 1991
The Sphinx. Chelsea, 1991

Evslin is an award-winning author of books on mythology and in this series he takes a look at 25 monsters from Greek, Norse, and Celtic folk traditions. Each volume presents the adventures of an individual monster, its origin, exploits and struggles with the gods and heroes of mythology. The books are rich in detail and imagery and can be useful as an introduction to mythology. There are a number of color reproductions of art pieces from around the world. Grades 5 and up.

MOVIE MONSTERS

GREEN, Carl, and **William SANFORD**

The Black Cat. Crestwood, 1988
Black Friday. Crestwood, 1985
Bride of Frankenstein. Crestwood, 1985
Dracula's Daughter. Crestwood, 1985
Ghost of Frankenstein. Crestwood, 1985
House of Fear. Crestwood, 1987
The House of Seven Gables. Crestwood, 1987
The Mole People. Crestwood, 1985
The Raven. Crestwood, 1985
The Revenge of the Creature. Crestwood, 1987
Tarantula. Crestwood, 1985
Werewolf of London. Crestwood, 1985

Horror movie buffs, at least those who appreciate the old ones, will flock to this series. The books retell the story, complete with photos from the movies. While the vocabulary is for grades 3-5, the subject matter makes this a good bet for reluctant readers. Crestwood's Monster series is very similar, accenting the creature rather than the film.

MY BEST FRIEND

MACMILLAN, Dianne, and **Dorothy FREEMAN**

Duc Tran (Vietnamese). Messner, 1987
Martha Rodriguez (Mexican). Messner, 1986
Mee-Yung Kim (Korean). Messner, 1989

YINGLING, Phylis S.

Elena Pappas (Greek). Messner, 1986
Tony Santos (Portuguese). Messner, 1988

Although this series employs fictional characters, the intent is to introduce readers to the ethnic lifestyles of various immigrant cultures. Some foreign words are introduced, along with holiday customs, foods, and dress. Written for grades 3-5. Glossary, bibliography.

MYSTERY OF...

ABELS, Harriette

Bermuda Triangle. Crestwood, 1987
Killer Bees. Crestwood, 1987
Loch Ness Monster. Crestwood, 1987
Lost City of Atlantis. Crestwood, 1987
Pyramids. Crestwood, 1987
Stonehenge. Crestwood, 1987

CHRISTIAN, Mary Blount

Bigfoot. Crestwood, 1987
UFO's. Crestwood, 1987

Right away the usability of this series suffers because there is no index, and the table of contents does not give a clue as to what each chapter is about. The subjects are interesting, the vocabulary is suitable for grades 4-6, but students will have tremendous difficulty finding information. Only for browsers.

MYTHS FOR MODERN CHILDREN

ESPELAND, Pamela

The Story of Arachne. Carolrhoda, 1980
The Story of Baucis and Philemon. Carolrhoda, 1981
The Story of Cadmus. Carolrhoda, 1980
The Story of King Midas. Carolrhoda, 1980
Theseus and the Road to Athens. Carolrhoda, 1981

Myths have fascinated people for centuries, so why not introduce children to them early? Unfortunately, this series is not really the way to do it. The stories are simply told, with a vocabulary suited to grades 2-4, but the illustrations are so unappealing that youngsters would hardly be tempted to pick them up in the first place.

NATIONAL PARKS

CAZIN, Lorraine Jolian

Yosemite. Crestwood, 1988

MCCORMICK, Maxine

Sequoia and Kings Canyon. Crestwood, 1988

MARRON, Carol

Yellowstone. Crestwood, 1989

MELL, Jan

Grand Canyon. Crestwood, 1989

PETERS, Lisa

Serengeti. Crestwood, 1989

ROM, Christine Sotnak

Everglades. Crestwood, 1989

ROOT, Phyllis

Glacier. Crestwood, 1988

ROOT, Phyllis, and **Maxine MCCORMICK**

Galapagos. Crestwood, 1989
Great Basin. Crestwood, 1988

SATEREN, Shelley

Banff. Crestwood, 1989

SOTNAK, Lewann

Carlsbad Caverns. Crestwood, 1989
Hawaii Volcanoes. Crestwood, 1989

Travellers and students alike will find this series on the national parks interesting. A brief overview of the national park concept is given, then the authors move on to the early history, natural and as related to man. Sights, activities, and special events are mentioned along with a list of rules, map, and index/glossary. Loads of color photos add to the appeal for grades 4-7.

NATURE WATCH

ARNOLD, Caroline

Ostriches and Other Flightless Birds. Carolrhoda, 1990
Saving the Peregrine Falcon. Carolrhoda, 1985
Tule Elk. Carolrhoda, 1989
Walk on the Great Barrier Reef. Carolrhoda, 1988

BUHOLZER, Theresa

Life of the Snail. Carolrhoda, 1987

CAJACOB, Thomas, and **Teresa BURTON**

Close to the Wild: Siberian Tigers in a Zoo. Carolrhoda, 1986

FEATHERLY, Jay

Ko-hoh: The Call of the Trumpeter Swan. Carolrhoda, 1986
Mustangs: Wild Horses of the American West. Carolrhoda, 1986

FISCHER-NAGEL, Heidrose, and **Andreas FISCHER-NAGEL**

Ant Colony. Carolrhoda, 1989
Fir Trees. Carolrhoda, 1989
Housefly. Carolrhoda, 1990
Inside the Burrow: The Life of the Golden Hamster. Carolrhoda, 1986
Life of the Butterfly. Carolrhoda, 1987
Life of the Honeybee. Carolrhoda, 1985
Life of the Ladybug. Carolrhoda, 1986
Look through the Mouse Hole. Carolrhoda, 1989
Season of the White Stork. Carolrhoda, 1985

ISENBART, Hans-Heinrich

Birth of a Foal. Carolrhoda, 1986

JOHNSON, Sylvia A.

Albatrosses of Midway Island. Carolrhoda, 1990

MALNIG, Anita

Where the Waves Break: Life at the Edge of the Sea. Carolrhoda, 1985

NICHOLSON, Darrell

Wild Boars. Carolrhoda, 1987

SCHNIEPER, Claudia

Amazing Spiders. Carolrhoda, 1989
Apple Tree. Carolrhoda, 1987
Chameleons. Carolrhoda, 1989
Lizards. Carolrhoda, 1990
On the Trail of the Fox. Carolrhoda, 1986

A wide variety of natural science topics are explored in this handsome series. Large color photos grace every page, as the authors describe the evolution and lifestyle of their subjects. New words are in boldface, later defined in a glossary. While there is no index, the coverage is thorough and appealing. Very good choices as needed. Grades 3-6.

NATURE'S HIDDEN WORLD

ALIBERT-KOURAGUINE, Daniel

Prairie Dwellers. Silver, 1983

CUISIN, Michael

Animals of the African Plains. Silver, 1980
Animals of the Countryside. Silver, 1987
Birds of Prey. Silver, 1980
Desert Dwellers. Silver, 1987
The Frozen North. Silver, 1983
Lakes and Rivers. Silver, 1980
Mountain Animals. Silver, 1980
Prehistoric Life. Silver, 1980
Woods and Forests. Silver, 1980

ROUX, Charles
Animals of the Seashore. Silver, 1983
ROUX, Charles, and **Paul-Henry PLAINTAIN**
Ocean Dwellers. Silver, 1985

Originally published in France, this oversize series emphasizes many large color drawings. Of the two pages devoted to each animal or species, only half a page is actual text. Some anatomical detail is illustrated, but only length and weight are regularly given. Lifestyles are touched on, as well as some interesting facts. The last page highlights the need to protect the environment. The lack of indexing and detailed information make these secondary choices for grades 4-6.

NEED TO KNOW LIBRARY

AYER, Eleanor H.
Everything You Need to Know about Teen Marriage. Rosen, 1990
BALL, Jacqueline
Everything You Need to Know about Drug Abuse. Rosen, 1988
BOUCHARD, Elizabeth
Everything You Need to Know about Sexual Harassment. Rosen, 1990
CARLSON, Linda
Everything You Need to Know about Your Parent's Divorce. Rosen, 1990
GLASSMAN, Bruce
Everything You Need to Know about Stepfamilies. Rosen, 1988
HAMMERSLOUGH, Jane
Everything You Need to Know about Teenage Motherhood. Rosen, 1990
HUGHES, Tracy
Everything You Need to Know about Teen Pregnancy. Rosen, 1988
KAHANER, Ellen
Everything You Need to Know about Growing up Female. Rosen, 1990
KEYISHIAN, Elizabeth
Everything You Need to Know about Smoking. Rosen, 1989
MUCCIOLO, Gary
Everything You Need to Know about Birth Control. Rosen, 1990
PALMER, Ezra
Everything You Need to Know about Prejudice. Rosen, 1990
ST. PIERRE, Stephanie
Everything You Need to Know about When Your Parents Are Out of Work. Rosen, 1990
SCHLEIFER, Jay
Everything You Need to Know about Teen Suicide. Rosen, 1988
SHUKER, Nancy
Everything You Need to Know about an Alcoholic Parent. Rosen, 1990
SHUKER-HAINES, Frances
Everything You Need to Know about Date Rape. Rosen, 1990
SPIES, Karen
Everything You Need to Know about Grieving. Rosen, 1990
STARK, Evan
Everything You Need to Know about Family Violence. Rosen, 1988
Everything You Need to Know about Sexual Abuse. Rosen, 1988
TAYLOR, Barbara
Everything You Need to Know about AIDS. Rosen, 1988
Everything You Need to Know about Alcohol. Rosen, 1988
THOMAS, Alicia
Everything You Need to Know about Romantic Breakup. Rosen, 1990
WOODS, Samuel
Everything You Need to Know about STD (Sexually Transmitted Diseases). Rosen, 1990

Many troubling social/moral/ethical problems that youngsters may face are dealt with in this series. Although aimed at grades 7-12, the reading level of 4.0-6.0 insures that younger children in need of this kind of bibliotherapy will also finds the books accessible. Background on each topic is supplied, along with a discussion of a youngster's possible reactions. The authors then talk about how to deal with the feelings and situations that can arise. A glossary, bibliography, addresses of helpful agencies, and index is provided in each work.

NEW DINOSAUR LIBRARY

DIXON, Dougal

The First Dinosaurs. Dell, 1990
Hunting the Dinosaurs. Dell, 1990
The Jurassic Dinosaurs. Dell, 1990
The Last Dinosaurs. Dell, 1990

Although the format of these books appears simple, with short paragraphs on each type of dinosaur, the opposing page has a drawing accompanied by more information. There is a small chart with basic statistics. A section of "fun facts" is included, along with a bibliography, glossary, and index. Grades 2-4.

NEW FRONTIERS

SANDAK, Cass

Arctic and the Antarctic. Watts, 1987
Remote Places. Watts, 1989
World of Space. Watts, 1989
World's Oceans. Watts, 1987

The challenges involved in the world's last remaining outposts are reviewed in the books in this series. Sandak describes the exploration during this century and how new technology has increased our knowledge of these areas. Included in each book are a chronology, glossary, and index. Sixth grade and up.

NEW THEORIES

LAMPTON, Christopher

New Theories on the Birth of the Universe. Watts, 1989
New Theories on the Dinosaurs. Watts, 1989
New Theories on the Origins of the Human Race. Watts, 1989

LEE, Sally

New Theories on Diet and Nutrition. Watts, 1990

These books explore the latest theories behind scientific issues. Each theory is carefully explained in order to sort out the complex nature that is often associated with such theories. These book are illustrated and also contain a glossary, index, and recommended reading lists. Grades 9 and up.

NEW TRUE BOOKS

BALLARD, Lois

Reptiles. Childrens, 1982

BROEKEL, Ray

Animal Observations. Childrens, 1990
Aquariums and Terrariums. Childrens, 1982
Baseball. Childrens, 1982
Dangerous Fish. Childrens, 1982
Experiments with Air. Childrens, 1988
Experiments with Light. Childrens, 1986
Experiments with Straws and Paper. Childrens, 1990
Experiments with Water. Childrens, 1988
Fire Fighters. Childrens, 1981
Football. Childrens, 1982

Gerbil Pets and Other Small Rodents. Childrens, 1983
Jet Planes. Childrens, 1987
Maps and Globes. Childrens, 1983
Police. Childrens, 1981
Snakes. Childrens, 1982
Sound Experiments. Childrens, 1983
Storms. Childrens, 1982
Trains. Childrens, 1981
Tropical Fish. Childrens, 1983
Trucks. Childrens, 1983
Your Five Senses. Childrens, 1984
Your Skeleton and Skin. Childrens, 1984

CARLISLE, Norman, and **Madelyn CARLISLE**
Bridges. Childrens, 1983
Rivers. Childrens, 1982

CARONA, Philip
Numbers. Childrens, 1982

CARTER, Katherine
Houses. Childrens, 1982
Oceans. Childrens, 1982
Ships and Seaports. Childrens, 1982

CHALLAND, Helen
Earthquakes. Childrens, 1982
Experiments with Chemistry. Childrens, 1988
Experiments with Electricity. Childrens, 1986
Experiments with Magnets. Childrens, 1986
Plants without Seeds. Childrens, 1986
Volcanoes. Childrens, 1983

CLARK, Mary Lou
Dinosaurs. Childrens, 1981

COLMAN, Warren
Bill of Rights. Childrens, 1987
Constitution. Childrens, 1987

DUVALL, Jill
Mohawk. Childrens, 1991
Seneca. Childrens, 1991

ELKIN, Benjamin
Money. Childrens, 1983

FAIN, James W.
Rodeos. Childrens, 1983

FRADIN, Dennis
Archaeology. Childrens, 1983
Astronomy. Childrens, 1983
Cancer. Childrens, 1988
Cheyenne. Childrens, 1988
Comets, Asteroids, and Meteors. Childrens, 1984
Continents. Childrens, 1986
Declaration of Independence. Childrens, 1988
Drug Abuse. Childrens, 1988
Earth. Childrens, 1989
Explorers. Childrens, 1984
Farming. Childrens, 1983
Flag of the United States. Childrens, 1988
Halley's Comet. Childrens, 1985
Heredity. Childrens, 1987

Jupiter. Childrens, 1989
Mars. Childrens, 1989
Mercury. Childrens, 1990
Moon Flights. Childrens, 1985
Movies. Childrens, 1983
Neptune. Childrens, 1990
Nuclear Energy. Childrens, 1987
Olympics. Childrens, 1983
Pawnee. Childrens, 1988
Pioneers. Childrens, 1984
Pluto. Childrens, 1989
Radiation. Childrens, 1987
Saturn. Childrens, 1989
Search for Extraterrestrial Intelligence. Childrens, 1987
Shoshoni. Childrens, 1988
Skylab. Childrens, 1984
Space Colonies. Childrens, 1985
Spacelab. Childrens, 1984
Space Telescope. Childrens, 1987
Thirteen Colonies. Childrens, 1988
Uranus. Childrens, 1989
Venus. Childrens, 1989
Voting and Elections. Childrens, 1985
Voyager *Space Probes*. Childrens, 1985

FREEMAN, Tony
Photography. Childrens, 1983

FRISKEY, Margaret
Birds We Know. Childrens, 1981
Space Shuttles. Childrens, 1982

FUJIMOTO, Patricia
Libraries. Childrens, 1984

GAFFNEY, Timothy R.
Kennedy Space Center. Childrens, 1985

GATES, Richard
Conservation. Childrens, 1982

GEORGES, D. V.
Africa. Childrens, 1986
Asia. Childrens, 1986
Australia. Childrens, 1986
Europe. Childrens, 1986
Glaciers. Childrens, 1986
North America. Childrens, 1986
South America. Childrens, 1986

GREENE, Carol
Astronauts. Childrens, 1984
Congress. Childrens, 1985
Holidays around the World. Childrens, 1982
How a Book Is Made. Childrens, 1988
Language. Childrens, 1983
Music. Childrens, 1983
Presidents. Childrens, 1984
Robots. Childrens, 1983
Supreme Court. Childrens, 1985
United Nations. Childrens, 1983

HAGMAN, Ruth
Crow. Childrens, 1990
HARGROVE, James
Microcomputers at Work. Childrens, 1984
HARMER, Mabel
Circus. Childrens, 1981
HEINRICHS, Susan
Atlantic Ocean. Childrens, 1986
Indian Ocean. Childrens, 1986
Pacific Ocean. Childrens, 1986
HENDERSON, Kathy
Christmas Trees. Childrens, 1989
Dairy Cows. Childrens, 1988
Great Lakes. Childrens, 1989
JACOBSEN, Karen
Argentina. Childrens, 1990
Brazil. Childrens, 1989
Chile. Childrens, 1991
China. Childrens, 1990
Computers. Childrens, 1982
Cuba. Childrens, 1990
Egypt. Childrens, 1990
Farm Animals. Childrens, 1981
Greece. Childrens, 1990
Health. Childrens, 1981
Japan. Childrens, 1982
Kenya. Childrens, 1991
Korea. Childrens, 1989
Laos. Childrens, 1991
Mexico. Childrens, 1982
South Africa. Childrens, 1989
Soviet Union. Childrens, 1990
Stamps. Childrens, 1983
Television. Childrens, 1982
Thailand. Childrens, 1989
Zimbabwe. Childrens, 1990
Zoos. Childrens, 1982
LEMASTER, Leslie Jean
Bacteria and Viruses. Childrens, 1985
Cells and Tissues. Childrens, 1985
Nutrition. Childrens, 1985
Your Brain and Nervous System. Childrens, 1984
Your Heart and Blood. Childrens, 1984
LEPTHIEN, Emilie U.
Bald Eagles. Childrens, 1989
Buffalo. Childrens, 1989
Cherokees. Childrens, 1985
Choctaw. Childrens, 1987
Koalas. Childrens, 1990
Manatees. Childrens, 1991
Mandan Indians. Childrens, 1989
Monarch Butterflies. Childrens, 1989
Penguins. Childrens, 1983
Seminole. Childrens, 1985

LEPTHIEN, Emilie U., and Joan KALBACKEN
Recycling. Childrens, 1991
LEWELLEN, John
Moon, Sun, and Stars. Childrens, 1981
LUMLEY, Kathryn Wentzel
Monkeys and Apes. Childrens, 1982
Work Animals. Childrens, 1983
MCKISSACK, Patricia
Apache. Childrens, 1984
Aztec Indians. Childrens, 1985
Inca. Childrens, 1985
Maya. Childrens, 1985
MARTINI, Teri
Cowboys. Childrens, 1981
Indians. Childrens, 1982
MILIOS, Rita
Sleeping and Dreaming. Childrens, 1987
MINER, O. Irene Sevrey
Plants We Know. Childrens, 1981
OLESKY, Walter
Experiments with Heat. Childrens, 1986
Lasers. Childrens, 1986
Video Revolution. Childrens, 1986
OSINSKI, Alice
Chippewa. Childrens, 1987
Eskimo. Childrens, 1986
Navajo. Childrens, 1987
Nez Perce. Childrens, 1988
Sioux. Childrens, 1984
Tlingit. Childrens, 1990
PAPAJANI, Janet
Museums. Childrens, 1983
PETERSEN, David
Airplanes. Childrens, 1981
Airports. Childrens, 1981
Apatosaurus. Childrens, 1989
Helicopters. Childrens, 1983
Newspapers. Childrens, 1983
Solar Energy at Work. Childrens, 1985
Submarines. Childrens, 1984
Tyrannosaurus Rex. Childrens, 1989
PODENDORF, Illa
Animal Homes. Childrens, 1982
Animals of Sea and Shore. Childrens, 1982
Baby Animals. Childrens, 1981
Energy. Childrens, 1982
Insects. Childrens, 1981
Jungles. Childrens, 1982
Pets. Childrens, 1981
Rocks and Minerals. Childrens, 1982
Seasons. Childrens, 1981
Space. Childrens, 1982
Spiders. Childrens, 1982
Trees. Childrens, 1982
Weeds and Wild Flowers. Childrens, 1981

POSELL, Elsa
Cats. Childrens, 1983
Deserts. Childrens, 1982
Dogs. Childrens, 1981
Elephants. Childrens, 1982
Horses. Childrens, 1981
Whales and Other Sea Mammals. Childrens, 1982
PURCELL, John Wallace
African Animals. Childrens, 1982
RICHARDS, Gregory B.
Satellites. Childrens, 1983
ROBERTS, Allan
Fossils. Childrens, 1983
Underground Life. Childrens, 1983
ROSENTHAL, Bert
Basketball. Childrens, 1983
Bears. Childrens, 1983
Soccer. Childrens, 1983
ROSENTHAL, Mark
Predators. Childrens, 1983
ROWAN, James P.
Butterflies and Moths. Childrens, 1983
Prairies and Grassland. Childrens, 1983
SNOW, Ted
Global Change. Childrens, 1990
STILLE, Darlene
Air Pollution. Childrens, 1990
Greenhouse Effect. Childrens, 1990
Ice Age. Childrens, 1990
Oil Spills. Childrens, 1991
Ozone Hole. Childrens, 1991
Soil Erosion and Pollution. Childrens, 1990
Spacecraft. Childrens, 1991
Water Pollution. Childrens, 1990
STONE, Lynn M.
Alligators and Crocodiles. Childrens, 1989
Antarctica. Childrens, 1985
Arctic. Childrens, 1985
Birds of Prey. Childrens, 1983
Endangered Animals. Childrens, 1984
Marshes and Swamps. Childrens, 1983
Mountains. Childrens, 1983
Pond Life. Childrens, 1983
TOMCHEK, Ann
Hopi. Childrens, 1987
WEBSTER, Vera
Plant Experiments. Childrens, 1982
Science Experiments. Childrens, 1982
Weather Experiments. Childrens, 1982
WILKIN, Fred
Machines. Childrens, 1986
Matter. Childrens, 1986
Microscopes and Telescopes. Childrens, 1983
WILKINSON, Sylvia
Automobiles. Childrens, 1982

WONG, Ovid
Experiments with Animal Behavior. Childrens, 1988
Giant Pandas. Childrens, 1987
Prehistoric People. Childrens, 1988
ZINER, Feenie, and **Elizabeth THOMPSON**
Time. Childrens, 1982
This far-reaching nonfiction series is one of the few written at the early reader (grades 1-3) level. Large print, color photos that occupy half of each page, and simple vocabulary make these an excellent purchase as needed. Each book includes a glossary and index.

NORTH AMERICAN INDIAN STORIES
MAYO, Gretchen Will
Earthmaker's Tales. Walker, 1989
More Earthmaker's Tales. Walker, 1990
More Star Tales. Walker, 1990
Star Tales. Walker, 1987
Young people, as well as storytellers, will love these books. This is a nicely put together collection of Indian legends from a number of American tribes. Each book also gives a brief history of the tale, and includes a glossary to help the reader understand some Indian phrases. Written for ages 10 and up.

NOVABOOKS
HADINGHAM, Evan, and **Janet HADINGHAM**
Garbage! Simon & Schuster, 1990
HARRAR, George
Radical Robots. Simon & Schuster, 1990
HARRAR, George, and **Linda HARRAR**
Signs of the Apes, Songs of the Whales. Simon & Schuster, 1989
HERBERMAN, Ethan
City Kid's Field Guide. Simon & Schuster, 1989
Great Butterfly Hunt. Simon & Schuster, 1990
ISBERG, Emily
Airborne: The Search for the Secret of Flight. Simon & Schuster, 1990
Peak Performance. Simon & Schuster, 1989
MAURER, Richard
Junk in Space. Simon & Schuster, 1989
Based on topics presented on PBS's *Nova* series, these books show the same level of expert coverage presented in an interesting, readable fashion. The text is interspersed with insets of related topics, often of a historical nature. Photos from the show liven the text. Index. Grades 4-8.

OCEAN WORLD LIBRARY
DAEGLING, Mary
Monster Seaweeds: The Story of Giant Kelps. Dillon, 1986
GILBREATH, Alice
Arctic and Antarctica: Roof and Floor of the World. Dillon, 1988
Continental Shelf: An Underwater Frontier. Dillon, 1986
Great Barrier Reef: A Treasure in the Sea. Dillon, 1986
Ring of Fire: And the Hawaiian Islands & Iceland. Dillon, 1986
River in the Ocean: The Story of the Gulf Stream. Dillon, 1986
GOLDNER, Kathryn A., and **Carole G. VOGEL**
Humphrey the Wrong Way Whale. Dillon, 1987
ROBINSON, W. Wright
Incredible Facts about the Ocean: How We Use It, How We Abuse It. Dillon, 1990
Incredible Facts about the Ocean: The Restless Blue Salt Water. Dillon, 1986
Incredible Facts about the Ocean: The Land Below, the Life Within. Dillon, 1987

SIBBALD, Jean

Homes in the Sea: From the Shore to the Deep. Dillon, 1986
Sea Babies: New Life in the Ocean. Dillon, 1986
Sea Creatures on the Move. Dillon, 1989
Sea Mammals: The Warm-Blooded Ocean Explorers. Dillon, 1988
Strange Eating Habits of Sea Creatures. Dillon, 1986

Lots of facts about oceans and the lives therein can be found in this series. There are maps, color photos, and illustrations to help young readers understand, as well as a glossary, bibliography, and index. There is a question and answer format used in the books by Robinson that, while making for interesting reading, forces the student to use the index constantly to locate subject material as it skips from page to page. Grades 5-8.

ONCE UPON AMERICA

GROSS, Virginia T.

The Day It Rained Forever. Viking, 1991
It's Only Goodbye. Viking, 1990

KUDLINSKI, Kathleen

Hero Over Here. Viking, 1990
Pearl Harbor Is Burning! Viking, 1991

ONEAL, Zibby

A Long Way to Go. Viking, 1990

This new historical fiction series aims to show readers what life was like for youngsters at certain important periods of American history. For example, one book features a girl whose suffragette grandmother raises her consciousness. Ages 7-11 may find these enlightening, but the treatment seems forced to convey the "message," rather than allowing for development of real character development and plotting. The American Girl series does a better job of showing real life at certain periods of time.

OPEN FAMILY

STEIN, Sara Bonnett

About Dying. Walker, 1984
About Handicaps. Walker, 1984
About Phobias. Walker, 1984
Adopted One. Walker, 1979
Hospital Story. Walker, 1984
Making Babies. Walker, 1974
On Divorce. Walker, 1984
That New Baby. Walker, 1984

These books are written at two levels to allow parents to discuss these often troublesome topics with their offspring. Each page has black and white photos, and a simple preschool to grade 2 level text in large print to be read to the child. On the same page, at the side and in smaller print is a discussion aimed at the parents, suggesting ways to comment on the text and content to make it more understandable to youngsters or to stimulate discussion. This should prove an excellent addition for a parent/child collection.

OPPOSING VIEWPOINTS

Abortion. Greenhaven, 1986
AIDS. Greenhaven, 1988
American Foreign Policy. Greenhaven, 1987
American Government. Greenhaven, 1988
American Values. Greenhaven, 1989
America's Children. Greenhaven, 1991
America's Elections. Greenhaven, 1988
America's Future. Greenhaven, 1990
America's Prisons. Greenhaven, 1985
Animal Rights. Greenhaven, 1989

Biomedical Ethics. Greenhaven, 1987
Censorship. Greenhaven, 1990
Central America. Greenhaven, 1990
Chemical Dependency. Greenhaven, 1985
China. Greenhaven, 1989
Civil Liberties. Greenhaven, 1988
Constructing a Life Philosophy. Greenhaven, 1985
Crime and Criminals. Greenhaven, 1989
Criminal Justice. Greenhaven, 1987
Death and Dying. Greenhaven, 1987
The Death Penalty. Greenhaven, 1986
Drug Abuse. Greenhaven, 1988
Eastern Europe. Greenhaven, 1990
Economics in America. Greenhaven, 1986
The Elderly. Greenhaven, 1990
The Environmental Crisis. Greenhaven, 1991
Euthanasia. Greenhaven, 1989
Genetic Engineering. Greenhaven, 1990
Global Resources. Greenhaven, 1991
The Health Crisis. Greenhaven, 1989
The Homeless. Greenhaven, 1990
Immigration. Greenhaven, 1990
Israel. Greenhaven, 1989
Japan. Greenhaven, 1989
Latin America and U.S. Foreign Policy. Greenhaven, 1988
Male/Female Roles. Greenhaven, 1989
The Mass Media. Greenhaven, 1988
The Middle East. Greenhaven, 1988
Nuclear War. Greenhaven, 1985
Paranormal Phenomena. Greenhaven, 1991
The Political Spectrum. Greenhaven, 1986
Poverty. Greenhaven, 1988
Problems of Africa. Greenhaven, 1986
Religion in America. Greenhaven, 1989
Science and Religion. Greenhaven, 1988
Sexual Values. Greenhaven, 1989
Social Justice. Greenhaven, 1990
The Soviet Union. Greenhaven, 1988
The Superpowers: A New Debate. Greenhaven, 1989
Teenage Sexuality. Greenhaven, 1988
Terrorism. Greenhaven, 1987
The Third World. Greenhaven, 1989
Trade. Greenhaven, 1991
The Vietnam War. Greenhaven, 1990
Violence in America. Greenhaven, 1990
War and Human Nature. Greenhaven, 1983
The War on Drugs. Greenhaven, 1990

Each of these books presents an issue of importance, through expert opinions, and creates a dialogue of essays on differing points of view, related to the topic. The essays are written by respected experts in the field, allowing students to see the many sides of the argument related to the issue. Each book contains illustrations, glossaries, chronologies, contact organizations, and complete index. This is a very well-respected series of books and they are a marvelous resource for classroom use and research source information. Highly recommended for public and high school libraries.

OPPOSING VIEWPOINTS JUNIORS

AIDS. Greenhaven, 1989
Alcohol. Greenhaven, 1989
Animal Rights. Greenhaven, 1989
Death Penalty. Greenhaven, 1989
Drugs and Sports. Greenhaven, 1989
The Environment. Greenhaven, 1990
Gun Control. Greenhaven, 1989
The Homeless. Greenhaven, 1990
Immigration. Greenhaven, 1989
Nuclear Power. Greenhaven, 1990
The Palestinian Conflict. Greenhaven, 1990
Patriotism. Greenhaven, 1989
Poverty. Greenhaven, 1989
Prisons. Greenhaven, 1990
Smoking. Greenhaven, 1989
Television. Greenhaven, 1990
Toxic Wastes. Greenhaven, 1989
The U.S. Constitution. Greenhaven, 1990
Working Mothers. Greenhaven, 1989
Zoos. Greenhaven, 1990

These are an elementary and junior high school version of the popular and well done Opposing Viewpoints Series. These are similar in content and utilize charts, graphs, photos, and cartoons to help present the materials. These are also well done and highly recommended.

OUR WORLD

BOOTH, Basil
Temperate Forests. Silver, 1989

LAMBERT, David
Grasslands. Silver, 1989
Polar Regions. Silver, 1987
Seas and Oceans. Silver, 1987

LYE, Keith
Coasts. Silver, 1989
Deserts. Silver, 1987
Mountains. Silver, 1987

PENNY, Malcolm
Pollution and Conservation. Silver, 1989

ROWLAND-ENTWISTLE, Theodore
Jungles and Rainforests. Silver, 1987
Rivers and Lakes. Silver, 1987

Climactic and geographic areas often have characteristics in common. This series explores these characteristics in terms of people, economy, weather, plants and animal life, and history. Ecological problems are also dealt with. Color photos and illustrations, glossary, bibliography, and index complete the picture for grades 5 and up.

OUTDOOR SCIENCE

WYLER, Rose
Grass and Grasshoppers. Messner, 1990
Puddles and Ponds. Messner, 1990
Raindrops and Rainbows. Messner, 1989
Seashore Surprises. Messner, 1991
The Starry Sky. Messner, 1989
The Wonderful Woods. Messner, 1990

Preschoolers through second graders can either read or have these books read to them with easy understanding of the information. The large color illustrations keep the feeling of picture books, while transmitting facts.

OVERVIEW SERIES

BOYD, Sunni
Animal Rights. Greenhaven, 1990
Endangered Species. Greenhaven, 1989

GAFFRON, Norma
Dealing with Death. Greenhaven, 1989

GANO, Lila
Smoking. Greenhaven, 1989

KEELER, Barbara
Energy Alternatives. Greenhaven, 1990

NARDO, Don
Drugs and Sports. Greenhaven, 1990

NICHELSON, Harry
Vietnam. Greenhaven, 1989

NIELSON, Nancy
Teen Alcoholism. Greenhaven, 1990

O'CONNOR, Karen
Garbage. Greenhaven, 1989
Homeless Children. Greenhaven, 1989

POWERS, Tom
Special Effects in the Movies. Greenhaven, 1989

RASMUSSEN, Richard Michael
The UFO Challenge. Greenhaven, 1990

STEWART, Gail
Acid Rain. Greenhaven, 1990
Drug Trafficking. Greenhaven, 1990

WARBURTON, Lois
The Beginning of Writing. Greenhaven, 1990

WILSON, Jonnie
AIDS. Greenhaven, 1989

These books presents an overview of a particular topic and are specifically written for use in writing school reports. There are bibliographies, illustrations, a glossary and an index in each book. Additionally, a list of contact organizations related to the book's subject is included. Grades 5-8.

PARKS FOR PEOPLE

RADLAUER, Ruth
Acadia National Park. Childrens, 1978
Bryce Canyon National Park. Childrens, 1987
Carlsbad Caverns National Park. Childrens, 1981
Denali National Park and Preserve. Childrens, 1988
Everglades National Park. Childrens, 1976
Glacier National Park. Childrens, 1984
Grand Canyon National Park. Childrens, 1984
Great Smoky Mountains National Park. Childrens, 1985
Haleakala National Park. Childrens, 1987
Hawaii Volcanoes National Park. Childrens, 1987
Mammoth Cave National Park. Childrens, 1987
Mesa Verde National Park. Childrens, 1984
Olympic National Park. Childrens, 1988
Rocky Mountain National Park. Childrens, 1984

Shenandoah National Park. Childrens, 1982
Yellowstone National Park. Childrens, 1985
Yosemite National Park. Childrens, 1984
Zion National Park. Childrens, 1988

Veteran author Radlauer takes young readers on a sightseeing trip through each of the National Parks. She spends a page on a famous location, natural formations, flora, and fauna. Color photos abound. There is no index, but the table of contents is explicit enough for student use. Large print and simple vocabulary makes this apropos for grades 2-5.

PASSPORT TO...

ADLER, Anne
Passport to West Germany. Watts, 1986
IRIZARRY, Carmen
Passport to Mexico. Watts, 1987
KEELER, Stephen
Passport to China. Watts, 1987
Passport to Soviet Union. Watts, 1988
LANGLEY, Andrew
Passport to Great Britain. Watts, 1986
LYE, Keith
Passport to Spain. Watts, 1987
MARIELLA, Cinzia
Passport to Italy. Watts, 1986
NORBROOK, Dominique
Passport to France. Watts, 1986
PEPPER, Susan
Passport to Australia. Watts, 1987
TAMES, Richard
Passport to Japan. Watts, 1988

These slender, oversize books give readers about a page and a half of information on such aspects of foreign life as religion, the arts, history, farming, etc. Each section is interspersed with a "fact file" of maps and graphs related to each topic. While visually appealing, some seem unnecessary, i.e., a graph of national holidays throughout the calendar year, rather than a simple listing. Grades 5-7.

PATHFINDERS IN EXPLORATION

Exploring Space. Silver, 1989
Exploring the Deserts. Silver, 1989
Exploring the Land. Silver, 1989
Exploring the Oceans. Silver, 1989
Exploring the Poles. Silver, 1989
Exploring the Rivers. Silver, 1989

These books present quite a mishmash of information. Each book discusses explorers and territories from all over the world and every era of time. The arrangement is chronological but jumps from place to place. Background is given on the explorer and why he/she explored, as well as why his/her discoveries were important. There are good maps and illustrations from the time. A quiz at the end, along with a glossary, and index completes the picture. Grades 4-7.

PEOPLE AND PLACES

ARDLEY, Brugette, and **Neil ARDLEY**
Greece. Silver, 1989
India. Silver, 1989
BENDER, Lionel
Canada. Silver, 1987
France. Silver, 1987

BROOKE-BALL, Peter, and Sue SEDDON
Southern Africa. Silver, 1989
BROWN, Susan
Pakistan and Bangladesh. Silver, 1989
CRANSHAW, Peter
Australia. Silver, 1988
GRANT, Neil
Ireland. Silver, 1989
United Kingdom. Silver, 1988
MASON, Antony
The Caribbean. Silver, 1989
Middle East. Silver, 1988
Southeast Asia. Silver, 1989
MORRISON, Marion
Argentina. Silver, 1989
Brazil. Silver, 1988
Central America. Silver, 1989
Italy. Silver, 1988
PARKER, Steve
Japan. Silver, 1987
PHILLPOTTS, Beatrice
Germany. Silver, 1989
TOLLHURST, Marilyn
China. Silver, 1987
Israel. Silver, 1989
Spain. Silver, 1989
U.S.S.R. Silver, 1987
WIDDOWS, Richard
Mexico. Silver, 1987
ZENFELL, Martha Ellen
U.S.A. Silver, 1988

These slim volumes give a very brief overview, loaded with maps and color illustrations of the country in question. Each subject area—religion, the arts, government—comprised two pages, one of which is illustrations. They will serve as good introductions for grades 3-6. Index.

PEOPLE IN FOCUS
CHAPLIK, Dorothy
Up with Hope: A Biography of Jesse Jackson. Dillon, 1986
DRIEMEN, J. E.
Atomic Dawn: A Biography of Robert Oppenheimer. Dillon, 1989
An Unbreakable Spirit: A Biography of Winston Churchill. Dillon, 1990
EMERSON, Kathy Lynn
Making Headlines: A Biography of Nellie Bly. Dillon, 1989
FINKELSTEIN, Norman H.
The Emperor General: A Biography of Douglas MacArthur. Dillon, 1988
GILLIES, John
Senor Alcalde: A Biography of Henry Cisneros. Dillon, 1988
GREENBERG, Morrie
The Buck Stops Here: A Biography of Harry Truman. Dillon, 1989
HADDOCK, Patricia
Standing up for America: A Biography of Lee Iacocca. Dillon, 1987
HARLAN, Judith
Sounding the Alarm: A Biography of Rachel Carson. Dillon, 1989

HENRY, Sondra, and **Emily TAITZ**
Everyone Wears His Name: A Biography of Levi Strauss. Dillon, 1990
One Woman's Power: A Biography of Gloria Steinem. Dillon, 1987
HUGHES, Libby
From Prison to Prime Minister: A Biography of Benazir Bhutto. Dillon, 1990
Madame Prime Minister: A Biography of Margaret Thatcher. Dillon, 1989
PEIFER, Charles Jr.
Soldier of Destiny: A Biography of George Patton. Dillon, 1988
SIMON, Sheridan
Unlocking the Universe: A Biography of Stephen Hawking. Dillon, 1991
TOMPERT, Ann
The Greatest Showman on Earth: A Biography of P. T. Barnum. Dillon, 1987
WOODS, Harold, and **Geraldine WOODS**
Equal Justice: A Biography of Sandra Day O'Connor. Dillon, 1985

People with an impact on today's lives are the focus of this series of biographies. The texts are factual, with thoughts, quotes, and experiences drawn from the writings of each subject, rather than the authors' imaginations. Photos and a bibliography are included. This is an excellent series for young adult readers.

PEOPLE OF DISTINCTION
BEATON, Margaret
Oprah Winfrey: TV Talk Show Host. Childrens, 1990
BROWN, Marion Marsh
Sacagawea: Indian Interpreter to Lewis and Clark. Childrens, 1988
ERICSSON, Mary Kentra
Morrie Turner: Creator of "Wee Pals". Childrens, 1986
FOSTER, Leila M.
Margaret Thatcher: First Woman Prime Minister of Great Britain. Childrens, 1990
GAFFNEY, Timothy
Chuck Yeager: First Man to Fly Faster Than Sound. Childrens, 1986
Jerrold Petrofsky: Biomedical Pioneer. Childrens, 1984
GREENE, Carol
Hans Christian Andersen: Teller of Tales. Childrens, 1986
Louisa May Alcott: Author, Nurse, Suffragette. Childrens, 1984
Marco Polo: Voyager to the Orient. Childrens, 1987
Marie Curie: Pioneer Physicist. Childrens, 1984
Simon Bolivar: South American Liberator. Childrens, 1989
Thomas Alva Edison: Bringer of Light. Childrens, 1985
Wolfgang Amadeus Mozart: Musician. Childrens, 1987
GUTNIK, Martin J.
Michael Faraday: Creative Scientist. Childrens, 1986
HARGROVE, Jim
Daniel Boone: Pioneer Trailblazer. Childrens, 1985
Diego Rivera: Mexican Muralist. Childrens, 1990
Mark Twain: The Story of Samuel Clemens. Childrens, 1984
Nelson Mandela: South Africa's Silent Voice of Protest. Childrens, 1989
Pablo Casals: Cellist of Conscience. Childrens, 1991
Richard M. Nixon: The Thirty-seventh President. Childrens, 1985
Steven Spielberg: Amazing Filmmaker. Childrens, 1988
HECKART, Barbara Hooper
Edmond Halley: The Man and His Comet. Childrens, 1984
HELLER, Jeffrey
Joan Baez: Singer with a Cause. Childrens, 1991

MCKISSACK, Patricia
Martin Luther King, Jr.: A Man to Remember. Childrens, 1984
Mary McLeod Bethune: A Great American Educator. Childrens, 1985
Paul Laurence Dunbar: A Poet to Remember. Childrens, 1984
MCKISSACK, Patricia, and **Fredrick MCKISSACK**
Frederick Douglass: The Black Lion. Childrens, 1987
OLESKY, Walter
Mikhail Gorbachev: A Leader for Soviet Change. Childrens, 1989
PARADIS, Adrian A.
Ida M. Tarbell: Pioneer Woman Journalist and Biographer. Childrens, 1985
PETERSEN, David, and **Mark COBURN**
Meriwether Lewis and William Clark: Soldiers, Explorers, and Partners in History. Childrens, 1988
RESNICK, Abraham
Lenin: Founder of the Soviet Union. Childrens, 1987
RICHARDS, Gregory
Jim Thorpe: World's Greatest Athlete. Childrens, 1984
ROSEN, Deborah N.
Anwar el-Sadat: A Man of Peace. Childrens, 1986

When assigned to read a biography, youngsters naturally gravitate toward those about well-known people. This series contains many about people of historical importance or currently in the news. The accounts are factual, and where scenes are re-created, they are drawn from actual writings of the subjects. There are a few illustrations and a list of important events in the person's life. Excellent biographies for ages 11 and up.

PEOPLES OF NORTH AMERICA
BACHELIS, Farren
The Central Americans. Chelsea, 1990
CARLTON, Claudia
The Bulgarian Americans. Chelsea, 1990
CAROLI, Betty
Immigrants Who Returned Home. Chelsea, 1990
CATALANO, Julie
The Mexican Americans. Chelsea, 1989
CORNELIUS, James
The English Americans. Chelsea, 1990
The Norwegian Americans. Chelsea, 1988
CULLISON, Alan
The South Americans. Chelsea, 1990
DALEY, William
The Chinese Americans. Chelsea, 1987
DARDY, Steven
The Hungarian Americans. Chelsea, 1990
DIAMOND, Arthur
The Romanian Americans. Chelsea, 1988
DIFRANCO, J. Philip
The Italian Americans. Chelsea, 1989
FORD, Doug
The Pacific Islanders. Chelsea, 1989
GALICICH, Anne
The German Americans. Chelsea, 1988
GERNAND, Renee
The Cuban Americans. Chelsea, 1988
GUTTMACHER, Peter
The Scotch-Irish Americans. Chelsea, 1988

HAUSER, Pierre
Illegal Aliens. Chelsea, 1990
ISRAEL, Fred
The Amish. Chelsea, 1986
The Dominican Americans. Chelsea, 1990
KISSINGER, Jerome
The Serbian Americans. Chelsea, 1990
KITANO, Henry
The Japanese Americans. Chelsea, 1987
KLEVAN, Miriam
The West Indian Americans. Chelsea, 1990
LEHRER, Brian
The Korean Americans. Chelsea, 1988
LICK, Sue
The Iberian Americans. Chelsea, 1990
MCGILL, Allyson
The Swedish Americans. Chelsea, 1988
MAGOCSI, Paul
The Carpatho-Rusyn Americans. Chelsea, 1990
The Russian Americans. Chelsea, 1989
MONOS, Dimitri
The Greek Americans. Chelsea, 1989
MORRICE, Polly
The French Americans. Chelsea, 1988
MUGGAMIN, Howard
The Jewish Americans. Chelsea, 1989
MUSSARI, Mark
The Danish Americans. Chelsea, 1988
NAFF, Alixa
The Arab Americans. Chelsea, 1988
OLSEN, Victoria
The Dutch Americans. Chelsea, 1988
OSBORN, Kevin
The Peoples of the Arctic. Chelsea, 1990
The Ukrainian Americans. Chelsea, 1989
REIMERS, David
The Immigrant Experience. Chelsea, 1989
SAKSON-FORD, Stephanie
The Czech Americans. Chelsea, 1989
SHAPIRO, Ellen
The Croatian Americans. Chelsea, 1989
SMEAD, Howard
The Afro-Americans. Chelsea, 1989
STERN, Jennifer
The Filipino Americans. Chelsea, 1989
STOLARIK, Mark
The Slovak Americans. Chelsea, 1988
TOBIER, Arthur
The Puerto Ricans. Chelsea, 1990
TOOR, Rachel
The Polish Americans. Chelsea, 1989
WALDSTREICHER, David
The Armenian Americans. Chelsea, 1989
WARTIK, Nancy
The French Canadians. Chelsea, 1989

WATTS, James

The Irish Americans. Chelsea, 1989

North America has long prided itself on its ethnic diversity. This series provides an in-depth account of many of those groups in the United States and Canada today. Each book highlights outstanding members of the particular immigrant group, reviews their place in history and takes a look at the many different cultures. Generously illustrated, each book also includes an index and bibliography. This is similar to Lerner's In America series, but is written for ages 12 and up.

PEOPLES OF THE PAST

BURLAND, Cottie

The Incas. Silver, 1978

GIBSON, Michael

The Vikings. Silver, 1977

KAN, Lai Po

The Ancient Chinese. Silver, 1980

MILLARD, Anne

The Egyptians. Silver, 1977

PLACE, Robin

The Celts. Silver, 1977

TRIGGS, Tony D.

The Saxons. Silver, 1979

Students of ancient history will find this series useful as it traces the origins of ancient peoples, describes what they were like, their towns and lifestyles, kinds of crafts, religion, holidays, and other customs. Famous people, maps, and timelines round off the presentation. Many of these cultures are not dealt with elsewhere in this depth. Grades 5 and up. Glossary, index, color illustrations.

PHYSICS FOR KIDS

WOOD, Robert W.

49 Easy Experiments with Acoustics. Tab, 1990

49 Easy Experiments with Electricity and Magnetism. Tab, 1990

49 Easy Experiments with Heat. Tab, 1989

49 Easy Experiments with Mechanics. Tab, 1989

49 Easy Experiments with Optics. Tab, 1990

Simple experiments that illustrate various physics principles are provided here. Necessary supplies are listed in a boxed head at the top of each page. Elementary school teachers will find these particularly useful for grades 3-8.

PICTURE ALBUMS

FROMMER, Harvey

150th Anniversary Album of Baseball. Watts, 1988

HANMER, Trudy J.

An Album of Rock and Roll. Watts, 1988

INGRAHAM, Gloria D., and **Leonard W. INGRAHAM**

An Album of American Women. Watts, 1987

KORAL, April

An Album of War Refugees. Watts, 1989

LAWSON, Don

An Album of the Vietnam War. Watts, 1986

SOLOMON, Maury

An Album of Voyager. Watts, 1990

VOGT, Gregory

An Album of Modern Spaceships. Watts, 1987

These history books give a firsthand look at these interesting subjects. Detailed from the beginning of the movement or invention, this series is a good starting point for students in grades six and up.

PICTURE BOOK BIOGRAPHIES

ADLER, David A.

A Picture Book of Abraham Lincoln. Holiday, 1990
A Picture Book of Benjamin Franklin. Holiday, 1990
A Picture Book of Christopher Columbus. Holiday, 1991
A Picture Book of Eleanor Roosevelt. Holiday, 1991
A Picture Book of George Washington. Holiday, 1990
A Picture Book of Helen Keller. Holiday, 1990
A Picture Book of Martin Luther King, Jr. Holiday, 1990
A Picture Book of Thomas Jefferson. Holiday, 1990

Readers ages 5-8 are the targets of this series. The format is that of a picture book, with a few lines of simple text accompanying a full-page color illustration. The basic information is presented, along with a list of important dates.

PICTURE HISTORY OF THE 20TH CENTURY

HEALEY, Tim

The 1960's. Watts, 1989
The 1970's. Watts, 1989

TAMES, Richard

The 1950's. Watts, 1990
The 1980's. Watts, 1990

UNSTEAD, R. J., and Tim WOOD

The 1940's. Watts, 1990

Increasingly students are being taught about recent history. These books will give them a good start. The highlight of each decade's events, trends, fashion, music, personalities, and other developments are touched on, accompanied by many photos. There is an index and a chronology. Grades 4-8.

PICTURE LIBRARY

BARRETT, N. S.

Airliners. Watts, 1989
Bears. Watts, 1988
Big Cats. Watts, 1988
BMX Bikes. Watts, 1989
Canoeing. Watts, 1990
Cats. Watts, 1990
Crocodiles and Alligators. Watts, 1989
Custom Cars. Watts, 1990
Deserts. Watts, 1990
Dogs. Watts, 1990
Dolphins. Watts, 1989
Dragsters. Watts, 1990
Elephants. Watts, 1988
Football. Watts, 1989
Gerbils. Watts, 1990
Guinea Pigs. Watts, 1990
Gymnastics. Watts, 1989
Hamsters. Watts, 1990
Helicopters. Watts, 1989
Hurricanes and Tornadoes. Watts, 1990
Ice Sports. Watts, 1989

Karting. Watts, 1989
Lasers and Holograms. Watts, 1985
Martial Arts. Watts, 1989
Monkeys and Apes. Watts, 1988
Mountains. Watts, 1990
Motorcycles. Watts, 1989
Pandas. Watts, 1988
Polar Animals. Watts, 1988
Polar Lands. Watts, 1990
Rabbits. Watts, 1990
Race Cars. Watts, 1990
Racing Cars. Watts, 1989
Rivers and Lakes. Watts, 1990
Satellites. Watts, 1985
Scuba Diving. Watts, 1989
Sharks. Watts, 1989
Snakes. Watts, 1989
Spiders. Watts, 1989
Stunt Riding. Watts, 1990
Trail Bikes. Watts, 1987
Trucks. Watts, 1989
Volcanoes. Watts, 1990
Whales. Watts, 1989

NORMAN, C. J.

Aircraft Carriers. Watts, 1986
Combat Aircraft. Watts, 1986
Military Helicopters. Watts, 1986
Submarines. Watts, 1989
Tanks. Watts, 1989
Warships. Watts, 1986

As the name implies, this series concentrates on the visual aspects of the subjects. The text is simple and in large type so that younger readers and reluctant readers will have no problems. Each page features large color action photos or drawings. A brief history of the sport or vehicle is presented, as well as a list of facts and records, glossary, and index. These will be a big hit with readers grades 3-8.

PICTURE LIFE BOOKS

ADAMS, Barbara Johnston

The Picture Life of Bill Cosby. Watts, 1986

BUSNAR, Gene

The Picture Life of Whitney Houston. Watts, 1988

CAULKINS, Janet

The Picture Life of Mikhail Gorbachev. Watts, 1989

HALLIBURTON, Warren J.

The Picture Life of Michael Jackson. Watts, 1984

LEATHER, Michael

The Picture Life of Steven Spielberg. Watts, 1988

NICKLAUS, Carol

The Picture Life of Cyndi Lauper. Watts, 1985

RASOF, Henry

The Picture Life of Charles and Diana. Watts, 1988

SCARIANO, Margaret M.

The Picture Life of Corazon Aquino. Watts, 1987

SCHNEIDERMAN, Ron

The Picture Life of George Bush. Watts, 1989

SOLOMON, Maury

The Picture Life of Dwight Gooden. Watts, 1986

The Picture Life books are not as easy as they sound. They do have photos every other page, but the text is not at a beginning reader level; rather, these are for grades 3-6. They hit the high spots of the subjects' lives in an easy reading format.

PICTURE STORY BIOGRAPHIES

ALVAREZ, Everett, Jr., and **Susan CLINTON**

Everett Alvarez, Jr.: A Hero for Our Times. Childrens, 1990

BEHRENS, June

Barbara Bush: First Lady of Literacy. Childrens, 1990
George Bush: Forty-First President of the United States. Childrens, 1989
Juliette Low: Founder of the Girl Scouts of America. Childrens, 1988
Miss Liberty: First Lady of the World. Childrens, 1986
Ronald Reagon—An All American. Childrens, 1981
Sally Ride: An American First. Childrens, 1984

BROWER, Pauline

Baden-Powell: Founder of the Boy Scouts. Childrens, 1989

DOUGLAS, Robert W.

John Paul II: The Pilgrim Pope. Childrens, 1980

GREENE, Carol

Desmond Tutu: Bishop of Peace. Childrens, 1986
Diana: Princess of Wales. Childrens, 1985
Elie Wiesel: Messenger from the Holocaust. Childrens, 1987
Indira Nehru Gandhi: Ruler of India. Childrens, 1985
Mother Teresa: Friend of the Friendless. Childrens, 1983
Sandra Day O'Connor: The First Woman on the Supreme Court. Childrens, 1982

JONES, Margaret B.

Martin Luther King, Jr. Childrens, 1968

LEPTHIEN, Emilie U.

Corazon Aquino: President of the Philippines. Childrens, 1987

MCKISSACK, Patricia, and **Fredrick MCKISSACK**

James Weldon Johnson: Lift Every Voice and Sing. Childrens, 1990

PETERSEN, David

Ishi: The Last of His People. Childrens, 1991

RIEHECKY, Janet

Caroline Herrera: International Fashion Designer. Childrens, 1991

ROBERTS, Naurice

Andrew Young: Freedom Fighter. Childrens, 1983
Barbara Jordan: The Great Lady from Texas. Childrens, 1984
Cesar Chavez and La Causa. Childrens, 1986
Harold Washington: Mayor with a Vision. Childrens, 1988
Henry Cisneros: Mexican-American Mayor. Childrens, 1986

SIMON, Charnan

Evelyn Cisneros: Prima Ballerina. Childrens, 1990

WILLIAMS, Sylvia

Leontyne Price: Opera Superstar. Childrens, 1984

Early readers grades 2-4 will find this series most approachable. The biographees are modern people found in today's headlines, so should have immediacy for readers. Limited to 32 pages, with large photos, and a brief list of outstanding events in the person's life, these will be good additions where simple biographies are needed.

PICTURE WORLD

BARRETT, Norman

The Picture World of Air Rescue. Watts, 1991
The Picture World of Airport Rescue. Watts, 1991
The Picture World of Ambulances. Watts, 1991
The Picture World of Astronauts. Watts, 1990
The Picture World of Fire Engines. Watts, 1991
The Picture World of Planets. Watts, 1990
The Picture World of Police Vehicles. Watts, 1991
The Picture World of Rockets and Satellites. Watts, 1990
The Picture World of Sea Rescue. Watts, 1991
The Picture World of Space Shuttles. Watts, 1990
The Picture World of Space Voyages. Watts, 1990
The Picture World of Sun and Stars. Watts, 1990

NORMAN, C. J.

The Picture World of Motorcycles. Watts, 1989
The Picture World of Racing Cars. Watts, 1989

STEPHEN, R. J.

The Picture World of Aircraft Carriers. Watts, 1990
The Picture World of Airliners. Watts, 1989
The Picture World of BMX. Watts, 1989
The Picture World of Combat Aircraft. Watts, 1990
The Picture World of Helicopters. Watts, 1989
The Picture World of Military Helicopters. Watts, 1990
The Picture World of Submarines. Watts, 1990
The Picture World of Tanks. Watts, 1990
The Picture World of Trucks. Watts, 1989
The Picture World of Warships. Watts, 1990

Very similar to a number of the titles in Watts's Picture Library series, these are aimed at a slightly younger age group, K-3. There are numerous color photos and diagrams, along with short overviews of different types of crafts, several pages of facts, and a glossary.

PIONEERS IN CHANGE

BURANELLI, Vincent

Thomas Alva Edison. Silver Burdette, 1989

CASTIGLIA, Julie

Margaret Mead. Silver Burdette, 1989

CURSON, Marjorie

Jonas Salk. Silver Burdette, 1990

DASH, Joan

The Triumph of Discovery: Women Scientists Who Won the Nobel Prize. Silver Burdette, 1991

FORCE, Eden

John Muir. Silver Burdette, 1990

GRAY, James Marion

George Washington Carver. Silver Burdette, 1990

IRELAND, Karin

Albert Einstein. Silver Burdette, 1989

PELTA, Kathy

Alexander Graham Bell. Silver Burdette, 1989

POTTER, Robert R.

Buckminster Fuller. Silver Burdette, 1990

TURNER, Glennette Tilley

Lewis Howard Latimer. Silver Burdette, 1990

WHEELER, Leslie A.

Jane Addams. Silver Burdette, 1990

Important people both in the natural and social sciences are profiled in this fine series. The main emphasis is on their scientific accomplishments, with only a brief chapter at beginning and end about childhood and decline. Many details about the intervening years and discoveries are presented, along with photos. There is a list of important dates, bibliography, and index. Grades 5-12.

PLACES IN THE NEWS

STEWART, Gail B.

China. Crestwood, 1990
Colombia. Crestwood, 1991
El Salvador. Crestwood, 1991
Ethiopia. Crestwood, 1991
Germany. Crestwood, 1990
Lebanon. Crestwood, 1990
Northern Ireland. Crestwood, 1990
Panama. Crestwood, 1990
Poland. Crestwood, 1990
Romania. Crestwood, 1991
South Africa. Crestwood, 1990
Soviet Union. Crestwood, 1990

These slim volumes are an attempt to bring current headlines to kids as fast as possible. All of these countries are in a state of upheaval nd change, and Stewart shows why. She begins with a brief run down of the current problem, then spends quite a bit of time on the historical background. The occasionally questionable place of U.S. political interests is touched upon, as well as a brief section on what the future may hold. A brief list of facts about the country is appended. These are far more detailed than magazine articles would be for students, but their very timeliness may outdate them too soon. Grades 5 and up. Glossary, index.

PLAY BOOKS

COCKEY, Tim

Playbook! Baseball ©2. SI, 1991

HAWKES, Bob

Playbook! Football ©2. SI, 1991

TEITELBAUM, Michael

Playbook! Baseball. SI, 1990
Playbook! Football. SI, 1990

Readers get a chance to play coach here, just like in the You Are the Coach series. The major difference is that the players and games here are fictional, while in the other series, real teams and games are used. Here the readers are given a player roster, with a list of strengths and weaknesses and a list of the opposing team, complete with strengths and weaknesses. The reader must choose which play to call, and then is led through the game, making either winning or losing choices. Good for sports buffs and reluctant readers grades 4-9.

PORTRAIT OF AMERICA

THOMPSON, Kathleen

Alabama. Raintree, 1988
Alaska. Raintree, 1988
Arizona. Raintree, 1986
Arkansas. Raintree, 1987
California. Raintree, 1987
Colorado. Raintree, 1987
Connecticut. Raintree, 1986
Delaware. Raintree, 1986

Florida. Raintree, 1986
Georgia. Raintree, 1986
Hawaii. Raintree, 1987
Idaho. Raintree, 1986
Illinois. Raintree, 1987
Indiana. Raintree, 1986
Iowa. Raintree, 1986
Kansas. Raintree, 1987
Kentucky. Raintree, 1987
Louisiana. Raintree, 1985
Maine. Raintree, 1985
Maryland. Raintree, 1985
Massachusetts. Raintree, 1985
Michigan. Raintree, 1987
Minnesota. Raintree, 1988
Mississippi. Raintree, 1987
Missouri. Raintree, 1986
Montana. Raintree, 1988
Nebraska. Raintree, 1988
Nevada. Raintree, 1986
New Hampshire. Raintree, 1988
New Jersey. Raintree, 1986
New Mexico. Raintree, 1986
New York. Raintree, 1988
North Carolina. Raintree, 1987
North Dakota. Raintree, 1986
Ohio. Raintree, 1988
Oklahoma. Raintree, 1987
Oregon. Raintree, 1985
Pennsylvania. Raintree, 1986
Puerto Rico. Raintree, 1986
Rhode Island. Raintree, 1987
South Carolina. Raintree, 1987
South Dakota. Raintree, 1987
Tennessee. Raintree, 1986
Texas. Raintree, 1986
Utah. Raintree, 1986
Vermont. Raintree, 1987
Virginia. Raintree, 1985
Washington. Raintree, 1987
Washington, D.C. Raintree, 1987
West Virginia. Raintree, 1988
Wisconsin. Raintree, 1986
Wyoming. Raintree, 1987

This series covers much the same ground, but with less detail than Children's Enchantment of America series. Almost half of the book relates historical facts, while the other half discusses people, economy, and life. There are interesting sections that profile residents and present their views on their state. Important events and a page of facts are included. While the text is not as simple as the Fradin books, this series falls somewhere between those and the Enchantment books, appealing to grades 3-6.

PORTRAITS OF THE NATIONS

ANDREWS, William G.

The Land and People of the Soviet Union. Lippincott, 1991

BLAIR, David N.
The Land and People of Bolivia. Lippincott, 1990
CHANDLER, David P.
The Land and People of Cambodia. Lippincott, 1991
CHENEY, Patricia
The Land and People of Zimbabwe. Lippincott, 1990
CLIFFORD, Mary L.
The Land and People of Afghanistan. Lippincott, 1989
FOX, Geoffrey
The Land and People of Argentina. Lippincott, 1990
HARRIS, Jonathan
The Land and People of France. Lippincott, 1989
LANDER, Patricia S., and **Claudette CHARBONNEAU**
The Land and People of Finland. Lippincott, 1990
MAHMOUD, Zaki N.
The Land and People of Egypt. Lippincott, 1972
MAJOR, John S.
The Land and People of China. Lippincott, 1989
The Land and People of Mongolia. Lippincott, 1990
MAREN, Michael
The Land and People of Kenya. Lippincott, 1989
MEEK, James
The Land and People of Scotland. Lippincott, 1990
ORTIZ, Victoria
The Land and People of Cuba. Lippincott, 1973
PATON, Jonathan
The Land and People of South Africa. Lippincott, 1990
SOLBERG, S. E.
The Land and People of Korea. Lippincott, 1991
SPENCER, William
The Land and People of Turkey. Lippincott, 1990

This fine series has been more than updated; it has been tremendously upgraded as well. All of the usual is included: culture, history, geography, religion, economy, government—but in considerably more detail than any other series. Photos, illustrations, maps, and tables are provided, albeit in black and white. A bibliography, filmography/discography and index are given. Excellent choices for grades 5 and up.

PREDICTING
LAMPTON, Christopher
Predicting AIDS and Other Epidemics. Watts, 1989
Predicting Nuclear and Other Technological Disasters. Watts, 1989
LEE, Sally
Predicting Violent Storms. Watts, 1989
VOGT, Gregory
Predicting Earthquakes. Watts, 1989

This series examines the causes of natural and man-made disasters and the technology that has allowed us to predict and avert them. These books provide easy to follow explanations of the causes of these disasters. Each book is well illustrated and includes a glossary, bibliography and index. Grades 9-12.

PREHISTORIC LIFE
MATTHEWS, Rupert
The Age of Mammals. Watts, 1990
The Dinosaur Age. Watts, 1989
The First People. Watts, 1990

The First Settlements. Watts, 1990
How Life Began. Watts, 1989
Ice Age Animals. Watts, 1990

This series explains in a simple language, theories regarding the origin of life and the universe and progress through to the beginnings of recorded history. Each book includes a glossary and index and is well illustrated with colorful drawings. These books were written for the junior high school aged student.

PRESIDENTIAL BIOGRAPHY SERIES

DEVANEY, John
Franklin Delano Roosevelt, President. Walker, 1987
Lyndon Baines Johnson, President. Walker, 1986
Ronald Reagan, President. Walker, 1990

RANDOLPH, Sallie
Gerald R. Ford, President. Walker, 1987
Richard M. Nixon, President. Walker, 1989
Woodrow Wilson, President. Walker, 1991

SMITH, Betsy Covington
Jimmy Carter, President. Walker, 1986

SMITH, Elizabeth Simpson
Five First Ladies. Walker, 1986

VAN STEENWYK, Elizabeth
Dwight David Eisenhower, President. Walker, 1987

These are excellent presidential biographies, written clearly to cover early beginnings and life after presidency, but primarily concentrating on the presidential years. Photos and indexes are a real plus for students. Although the publisher suggests ages 10 and up, these are thorough enough for the junior/senior high students.

PROFILES IN SCIENCE FOR YOUNG PEOPLE: SOLUTIONS

CWIKLIK, Robert
Albert Einstein and the Theory of Relativity. Childrens, 1988

EGAN, Louise
Thomas A. Edison: The Great American Inventor. Childrens, 1988

SKELTON, Renee
Charles Darwin and the Theory of Natural Selection. Childrens, 1988

STEINKE, Ann
Marie Curie and the Discovery of Radium. Childrens, 1988

Originally published in paperback as part of Barron's Educational Series, these biographies cover the usual ground, using line drawings and fictionalized conversations. There is a glossary, index, bibliography, and list of discussion topics. There are better books available for grades 5-9.

PROFILES OF GREAT AMERICANS FOR YOUNG PEOPLE: HENRY STEELE COMMAGER'S AMERICANS

CLAFLIN, Edward Beecher
Sojourner Truth and the Struggle for Freedom. Childrens, 1988

GUTMAN, William
Andrew Jackson and the New Populism. Childrens, 1988

SHEBAR, Sharon
Franklin D. Roosevelt and the New Deal. Childrens, 1988

SHORTO, Russell
Thomas Jefferson and the American Ideal. Childrens, 1988

Several important historical figures are profiled here. Aimed at grades 5 and up, each volume has a brief introduction by noted historian Henry Steele Commager. Unfortunately, the remainder of the contents do not live up to that beginning. There is much use of "conversation" and numerous statements about people's emotions that are not backed up by any source material. Furthermore, small, uninteresting illustrations sprinkle the text where using reproductions of real portraits and drawings of the subject would be far more effective. For a younger age, these problems might be forgiven in the interest of appealing to a young reader's interest, but at this level, accuracy is far more important. There are plenty of other biographical sources for these figures.

PROJECT WILDLIFE

BRIGHT, Michael

Alligators and Crocodiles. Watts, 1990
Elephants. Watts, 1990
Giant Panda. Watts, 1989
Humpback Whale. Watts, 1990
Koalas. Watts, 1990
Mountain Gorilla. Watts, 1989
Polar Bear. Watts, 1989
Tiger. Watts, 1989

Like Watts's Survival series, this one profiles endangered species. Human harvesting of the animals is examined, but so is man's effect on the animals' habitats. Future possibilities and suggestions for preserving the animals and their homes are given. There are also 6 pages of facts on the species, including anatomy and lifestyle, that should prove useful for school reports. Lots of color photos enhance the text. Grades 5-8.

PROJECTS FOR YOUNG SCIENTISTS

DUNBAR, Robert E.

Heart and Circulatory System Projects for Young Scientists. Watts, 1989

GARDNER, Robert

Energy Projects for Young Scientists. Watts, 1989

GOODWIN, Peter H.

Engineering Projects for Young Scientists. Watts, 1989

GUTNIK, Martin J.

Ecology Projects for Young Scientists. Watts, 1989
Genetics Projects for Young Scientists. Watts, 1989

MCKAY, David E., and **Bruce G. SMITH**

Space Science Projects for Young Scientists. Watts, 1989

RAINIS, Kenneth G.

Nature Projects for Young Scientists. Watts, 1989

THOMAS, David A.

Math Projects for Young Scientists. Watts, 1989

TOCCI, Salvatore

Biology Projects for Young Scientists. Watts, 1989

Unlike Watts's series, Experimental Science, this one is not so much intended for science fair projects as it is for classroom or home experiments to learn about various scientific processes. The experiments lead logically from one to the other and so would work well in the classroom setting. The authors emphasize safety so much that it seems most of the projects would best be done under supervision. Each chapter ends with suggestions for further readings. There is also an appendix listing where special materials may be obtained. Best for the serious young scientist or teacher. Grades 5-12.

QUACKENBUSH BIOGRAPHIES

QUACKENBUSH, Robert

Clear the Cow Pasture, I'm Coming in for a Landing! S&S, 1990
Don't You Dare Shoot That Bear! S&S, 1984
Mark Twain? What Kind of Name Is That? S&S, 1984
Old Silver Leg Takes Over. S&S, 1986
Once upon a Time! S&S, 1985

These are easy to read biographies with the trademark cartoon-like Quackenbush illustrations. They will appeal to young readers and do present the salient facts. No index or table of contents. Ages 7-10.

QUESTION AND ANSWER BOOKS

GABB, Michael

Creatures Great and Small. Lerner, 1980

Everyday Science. Lerner, 1980

HARVEY, Anthony

The World of Dinosaurs. Lerner, 1980

HARVEY, T.

Railroads. Lerner, 1980

KERROD, Robin

The Challenge of Space. Lerner, 1980

Mission Outer Space. Lerner, 1980

The Mysterious Universe. Lerner, 1980

Race for the Moon. Lerner, 1980

LYE, Keith

Our Planet the Earth. Lerner, 1980

MAYNARD, Christopher

War Vehicles. Lerner, 1980

SQUIRE, David

Wheels. Lerner, 1980

TUNNEY, Christopher

Aircraft. Lerner, 1980

As the title implies, the format involves questions and answers. Each oversize page is full color, with several questions presented in large print and an accompanying illustration. The reply is underneath in smaller print, so the page has eye appeal. In terms of school reports, there is not a superabundance of information, but there is a lot of browse-appeal for ages 10-13. Index.

RANDOM HOUSE LIBRARY OF KNOWLEDGE

BLAIR, Carvel Hall

Exploring the Sea. Random, 1986

BRUUN, Ruth Dowling, and **Bertel BRUUN**

Human Body. Random, 1982

HAMMOND, editors

World Atlas. Random, 1982

MOCHE, Dinah L.

Astronomy Today. Random, 1982

SILVER, Donald M.

Animal World. Random, 1987

Earth: The Ever-Changing Planet. Random, 1989

Life on Earth. Random, 1983

ZALLINGER, Peter

Dinosaurs. Random, 1986

Here is a colorful oversize series that covers a number of scientific topics. Each volume gives a thorough examination of its subject with plentiful color illustrations and diagrams that will be very useful to students from elementary through high school.

READ ABOUT

ATTMORE, Stephen

Read about Horses and Ponies. Watts, 1989

CASTLE, Kate

Read about Ballet. Watts, 1989

JEFFERIS, David
Read about Helicopters. Watts, 1990
Read about Submarines. Watts, 1990
KERROD, Robin
Read about Jet Airliners. Watts, 1989
Read about Out in Space. Watts, 1989
LAMBERT, David
Read about Dinosaurs. Watts, 1990
WOOD, Jenny
Read about Jungle Animals. Watts, 1990
WOOD, Tim
Read about Castles. Watts, 1990

These slim, colorful volumes are intended to introduce readers to facts on a variety of scientific topics. Simple vocabulary make these appropriate for ages 8-11. Included are suggestions for making projects. Glossary, index.

RECENT AMERICAN IMMIGRANTS
GORDON, Susan
Asian Indians. Watts, 1990
GRENQUIST, Barbara
Cubans and Caribbean Islanders. Watts, 1991
MAYBERRY, Jodine
Chinese. Watts, 1990
Eastern Europeans. Watts, 1991
Filipinos. Watts, 1990
Koreans. Watts, 1991
Mexicans. Watts, 1990
MCGUIRE, William
Southeast Asians. Watts, 1991

It has been a while since there has been series coverage of the ethnic groups that make up America. These books describe the country of origin and explain the various waves of immigration: why they happened, how they were received in the U.S., and what they brought to this country. Religion, festivals, famous people, families, and problems faced are also examined. Grades 5 and up. Bibliography, index.

REMARKABLE ANIMALS SERIES
BEERS, Dorothy Sands
The Gecko. Dillon, 1990
The Prairie Dog. Dillon, 1990
HARRIS, Lorle K.
The Caribou. Dillon, 1988
LABONTE, Gail
The Arctic Fox. Dillon, 1989
The Llama. Dillon, 1989
The Miniature Horse. Dillon, 1990
The Tarantula. Dillon, 1991
PEMBLETON, Seliesa
The Pileated Woodpecker. Dillon, 1989
SIBBALD, Jean H.
The Manatee. Dillon, 1990
STONE, Lynn
The Pelican. Dillon, 1990
VOELLER, Edward
The Red-Crowned Crane. Dillon, 1989

The anatomy, habits and habitats, and life cycles of these unusual animals are presented in this series. There are color photos, a glossary, an index, and fact sheet in each book. These have plentiful information for grades 5-8, where coverage of these animals is needed.

RESOURCES TODAY

CACKETT, Sue

Glass. Watts, 1988

MERCER, Ian

Oils. Watts, 1989

WHYMAN, Kathryn

Metals and Alloys. Watts, 1988
Plastics. Watts, 1988
Rocks and Minerals. Watts, 1989
Textiles. Watts, 1988

The resources of the world, both natural and man-made, are explored here. First the author describes the origin of the product, then how it is converted into usable form. The many ways it is used are described, with ecological impact emphasized. Color illustrations, glossaries, indexes, and fact files complete the package. Grades 3-9.

RIVERS OF THE WORLD

ANSON, Robert Sam

The Yellow River. Silver, 1980

BATCHELOR, John, and **Julie BATCHELOR**

The Congo. Silver, 1980

DARRELL-BROWN, Susan

The Mississippi. Silver, 1978

DOUGLAS, Gina

The Ganges. Silver, 1978

HILLS, C. A. R.

The Danube. Silver, 1980
The Rhine. Silver, 1978
The Seine. Silver, 1980

LIGHTFOOT, Paul

The Mekong. Silver, 1980

LYTE, Charles

The Thames. Silver, 1980

STRAUSS, Raymond

The Rio Grande. Silver, 1980

WATSON, Jane Werner

The Volga. Silver, 1980

WINKS, Honor Lee

The Colorado. Silver, 1980

WINKS, Honor Lee, and **Robin W. WINKS**

The St. Lawrence. Silver, 1980

WORTHINGTON, E. Barton

The Nile. Silver, 1978

These books spend more time discussing the towns, peoples, agriculture, and flora and fauna of the surrounding area than on the actual formation and geographical/geological makeup of the river itself. Politics, government, and history are also included. Information on the rivers themselves is more easily accessed in encyclopedias. Grades 5-9. Glossary, bibliography, index.

ROOKIE BIOGRAPHIES

GREENE, Carol

Abraham Lincoln: President of a Divided Country. Childrens, 1989
Benjamin Franklin: A Man with Many Jobs. Childrens, 1988

Black Elk: A Man with a Vision. Childrens, 1990
Christopher Columbus: A Great Explorer. Childrens, 1989
Daniel Boone: Man of the Forests. Childrens, 1990
Elizabeth Blackwell: First Woman Doctor. Childrens, 1991
Elizabeth the First: Queen of England. Childrens, 1990
George Washington: First President of the United States. Childrens, 1991
Hans Christian Andersen: Prince of Storytellers. Childrens, 1991
Jackie Robinson: Baseball's First Black Major Leaguer. Childrens, 1990
Jacques Cousteau: Man of the Oceans. Childrens, 1990
John Muir: Man of the Wild Places. Childrens, 1991
Laura Ingalls Wilder: Author of the Little House Books. Childrens, 1990
Louis Pasteur: Enemy of Disease. Childrens, 1990
Ludwig Van Beethoven: Musical Pioneer. Childrens, 1989
Martin Luther King, Jr.: A Man Who Changed Things. Childrens, 1989
Pocahontas: Daughter of a Chief. Childrens, 1988
Robert E. Lee: Leader in War and Peace. Childrens, 1989

Early readers will find this biography series a perfect choice. The vocabulary is limited, sentences are short, the print is large, and each life is told briefly but with the salient details. Illustrations on every page, some in color, will keep interest, and help understand the text. There is an index and list of important dates. Grades 2-3.

ROSEN PHOTO GUIDES

HAMMER, Arnold

Rosen Photo Guide to a Career in Health and Fitness. Rosen, 1988

JEFFERS, Susan

Rosen Photo Guide to a Career in Animal Care. Rosen, 1988

LASLO, Cynthia

Rosen Photo Guide to a Career in the Circus. Rosen, 1988

WILLIAMS, Randal

Rosen Photo Guide to a Career in Magic. Rosen, 1988

This is a career series aimed at reluctant readers, with only 64 pages and a reading level set at 4.0. The publisher has sought to make the books appealing by choosing unusual careers. While health and fitness and working with animals are possible career areas for reluctant readers, one wonders just how many job opportunities are available in the circus or magic fields! The books do provide brief explanations of different jobs available with a mention of possible training requirements and salaries. Suggestions of where to write for further information are given. Only the first two titles are recommended for this series.

SAVE OUR EARTH

HARE, Tony

Acid Rain. Watts, 1990
The Greenhouse Effect. Watts, 1990
The Ozone Layer. Watts, 1990
Rainforest Destruction. Watts, 1990

More recently published than Watts's Issues series, this one covers much the same territory. Clear explanations, well illustrated, of these current topics can be found in these oversize books. While the approach is the same, this series also includes a section on "What You Can Do," and several pages of "Fact Files" that synopsize the high points of the text. Good choices for grades 5-8.

SAVE OUR SPECIES

BAILEY, Jill

Gorilla Rescue. Steck, 1990
Mission Rhino. Steck, 1990
Operation Elephant. Steck, 1991
Polar Bear Rescue. Steck, 1991

Project Panda. Steck, 1990
Project Whale. Steck, 1991
Save the Snow Leopard. Steck, 1991
Save the Tiger. Steck, 1990

Many series are turning their attention to aspects of environmental and conservation concerns. This one differs in that it emphasizes individual species that are in danger. The author tells why the species has become endangered, particularly man's role. Unfortunately, perhaps to add interest, the information is buried in a series of stories sprinkled with realistic photos and illustrations. There is an index, but nonetheless, these will be tough to use for school reports. The most useful section is the final page that gives a statistical update on the animal. Grades 3-6.

SCHOOL SMARTS
GILBERT, Sara
How to Take Tests. Lothrop, 1983
JAMES, Elizabeth, and **Carol BARKIN**
How to Be School Smart. Lothrop, 1988
How to Write Your Best Book Report. Lothrop, 1986
How to Write a Great School Report. Lothrop, 1983
How to Write a Term Paper. Lothrop, 1980

Students will benefit from these excellent study helpers. The authors take the reader step-by-step through a project, from choosing a topic, to taking notes, to how to research, to writing. There are many samples to give them ideas of how to organize and how a source will look. These are the next best thing to in-person instruction. Grades 5 and up. Index.

SCHWARTZ, David M.
The Hidden Life of the Desert. Crown, 1990
The Hidden Life of the Forest. Crown, 1988
The Hidden Life of the Meadow. Crown, 1988
The Hidden Life of the Pond. Crown, 1988

This series looks at the various forms of life that congregate in these locales. Birds, insects, reptiles, even microscopic life are (very) briefly described and accompanied by a color photo. Not enough information for reports on individual species, these are best used for the overview they present. Grades 3-5.

SCIENCE ACTIVITIES
CHALLAND, Helen J.
Activities in the Earth Sciences. Childrens, 1982
Activities in the Life Sciences. Childrens, 1982
Activities in the Physical Sciences. Childrens, 1984
Science Projects and Activities. Childrens, 1985
WONG, Ovid K.
Is Science Magic? Childrens, 1989
Your Body and How It Works. Childrens, 1986

It's science project time and you aren't sure where to turn. A good start would be with any of the books in this series from Childrens Press. The experiments and explanations are easy to read and understand. Numerous illustrations are spread throughout the books to help the reader understand by visually explaining a step or concept. The books are indexed thoroughly and are a good beginning source for the future scientist.

SCIENCE ALIVE
KERROD, Robin
All Around. Silver, 1986
Changing Things. Silver, 1986
Living Things. Silver, 1986
Moving Things. Silver, 1986

The books in this series are intended to complement each other, so there is a code at the top of the page to refer the reader to a relevant page in one of the other three books in the series. The first two-thirds of each book contains simply explained scientific concepts, complete with diagrams and illustrations. The last one-third has related science experiments and projects, using easily obtainable materials. Children in grades 2-5 will find these decent introductions. Glossary, index.

SCIENCE AND ITS SECRETS

Animals. Raintree, 1988
Archaeology. Raintree, 1988
Astronomy. Raintree, 1988
Birds. Raintree, 1988
Dolphins. Raintree, 1988
Energy. Raintree, 1988
Prehistoric Animals. Raintree, 1988
The Poles. Raintree, 1988
Volcanoes. Raintree, 1988
Weather. Raintree, 1988

Each volume in this series concentrates on an area of interest in the sciences. It is designed to capture the interest of reluctant readers and does so by including many vivid illustrations. Each title asks the reader a question that relates to that particular area of science, and then goes on to answer the question. For example, "What are the seven wonders of the ancient world?" The text is easy to read and should be appreciated by students in grades 5-10.

SCIENCE AND TECHNOLOGY

CROSS, Wilbur
Coal. Childrens, 1983
Petroleum. Childrens, 1983
Solar Energy. Childrens, 1984

CROSS, Wilbur, and **Susanna CROSS**
Space Shuttle. Childrens, 1985

HARGROVE, Jim
Computer Wars. Childrens, 1985

OLEKSY, Walter
Miracles of Genetics. Childrens, 1986

These titles include numerous photographs to enrich the comprehensive format. The basic information is clear and easy to read. Each book is indexed with a glossary and bibliography. Good books for 10-15 year olds.

SCIENCE BOOK SERIES

POPE, Joyce
Do Animals Dream? Viking, 1986

WHITFIELD, Philip, and **Joyce POPE**
Can the Whales Be Saved? Viking, 1989
Why Do the Seasons Change? Viking, 1987
Why Do Volcanoes Erupt? Viking, 1990

WHITFIELD, Philip, and **Ruth WHITFIELD**
Why Do Our Bodies Stop Growing? Viking, 1988

While the information in this series is excellent, the question and answer format will limit usefulness to students tremendously. The table of contents lists the questions, but there is no indication of chapter or general topic headings. The index is helpful, but with the plethora of materials on the natural world, this seems of marginal usefulness. Grades 5 and up.

SCIENCE CLUB SERIES

SMITH, Henry

Amazing Air. Lothrop, 1983

WATSON, Philip

Light Fantastic. Lothrop, 1983

Liquid Magic. Lothrop, 1983

Super Motion. Lothrop, 1983

These are science experiment/project books. A list of supplies and skills precedes the text. The presentation is somewhat confusing: sets of steps are listed, but separated from other steps relating to the same experiment by boxing; some projects occupy one page, with steps numbered from top to bottom, while others cover two pages and are numbered horizontally. There is a glossary and index.

SCIENCE FAIR PROJECT SERIES

BONNET, Robert L., and G. Daniel KEEN

Botany: 49 Science Fair Projects. Tab, 1989

Botany: 49 More Science Fair Projects. Tab, 1990

Computers: 49 Science Fair Projects. Tab, 1990

Earth Science: 49 Science Fair Projects. Tab, 1989

Environmental Science: 49 Science Fair Projects. Tab, 1990

One of several Tab Books series with science fair projects for youngsters, these begin with a description of the project, then give a list of supplies. The procedure is then outlined step by step. There is also a list of further experiments that can be made. The need for parental supervision is spelled out as needed just under the title of the project. Not all of the supplies are readily on hand, but there is a nice mix of easy with more ambitious projects. There is a list of sources for supplies, a glossary, and index. Excellent choice for grades 5-12.

SCIENCE FOR KIDS

WOOD, Robert W.

Science for Kids: 39 Easy Animal Biology Experiments. Tab, 1991

Science for Kids: 39 Easy Astronomy Experiments. Tab, 1991

Science for Kids: 39 Easy Chemistry Experiments. Tab, 1991

Science for Kids: 39 Easy Engineering Experiments. Tab, 1991

Science for Kids: 39 Easy Geography Activities. Tab, 1991

Science for Kids: 39 Easy Geology Experiments. Tab, 1991

Science for Kids: 39 Easy Meteorology Experiments. Tab, 1991

Science for Kids: 39 Easy Plant Biology Experiments. Tab, 1991

Like Tab's Physics & Chemistry for Kids series, this one features experiments using common household supplies that can illustrate and teach or be used for science fairs. Each experiment is preceded by a list of supplies, drawings accompany directions, and an explanation as to why the project works is also provided. Grades 4-8. Glossary, index.

SCIENCE FRONTIERS

BRAMWELL, Martyn

Oceanography. Watts, 1989

GRAHAM, Ian

Communications. Watts, 1989

Transportation. Watts, 1989

MCKIE, Robin

Energy. Watts, 1989

Some very large subjects are tackled in these slender oversize volumes. The overview is *very* brief, as the authors try to cover the many phases of their topics. Several paragraphs are dedicated to each subject, complete with a photo or illustration. Browsers will enjoy, but there is not enough information for report-writers. Grades 5-9.

SCIENCE FUN

WYLER, Rose

Science Fun with a Homemade Chemistry Set. Messner, 1987
Science Fun with Drums, Bells, and Whistles. Messner, 1987
Science Fun with Mud and Dirt. Messner, 1987
Science Fun with Peanuts and Popcorn. Messner, 1987
Science Fun with Toy Boats and Planes. Messner, 1987
Science Fun with Toy Cars and Trucks. Messner, 1988

This is an early science series designed to introduce learners 6-9 to basic concepts, primarily through experimentation. Biological and mechanical principles are explained simply, with many large illustrations. The experiments are simple enough to do at home, or in the classroom. A little history, a few games, and some riddles round out each book. These should prove an enjoyable start for young scientists.

SCIENCE SPIRALS

FITZPATRICK, Julia

Balancing. Silver, 1990
Bounce, Stretch, and Spring. Silver, 1990
In the Air. Silver, 1988
Magnets. Silver, 1988
Mirrors. Silver, 1988
Towers and Bridges. Silver, 1988
Wheels. Silver, 1988

The youngest readers are the target audience for these simple science experiments. Each experiment illustrates a scientific principle, so their best use is for home or classroom learning. The format is a bit odd, with simple sentences used, but filling only the left-hand side of the page. This forces a beginning reader to read part of a sentence on one line, then move on to the next line to complete it, when the entire sentence could fit (and be more easily read) on one line. The index only lists the title of each project; no other terms are included. Grades K-3.

SCIENCE STARTERS

TAYLOR, Barbara

Bouncing and Bending Light. Watts, 1990
Color and Light. Watts, 1990
Electricity and Magnets. Watts, 1990
Energy and Power. Watts, 1990
Force and Movement. Watts, 1990
Weight and Balance. Watts, 1990

Various scientific principles are illustrated here, with plentiful color illustrations and simple experiments. While the majority of these experiments are more suitable for classroom (or home) learning, there are a few under "More Things to Do" that could be used for science fairs. There is a glossary, index, and fact list. Grades 3-6.

SCIENCE TODAY

PETTIGREW, Mark

Music and Sound. Watts, 1987
Weather. Watts, 1987

WHYMAN, Kathryn

Electricity and Magnetism. Watts, 1986
Heat and Energy. Watts, 1986
Light and Lasers. Watts, 1986
Living Things. Watts, 1987
Solar System. Watts, 1987

Like many of Watts's other science series, this one features a page of explanation alternating with a page of illustrations in an oversize format. Unlike the other series, though, this British import's illustrations are not clear enough. For example, in *Weather*, a drawing of a weather map never explains all the symbols seen in it; another drawing showing how the snow line varies depending on the distance from the equator never explains the color key used. Grades 5-8.

SEA LIFE

BEHRENS, June

Dolphins! Childrens, 1989
Sharks! Childrens, 1990
Whales of the World. Childrens, 1987
Whalewatch! Childrens, 1978

Whales, dolphins, and sharks continue to fascinate children of all ages. Even the youngest readers will enjoy these entries. Written simply, with large print and colorful photos, readers grades 2-4 should be able to handle these; younger children will comprehend them easily when read aloud. Both a glossary and index are provided.

SEA WORLD BOOKS

BUNTING, Eve

Sea World Book of Sharks. Harcourt, 1980
Sea World Book of Whales. Harcourt, 1980

EVANS, Phyllis Roberts

Sea World Book of Seals and Sea Lions. Harcourt, 1986

LEATHERWOOD, Stephen, and **Randall REEVES**

Sea World Book of Dolphins. Harcourt, 1987

TODD, Frank S.

Sea World Book of Penguins. Harcourt, 1981

There is much detailed information on sea creatures in these books. Much of the information is drawn from research teams, although the Sea World staff also has considerable scientific background and expertise to offer. There are some color photos and an index. The endangered species aspects are also dealt with. Grades 5-12.

SEAS AND OCEANS

HARGREAVES, Pat

The Antarctic. Silver, 1980
The Arctic. Silver, 1981
The Atlantic. Silver, 1980
The Caribbean and Gulf of Mexico. Silver, 1980
The Indian Ocean. Silver, 1981
The Mediterranean. Silver, 1980
The Pacific. Silver, 1981
The Red Sea and the Persian Gulf. Silver, 1981

Historic and scientific information about the seas can be found in these books. Varieties of life existing in each body of water, water resources, and economy are all examined. There is a wealth of information here for readers grades 5-9, complete with photos, glossary, and index.

SEASONS

WHITLOCK, Ralph

Autumn. Watts, 1990
Spring. Watts, 1987
Summer. Watts, 1987
Winter. Watts, 1987

Teachers will applaud these books. Why the seasons occur, what happens to wildlife at each time, festivals, folklore, and sports enjoyed at each season are touched upon. Scientific observations and projects are also given. Although written at the third to sixth grade level, teachers of younger kids could read sections aloud and adapt to younger groups. Many color illustrations. Glossary, bibliography, index.

SECRET WORLDS

TAYLOR, Kim

Hidden by Darkness. Delacorte, 1990
Hidden Inside. Delacorte, 1990
Hidden Underwater. Delacorte, 1990
Hidden Underneath. Delacorte, 1990
Too Clever to See. Delacorte, 1990

Young scientists will enjoy these peeks into "hidden worlds" and the animals who inhabit them. Cave dwellers, forest and water creatures are all examined, albeit briefly. A two-page spread is devoted to most, with much of that space used by color photos. Some really unusual animals show up here, so even though there is not enough material for reports, browsers grades 3-6 will get a kick out of them. Index.

SEE INSIDE

KERROD, Robin

See Inside a Space Station. Watts, 1988

RUTLAND, Jonathan

See Inside a Submarine. Watts, 1988
See Inside an Airport. Watts, 1988
See Inside an Oil Rig and Tanker. Watts, 1988

Readers will get an up-close tour of these facilities in these oversize, heavily illustrated books. The authors touch on history and development, what kinds of tasks are done and where, as well as future possibilities. There is a glossary, index, and list of important dates. Grades 5-8.

SEE THE USA

CORNING, Josie

Denver, Colorado. Crestwood, 1989

DEEGAN, Paul

Nashville, Tennessee. Crestwood, 1989
New York, New York. Crestwood, 1989

LEE, Gregory

Los Angeles, California. Crestwood, 1989

NIELSEN, Nancy

Boundary Waters Canoe Area, Minnesota. Crestwood, 1989

STEPHENSON, Sallie

Orlando, Florida. Crestwood, 1989

TURCK, Mary

Chicago, Illinois. Crestwood, 1989
Washington, D.C. Crestwood, 1989

Unlike Great Cities of the World, this series concentrates only on American cities and are more like tour guides for kids. Coverage is only on the sights (and sites) a child visitor will see, with a little background on, and pictures of, what can be seen there, but no information on economy or history, etc. There is a city map, fact page, index, and list of tourist addresses. Grades 4-7.

SEXUALITY DECISION MAKING SERIES

DEVAULT, Christine

Don't Let It Get Around. Network, 1989
Taking Chances with Sex. Network, 1989
Too Soon for Sex. Network, 1989

These interactive books place the reader into the lives of teens at Rosemont High. When a character is faced with making a decision about sexual involvement, the reader makes the decision and faces the consequences. The reader is drawn into these stories that relay good information about abstinence, contraception and sexually transmitted diseases. These books are fantastic. They are easy to read and designed for teenagers. Caution, however: the subject matter and contents can be extremely controversial, but don't let that stop you from adding this series to your school or public library.

SHAKESPEARE MADE EASY

DURBAND, Alan (editor)

Hamlet. Barrons, 1986
Henry IV, Part One. Barrons, 1985
Julius Caesar. Barrons, 1985
King Lear. Barrons, 1986
Macbeth. Barrons, 1985
The Merchant of Venice. Barrons, 1985
A Midsummer Night's Dream. Barrons, 1984
Romeo and Juliet. Barrons, 1985
The Tempest. Barrons, 1985
Twelfth Night. Barrons, 1985

At last, Shakespeare really is made easy. In this series, the complete original text is laid out side-by-side with a fully translated modern version. Also included in each book are study questions and review material. Excellent for the first-time high school Shakespeare reader.

SILVER BURDETTE COLOR LIBRARY

BOORER, Michael
Animals. Silver, 1983

LYE, Keith
The Earth. Silver, 1983

MAY, Robin
The American West. Silver, 1983

RIDPATH, Ian
Space. Silver, 1983

RUTLAND, Jonathan
The Sea. Silver, 1983

WHITLOCK, Ralph
Insects. Silver, 1984

These are *very* oversize books—perhaps too big to fit a shelf. For some reason, chapter headings are printed vertically on the far left side of the page, so that a youngster in a hurry could miss the fact that they are in a new section. Illustrations are plentiful, many in color and many from the era under discussion. Grades 5-8. Index.

SILVERSTEIN, Alvin, and **Virginia SILVERSTEIN**

The Story of Your Ear. Coward, 1981
The Story of Your Foot. Putnam, 1987
The Story of Your Mouth. Coward, 1984

As always, the Silversteins present a thorough examination of their topic, in this case, anatomy. The text dominates, with a detailed commentary on the exterior and interior workings of each body part under discussion, followed by information on various health and social aspects. There are occasional black and white illustrations, but other texts are stronger in this area. Grades 5 and up.

SIMON AND SCHUSTER COLOR ILLUSTRATED QUESTION AND ANSWER BOOKS

How Things Work. Simon & Schuster, 1984
Simon & Schuster Color Illustrated Book of Questions and Answers. Simon & Schuster, 1989
What Is It? Simon & Schuster, 1984
When Did It Happen? Simon & Schuster, 1986
Where Is It? Simon & Schuster, 1985
Who Were They? Simon & Schuster, 1985
Why Things Are. Simon & Schuster, 1984

These oversize volumes use a question-and-answer format to cover a gamut of topics, primarily in the sciences. There is an index. Good for casual readers grades 5-9.

SKILLS ON STUDYING

BERRY, Marilyn

Help Is on the Way for Book Reports. Childrens, 1984
Help Is on the Way for Charts & Graphs. Childrens, 1986
Help Is on the Way for Grammar. Childrens, 1987
Help Is on the Way for Group Reports. Childrens, 1987
Help Is on the Way for Library Skills. Childrens, 1985
Help Is on the Way for Listening Skills. Childrens, 1987
Help Is on the Way for Maps & Globes. Childrens, 1987
Help Is on the Way for Math Skills. Childrens, 1986
Help Is on the Way for Memory Skills. Childrens, 1985
Help Is on the Way for Oral Reports. Childrens, 1987
Help Is on the Way for Outlining Skills. Childrens, 1986
Help Is on the Way for Punctuation. Childrens, 1987
Help Is on the Way for Reading Skills. Childrens, 1984
Help Is on the Way for Schoolwork. Childrens, 1984
Help Is on the Way for Science Skills. Childrens, 1987
Help Is on the Way for Spelling Skills. Childrens, 1986
Help Is on the Way for Study Habits. Childrens, 1985
Help Is on the Way for Taking Notes. Childrens, 1986
Help Is on the Way for Tests. Childrens, 1985
Help Is on the Way for Thinking Skills. Childrens, 1987
Help Is on the Way for Using Resource Materials. Childrens, 1986
Help Is on the Way for Word Skills. Childrens, 1986
Help Is on the Way for Writing Skills. Childrens, 1987
Help Is on the Way for Written Reports. Childrens, 1984

The focus of this series is study tips for students. They are presented in brief, readable form with cartoon-type illustrations that will appeal to readers. While the 48-page limit makes them approachable, quick reading, they might be more useful (and economical) if they were consolidated in fewer, larger volumes. In the meantime, libraries will have to limit themselves to those topics most often asked for by students and their parents, grades 3-8.

SKYLIGHT BOOKS

ANDERSON, Norman D.

Lemurs. Putnam, 1984

BILLINGS, Charlene W.

Fiber Optics. Putnam, 1986
The Loon. Putnam, 1988
Microchip. Putnam, 1984
Space Station. Putnam, 1986

BLASSINGAME, Wyatt

Porcupines. Putnam, 1982
The Strange Armadillo. Putnam, 1983

CASEY, Denise

The American Marten. Putnam, 1988
Black-Footed Ferret. Putnam, 1985

CHACE, Earl G.

Rattlesnakes. Putnam, 1984

HOPF, Alice L.

Bats. Putnam, 1985
Hyenas. Putnam, 1983

HUNT, Patricia
Gibbons. Putnam, 1983
Snowy Owls. Putnam, 1982
Tigers. Putnam, 1981
LEWIS, Bruce
Meet the Computer. Putnam, 1977
MCDEARMON, Kay
Orangutans. Putnam, 1983
MINTA, Kathryn A.
The Digging Badger. Putnam, 1985
NIXON, Hershell H., and **Joan Lowery NIXON**
Land under the Sea. Putnam, 1985

Primarily, this series covers natural science, particularly animals. The books provide good introductory material, with scientific history and descriptive chapters. There are black and white photos. The reading level is appropriate for grades 5 and up. Many of these animals are not found in individual treatments elsewhere.

SMALL WORLD
PETTY, Kate
Arctic Lands. Watts, 1988
Bees and Wasps. Watts, 1987
Dinosaurs. Watts, 1988
Eskimos. Watts, 1987
Plains Indians. Watts, 1988
Reptiles. Watts, 1987
Vikings. Watts, 1987
Whales. Watts, 1988

This is a super series for young readers that explores science and social studies topics. Color drawings accompany simple but informative texts written at the 2nd-4th grade level. An index is provided.

SPACE AND AVIATION
BERLINER, Don
Airplanes of the Future. Lerner, 1987
Before the Wright Brothers. Lerner, 1989
Distance Flights. Lerner, 1989
Research Airplanes: Testing the Boundaries of Flight. Lerner, 1988
Research Balloons: Exploring Hidden Worlds. Lerner, 1988
BRIGGS, Carole S.
Women in Space: Reaching the Last Frontier. Lerner, 1988
MOULTON, Robert R.
First to Fly. Lerner, 1983
WINTER, Frank H.
Comet Watch: The Return of Halley's Comet. Lerner, 1986

Kids with a fascination for aviation will gravitate to this series. The titles run the gamut from the early days of aircraft clear up to modern testing practices. A little background is presented first, then brief write ups of specific models are given, with an accompanying photo. Grades 4 and up. Index.

SPACE LIBRARY
VOGT, Gregory
Space Explorers. Watts, 1990
Space Laboratories. Watts, 1989
Space Satellites. Watts, 1987
Space Stations. Watts, 1990

Space Walking. Watts, 1987
Spaceships. Watts, 1989
Like Watts's Space Scientist series, this one covers topics related to space exploration. This one emphasizes text coverage more than illustration, although there are a number of color photos. Historical developments, current endeavors, and future possibilities are all examined. The author provides a chronology of important dates, glossary, and index. Grades 5-12.

SPACE SCIENTIST
COUPER, Heather
Space Probes and Satellites. Watts, 1987
Telescopes and Observatories. Watts, 1987
COUPER, Heather, and **Nigel HENBEST**
Galaxies and Quasars. Watts, 1987
The Moon. Watts, 1987
Space aficionados will find a lot to like in this series. These oversize books with plentiful color illustrations explain in a detailed manner a number of space-related subjects. Note: not only are American achievements noted, but also those of other countries. There is a glossary, index, and information on places and groups to contact for further information. Grades 5-8.

SPORTS ACHIEVERS
AASENG, Nathan
Carl Lewis. Lerner, 1985
Dwight Gooden. Lerner, 1988
Eric Heiden. Lerner, 1980
Florence Griffith Joyner. Lerner, 1990
Jose Canseco. Lerner, 1990
Pete Rose. Lerner, 1981
Steve Carlton. Lerner, 1984
DEEGAN, Paul J.
Michael Jordan. Lerner, 1988
RABER, Thomas R.
Bo Jackson. Lerner, 1990
Joe Montana. Lerner, 1990
WASHINGTON, Rosemary G.
Mary Lou Retton. Lerner, 1985
Sports fans will enjoy this series, loaded with biographical and statistical information on current sports figures. Black and white photos. Grades 4-7. No index.

SPORTS CLOSE-UPS 2
CREIGHTON, Susan
Greg Norman. Crestwood, 1988
DUDEN, Jane
Shirley Muldowney. Crestwood, 1988
ELIOT, Chip
Ivan Lendl. Crestwood, 1988
GLOECKNER, Carolyn
Fernando Valenzuela. Crestwood, 1985
GOODMAN, Michael
Lawrence Taylor. Crestwood, 1988
Magic Johnson. Crestwood, 1988
LEDER, Jane Mersky
Marcus Allen. Crestwood, 1985
Martina Navratilova. Crestwood, 1985
Walter Payton. Crestwood, 1985
Wayne Gretsky. Crestwood, 1985

MCCUNE, Dan
Michael Jordan. Crestwood, 1988
MONROE, Judy
Dave Winfield. Crestwood, 1988
John Elway. Crestwood, 1988
Steffi Graf. Crestwood, 1988
NEWMAN, Matthew
Dwight Gooden. Crestwood, 1986
Larry Bird. Crestwood, 1986
Lynette Woodard. Crestwood, 1986
Mary Decker Slaney. Crestwood, 1986
Patrick Ewing. Crestwood, 1986
NIELSEN, Nancy
Eric Dickerson. Crestwood, 1988
PHILLIPS, Louis
Willie Shoemaker. Crestwood, 1988
WEBER, Bruce
Sparky Anderson. Crestwood, 1988

Like most sports bios, these begin with a little information about the early years, especially as they relate to athletic development. The balance of the material deals with their sports life and discusses important games. There are black and white photos throughout, and a list of statistics at the end. No index.

SPORTS FOR ME BOOKS
BRIGGS, Carole S.
Diving Is for Me. Lerner, 1983
Skin Diving Is for Me. Lerner, 1981
Waterskiing Is for Me. Lerner, 1986
CHAPPELL, Annette Jo
Skiing Is for Me. Lerner, 1978
CHILDRESS, Valerie, and **Jane NELSON**
Drill Team Is for Me. Lerner, 1986
DICKMEYER, Lowell A.
Baseball Is for Me. Lerner, 1978
Basketball Is for Me. Lerner, 1980
Football Is for Me. Lerner, 1979
Hockey Is for Me. Lerner, 1978
Skateboarding Is for Me. Lerner, 1978
DICKMEYER, Lowell A., and **Lin ROLENS**
Ice Skating Is for Me. Lerner, 1980
HAMMOND, Mildred
Square Dancing Is for Me. Lerner, 1983
HAWKINS, Jim W.
Baton Twirling Is for Me. Lerner, 1982
Cheerleading Is for Me. Lerner, 1981
HOLM, John Ralph, and **Lori HARMAN**
Judo Is for Me. Lerner, 1986
HYDEN, Tom, and **Tim ANDERSON**
Rock Climbing Is for Me. Lerner, 1984
LERNER, Mark
Bowling Is for Me. Lerner, 1981
Golf Is for Me. Lerner, 1982
Quarter-Midget Racing Is for Me. Lerner, 1981
Racquetball Is for Me. Lerner, 1983

MORAN, Tom
Bicycle Motocross Is for Me. Lerner, 1982
Canoeing Is for Me. Lerner, 1984
Frisbee Disc Flying Is for Me. Lerner, 1982
NEFF, Fred
Karate Is for Me. Lerner, 1980
Running Is for Me. Lerner, 1980
PRESTON-MAUKS, Susan
Field Hockey Is for Me. Lerner, 1983
Synchronized Swimming Is for Me. Lerner, 1983
TEMPLE, Nancy Marie, and **Rande ARONSON**
Juggling Is for Me. Lerner, 1986
TERKEL, Susan Neiburg
Yoga Is for Me. Lerner, 1982
THOMAS, Art
Bicycling Is for Me. Lerner, 1979
Fencing Is for Me. Lerner, 1982
Fishing Is for Me. Lerner, 1980
Wrestling Is for Me. Lerner, 1979
THOMAS, Art, and **Laura STORMS**
Boxing Is for Me. Lerner, 1982
WASHINGTON, Rosemary G.
Cross-Country Skiing Is for Me. Lerner, 1982
Gymnastics Is for Me. Lerner, 1979

Younger readers can learn about a wide variety of sports in this series. Told in the first person, with black and white photos of the children at play, these books follow youngsters as they learn and participate in a sport. A little history, description of equipment, and basic how-tos are provided. A child really could not learn how to do a sport from this series, but they could learn enough to want to take lessons. Grades 2-5. Glossary.

***SPORTS HEROES LIBRARY**
AASENG, Nathan
Baseball's Ace Relief Pitchers. Lerner, 1984
Baseball's Brilliant Managers. Lerner, 1982
Baseball's Finest Pitchers. Lerner, 1980
Baseball's Power Hitters. Lerner, 1983
Basketball's High Flyers. Lerner, 1980
Basketball's Playmakers. Lerner, 1983
Basketball's Power Players. Lerner, 1985
Basketball's Sharpshooters. Lerner, 1983
Comeback Stars of Pro Sports. Lerner, 1983
Football's Breakaway Backs. Lerner, 1980
Football's Crushing Blockers. Lerner, 1982
Football's Cunning Coaches. Lerner, 1981
Football's Daring Defensive Backs. Lerner, 1984
Football's Fierce Defenses. Lerner, 1980
Football's Hard-Hitting Linebackers. Lerner, 1984
Football's Punishing Pass Rushers. Lerner, 1984
Football's Steadiest Kickers. Lerner, 1981
Football's Super Bowl Champions I-VIII. Lerner, 1982
Football's Super Bowl Champions IX-XVI. Lerner, 1982
Football's Sure-Handed Receivers. Lerner, 1980
Football's Toughest Tight Ends. Lerner, 1981
Football's Winning Quarterbacks. Lerner, 1980
Hockey's Fearless Goalies. Lerner, 1984

Hockey's Super Scorers. Lerner, 1984
Little Giants of Pro Sports. Lerner, 1983
Memorable World Series Moments. Lerner, 1982
Superstars Stopped Short. Lerner, 1982
Supersubs of Pro Sports. Lerner, 1983
Track's Magnificent Milers. Lerner, 1981
Winning Men of Tennis. Lerner, 1981
Winning Women of Tennis. Lerner, 1981
World-Class Marathoners. Lerner, 1982

This sports series features write ups of outstanding players, with the emphasis on their athletic achievements. Career and game highlights are presented, along with black and white photos from their games. Ages 10-14. No index.

SPORTS LEGENDS

HAHN, James, and **Lynn HAHN**
Casey! Crestwood, 1981
Killy! Crestwood, 1981
King! Crestwood, 1981
Patty! Crestwood, 1981
Thorpe! Crestwood, 1981
Zaharias! Crestwood, 1981

This series emphasizes the sports career of each person, with several chapters on their early development. Only a brief afterword mentions what they are doing now. Although the vocabulary is 3rd to 4th grade level, the style is for older readers, which makes these good choices for reluctant readers. No index.

SPORTS STARS

BUCK, Ray
Cal Ripken, Jr.: All-Star Shortstop. Childrens, 1985
Pete Rose: "Charlie Hustle". Childrens, 1986
Tiffany Chin: A Dream on Ice. Childrens, 1986

CONRAD, Dick
Tony Dorsett: From Heisman to Super Bowl in One Year. Childrens, 1979

DONOVAN, Pete
Carol Johnston: The One-armed Gymnast. Childrens, 1982

HENKEL, Cathy
Mary Decker: America's Nike. Childrens, 1984

HERBERT, Mike
Michael Jordan: The Bulls' Air Power. Childrens, 1987

JANOFF, Barry
Alan Trammell: Tiger on the Prowl. Childrens, 1985
Hulk Hogan: Eye of the Tiger. Childrens, 1986

LEVIN, Richard
Magic Johnson: Court Magician. Childrens, 1981

LITTWIN, Mike
Fernando Valenzuela: The Screwball Artist. Childrens, 1983

LUNDGREN, Hal
Calvin Murphy: The Giant Slayer. Childrens, 1982
Dale Murphy: A Gentleman. Childrens, 1986
Mary Lou Retton: Gold Medal Gymnast. Childrens, 1985
Moses Malone: Philadelphia's Peerless Center. Childrens, 1983
Ryne Sandberg: The Triple Threat. Childrens, 1986

ROBERTS, Andre
William Perry: The Refrigerator. Childrens, 1986

ROSENTHAL, Bert
Carl Lewis: The Second Jesse Owens. Childrens, 1984

Darryl Dawkins: The Master of Disaster. Childrens, 1982
Dwight Gooden: King of the K's. Childrens, 1985
Isaiah Thomas: Pocket Magic. Childrens, 1983
Larry Bird: Cool Man on the Court. Childrens, 1981
Lynette Woodard: The First Female Globetrotter. Childrens, 1986
Sugar Ray Leonard: The Baby-faced Boxer. Childrens, 1982
Wayne Gretzky: The Great Gretzky. Childrens, 1983

RUBIN, Bob
Dan Marino: Wonder Boy Quarterback. Childrens, 1985

STEIN, R. Conrad
Walter Payton: Record-Breaking Runner. Childrens, 1987

Young sports fans will be delighted with this entry. Written at the 2nd-4th grade level, many photos accompany the easy-to-read text. A little information on the sports hero's childhood and personality is given, but the primary emphasis is on the career. Appended to the text is a chronology.

SPORTS TALK

AASENG, Nate
Baseball's Greatest Teams. Lerner, 1985
Baseball's Worst Teams. Lerner, 1985
College Football's Hottest Rivalries. Lerner, 1987
Football's Incredible Bulks. Lerner, 1987
Football's Most Controversial Calls. Lerner, 1985
Football's Most Shocking Upsets. Lerner, 1985
Great Summer Olympic Moments. Lerner, 1990
Great Winter Olympic Moments. Lerner, 1990
Pro Sports' Greatest Rivalries. Lerner, 1985
Record Breakers of Pro Sports. Lerner, 1987
Ultramarathons. Lerner, 1987

Lerner has a number of sports highlights books; these profile individual stars or events with 3 pages per person, accompanied by black and white photos. Sports fans and reluctant readers will check these out. Records are provided at the end. Grades 5-8. No index.

STARTING POINTS

PETTY, Kate
Fire. Watts, 1990

SWALLOW, Su
Water. Watts, 1990

THOMSON, Ruth
Autumn. Watts, 1989
Spring. Watts, 1990
Summer. Watts, 1990
Winter. Watts, 1989

Wonderful choices for early education teachers or parents with young children, this series combines information with experiences and crafts that are colorful, do-able, and utilize easily found materials. The titles relating to the seasons are particularly useful, with seasonal signs to observe, plants to collect, and simple crafts. Highly recommended for preschool-3rd grade.

STATE REPORTS

AYLESWORTH, Thomas G., and **Virginia L. AYLESWORTH**
Atlantic: Virginia, West Virginia, District of Columbia. Chelsea, 1991
Eastern Great Lakes: Ohio, Indiana, Michigan. Chelsea, 1991
Great Plains: Montana, North Dakota, South Dakota, Wyoming, Nebraska. Chelsea, 1991
Lower Atlantic: North Carolina, South Carolina. Chelsea, 1991

Mid-Atlantic: Pennsylvania, Delaware, Maryland. Chelsea, 1991
Northern New England: Maine, Vermont, New Hampshire. Chelsea, 1991
Northwest: Washington, Oregon, Alaska, Idaho. Chelsea, 1991
Pacific: California, Hawaii. Chelsea, 1991
South: Mississippi, Alabama, Florida. Chelsea, 1991
South Central: Louisiana, Arkansas, Missouri, Kansas, Oklahoma. Chelsea, 1991
Southeast: Kentucky, Tennessee, Georgia. Chelsea, 1991
Southern New England: Connecticut, Massachusetts, Rhode Island. Chelsea, 1991
Southwest: Texas, New Mexico, Colorado. Chelsea, 1991
Upper Atlantic: New York, New Jersey. Chelsea, 1991
U.S. Territories and Possessions: Guam, Puerto Rico, U.S. Virgin Islands, American Samoa, North Mariana Islands. Chelsea, 1991
West: Arizona, Nevada, Utah. Chelsea, 1991
Western Great Lakes: Illinois, Iowa, Wisconsin, Minnesota. Chelsea, 1991

This series is a companion to Let's Discover the States. Here the authors take the same information on the states: geography, economy, government, plus the ever-popular state seal, bird, tree, song, etc., but in an easy to find tabular format. There is also a biographical section. Color photos, maps, bibliography, index. Grades 4 and up.

STOPWATCH

BACK, Christine

Bean and Plant. Silver Burdette, 1986

BACK, Christine, and **Jens OLESEN**

Chicken and Egg. Silver Burdette, 1986

BACK, Christine, and **Barrie WATTS**

Spider's Web. Silver Burdette, 1986
Tadpole and Frog. Silver Burdette, 1986

COLDREY, Jennifer

Strawberry. Silver Burdette, 1989

OLESEN, Jens

Snail. Silver Burdette, 1986

WATTS, Barrie

Apple Tree. Silver Burdette, 1987
Birds' Nest. Silver Burdette, 1987
Butterfly and Caterpillar. Silver Burdette, 1989
Dandelion. Silver Burdette, 1987
Dragonfly. Silver Burdette, 1989
Hamster. Silver Burdette, 1986
Honeybee. Silver Burdette, 1990
Ladybug. Silver Burdette, 1987
Moth. Silver Burdette, 1991
Mushroom. Silver Burdette, 1986
Potato. Silver Burdette, 1989
Tomato. Silver Burdette, 1990

These early science books show the youngest readers how these species live and develop. The color photos are excellent; a section at the end ties the photos in with refresher questions. Ages 4-9.

STORY OF...

ANDERSON, Dave

The Story of Basketball. Morrow, 1988
The Story of Football. Morrow, 1985

RITTER, Lawrence S.

The Story of Baseball. Morrow, 1983

Written by well-known sports writers, these three books are fantastic. They chronicle the beginnings of the three most popular sports in America and end up with the current situations in each sport. Explanations are given for who, what, when, why and how. These books will go well in any junior or senior high school library and are great pleasure reading.

STORY OF THE EARTH

BENDER, Lionel

Cave. Watts, 1989
Desert. Watts, 1989
Glacier. Watts, 1989
Island. Watts, 1989
Lake. Watts, 1989
Mountain. Watts, 1989
River. Watts, 1988
Volcano. Watts, 1988

This outstanding new series touches all the bases in earth studies. The landform is described, as well as the prevailing characteristics. Diagrams and photos clarify land conditions, and maps indicate where these landforms are located. The impact of the elements in forming the earth's landscapes is examined, and famous examples are given. Flora and fauna, technology, and human adaptations to each situation are presented. An excellent glossary is appended.

SULLIVAN, George

Famous Air Force Bombers. Putnam, 1985
Famous Air Force Fighters. Putnam, 1985
Famous Blimps and Airships. Putnam, 1988
Famous Navy Attack Planes. Putnam, 1986
Famous Navy Fighter Planes. Putnam, 1986
Famous U.S. Spy Planes. Putnam, 1987

Each of these books describes famous ships in the U.S. air fleet; for example, the book about airships includes the airship *Akron* and the *Graf Zeppelin*. There are 2 or more pages of description and photos of each plane, along with statistical and historical data. Aircraft buffs grades 4 and up will enjoy these.

SUPER-CHARGED!

ANDERSEN, T. J.

Baja Cars. Crestwood, 1988
Power Boat Racing. Crestwood, 1988

CREIGHTON, Susan

Funny Cars. Crestwood, 1988

ESTREM, Paul

ATVs. Crestwood, 1987
BMXs. Crestwood, 1987
Motocross Cycles. Crestwood, 1987
Rocket-Powered Cars. Crestwood, 1987

GRIMM, Rosemary

Stunt Planes. Crestwood, 1988
Truck and Tractor Pullers. Crestwood, 1988

HARRIS, Jack

Dream Cars. Crestwood, 1988
Personal Watercraft. Crestwood, 1988

HOLDER, Bill

Monster 4-Wheelers. Crestwood, 1987

KEATON, Phyllis Hersh

Buggies. Crestwood, 1988

LEDER, Jane Mersky
Exotic Cars. Crestwood, 1987
LORD, Suzanne
Radio-Controlled Model Airplanes. Crestwood, 1988
NIELSEN, Nancy
Bicycle Racing. Crestwood, 1988
ROBINSON, Scott
Indy Cars. Crestwood, 1988
SCHLABACH, Cara
Touring Cycles. Crestwood, 1987
SOSA, Maria
Dragsters. Crestwood, 1987
STEWART, Gail
Motorcycle Racing. Crestwood, 1988

These are high-interest hobby areas, written for grades 5 and up. Each book begins with a brief history, then concentrates on technical advancements, how-tos of the hobby, and even discusses meets, shows, and competitions. There are color photos, addresses for further information, and a glossary/index.

SUPERWHEELS AND THRILL SPORTS
AYRES, Carter M.
Soaring. Lerner, 1985
BENSON, Rolf
Skydiving. Lerner, 1979
BERLINER, Don
Aerobatics. Lerner, 1980
Airplane Racing. Lerner, 1979
Helicopters. Lerner, 1983
Home-Built Airplanes. Lerner, 1979
Personal Airplanes. Lerner, 1982
Record-Breaking Airplanes. Lerner, 1985
Unusual Airplanes. Lerner, 1985
Yesterday's Airplanes. Lerner, 1980
BRIGGS, Carole S.
Ballooning. Lerner, 1985
Sport Diving. Lerner, 1982
DAVID, Andrew, and **Tom MORAN**
River Thrill Sports. Lerner, 1983
DEXLER, Paul R.
Yesterday's Cars. Lerner, 1979
DORIN, Patrick C.
Yesterday's Trucks. Lerner, 1982
GEORGE, Barbara
Bicycle Road Racing. Lerner, 1977
Bicycle Track Racing. Lerner, 1977
GRIFFIN, John Q.
Motorcycles on the Move. Lerner, 1976
HARGROVE, Jim, and **S. A. JOHNSON**
Mountain Climbing. Lerner, 1983
HATMAN, Paul W.
Yesterday's Fire Engines. Lerner, 1980
JONES, Claire
Sailboat Racing. Lerner, 1981

KNUDSON, Richard L.
Classic Sports Cars. Lerner, 1979
Land Speed Record Breakers. Lerner, 1981
Model Cars. Lerner, 1981
Racing Yesterday's Cars. Lerner, 1985
Rallying. Lerner, 1981
Restoring Yesterday's Cars. Lerner, 1983
KRISHEF, Robert K.
The Indianapolis 500. Lerner, 1978
MORAN, Tom
Bicycle Motocross Racing. Lerner, 1985
MUNDALE, Susan
Mopeds: The Go-Everywhere Bikes. Lerner, 1979
POPP, Dennis
Ice Racing. Lerner, 1973
PULEO, Nicole
Drag Racing. Lerner, 1973
PURSELL, Thomas F.
Bicycles on Parade. Lerner, 1980
RAE, Rusty
The World's Biggest Motorcycle Race: The Daytona 200. Lerner, 1978
STRUTHERS, John
Dinosaur Cars: Late Great Cars from 1945-1966. Lerner, 1977
WASHINGTON, Rosemary G.
Karting: Racing's Fast Little Cars. Lerner, 1980
YAW, John, and **Rusty RAE**
Grand National Championship Races. Lerner, 1978

Wheeled vehicles of many kinds capture the interest of younger readers, especially boys, so this series has a natural audience. The history of its development and the mechanics of how it works are tackled first. Then the authors describe the many varieties of vehicle that are available and even provide basic specifications for them. Many illustrations add to the appeal. Grades 4-8. No glossary or index.

SURVIVAL
EAST, Ben
1—*Danger in the Air*. Crestwood, 1979
2—*Desperate Search*. Crestwood, 1979
3—*Frozen Terror*. Crestwood, 1979
4—*Mistaken Journey*. Crestwood, 1979
5—*Trapped in Devil's Hole*. Crestwood, 1979

Ben East was an editor of *Outdoor Life* magazine. These stories are real life adventures told to him and recounted by those involved. The writing is spare and factual but hardly as exciting as it could be. Marginal choices for grades 3-6.

SURVIVAL
BARTON, Miles
Animal Rights. Watts, 1987
Zoos and Game Reserves. Watts, 1988
BRIGHT, Michael
The Dying Sea. Watts, 1988
Killing for Luxury. Watts, 1988
Saving the Whale. Watts, 1987
BURTON, John
Close to Extinction. Watts, 1988

With renewed interest in the survival of the planet, this timely series should find a lot of users. Like others published by Watts, this one is oversize, with plentiful color photos and lots of factual information. The series pulls no punches, using graphic photos and facts to get across the message about wildlife facing extinction. The fact section at the end of each volume is truly horrifying. Pertinent addresses are given. Grades 5-8.

TAKE A TRIP TO...

GRIFFITHS, John

Take a Trip to Haiti. Watts, 1989
Take a Trip to Panama. Watts, 1989
Take a Trip to Puerto Rico. Watts, 1989

LYE, Keith

Take a Trip to Austria. Watts, 1987
Take a Trip to Cuba. Watts, 1987
Take a Trip to East Germany. Watts, 1987
Take a Trip to Finland. Watts, 1986
Take a Trip to Hawaii. Watts, 1988
Take a Trip to Hungary. Watts, 1986
Take a Trip to Jamaica. Watts, 1988
Take a Trip to Morocco. Watts, 1988
Take a Trip to Nepal. Watts, 1988
Take a Trip to Nicaragua. Watts, 1988
Take a Trip to Peru. Watts, 1987
Take a Trip to Romania. Watts, 1988
Take a Trip to Syria. Watts, 1988
Take a Trip to Thailand. Watts, 1986
Take a Trip to Turkey. Watts, 1987
Take a Trip to Venezuela. Watts, 1988
Take a Trip to Wales. Watts, 1986
Take a Trip to Yugoslavia. Watts, 1987
Take a Trip to Zimbabwe. Watts, 1987

SAMARASEKARA, Dhanapala

Take a Trip to Sri Lanka. Watts, 1987

TAMES, Richard

Take a Trip to Iran. Watts, 1989
Take a Trip to Iraq. Watts, 1989
Take a Trip to Lebanon. Watts, 1989
Take a Trip to Libya. Watts, 1989

Aimed at the youngest readers (grades K-3), this series features a controlled vocabulary and color photos. The coverage is sufficient to arouse interest, but not really enough if the child needs to do a report.

TAKING A STAND

HANMER, Trudy J.

Taking a Stand against Sexism and Sex Discrimination. Watts, 1990

KRONENWETTER, Michael

Taking a Stand against Human Rights Abuses. Watts, 1990

MCKISSACK, Patricia, and **Frederick MCKISSACK**

Taking a Stand against Racism and Racial Discrimination. Watts, 1990

NEWTON, David E.

Taking a Stand against Environmental Pollution. Watts, 1990

THRO, Ellen

Taking a Stand against Nuclear War. Watts, 1990

This series provides its readers with background information on the issues that face the world today. These books emphasize how a high school student can become involved in these issues, by providing historical background, opposing viewpoints and profiles of people who are already involved. This series provides a good look at today's issues for high school students. Each book includes an index and bibliography.

TAKING CARE OF YOUR PET

POPE, Joyce

Taking Care of Your Cat. Watts, 1990
Taking Care of Your Dog. Watts, 1990
Taking Care of Your Fish. Watts, 1990
Taking Care of Your Gerbil. Watts, 1990
Taking Care of Your Guinea Pig. Watts, 1990
Taking Care of Your Hamster. Watts, 1990
Taking Care of Your Rabbit. Watts, 1990
Taking Care of Your Rats and Mice. Watts, 1990

Kids want pets, and this series will show even the youngest how to care for them. Each volume opens with a list of petkeepers' responsibilities. Next comes an overview of what kind of pet the animal will be and what to expect of it. All the basics are covered: housing, feeding, exercise, and health. The vocabulary is suitable for 2nd grade and up, with large color photos to enhance the text. There is a quiz at the end, and a checklist for choosing and caring for the pet. Each is indexed.

TAKING PART

BANKS, David
Sarah Ferguson: The Royal Redhead. Dillon, 1987

BLACKNALL, Carolyn
Sally Ride: America's First Woman in Space. Dillon, 1984

CALLAHAN, Dorothy S.
Julie Krone: A Winning Jockey. Dillon, 1990

CLARK, Steve
Wade Boggs: Baseball's Star Hitter. Dillon, 1988

COLLINS, Tom
Steven Spielberg: Creator of E.T. Dillon, 1983

DIFRANCO, Anthony
Pope John Paul II: Bringing Love to a Troubled World. Dillon, 1983

GALICICH, Anne
Samantha Smith: A Journey for Peace. Dillon, 1987

LEE, Betsy
Judy Blume's Story. Dillon, 1981

MICKLOS, John Jr.
Leonard Nimoy: A Star's Trek. Dillon, 1988

ROBISON, Nancy
Janet Jackson: In Control. Dillon, 1987

SPIES, Karen
Raffi: The Children's Voice. Dillon, 1989

WENZEL, Dorothy
Ann Bancroft: On Top of the World. Dillon, 1989

WESTMAN, Paul
Jacques Cousteau: Free Flight Undersea. Dillon, 1980

WOODS, Geraldine
Jim Henson: From Puppets to Muppets. Dillon, 1987

WOODS, Harold, and **Geraldine WOODS**
Bill Cosby: Making America Laugh and Learn. Dillon, 1983

Good factual biographies for readers grades 2-5, these present the early life, but stress events that led to fame. The biographees are all current people of interest to kids, but there are 2 drawbacks: line drawings are used rather than photos, which should be easily obtainable, and there is no index.

TECH TALK BOOKS

RADLAUER, Ed, and **Ruth RADLAUER**

Auto Tech Talk. Childrens, 1987

Nuclear Tech Talk. Childrens, 1985

RADLAUER, Ruth, and **Ed RADLAUER**

Computer Tech Talk. Childrens, 1984

Radio Tech Talk. Childrens, 1984

Robot Tech Talk. Childrens, 1985

Tech Talk books are actually mini specialized illustrated dictionaries. Definitions, descriptions, and cross-references to related words are given. Most students need material for reports or extended subject reading. This series will not fill either function, but may be useful where specialized scientific definitions are explained on the 4th-8th grade level.

TECHNOLOGY IN ACTION

LAMBERT, Mark

Aircraft Technology. Watts, 1990

Car Technology. Watts, 1990

Farming Technology. Watts, 1990

Ship Technology. Watts, 1990

TV and Video Technology. Watts, 1990

MASON, John

Spacecraft Technology. Watts, 1990

POLLARD, Michael

Train Technology. Watts, 1990

RAYNER, Ralph

Undersea Technology. Watts, 1990

The development of technology is examined in this series, beginning with its early history up to current trends. Types of equipment and how they are constructed and used are also explored. There is a glossary, index, and bibliography. Lots of illustrations. Grades 5-9.

TEEN GUIDES

BROWN, Fern G.

Teen Guide to Caring for Your Unborn Baby. Watts, 1989

Teen Guide to Childbirth. Watts, 1988

FRIEDRICH, Liz

Teen Guide to Married Life. Watts, 1989

HAWKSLEY, Jane

Teen Guide to Pregnancy, Drugs and Smoking. Watts, 1989

NOURSE, Alan E.

Teen Guide to AIDS Prevention. Watts, 1990

Teen Guide to Birth Control. Watts, 1988

Teen Guide to Safe Sex. Watts, 1988

Teen Guide to Survival. Watts, 1990

SILVERSTEIN, Herma

Teen Guide to Single Parenting. Watts, 1989

These guides provide an excellent resource for teens of all ages by providing information that can help them make responsible decisions. Most of the titles deal with sexual awareness and are greatly needed, especially books such as these that are written for the reluctant reader. Each book includes a glossary, color photographs, illustrations and an index. These are also good for parents to read and give to their children.

THINK SERIES

ASIMOV, Isaac

Space. Walker, 1990

BOUVIER, Leon

Immigration. Walker, 1988

COONEY, James A.
Foreign Policy. Walker, 1988
HAWLEY, Richard
Drugs and Society. Walker, 1990
JAKOBSON, Cathryn
Teenage Pregnancy. Walker, 1988
KENNEDY, Moorhead, and **Terrell ARNOLD**
Terrorism. Walker, 1988
NAM, Charles
Our Population. Walker, 1988
SMOKE, Richard
Nuclear Arms Control. Walker, 1988
WILSON, Reginald
Our Rights. Walker, 1988
WOODS, Daniel, and **John WILLIAMSON**
Poverty. Walker, 1988

The Think Series takes a look at some of the important issues of the day. The subject content follows a similar format: definition of the issue, its history, contemporary analysis, and future possibilities. The books contain a glossary, index, and bibliography and there are some illustrations. Good for school reports for grades 7-10.

THIRTEEN COLONIES
FRADIN, Dennis
The Connecticut Colony. Childrens, 1990
The Georgia Colony. Childrens, 1989
The Maryland Colony. Childrens, 1990
The Massachusetts Colony. Childrens, 1986
The New Hampshire Colony. Childrens, 1987
The New Jersey Colony. Childrens, 1991
The New York Colony. Childrens, 1988
The Pennsylvania Colony. Childrens, 1988
The Rhode Island Colony. Childrens, 1989
The Virginia Colony. Childrens, 1986

These handsome books provide a thorough examination of the pre-colonial states, as well as their settlement and development as colonies. Daily life and attitudes in each colony are explored. An especially nice touch is the inclusion of 1+ pages of biographical material on several important figures in each colony's history. There are reproductions of maps, engravings, and paintings of the period to add flavor. A colonial time line ends each volume. An excellent choice for grades 5-12.

THOSE AMAZING...
HALTON, Cheryl Mays
Those Amazing Bats. Dillon, 1991
Those Amazing Eels. Dillon, 1990
Those Amazing Leeches. Dillon, 1990

So far author Halton is concentrating on pretty repulsive creatures, but she is doing a really good job of it. First, she discusses why the creature is reviled, then tells about their physical capabilities, their history, and how they are used today, including their cultivation. There is a section on how to collect and keep the animal, with possible experiments involving them included. An appendix tells about the scientific classifications and where one can obtain them by mail. Color photos, bibliography, glossary, index. Grades 4-8.

THROUGH THE MICROSCOPE

BENDER, Lionel

Atoms and Cells. Watts, 1990

The Body. Watts, 1989

Forensic Detection. Watts, 1990

CORBISHLEY, Mike

Detecting the Past. Watts, 1990

STIDWORTHY, John

Insects. Watts, 1989

Plants and Seeds. Watts, 1990

A page introduces the workings of the microscope. Then, fascinating color photos show various lifeforms, from cells to plants to insects as they appear microscopically. A drawing shows the atomic structure of some things. A brief project section, as well as another discussing microphotography or other related modern developments is included. Grades 5-9. Glossary, index.

TIME DETECTIVES SERIES

BERRILL, Margaret

Mummies, Masks, & Mourners. Lodestar, 1990

CORBISHLEY, Mike, and **Roger W. WALKER**

Secret Cities. Lodestar, 1989

RYAN, Peter

Explorers & Mapmakers. Lodestar, 1990

TREASE, Geoffrey

Hidden Treasure. Lodestar, 1989

Transplanted from England, this oversize series specializes in outstanding illustrations accompanying the texts. In addition to the obvious aspects of the subject, like Egyptian mummies in the first book, the authors also explore the less well-known, like the American basket mummies and the Viking burials. "Fact Boxes" define terms and offer statistics for further knowledge. For grades 4-12.

TIME QUEST BOOKS

BALLARD, Robert D.

The Lost Wreck of the Isis. Scholastic, 1990

The Secrets of Vesuvius. Scholastic, 1991

Exploring the Bismarck. Scholastic, 1991

The Spirit of Columbus. Scholastic, 1992

The Lost Expedition. Scholastic, 1992

The first book in this new series by adventurer/discoverer Robert Ballard (who found the *Titanic*) alternates the tale of his search for a sunken Greek sailing vessel, *Isis*, with the story of the vessel's origins and the culture of the time she was built. There are loads of illustrations. History buffs, archaeology mavens, and adventure lovers grades 5 and up will find this fascinating reading. Glossary, no index.

TIMELINES

STEWART, Gail B.

1900's. Crestwood, 1989

1910's. Crestwood, 1989

1920's. Crestwood, 1989

1930's. Crestwood, 1989

DUDEN, Jane

1940's. Crestwood, 1989

1950's. Crestwood, 1989

1960's. Crestwood, 1989

1970's. Crestwood, 1989

DUDEN, Jane, and **Gail B. STEWART**

1980's. Crestwood, 1991

While Decades begins recently, covering only from the 1950s to the present, this series starts much earlier. These books are smaller and use black and white photos from the time to highlight the text. Rather than give an overview, these hit the high spots for each year of the decade in politics, sports, inventions, economy, and leisure activities. Grades 4-8. Index.

TODAY'S WORLD

ARDLEY, Neil

Language and Communications. Watts, 1989
The World of the Atom. Watts, 1989

BENDER, Lionel

Birds and Mammals. Watts, 1988
Fish to Reptiles. Watts, 1988
Invertebrates. Watts, 1988
Plants. Watts, 1988

DIXON, Dougal

The Planet Earth. Watts, 1989

GAMLIN, Linda

The Human Body. Watts, 1988
The Human Race. Watts, 1988
Life on Earth. Watts, 1988
Origins of Life. Watts, 1988

JOHNSTONE, Hugh

Aircraft and Rockets. Watts, 1989
Land and Sea Transport. Watts, 1989

KERROD, Robin

Future Energy and Resources. Watts, 1990
The Revolution in Industry. Watts, 1990

LAFFERTY, Peter

Energy and Light. Watts, 1989

LYE, Keith

Africa. Watts, 1987
The Americas. Watts, 1987
Asia and Australia. Watts, 1987
Europe. Watts, 1987

THOMAS, Jane

Population and Food. Watts, 1990

TIMMS, Howard

Living in the Future. Watts, 1990
Measuring and Computing. Watts, 1989

VBROVA, Zuza

Space and Astronomy. Watts, 1989

A wide variety of subjects are touched on in this series featuring the usual Watts format of oversize material with excellent color illustrations. Current developments, technology, and discoveries, possibilities of the future, anatomy, life cycles, and ecology are all addressed. Excellent choices for grades 5-8 as the subjects are needed.

TOP DOG

CASANOVA, Mary

The Golden Retriever. Crestwood, 1990

LORD, Suzanne

The Labrador Retriever. Crestwood, 1990

SANFORD, William, and **Carl GREEN**
The American Pit Bull Terrier. Crestwood, 1989
The Beagle. Crestwood, 1990
The Cocker Spaniel. Crestwood, 1990
The Dachshund. Crestwood, 1990
The Dalmation. Crestwood, 1989
The Doberman Pinscher. Crestwood, 1989
The German Shepherd. Crestwood, 1990
The Greyhound. Crestwood, 1989
The Old English Sheepdog. Crestwood, 1989
The Poodle. Crestwood, 1990
The Samoyed. Crestwood, 1989
The Shih Tzu. Crestwood, 1989
ZENK, Heather
The Siberian Husky. Crestwood, 1990

Many popular dog breeds are covered in this series. The history of the breed, physical and temperamental characteristics, choosing, caring for, and breeding of the animal is discussed. Potential problem aspects of the dog, as with the American Pit Bull, are also examined. Color photos will add to the appeal for dog lovers and owners ages 8 and up. Glossary, index.

TOPICS

BRIERS, Audrey
Money. Watts, 1987
CONNER, Edwina
Ghosts and the Supernatural. Watts, 1987
COOKE, Jean
Archaeology. Watts, 1987
Costumes and Clothes. Watts, 1987
CRAWFORD, Sue
The Seasons. Watts, 1988
DINEEN, Jacqueline
Ships. Watts, 1988
FRASER, Duncan
Photography. Watts, 1987
GRAHAM, Ian
Inventions. Watts, 1987
GUNSTON, Bill
Railroads. Watts, 1988
HOLLAND, Rowena
Farm Animals. Watts, 1987
LAMBERT, David
Earthquakes and Volcanoes. Watts, 1986
Maps and Globes. Watts, 1987
LANGLEY, Andrew
Jungles. Watts, 1987
Peoples of the World. Watts, 1986
The World of Sharks. Watts, 1988
MOSS, Miriam
Language and Writing. Watts, 1988
Zoos. Watts, 1987
RICKARD, Graham
Airports. Watts, 1987
Canals. Watts, 1988
Helicopters. Watts, 1988
Prisons and Punishment. Watts, 1987

Spacecraft. Watts, 1987
Tunnels. Watts, 1988
ROWLAND-ENTWISTLE, Theodore
Flags. Watts, 1988
Guns. Watts, 1988
TATLOW, Peter
The Olympics. Watts, 1988
Young readers will find this introductory series full of information. The authors provide historical background, illustrate how things work, and their many uses. Glossary vocabulary is highlighted. Grades 2-4.

TOUGH WHEELS
CHIRINIAN, Alain
Motorcycles. Messner, 1989
Muscle Cars. Messner, 1989
Race Cars. Messner, 1989
Weird Wheels. Messner, 1989
Kids are fascinated with cars, so this series will hit the mark with many, especially reluctant readers. The author spends several pages on a car model, first listing the specifications, then spending several paragraphs describing what is unusual about the vehicle. A photo of each car is provided in black and white. Grades 4-9. Glossary, index.

TUNDRA SPECIAL INTEREST BOOKS
KURELEK, William, and **Margaret S. ENGELHART**
They Sought a New World. Childrens, 1985
SHEMIE, Bonnie
Houses of Bark. Childrens, 1991
TAKASHIMA, Shizuye
A Child in Prison Camp. Childrens, 1991
TAYLOR, C. J.
How Two-Feather Was Saved from Loneliness. Childrens, 1991
The Tundra Books are meant to introduce young readers to unusual ethnic peoples and their lifestyles. They are so readable, they are almost like novels, with a low-key retelling of what life is or was like. There are many quotes from firsthand accounts of settlers and residents. There is a fact page, but these are really more for personal interest than school reports. No index.

TURNING POINTS IN AMERICAN HISTORY
COFFEY, Vincent J.
The Battle of Gettysburg. Silver, 1989
GLASSMAN, Bruce
The Crash of '29 and the New Deal. Silver, 1989
MCGRATH, Patrick
The Lewis and Clark Expedition. Silver, 1985
MCPHILLIPS, Martin
Battle of Trenton. Silver, 1985
The Constitutional Convention. Silver, 1986
Hiroshima. Silver, 1985
MILLER, Marilyn
The Bridge at Selma. Silver, 1985
D-Day. Silver, 1986
The Trans-Continental Railroad. Silver, 1985
OCHOA, George
The Fall of Mexico City. Silver, 1989
The Fall of Quebec. Silver, 1990

SIMONDS, Christopher
Samuel Slater's Mill. Silver, 1990
SMITH, Betsy Covington
Women Win the Vote. Silver, 1989
SMITH, Carter
The Korean War. Silver, 1990
One Giant Leap for Mankind. Silver, 1989
WESTERFIELD, Scott
The Berlin Airlift. Silver, 1989
WILLS, Charles
The Battle of the Little Bighorn. Silver, 1990
The Tet Offensive. Silver, 1989

These books provide detailed treatments of important historical events. The crisis is presented, the historical background is discussed, then the event itself comes under scrutiny. Original maps, paintings, and photographs are employed. Index, bibliography. Grades 5-8.

TWENTIETH CENTURY AMERICAN HISTORY
FEINBERG, Barbara S.
Watergate: Scandal in the White House. Watts, 1990
MCGOWEN, Tom
The Great Monkey Trial. Watts, 1990
SCHRAFF, Anne E.
The Great Depression and the New Deal. Watts, 1990

These books were written to allow young adults to have a better understanding of contemporary American history. Each book takes a look at the particular event from a political, economic and cultural viewpoint, and the lasting impact of the events is also discussed. Chronologies, bibliographies, indexes and notes are all included to make the events more readable. Grades 9 and up.

UNDERSTANDING DISEASE
STEDMAN, Nancy
The Common Cold and Influenza. Messner, 1987
TIGER, Steven
Arthritis. Messner, 1986
Diabetes. Messner, 1988
Heart Disease. Messner, 1986

While there are a number of books on the human body, there are very few on diseases, so this new series is very welcome. The basic operation of the well body is discussed first; then the disease is described; then current treatment. While the information provided on the diseases is accurate and informative, a mere page and a half is given over to treatment. A child doing a report might need more information in this area, and certainly a child researching their own ailment could use more complete coverage. The black and white illustrations are adequate, but the addition of color in the central reproductions adds a lot. In all, a must buy for grades 5-12.

UNDERSTANDING DRUGS
ALGEO, Philippa
Acid and Hallucinogens. Watts, 1990
BEVAN, Nicholas
AIDS and Drugs. Watts, 1988
CHOMET, Julian
Cocaine and Crack. Watts, 1987
Speed and Amphetamines. Watts, 1990
CONDON, Judith
The Pressure to Take Drugs. Watts, 1990

GODFREY, Martin
Heroin. Watts, 1987
Marijuana. Watts, 1987
HARRIS, Neil
Drugs and Crime. Watts, 1989
MADSEN, Christine
Drinking and Driving. Watts, 1989
MOHUN, Janet
Drugs, Steroids and Sports. Watts, 1988
POWNALL, Mark
Inhalants. Watts, 1987
RANDALL, Denise
Drugs and Organized Crime. Watts, 1990
STEPNEY, Rob
Alcohol. Watts, 1987
Tobacco. Watts, 1987

For the middle school set, these books delve into the drug problem, explaining what the composition of each drug is, its short- and long-term effects, health consequences, and the like. There are color photos of the substances themselves, as well as users and victims. Quotes from and about victims are highlighted on each page. There is an index, factfile, drug profile, glossary, and addresses of help agencies. Very good sources.

UNDERSTANDING PRESSURE

KUNZ, Roxane Brown, and **Judy Harris SWENSON**
Cancer: The Whispered Word. Dillon, 1986
Feeling Down: The Way Back Up. Dillon, 1986
Learning My Way: I'm a Winner. Dillon, 1986
No One Like Me. Dillon, 1985

Youngsters with stress-inducing personal problems are the targets of these books. Coping with cancer, learning disability, suicide, and differences are encouraged in these first-person accounts of each child's problem. Glossary terms are highlighted; there is an adult resource guide describing the problem simply for parent or teacher; ideas for discussion, activities, symptoms, and resources fill out the remainder of each book. These are similar to the Concept series, and aimed at the same age 7-9 audience.

UNDERSTANDING SCIENCE

ARDLEY, Neil
Understanding Energy. Silver, 1985
BENDER, Lionel
Understanding Communications and Control. Silver, 1985
HANCOCK, Ralph
Understanding Movement. Silver, 1985
IRVINE, Mat
Understanding the Cosmos. Silver, 1985
KERROD, Robin
Understanding Structures and Materials. Silver, 1985
LAMBERT, Mark
Understanding Living Things. Silver, 1985
STARRS, Graham
Understanding the Senses. Silver, 1985
WILLIAMSON, Tom
Understanding the Earth. Silver, 1985

The physical world is explored in a series of slim, illustrated volumes. The basics are touched on, sometimes with an unusual emphasis. For example, the book on energy spends little more than 10 pages on various types of energy; most of the discussion involves the principles of energy. There are a few very simple experiments included, acceptable for learning, but not complex enough for science projects. Index. Grades 5-8.

UNDERSTANDING SOCIAL ISSUES

ARMSTRONG, Ewan
The Impact of AIDS. Watts, 1990

FAGAN, Margaret
The Fight against Homelessness. Watts, 1990

HODDER, Elizabeth
Stepfamilies. Watts, 1990

PARK, Angela
Child Abuse. Watts, 1988

ROBINS, Dave
Just Punishment. Watts, 1990

VAN ZWANENBERG, Fiona
Caring for the Aged. Watts, 1989

WHARTON, Mandy
Abortion. Watts, 1989
Rights of Women. Watts, 1989

WHITE, Peter
Disabled People. Watts, 1989

Controversial current topics are addressed here, with a balanced, dispassionate presentation of the issue, explanations of why it is an issue, and alternative viewpoints. The text is sprinkled with quotes both pro and con, and each chapter is interspersed with a case study. There is an index, bibliography, glossary, and list of useful addresses. Grades 5-12.

VALUES LIBRARY

BOWMAN, John S.
Sportsmanship. Rosen, 1990

EARLE, Vana
Honesty. Rosen, 1990

JOHNSON, Linda Carlson
Patriotism. Rosen, 1990
Responsibility. Rosen, 1990

KAHANER, Ellen
Courage. Rosen, 1990

MARGULIES, Alice
Compassion. Rosen, 1990

OSBORN, Kevin
Tolerance. Rosen, 1990

SCHLEIFER, Jay
Citizenship. Rosen, 1990

Ethics, morality, values—many people decry their demise. Some say they should be taught at home, some say at school. Wherever it should be done, there has been precious little material, other than religiously oriented, to do it with. This fine series fills the void. The authors discuss the many ways the subject is viewed, as well as current attitudes as opposed to those of earlier times. Behavior of adults and famous people is used to clarify the issues and point youngsters in the right direction. Practical advice and suggestions for behavior are given. Grades 5 and up. Glossary, bibliography, index.

VENTURE BOOKS

ANDERSON, Madelyn
Arthritis. Watts, 1989

ARNOLD, Caroline
Heart Disease. Watts, 1990

BLEIFELD, Maurice
Experimenting with a Microscope. Watts, 1988
BORTZ, Fred
Superstuff. Watts, 1990
CHAPLE, Jr., Glenn F.
Exploring with a Telescope. Watts, 1988
DAYEE, Frances S.
Babysitting. Watts, 1990
DUNNAHOO, Terry
How to Win a School Election. Watts, 1989
U.S. Territories and Freely Associated States. Watts, 1988
GARDNER, Robert
Experimenting with Illusions. Watts, 1990
Experimenting with Inventions. Watts, 1990
Science and Sports. Watts, 1988
GOODHEART, Barbara
Diabetes. Watts, 1990
GUTNICK, Martin J.
Immunology. Watts, 1989
HANMER, Trudy J.
Uganda. Watts, 1989
HERDA, D. J.
Cancer. Watts, 1989
KERBY, Mona
Asthma. Watts, 1989
MACFARLANE, Ruth B.
Making Your Own Nature Museum. Watts, 1989
MCGOWEN, Tom
Chemistry. Watts, 1989
Epilepsy. Watts, 1989
MAZZENGA, Isabel B.
Compromise or Confrontation. Watts, 1989
METOS, Thomas
The Human Mind. Watts, 1990
NEWTON, David E.
Particle Accelerations. Watts, 1989
NOURSE, Alan E.
Radio Astronomy. Watts, 1989
Your Immune System. Watts, 1989
PACKER, Kenneth L.
Puberty. Watts, 1989
REISER, Howard
Skateboarding. Watts, 1989
ROSSEL, Seymour
The Holocaust. Watts, 1989
SILVERSTEIN, Herma
Alcoholism. Watts, 1990
SMITH, Norman F., and **Douglas H. SMITH**
Simulations. Watts, 1989
TANNENBAUM, Beulah, and **Harold E. TANNENBAUM**
Making and Using Your Own Weather Station. Watts, 1989
TAUBER, Gerald E.
Relativity. Watts, 1988
WALKER, Ormiston H.
Experimenting with Air and Flight. Watts, 1989

YOUNG, John K.
Cells. Watts, 1990
ZEINERT, Karen
The Salem Witchcraft Trials. Watts, 1989
For those high school students needing more advanced information this series can be a valuable resource. Covering subject areas in science, social studies and health, these books are of special interest because of the depth of information in them. The subject matter is comprehensive. A number of illustrations are used along with a bibliography, glossary (in some) and an index. Good books for students in grades 9-12.

VERY YOUNG
KREMENTZ, Jill
A Very Young Circus Flyer. Knopf, 1979
A Very Young Dancer. Knopf, 1976
A Very Young Gymnast. Knopf, 1978
A Very Young Gardener. Dial, 1990
A Very Young Musician. S&S, 1991
A Very Young Rider. Knopf, 1977
A Very Young Skater. Knopf, 1979
A Very Young Skier. Knopf, 1990
Like her How It Feels series, this one spotlights Krementz's outstanding photos as a vehicle for communicating the various aspects of each activity. One youngster is profiled in each book, and the charm and accessibility of the series lies in the very real interviews that readers will identify with. These will serve to introduce neophytes or elicit knowing nods from other practitioners of the sports. Grades 4-8.

VISUAL GEOGRAPHY
Afghanistan in Pictures. Lerner, 1989
Argentina in Pictures. Lerner, 1988
Australia in Pictures. Lerner, 1990
Austria in Pictures. Lerner, 1991
Belgium in Pictures. Lerner, 1991
Bolivia in Pictures. Lerner, 1987
Botswana in Pictures. Lerner, 1990
Brazil in Pictures. Lerner, 1987
Bulgaria in Pictures. Lerner, 1991
Cameroon in Pictures. Lerner, 1989
Canada in Pictures. Lerner, 1989
Central African Republic in Pictures. Lerner, 1989
Chile in Pictures. Lerner, 1988
China in Pictures. Lerner, 1989
Colombia in Pictures. Lerner, 1987
Costa Rica in Pictures. Lerner, 1987
Cote d'Ivoire in Pictures. Lerner, 1988
Cuba in Pictures. Lerner, 1987
Czechoslovakia in Pictures. Lerner, 1991
Denmark in Pictures. Lerner, 1991
Dominican Republic in Pictures. Lerner, 1988
East Germany in Pictures. Lerner, 1991
Ecuador in Pictures. Lerner, 1987
Egypt in Pictures. Lerner, 1988
El Salvador in Pictures. Lerner, 1987
England in Pictures. Lerner, 1990
Ethiopia in Pictures. Lerner, 1988
Finland in Pictures. Lerner, 1991

France in Pictures. Lerner, 1991
Ghana in Pictures. Lerner, 1988
Greece in Pictures. Lerner, 1991
Guatemala in Pictures. Lerner, 1987
Guyana in Pictures. Lerner, 1988
Haiti in Pictures. Lerner, 1987
Honduras in Pictures. Lerner, 1987
Hungary in Pictures. Lerner, 1991
Iceland in Pictures. Lerner, 1991
India in Pictures. Lerner, 1989
Indonesia in Pictures. Lerner, 1990
Iran in Pictures. Lerner, 1988
Iraq in Pictures. Lerner, 1990
Ireland in Pictures. Lerner, 1991
Israel in Pictures. Lerner, 1988
Italy in Pictures. Lerner, 1991
Jamaica in Pictures. Lerner, 1987
Japan in Pictures. Lerner, 1989
Jordan in Pictures. Lerner, 1988
Kenya in Pictures. Lerner, 1988
Kuwait in Pictures. Lerner, 1989
Lebanon in Pictures. Lerner, 1988
Liberia in Pictures. Lerner, 1988
Madagascar in Pictures. Lerner, 1988
Malawi in Pictures. Lerner, 1988
Malaysia in Pictures. Lerner, 1989
Mali in Pictures. Lerner, 1990
Mexico in Pictures. Lerner, 1988
Morocco in Pictures. Lerner, 1988
Nepal in Pictures. Lerner, 1989
Netherlands in Pictures. Lerner, 1991
New Zealand in Pictures. Lerner, 1990
Nicaragua in Pictures. Lerner, 1987
Nigeria in Pictures. Lerner, 1988
Norway in Pictures. Lerner, 1990
Pakistan in Pictures. Lerner, 1989
Panama in Pictures. Lerner, 1987
Paraguay in Pictures. Lerner, 1987
Peru in Pictures. Lerner, 1987
Philippines in Pictures. Lerner, 1990
Poland in Pictures. Lerner, 1991
Portugal in Pictures. Lerner, 1991
Puerto Rico in Pictures. Lerner, 1987
Romania in Pictures. Lerner, 1991
Saudi Arabia in Pictures. Lerner, 1989
Scotland in Pictures. Lerner, 1991
Senegal in Pictures. Lerner, 1988
South Africa in Pictures. Lerner, 1988
South Korea in Pictures. Lerner, 1990
Soviet Union in Pictures. Lerner, 1989
Spain in Pictures. Lerner, 1991
Sri Lanka in Pictures. Lerner, 1988
Sudan in Pictures. Lerner, 1988
Sweden in Pictures. Lerner, 1991
Switzerland in Pictures. Lerner, 1991

Syria in Pictures. Lerner, 1990
Taiwan in Pictures. Lerner, 1989
Tanzania in Pictures. Lerner, 1988
Thailand in Pictures. Lerner, 1989
Tunisia in Pictures. Lerner, 1989
Turkey in Pictures. Lerner, 1988
United States in Pictures. Lerner, 1991
Uruguay in Pictures. Lerner, 1987
Venezuela in Pictures. Lerner, 1987
Wales in Pictures. Lerner, 1991
West Germany in Pictures. Lerner, 1991
Yugoslavia in Pictures. Lerner, 1991
Zimbabwe in Pictures. Lerner, 1988

The series title is a misnomer; while photos, both color and black and white, abound here, there is also text which covers the basics: the land, history, people, and economy. The print is small and the vocabulary makes these appropriate for grades 5-12. Collections geared to younger readers may want to choose some titles because the coverage is unavailable elsewhere. Index.

VOICES

Voices from America's Past. Steck, 1990
Voices from around the World. Steck, 1990
Voices from Distant Lands. Steck, 1990
Voices from Our Nation. Steck, 1990

First-hand accounts of human experiences form the basis of this interesting series. Some of the writings are contemporary, some historical. They all relate adventures, thoughts, experiences, or lifestyles of different people in many lands. Four pages are devoted to each author. There are several color photos with each account, a glossary to the left of the text, and a final paragraph about the author. Social studies classes could find this material interesting, and the casual reader will be engrossed as well. Grades 5 and up.

VOYAGE THROUGH THE UNIVERSE

The Cosmos. Time-Life, 1988
Far Planets. Time-Life, 1988
Galaxies. Time-Life, 1988
Lifesearch. Time-Life, 1989
The Near Planets. Time-Life, 1989
The New Astronomy. Time-Life, 1989
Outbound. Time-Life, 1989
Spacefarers. Time-Life, 1989
Stars. Time-Life, 1988
The Sun. Time-Life, 1990
The Third Planet. Time-Life, 1989

As in many other Time-Life series, this one excels in the graphics. The photos, maps, charts, and drawings are striking, and sure to draw readers ages 12 and up. The text is presented in a newsy, informative style that does not always lend itself to easy use by the homework brigade, however. General topics are covered, and those in search of research material must use the index heavily. Some of the texts will prove more useful for research, while others lend themselves more to the inquiring pleasure reader.

WAR IN VIETNAM

WRIGHT, David K.

Eve of Battle (Prehistory to 1965). Childrens, 1989
A Wider War. Childrens, 1989
Vietnamization. Childrens, 1989
The Fall of Vietnam. Childrens, 1989

This excellent series charts the Vietnam War from its earliest pre-U.S. days through the "military advisor" stage through total involvement through the withdrawal of forces. Citizen responses, both in the U.S. and abroad are mentioned, and a balanced, informative picture is created. A timeline for the period under discussion begins each volume; the end of the text finds a timeline of Vietnamese history, a glossary, and index. There are many black and white photos. Grades 5-12.

WARWICK HISTORICAL ATLAS

ADAMS, Simon

The Middle Ages: A.D. 456-1450. Watts, 1990

BRIQUEBEC, John

The Ancient World: 30,000 B.C.-A.D. 456. Watts, 1990

KRAMER, Ann

Exploration and Empire: 1450-1760. Watts, 1990

Revolution and Technology: 1760-Present Day. Watts, 1990

These historical atlases combine maps with color illustrations and explanatory text. Readers get a brief overview not only of the geography of each area, but also the architecture, writing, art, religions, and history. There is a glossary, time line, and index. Grades 5-8.

WASTE CONTROL

CONDON, Judith

Recycling Glass. Watts, 1991

Recycling Paper. Watts, 1990

PALMER, Joy

Recycling Metal. Watts, 1991

Recycling Plastic. Watts, 1990

Another in Watts' fine series on conservation, this one deals with recycling—an overview of the garbage problem, followed by a brief discussion of how the substance is produced, how it is recycled, costs, and how individuals and governments can help. Lots of color pictures, a glossary, list of addresses, and index will aid readers 8-12.

WHAT MADE THEM GREAT

BREWSTER, Scott

Ferdinand Magellan. Silver, 1990

CRAWFORD, Gail

Albert Schweitzer. Silver, 1990

MARSHALL, Norman F.

Leonardo Da Vinci. Silver, 1990

MONTGOMERY, Mary

Marie Curie. Silver, 1990

MORGAN, Lee

Abraham Lincoln. Silver, 1990

Christopher Columbus. Silver, 1990

SHORE, Donna

Florence Nightingale. Silver, 1990

TYLER, Laura

Anne Frank. Silver, 1990

This is an exceptionally good biographical series. The authors present background on the time as well as the person, so that the reader can see why they were important. Their entire lives are examined in a realistic fashion. Sometimes excerpts from their own writings are provided. A timeline of their life in context with a world timeline is also given. Grades 5 and up. Bibliography, index.

WHAT WAS IT LIKE?

POLCOVAR, Jane

Helen Keller. Childrens, 1988

WEINBERG, Lawrence

Abraham Lincoln. Childrens, 1988
Benjamin Franklin. Childrens, 1988
George Washington. Childrens, 1988
Harriet Tubman. Childrens, 1988
Jackie Robinson. Childrens, 1988
Paul Revere. Childrens, 1988
Thomas Edison. Childrens, 1988

These biographies are written in the first person, to give the illusion that the reader is right there with the biographee. Conversations are not reconstructed and only documented events and historical background are related, so they are accurate. These are small books with large print and a vocabulary level that makes them suitable for grades 3-6. There are line drawings and a chronology, but no index. The side margins are only ¼", so they are not as attractive to the eye as other biographies.

WHEELS

LAFFERTY, Peter, and David JEFFERIS

Pedal Power: The History of Bicycles. Watts, 1990
Superbikes: The History of Motorcycles. Watts, 1990
To the Rescue: The History of Emergency Vehicles. Watts, 1990
Top Gear: The History of Automobiles. Watts, 1990

This attractive new series is bound to draw raves from the many fans of wheeled vehicles. The earliest history is given, along with comparisons of new and old vehicles. Pioneers and developments in other lands are noted, as well as outstanding manufacturers. Future possibilities, technology, and facts and records are included. Loads of color illustrations add to the appeal. Reluctant readers will enjoy. Index. Grades 4-8.

WILD WINGS

EMERT, Phyllis

Fighter Planes. Messner, 1990
Helicopters. Messner, 1990
Special Task Aircraft. Messner, 1990
Transports and Bombers. Messner, 1990

Lots of kids enjoy reading about aircraft, and the Gulf War has only heightened that interest. These books will please fans. There is a (small) clear photo of each craft, accompanied by a page of vital statistics. Two more pages describe the history and design of the plane. Grades 5 and up. Glossary. No index.

WILDLIFE (HABITS & HABITAT)

AHLSTROM, Mark

Black Bear. Crestwood, 1985
Canada Goose. Crestwood, 1984
Coyote. Crestwood, 1985
Elk. Crestwood, 1985
Foxes. Crestwood, 1983
Moose. Crestwood, 1985
Mule Deer. Crestwood, 1987
Polar Bear. Crestwood, 1986
Pronghorn. Crestwood, 1986
Sheep. Crestwood, 1984
Snow Goose. Crestwood, 1986
Whitetail. Crestwood, 1983
Wild Pigs. Crestwood, 1986

CREIGHTON, Susan
Giant Lizard. Crestwood, 1988
CROFFORD, Emily
Opossum. Crestwood, 1990
DUDEN, Jane
Ferret. Crestwood, 1990
Harp Seal. Crestwood, 1990
FINE, Edith Hope
Python and Anaconda. Crestwood, 1988
Turtle and Tortoise. Crestwood, 1988
GREEN, Carl, and **William SANFORD**
African Lion. Crestwood, 1987
African Rhinos. Crestwood, 1987
Asiatic Elephant. Crestwood, 1987
Badger. Crestwood, 1986
Bengal Tiger. Crestwood, 1986
Bison. Crestwood, 1985
Boa Constrictor. Crestwood, 1987
Bottlenose Dolphin. Crestwood, 1987
Camel. Crestwood, 1988
Cape Buffalo. Crestwood, 1987
Cobra. Crestwood, 1986
Elephant Seal. Crestwood, 1987
Giant Panda. Crestwood, 1987
Giraffe. Crestwood, 1987
Gorilla. Crestwood, 1986
Great White Shark. Crestwood, 1985
Hippopotamus. Crestwoood, 1988
Humpback Whale. Crestwood, 1985
Hyena. Crestwood, 1988
Kangaroos. Crestwood, 1987
Koala. Crestwood, 1987
Little Brown Bat. Crestwood, 1986
Octopus. Crestwood, 1988
Orangutan. Crestwood, 1987
Ostrich. Crestwood, 1987
Pelicans. Crestwood, 1987
Peregrine Falcon. Crestwood, 1986
Porcupine. Crestwood, 1985
Rabbit. Crestwood, 1988
Rattlesnake. Crestwood, 1984
Striped Skunk. Crestwood, 1987
Tarantulas. Crestwood, 1987
Walrus. Crestwood, 1986
Wild Horses. Crestwood, 1986
Zebra. Crestwood, 1988
HOLMGREN, Virginia
Pheasant. Crestwood, 1983
HORN, Gabriel
Crane. Crestwood, 1988
JOSEPHSON, Judith Pinkerton
Loon. Crestwood, 1988
Monarch Butterfly. Crestwood, 1988

MCCONOUGHEY, Jana
Bald Eagle. Crestwood, 1983
Squirrels. Crestwood, 1983
Wolves. Crestwood, 1983
MCCORMICK, Maxine
Chimpanzee. Crestwood, 1990
MELL, Jan
Scorpion. Crestwood, 1990
MORRISON, Susan Dudley
Alligator. Crestwood, 1984
NENTL, Jerolyn
Beaver. Crestwood, 1983
Caribou. Crestwood, 1984
Grizzly. Crestwood, 1984
Mallard. Crestwood, 1983
Raccoon. Crestwood, 1984
Wild Cats. Crestwood, 1984
NIELSEN, Nancy
Black Widow Spider. Crestwood, 1990
PETERS, Lisa Westberg
Condor. Crestwood, 1990
SATEREN, Shelley Swanson
Black Panther. Crestwood, 1990
STONE, Lynn
Great Horned Owl. Crestwood, 1987
Killer Whale. Crestwood, 1987
Penguins. Crestwood, 1987

For some reason these books open with a fictionalized prologue before going on to the meat of the subject. The authors describe types of the animals, their habits and habitats, and reproduction. Myths and stories about the creature and its usefulness to man is also explored. Some of these animals are difficult to find information on, while others have been covered better elsewhere. Grades 4-6. Glossary/index.

WINDOWS ON THE WORLD BOOKS
CASELLI, Giovanni
Life through the Ages. Grosset, 1987
FELTWELL, John
Animals and Where They Live. Grosset, 1988
PARKER, Steve
Dinosaurs and Their World. Grosset, 1988

This oversize British series has been imported by Grosset. Large color illustrations are the hallmark of these books. The dinosaur book will be especially appealing to young fans grades 3 and up.

WINGS: THE CONQUEST OF THE AIR
JEFFERIS, David
Epic Flights. Watts, 1988
The First Flyers. Watts, 1988
Giants of the Air. Watts, 1988
Helicopters. Watts, 1989
The Jet Age. Watts, 1988
Supersonic Flight. Watts, 1989
MAYNARD, Christopher, and **David JEFFERIS**
The Aces. Watts, 1987
Air Battles. Watts, 1987

Lots of youngsters are fascinated by the hardware of war: its history, current technology, and famous planes, flyers, and battles. This series will find a ready audience with them. Lots of illustrations, index, glossary, and aircraft data.

WITNESS HISTORY

HARPER, Paul

The Arab-Israeli Conflict. Watts, 1990

HARRIES, Ann

South Africa since 1948. Watts, 1989

HEATER, Derek

The Cold War. Watts, 1989

ROSS, Stewart

China since 1945. Watts, 1989

The Origins of World War I. Watts, 1989

The Russian Revolution. Watts, 1989

The United Nations. Watts, 1990

SMITH, Nigel

The United States since 1945. Watts, 1990

WILLIAMSON, David

The Third Reich. Watts, 1989

This series examines important historical topics by using a clearly written, yet in-depth text and numerous illustrations. The events discussed are also analyzed to give further assistance in understanding the importance of the topic. Included are brief biographies of important people, diagrams, chronologies, glossaries, and suggestions for further reading. Grades 8-12.

WOMEN HISTORY MAKERS

BRYAN, Jenny

Health and Science. Watts, 1988

MACDONALD, Fiona

A Chance to Learn. Watts, 1989

Working for Equality. Watts, 1988

SPROULE, Anna

New Ideas in Industry. Watts, 1988

Solidarity. Watts, 1988

STOTT, Carole

Into the Unknown. Watts, 1989

Women's history is the accent here, with important events and developments that women were involved in (but are seldom taught about in schools) described. First, a general background is given, then specific female contributions are presented. Interspersed with the illustrations are "witness" sections that directly quote contemporaries of the event. In addition, the authors provide an index, time chart, glossary, and list of places to visit. Grades 5-9.

WOMEN OF OUR TIME

ADLER, David A.

Our Golda. Viking, 1984

FABER, Doris

Eleanor Roosevelt. Viking, 1985

Margaret Thatcher. Viking, 1985

GHERMAN, Beverly

Sandra Day O'Connor. Viking, 1991

GIFF, Patricia Reilly

Diana: Twentieth-Century Princess. Viking, 1991

Laura Ingalls Wilder. Viking, 1987

Mother Teresa. Viking, 1986

HASKINS, James
Diana Ross. Viking, 1985
Shirley Temple Black. Viking, 1988
HOWE, James
Carol Burnett. Viking, 1987
HURWITZ, Johanna
Astrid Lindgren. Viking, 1989
KERBY, Mona
Amelia Earhart: Courage in the Sky. Viking, 1990
Beverly Sills. Viking, 1989
KNUDSON, R. R.
Babe Didrikson. Viking, 1986
Julie Brown. Viking, 1988
Martina Navratilova. Viking, 1986
KUDLINSKI, Kathleen V.
Helen Keller. Viking, 1989
Juliette Gordon Low. Viking, 1989
Rachel Carson. Viking, 1988
KUSTANOWITZ, Shulamit E.
Henrietta Szold: Israel's Helping Hand. Viking, 1990
MELTZER, Milton
Betty Friedan. Viking, 1985
Dorothea Lange. Viking, 1985
Mary McLeod Bethune. Viking, 1987
Winnie Mandela. Viking, 1986
ONEAL, Zibby
Grandma Moses. Viking, 1986
SAUNDERS, Susan
Dolly Parton. Viking, 1985
Margaret Mead. Viking, 1987

This highly readable biography series should prove to be a popular one with readers and students. The subjects are all contemporary enough that youngsters will have heard of them and can relate to their lives. They cover the spectrum of religious, artistic, show biz, and political personalities. The texts are conversational, with occasional illustrations. A very good choice for readers grades 3-6.

WONDERS OF...
BLASSINGAME, Wyatt
Wonders of Egrets, Bitterns, and Herons. Putnam, 1982
Wonders of Sharks. Putnam, 1984
LAVINE, Sigmund A.
Wonders of Badgers. Putnam, 1985
Wonders of Donkeys. Putnam, 1979
Wonders of Goats. Putnam, 1980
Wonders of Mice. Putnam, 1980
Wonders of Mules. Putnam, 1982
Wonders of Peacocks. Putnam, 1982
Wonders of Rhinos. Putnam, 1982
Wonders of Tigers. Putnam, 1987
MCFALL, Christie
Wonders of Dust. Putnam, 1980
SCURO, Vincent
Wonders of Dairy Cattle. Putnam, 1986

Scientific information about various animals forms the basis for this series. The animals are described: development, habitat, lifestyle, and anatomy. Legends and lore and the animals' relationship to man are also explored. The text is informative, including material on scientific studies that readers grades 5 and up will find of interest. Some of the animals are popular reading matter, others are unusual and hard to find.

WORKING DOGS

EMERT, Phyllis Raybin

Guide Dogs. Crestwood, 1985
Hearing-Ear Dogs. Crestwood, 1985
Law Enforcement Dogs. Crestwood, 1985
Military Dogs. Crestwood, 1985
Search and Rescue Dogs. Crestwood, 1985
Sled Dogs. Crestwood, 1985

LEDER, Jane Mersky

Stunt Dogs. Crestwood, 1985

NEWMAN, Matthew

Watch/Guard Dogs. Crestwood, 1985

Dog lovers will enjoy being able to find out about the various jobs that dogs have, in addition to being pets! The books begin with a story (not indicating that the events are really factual) about a dog involved in each line of work; this is followed by a brief history of the occupation. Then the breeds of dogs used and how they are trained makes up the balance of the information. Grades 5 and up. Glossary, no index.

WORKING MOMS

BRYANT, Jennifer

Anna Abrams: Engineer Drafter. Childrens, 1991
Carol Thomas-Weaver: Music Teacher. Childrens, 1991
Ubel Velez: Lawyer. Childrens, 1991
Zoe McCully: Park Ranger. Childrens, 1991

SHULMAN, Jeffrey

Karen Strange: Children's Theater Producer. Childrens, 1991
Sahron Oehler: Pediatrician. Childrens, 1991

This series really has a good idea for the younger reader: it shows what life is like for real mothers who are also career people. The books begin with a picture of what each person does as a mom—and emphasizes how important that is, as well as how important her family is to her. Then the reader sees her on the job, where her activities are described. These give an honest picture of what supermoms deal with daily, while still furnishing career information and reassurance for kids that their moms love them even though they are not at home. These can be read to preschoolers and up or read alone by grades 3-6.

WORLD AT WAR

SKIPPER, G. C.

Battle of the Atlantic. Childrens, 1981
Battle of Britain. Childrens, 1980
Battle of the Coral Sea. Childrens, 1981
Battle of Leyte Gulf. Childrens, 1981
Battle of Midway. Childrens, 1980
D-Day. Childrens, 1982
Death of Hitler. Childrens, 1980
Invasion of Poland. Childrens, 1983
Invasion of Sicily. Childrens, 1981
MacArthur and the Philippines. Childrens, 1982
Pearl Harbor. Childrens, 1983
Submarines in the Pacific. Childrens, 1980

STEIN, R. Conrad

Battle of Guadalcanal. Childrens, 1983
Battle of Okinawa. Childrens, 1985
Dunkirk. Childrens, 1982
Fall of Singapore. Childrens, 1982
Fighter Planes. Childrens, 1986
Hiroshima. Childrens, 1982
Hitler Youth. Childrens, 1985
The Holocaust. Childrens, 1986
The Home Front. Childrens, 1986
Invasion of Russia. Childrens, 1985
Nisei Regiment. Childrens, 1985
Prisoners of War. Childrens, 1987
Resistance Movements. Childrens, 1982
Road to Rome. Childrens, 1984
Siege of Leningrad. Childrens, 1983
Warsaw Ghetto. Childrens, 1985

These slim volumes (under 50 pages) cover important events and aspects of World War II. The vocabulary is simple enough for an interested 4th grader, but complete enough to fill report needs. There are numerous black and white photos and maps. Although there are no chapter divisions or table of contents, there is an adequate index. There is also a brief list of important events in both theaters of war. As needed, grades 4-6.

WORLD CITIES

Chicago. Raintree, 1990
London. Raintree, 1990
Los Angeles. Raintree, 1990
Mexico City. Raintree, 1990
Moscow. Raintree, 1990
New York. Raintree, 1990
Tokyo. Raintree, 1990
Washington, D.C. Raintree, 1990

Students can learn about the history, culture, geography and economy of these world cities by reading this series for junior high schoolers. The reader learns why each city is important in the world today and gains a view of the role each city plays. The books are illustrated with many photographs, maps, and a timeline. There is also an almanac of facts and index.

WORLD DISASTERS

BIEL, Timothy Levi

The Black Death. Greenhaven, 1989
The Challenger. Greenhaven, 1990
Pompeii. Greenhaven, 1989

DIAMOND, Arthur

The Bhopal Chemical Leak. Greenhaven, 1989

ENGHOLM, Chris

The Armenian Earthquake. Greenhaven, 1989

FARRIS, John

The Dust Bowl. Greenhaven, 1989
Hiroshima. Greenhaven, 1990

GLASER, Elizabeth, and **Timothy Levi BIEL**

The Ethiopian Famine. Greenhaven, 1990

HOUSE, James, and **Bradley STEFFENS**

The San Francisco Earthquake. Greenhaven, 1989

MIGNECO, Ronald, and **Timothy Levi BIEL**

The Crash of 1929. Greenhaven, 1989

NARDO, Don
Chernobyl. Greenhaven, 1990
The Irish Potato Famine. Greenhaven, 1990
Krakatoa. Greenhaven, 1990
STACEY, Tom
The Hindenburg. Greenhaven, 1990
The Titanic. Greenhaven, 1989
WARBURTON, Lois
The Chicago Fire. Greenhaven, 1989

The most perilous disasters of all time are dealt with in this series of books. Each book discusses the history of the time period and the culture in which the disaster occurred. All the books contain a glossary, bibliography, and index. Grades 5-8.

WORLD DISASTERS
KNAPP, Brian
Drought. Steck, 1990
Earthquake. Steck, 1990
Fire. Steck, 1990
Flood. Steck, 1990
Storm. Steck, 1990
Volcano. Steck, 1990

This new series covers a variety of natural disasters. Author Knapp begins by giving the scientific whys and wherefores, then discussing various types of disasters, how nature protects itself, and ending with famous examples. Safety precautions are included. Glossary, index. Grades 5-8.

WORLD EXPLORERS
ALLEN, John L.
Jedediah Smith and the Mountain Men of the American West. Chelsea, 1991
BERNHARD, Brenda
Pizarro, Orellana, and the Exploration of the Amazon. Chelsea, 1991
BROWN, Warren
Search for the Northwest Passage. Chelsea, 1991
COULTER, Tony
LaSalle and the Explorers of the Mississippi. Chelsea, 1991
DODGE, Steven
Christopher Columbus and the First Voyages to the New World. Chelsea, 1991
GAINES, Ann
Alexander von Humboldt, Colossus of Exploration. Chelsea, 1991
HANEY, David
Captain James Cook and the Explorers of the Pacific. Chelsea, 1991
HARRIS, Edward
John Charles Fremont and the Great Western Reconnaisance. Chelsea, 1990
KENNEDY, Gregory
First Men in Space. Chelsea, 1991
MOULTON, Gary
Lewis and Clark and the Route to the Pacific. Chelsea, 1991
POWELL, Thomas
Daniel Boone and the Opening of the Ohio Country. Chelsea, 1991
STALLONES, Jared
Zebulon Pike and the Explorers of the American Southwest. Chelsea, 1991
STEFOFF, Rebecca
Ferdinand Magellan and the Discovery of the World Ocean. Chelsea, 1990
WHITMAN, Sylvia
Hernando de Soto and the Explorers of the American South. Chelsea, 1991

WOLF, Cheri

Lt. Charles Wilkes and the Great U.S. Exploring Expedition. Chelsea, 1991

This excellent in-depth series combines biography and history to give a picture of the man and his times: what made him the way he was, what he did, and why it was so important. The text is dotted with reproductions of photos, maps, and drawings of the period. Family life is discussed as well as exploits. The publisher intends to bring the series into the present day, with books planned about undersea and space exploration. Grades 5 and up. Bibliography, chronology, index.

WORLD HISTORY

ADDISON, John

Suleyman and the Ottoman Empire. Greenhaven, 1980
Traditional Africa. Greenhaven, 1980

AMEY, Peter

Imperalism. Greenhaven, 1980
Leonardo da Vinci. Greenhaven, 1980
Luther, Erasmus and Loyola. Greenhaven, 1980
Pax Romana. Greenhaven, 1980
The Scientific Revolution. Greenhaven, 1980

BOOTH, Martin

Bismarck. Greenhaven, 1980

CLIFFORD, Alan

The Middle Ages. Greenhaven, 1980

CRIPWELL, Kenneth

Language. Greenhaven, 1980

DUCKWORTH, John

Muhammed and the Arab Empire. Greenhaven, 1980

DUNCASTER, Islay

Traditional China. Greenhaven, 1980

GARRETT, Sean

The Suez Canal. Greenhaven, 1980

GUYATT, John

The American Revolution. Greenhaven, 1980
Ancient America. Greenhaven, 1980
Bolivar. Greenhaven, 1980

HARRISON, John

Akbar and the Mughal Empire. Greenhaven, 1980

KANTIKER, Helen

Asoka and Indian Civilization. Greenhaven, 1980

KILLINGRAY, David

The American Frontier. Greenhaven, 1980
The Atom Bomb. Greenhaven, 1980
Henry Ford. Greenhaven, 1980
The Mexican Revolution. Greenhaven, 1980
Neolithic Revolution. Greenhaven, 1980
Nyerere and Nkrumah. Greenhaven, 1980
Population. Greenhaven, 1980
The Russian Revolution. Greenhaven, 1980
Slave Trade. Greenhaven, 1980
Stalin. Greenhaven, 1980
The Two World Wars. Greenhaven, 1980
World Economy. Greenhaven, 1980

KILLINGRAY, David, and **Malcolm YAPP**

The Enlightenment. Greenhaven, 1980
Hollywood. Greenhaven, 1980

KILLINGRAY, Margaret
The Agricultural Revolution. Greenhaven, 1980
Ancient Greece. Greenhaven, 1980
Constantine. Greenhaven, 1980
KNOX, Diana
The Industrial Revolution. Greenhaven, 1980
NICHOLSON, Alasdair
The Cold War. Greenhaven, 1980
O'CONNER, Edmund
Darwin. Greenhaven, 1980
Education. Greenhaven, 1980
Japan's Modernization. Greenhaven, 1980
Roosevelt. Greenhaven, 1980
Wealth of Japan. Greenhaven, 1980
PAINTER, Desmund
Columbus. Greenhaven, 1980
Mao Tse-tung. Greenhaven, 1980
Religion. Greenhaven, 1980
PEARSON, Eileen
Hitler's Reich. Greenhaven, 1980
READ, James
Law. Greenhaven, 1980
TAMES, Richard
Cities. Greenhaven, 1980
The French Revolution. Greenhaven, 1980
Napoleon. Greenhaven, 1980
TOWSON, Duncan
Alexander. Greenhaven, 1980
Spices and Civilizations. Greenhaven, 1980
WESTCH, Anthony
The Chinese Revolution. Greenhaven, 1980
WRANGHAM, Elizabeth
The Family. Greenhaven, 1980
YAPP, Malcolm
The Ancient Near East. Greenhaven, 1980
The British Raj and Indian Nationalism. Greenhaven, 1980
Chingis Khan and the Mongol Empire. Greenhaven, 1980
Gandhi. Greenhaven, 1980
The Growth of the State. Greenhaven, 1980
Iba Sina and the Muslim World. Greenhaven, 1980
Nationalism. Greenhaven, 1980

Written in the United Kingdom, these books have been adapted for use by American students in grades 7-9. The books are readable and contain a different point of view from most domestic history books. Recommended only as supplemental additions to an in-depth young adult history collection.

WORLD IN VIEW
ANGELILLO, Barbara
Italy. Steck, 1990
ASHFORD, Moyra
Brazil. Steck, 1991
DAVIES, Katherine
Wales. Steck, 1990
FYSON, Nance Lui
Hong Kong. Steck, 1990
Indonesia. Steck, 1990

GARRETT, Dan
Scandinavia. Steck, 1991
GARRETT, Dan, and **Warrill GRINDROD**
Australia. Steck, 1990
KRONE, Chester
United States of America. Steck, 1990
MILNER, Cate
France. Steck, 1990
MORRIS, Emily
Cuba. Steck, 1991
PEPLOW, Mary, and **Debra SHIPLEY**
England. Steck, 1990
Ireland. Steck, 1990
ROGOFF, Mike
Israel. Steck, 1990
STEELE, Philip
China. Steck, 1990
TAYLOR, Doreen
Scotland. Steck, 1990

Like the Enchantment of the World series, this one gives geography, history, culture, and economy. These books are smaller, with smaller print and pictures, so they have less eye appeal. Grades 4-8. Index.

WORLD LEADERS PAST AND PRESENT
AMDUR, Richard
Chaim Weizmann. Chelsea, 1988
Menachim Begin. Chelsea, 1988
Moshe Dayan. Chelsea, 1989
AUFDERHEIDE, Patricia
Anwar Sadat. Chelsea, 1987
BANFIELD, Susan
Charlemagne. Chelsea, 1987
Charles de Gaulle. Chelsea, 1985
Joan of Arc. Chelsea, 1986
BARLOW, Jeffrey
Sun Yat-sen. Chelsea, 1987
BEILENSON, John
Sukarno. Chelsea, 1990
BERMAN, Russell
Paul von Hindenburg. Chelsea, 1987
BERRY, Lynn
Wojciech Jaruzelski. Chelsea, 1989
BRAND, Eric
William Gladstone. Chelsea, 1986
BRANNER, Steven
Leon Blum. Chelsea, 1987
BRUNS, Roger
Abraham Lincoln. Chelsea, 1987
George Washington. Chelsea, 1987
Julius Caesar. Chelsea, 1987
Thomas Jefferson. Chelsea, 1987
BUSH, Catherine
Elizabeth I. Chelsea, 1986
Mohandas K. Gandhi. Chelsea, 1985

BUTLER, Francelia
Indira Gandhi. Chelsea, 1986
BUTSON, Thomas
Ivan the Terrible. Chelsea, 1987
Mikhail Gorbachev. Chelsea, 1986
Pierre Elliott Trudeau. Chelsea, 1987
CARSON, S. L.
Maximilien Robespierre. Chelsea, 1988
CHUA-EOAN, Howard
Corazon Aquino. Chelsea, 1988
CLUCAS, Joan
Mother Teresa. Chelsea, 1988
COCKROFT, James
Mohammed Reza Pahlavi. Chelsea, 1989
COELHO, Tony
John Quincy Adams. Chelsea, 1990
CONDIT, Erin
Francois and Jean-Claude Duvalier. Chelsea, 1989
CUDLIPP, Edythe
Konrad Adenour. Chelsea, 1985
DECHANCIE, John
Gamal Abdel Nasser. Chelsea, 1988
Peron. Chelsea, 1987
DOHERTY, Paul
King Arthur. Chelsea, 1987
DOLAN, Sean
Chiang Kai-shek. Chelsea, 1988
DRAMER, Kim
Kublai Khan. Chelsea, 1990
DWYER, Frank
Danton. Chelsea, 1987
Henry VIII. Chelsea, 1988
John Adams. Chelsea, 1989
EBON, Martin
Nikita Khrushchev. Chelsea, 1986
EIDE, Lorraine
Robert Mugabe. Chelsea, 1989
FINCK, Lila
Jawaharlal Nehru. Chelsea, 1987
FORTIER, E. H.
Judas Maccabeus. Chelsea, 1988
FRIESE, Kai
Tenzin Gyatso. Chelsea, 1990
GARFINKEL, Bernard
Margaret Thatcher. Chelsea, 1985
GARZA, Hedda
Francisco Franco. Chelsea, 1987
Leon Trotsky. Chelsea, 1987
Mao Zedong. Chelsea, 1988
Salvador Allende. Chelsea, 1989
GLOSSOP, Pat
Cardinal Richelieu. Chelsea, 1989
GORDON, Matthew
Ayatollah Khomeini. Chelsea, 1986
The Gemayels. Chelsea, 1988
Hafez al-Assad. Chelsea, 1989

GOTTFRIED, Ted
Georges Clemenceau. Chelsea, 1989
GROSS, Albert
Henry of Navarre. Chelsea, 1988
HANEY, John
Cesare Borgia. Chelsea, 1987
Charles Stewart Parnell. Chelsea, 1989
Clement Attlee. Chelsea, 1988
Vladimir Lenin. Chelsea, 1988
HARTINIAN, Larry
Benito Mussolini. Chelsea, 1988
HOOBLER, Dorothy
Joseph Stalin. Chelsea, 1985
HOOBLER, Dorothy, and **Thomas HOOBLER**
Cleopatra. Chelsea, 1987
Zhou Enlai. Chelsea, 1986
HOOBLER, Thomas
Toussaint L'Ouverture. Chelsea, 1990
HORN, Pierre
King Louis XIV. Chelsea, 1986
Marquis de Lafayette. Chelsea, 1989
HUMPHREY, Judy
Genghis Khan. Chelsea, 1986
ISRAEL, Fred
Franklin Delano Roosevelt. Chelsea, 1985
Henry Kissinger. Chelsea, 1986
JAKOUBEK, Robert
Martin Luther King, Jr. Chelsea, 1989
KAPLAN, Lawrence
Oliver Cromwell. Chelsea, 1986
KAPLAN, Zoe
Eleanor of Aquitaaine. Chelsea, 1987
KAYE, Tony
Lech Walesa. Chelsea, 1989
Lyndon B. Johnson. Chelsea, 1988
KELLNER, Douglas
Ernesto "Che" Guevara. Chelsea, 1989
Nkrumah. Chelsea, 1987
KING, Perry
Jefferson Davis. Chelsea, 1990
Pericles. Chelsea, 1988
KITTREDGE, Mark
Frederick the Great. Chelsea, 1987
Marc Antony. Chelsea, 1988
KYLE, Benjamin
Muammar el-Qaddafi. Chelsea, 1987
LEAVELL, Perry
Harry S. Truman. Chelsea, 1988
James Madison. Chelsea, 1988
Woodrow Wilson. Chelsea, 1987
LEWIS, Gavin
Tomas Masaryk. Chelsea, 1990
LLOYD, Dana
Ho Chi Minh. Chelsea, 1987

LLYWELYN, Morgan
Xerxes. Chelsea, 1987
LOOBY, Chris
Benjamin Franklin. Chelsea, 1990
LUBETKIN, Wendy
Deng Xiaoping. Chelsea, 1988
George Marshall. Chelsea, 1989
MCAULEY, Karen
Eleanor Roosevelt. Chelsea, 1987
Golda Meir. Chelsea, 1985
MCDERMOTT, Kathleen
Peter the Great. Chelsea, 1991
MCGUIRE, Leslie
Catherine the Great. Chelsea, 1986
Napoleon Bonaparte. Chelsea, 1986
MCGUIRK, Carol
Benjamin Disraeli. Chelsea, 1987
MACNAMARA, Desmond
Eamon De Valera. Chelsea, 1988
MARKHAM, Lois
Theodore Roosevelt. Chelsea, 1985
MATUSKY, Gregory
Hussein. Chelsea, 1987
NAVAZELSKIS, Ina
Alexander Dubcek. Chelsea, 1989
Leonid Brezhnev. Chelsea, 1987
NEGASH, Askele
Haile Selassie. Chelsea, 1989
O'BRIEN, Steven
Alexander Hamilton. Chelsea, 1989
Ulysses S. Grant. Chelsea, 1990
PETRILLO, Daniel
Robert F. Kennedy. Chelsea, 1989
POWERS, Elizabeth
Nero. Chelsea, 1988
RAGAN, John
Emiliano Zapata. Chelsea, 1989
RANDALL, Marta
John F. Kennedy. Chelsea, 1988
RIPLEY, C. Peter
Richard Nixon. Chelsea, 1987
RODGERS, Judith
Winston Churchill. Chelsea, 1987
ROSE, Jonathan
Bismarck. Chelsea, 1987
SAMUELS, Steven
Ronald Reagan. Chelsea, 1991
SANDBERG, Peter
Dwight D. Eisenhower. Chelsea, 1987
SCHIFFMAN, Ruth
Josip Broz Tito. Chelsea, 1987
SEVERNS, Karen
Hirohito. Chelsea, 1988
SHEARMAN, Deidre
David Lloyd George. Chelsea, 1988
Queen Victoria. Chelsea, 1987

SHELDON, Richard
Hammarskjold. Chelsea, 1987
SLACK, Gordy
Ferdinand Marcos. Chelsea, 1988
SLAVIN, Ed
Jimmy Carter. Chelsea, 1989
STEFOFF, Rebecca
Faisal. Chelsea, 1989
Yasir Arafat. Chelsea, 1988
STEPANEK, Sally
John Calvin. Chelsea, 1987
Martin Luther. Chelsea, 1987
Mary, Queen of Scots. Chelsea, 1987
STEVENS, Paul
Ferdinand and Isabella. Chelsea, 1988
STOCKWELL, John
Daniel Ortega. Chelsea, 1989
TACHAU, Frank
Kemal Ataturk. Chelsea, 1987
VAIL, John
David Ben-Gurion. Chelsea, 1987
Fidel Castro. Chelsea, 1988
Nelson and Winnie Mandela. Chelsea, 1989
Thomas Paine. Chelsea, 1990
VIOLA, Herman
Andrew Jackson. Chelsea, 1986
VIOLA, Tom
Giuseppe Garibaldi. Chelsea, 1988
Willy Brandt. Chelsea, 1988
VOGT, George
Nicholas II. Chelsea, 1987
VON DER HEIDE, John
Klemens von Metternich. Chelsea, 1988
VOROTY, Steve
Attila. Chelsea, 1990
WALCH, Timothy
John Paul II. Chelsea, 1989
John XXIII. Chelsea, 1987
WALWORTH, Nancy
Augustus Caesar. Chelsea, 1989
Constantine. Chelsea, 1989
WEPMAN, Dennis
Adolf Hitler. Chelsea, 1986
Alexander the Great. Chelsea, 1986
Benito Juarez. Chelsea, 1987
Hernan Cortes. Chelsea, 1987
Jomo Kenyatta. Chelsea, 1985
Simon Bolivar. Chelsea, 1985
Tamerlane. Chelsea, 1987
WETZEL, Charles
James Monroe. Chelsea, 1989

An exhaustive series of reference books that presents the men and women whose ideas and actions have influenced history. Each title is well illustrated with photographs, maps, and engravings. A bibliography and index are also included. Junior and senior high school students will find these books to be excellent reference tools for reports or for reading on their own. A number of these books have been chosen by the New York Public Library as Best Books for the Teen Age.

WORLD OF SPORT
BARTLETT, E. G.
Judo. Silver, 1987
JARMAN, Katherine
Freshwater Fishing. Silver, 1987
RILEY, John
Soccer. Silver, 1987
TATLOW, Peter
Gymnastics. Silver, 1987
TRUMAN, Christine
Tennis. Silver, 1987
WILSON, C. G.
Swimming and Diving. Silver, 1987
Originally published in England, this informative sports series is international in approach. Information on the history of the sport is given; variations and techniques in playing worldwide are also presented. Much emphasis is placed on tournaments and competitions. Clothing, equipment, rules, and feats are explored. Glossary, index, and list of pertinent addresses are provided. Grades 5 and up.

WORLD OF WORK
VAUGHAN, Jenny
Airport. Silver, 1988
Bank. Silver, 1988
Hospital. Silver, 1988
Hotel. Silver, 1988
Mine. Silver, 1988
Ship. Silver, 1988
The series title is something of a misnomer; these are not career books or books that show people at work. Rather, they present an overview of the history of these institutions, as well as present-day workings and services. Perhaps because they originated in England, the thrust of the material is international, with lots of photos from other countries and information on the international scene. These are certain to give the 10-14 year old set a nice introduction to the topics. Glossary, index.

WORLD'S CHILDREN
HARKONEN, Reijo
Children of China. Carolrhoda, 1990
Children of Egypt. Carolrhoda, 1990
Children of Nepal. Carolrhoda, 1990
Originally published in Finland, this new series is being imported now to the United States. Several children are briefly profiled, then the thrust becomes more general as the author touches on history, geography, economics, and lifestyle. Although there is an index, the information is presented very briefly and conversationally. They make for interesting reading, especially with the plentiful outstanding photos. Their usefulness for school assignments is limited, however. Grades 3-6.

WORLD'S GREAT EXPLORERS
ASH, Maureen
Vasco Nunez de Balboa: Expedition to the Pacific Ocean. Childrens, 1990
CLINTON, Susan
Henry Stanley and David Livingstone: Explorers of Africa. Childrens, 1990

FITZ-GERALD, Christine A.

Meriwether Lewis and William Clark: The Northwest Expedition. Childrens, 1991

GAFFNEY, Timothy R.

Edmund Hillary: First to Climb Mount Everest. Childrens, 1990

HARGROVE, Jim

Ferdinand Magellan: First around the World. Childrens, 1990

Rene-Robert Cavelier, Sieur de la Salle: Explorer of the Mississippi River. Childrens, 1990

SIMON, Charnan

Explorers of the Ancient World. Childrens, 1990

Leif Eriksson and the Vikings: The Norse Discovery of America. Childrens, 1991

Richard Burton: Explorer of Arabia and Africa. Childrens, 1991

SINNOTT, Susan

Zebulon Pike: Up the Mississippi and Out to the Rockies. Childrens, 1990

SIPIERA, Paul

Roald Amundsen and Robert Scott: Race for the South Pole. Childrens, 1990

STEIN, R. Conrad

Hernando Cortes: Conqueror of Mexico. Childrens, 1991

This excellent new series resembles Childrens' Enchantment series: thorough coverage, solid illustrations, glossy pages. The biographees are placed in their time; their importance both then and in the historical scheme is examined. Timeline, glossary, bibliography, and index. Grades 5-12.

WORLDS OF WONDER

BELL, Robert A., and **Rosanna HANSEN**

My First Book of Space. Simon & Schuster, 1985

ELTING, Mary

Snakes and Other Reptiles. Simon & Schuster, 1987

Volcanoes and Earthquakes. Simon & Schuster, 1990

MILLER, Susanne Santoro

Prehistoric Mammals. Simon & Schuster, 1984

Whales and Sharks and Other Creatures of the Deep. Simon & Schuster, 1982

PACKARD, Mary

Dinosaurs. Simon & Schuster, 1981

TOMB, Howard

Living Monsters. Simon & Schuster, 1990

WHAYNE, Susanne Santoro

The World of Insects. Simon & Schuster, 1990

Large, attractive color illustrations dominate these oversize volumes. The authors present an overview of the subject, then move into more information on individual creatures. There are *no* indexes. Grades 3-6.

WORLD WAR II BIOGRAPHIES

BRADLEY, Catherine

Hitler and the Third Reich. Watts, 1990

BRADLEY, John

Churchill and the British. Watts, 1990

CROSS, Robin

Roosevelt and the Americans at War. Watts, 1990

MULVIHILL, Margaret

Mussolini and Italian Fascism. Watts, 1990

World War II buffs and students alike will find these books fascinating. The formative years of the subject are described in a chapter; the remainder of the book concentrates on the war and its conduct by the biographee. Historical photos combine with maps to present a clear picture of events. There is a chronology, glossary, bibliography, and index. Grades 5-12.

YEAR IN THE LIFE

STIDWORTHY, John

Chimpanzee. Silver, 1987
Elephant. Silver, 1986
Owl. Silver, 1987
Tiger. Silver, 1986
Whale. Silver, 1986

In order to teach about animals, this series personalizes things by showing a year in the life of a particular tiger, owl, etc. The first two pages introduce the species with basic facts and statistics. The year then commences, showing feeding habits, hunting, lifestyle, mating, and rearing the young. The last page emphasizes the need for conservation. While the format and illustrations seem aimed at younger readers, the text is really more apropos for grades 4-7. Index.

YOU AND YOUR PET

STEINBERG, Phil

You and Your Pet: Cats. Lerner, 1978
You and Your Pet: Dogs. Lerner, 1978
You and Your Pet: Rodents and Rabbits. Lerner, 1979
You and Your Pet: Terrarium Pets. Lerner, 1979

These are decent books to teach kids about pets and pet care. They begin with an overview of the history of the animal and how it came to become domesticated. Brief information on breeds is given, along with black and white drawings. The author then goes on to the issue of how to choose the right pet, training, health, feeding, etc. Grades 4-8. Index.

YOU ARE THE COACH

AASENG, Nathan

Baseball: It's Your Team. Lerner, 1985
Baseball: You Are the Manager. Lerner, 1983
Basketball: You Are the Coach. Lerner, 1983
College Basketball: You Are the Coach. Lerner, 1984
College Football: You Are the Coach. Lerner, 1984
Football: It's Your Team. Lerner, 1985
Football: You Are the Coach. Lerner, 1983
Hockey: You Are the Coach. Lerner, 1983

This unusual series is almost like a real life Choose Your Own Adventure! A situation that a real pro team faced is described along with the players involved. The reader is then asked to act as coach and decide which play to run. The next page describes what really happened and why that choice was made. Readers are encouraged to test their knowledge of tactics, as well as be taught some sports history. Grades 4 and up. No index, glossary.

YOUNG DISCOVERY LIBRARY

BOMBARDE, Odile

The Barbarians. Childrens, 1988

BOMBARDE, Odile, and **Claude MOATTI**

Living in Ancient Rome. Childrens, 1988

BRICE, Raphaelle

From Oil to Plastic. Childrens, 1988
Rice: The Little Grain That Feeds the World. Childrens, 1991

COURTALON, Corinne

On the Banks of the Pharaoh's Nile. Childrens, 1988

COURTAULT, Martine

Going West: Cowboys and Pioneers. Childrens, 1990

DE BEAUREGARD, Diane Costa
Animals in Jeopardy. Childrens, 1991
The Blue Planet: Seas and Oceans. Childrens, 1990
DESAIRIGNE, Catherine
Animals in Winter. Childrens, 1988
DIEVART, Roger
Teeth, Tusks and Fangs. Childrens, 1991
FARRE, Marie
Crocodiles and Alligators. Childrens, 1988
Long Ago in a Castle. Childrens, 1988
FONTANEL, Beatrice
Cats, Big and Little. Childrens, 1991
GANDIOL-COPPIN, Brigitte
Cathedrals: Stone upon Stone. Childrens, 1990
GEISTDOERFER, Patrick
Undersea Giants. Childrens, 1988
GRENIER, Nicolas
Following Indian Trails. Childrens, 1988
HENRY-BIABAUD, Chantal
Living in the Heart of Africa. Childrens, 1991
Living in South America. Childrens, 1991
JOBIN, Claire
All about Wool. Childrens, 1988
JOLY, Dominique
Grains of Salt. Childrens, 1988
LAURENCIN, Genevieve
Music! Childrens, 1990
LIMOUSIN, Odile
The Story of Paper. Childrens, 1988
LUCAS, Andre
Monkeys, Apes and Other Primates. Childrens, 1990
OTTENHEIMER, Laurence
Japan: Land of Samurai and Robots. Childrens, 1988
PFEFFER, Pierre
Bears, Big and Little. Childrens, 1990
Elephants: Big, Strong, and Wise. Childrens, 1988
PLANCHE, Bernard
Living on a Tropical Island. Childrens, 1988
Living with the Eskimos. Childrens, 1988
PROT, Viviane Abel, and **Philippe DELORME**
The Story of Birth. Childrens, 1991
REYMOND, Jean-Pierre
Metals: Born of Earth and Fire. Childrens, 1988
RUFFAULT, Charlotte
Animals Underground. Childrens, 1988
SINGH, Anne
Living in India. Childrens, 1988
STANLEY-BAKER, Penny
Australia: On the Other Side of the World. Childrens, 1988
TORDJMAN, Nathalie
The Living Pond. Childrens, 1991
VERDET, Jean-Pierre
The Sky: Stars and Night. Childrens, 1991

Written by an international selection of authors, this series of slim, pocket-size books contains nuggets of interesting facts that will pique the curiosity of interested readers. There is not, however, enough information here to serve as the basis for a report. Ages 7-10.

***YOUNG PEOPLE'S HISTORY OF AMERICA'S WARS**

LAWSON, Don

The United States in the Civil War. Harper, 1977
The United States in the Mexican War. Harper, 1976
The United States in the Spanish-American War. Harper, 1976
The United States in the Vietnam War. Harper, 1981

These are the final four volumes in this series. The previous seven books were reviewed in an earlier *YPLIS*. These books are written so young people can understand the issues and causes of the conflicts. All were well received: the book on the Vietnam War was chosen as an ALA Best Book for Young Adults. The books have many illustrations, recommendations for further reading and indexes. Junior high and up, well suited for classroom use.

YOUNG PEOPLE'S STORIES OF OUR STATES

FRADIN, Dennis

Alabama: In Words and Pictures. Childrens, 1980
Alaska: In Words and Pictures. Childrens, 1977
Arizona: In Words and Pictures. Childrens, 1980
Arkansas: In Words and Pictures. Childrens, 1980
California: In Words and Pictures. Childrens, 1977
Colorado: In Words and Pictures. Childrens, 1980
Connecticut: In Words and Pictures. Childrens, 1980
Delaware: In Words and Pictures. Childrens, 1980
District of Columbia: In Words and Pictures. Childrens, 1981
Florida: In Words and Pictures. Childrens, 1980
Georgia: In Words and Pictures. Childrens, 1981
Hawaii: In Words and Pictures. Childrens, 1980
Idaho: In Words and Pictures. Childrens, 1980
Illinois: In Words and Pictures. Childrens, 1976
Indiana: In Words and Pictures. Childrens, 1980
Iowa: In Words and Pictures. Childrens, 1980
Kansas: In Words and Pictures. Childrens, 1980
Kentucky: In Words and Pictures. Childrens, 1981
Louisiana: In Words and Pictures. Childrens, 1981
Maine: In Words and Pictures. Childrens, 1980
Maryland: In Words and Pictures. Childrens, 1980
Massachusetts: In Words and Pictures. Childrens, 1981
Michigan: In Words and Pictures. Childrens, 1980
Minnesota: In Words and Pictures. Childrens, 1980
Mississippi: In Words and Pictures. Childrens, 1980
Missouri: In Words and Pictures. Childrens, 1980
Montana: In Words and Pictures. Childrens, 1981
Nebraska: In Words and Pictures. Childrens, 1980
Nevada: In Words and Pictures. Childrens, 1981
New Hampshire: In Words and Pictures. Childrens, 1981
New Jersey: In Words and Pictures. Childrens, 1980
New Mexico: In Words and Pictures. Childrens, 1981
New York: In Words and Pictures. Childrens, 1981
North Carolina: In Words and Pictures. Childrens, 1980
North Dakota: In Words and Pictures. Childrens, 1981
Ohio: In Words and Pictures. Childrens, 1977
Oklahoma: In Words and Pictures. Childrens, 1981
Oregon: In Words and Pictures. Childrens, 1980
Pennsylvania: In Words and Pictures. Childrens, 1980
Rhode Island: In Words and Pictures. Childrens, 1981
South Carolina: In Words and Pictures. Childrens, 1981

South Dakota: In Words and Pictures. Childrens, 1981
Tennessee: In Words and Pictures. Childrens, 1980
Texas: In Words and Pictures. Childrens, 1981
Utah: In Words and Pictures. Childrens, 1980
Vermont: In Words and Pictures. Childrens, 1980
Virginia: In Words and Pictures. Childrens, 1976
Washington: In Words and Pictures. Childrens, 1980
West Virginia: In Words and Pictures. Childrens, 1980
Wisconsin: In Words and Pictures. Childrens, 1977
Wyoming: In Words and Pictures. Childrens, 1980

For readers grades 1-4, this is the only series available on their reading level on the states. There is an index and a section of facts and historical timeline at the end, which is really necessary since there is no table of contents at the front. The presentation begins with ancient history and finally moves into current facts. There are some photos, mingled with mediocre color illustrations. Pronunciation of unfamiliar terms is spelled out parenthetically within the text, but so frequently, that young readers may find it more of an annoyance than a help.

YOUNG PRESIDENTS SERIES
HILTON, Suzanne

The World of Young Andrew Jackson. Walker, 1988
The World of Young George Washington. Walker, 1987
The World of Young Herbert Hoover. Walker, 1987
The World of Young Tom Jefferson. Walker, 1986

In this series, author Hilton covers only the childhood years of her subject. Her thesis is that this period, often skimmed over in other books, forms the characters and influences the molding of the future adult. The author uses direct sources like diaries for her presentation of what life was like during that time. Well researched and well written, each volume includes a chronological section on the deeds of the adult, as well as a bibliography and index. Excellent choice for grades 4-8.

YOUNG SCIENTIST INVESTIGATES
JENNINGS, Terry

Air. Childrens. 1989
Birds. Childrens, 1989
Electricity and Magnetism. Childrens, 1989
Energy. Childrens, 1989
Everyday Chemicals. Childrens, 1989
Flowers. Childrens, 1989
Food. Childrens, 1989
Heat. Childrens, 1989
The Human Body. Childrens, 1989
Light and Color. Childrens, 1989
Materials. Childrens, 1989
Pond Life. Childrens, 1989
Rocks and Soil. Childrens, 1989
Sea and Seashore. Childrens, 1989
Seeds and Seedlings. Childrens, 1989
Small Garden Animals. Childrens, 1989
Sounds. Childrens, 1989
Structures. Childrens, 1989
Trees. Childrens, 1989
Water. Childrens, 1989

Originally published by Oxford University Press, this series features large colorful illustrations and diagrams, along with clear, simply written texts for grades 3-6. School libraries will find them particularly useful, because there are several sections in each book that ask review questions and suggest projects and experiments for students to do.

Fiction Series Title Index

Non-Fiction Series Title Index

Non-Fiction Series Subject Index

Combined Author/Title Index